TRAGEDY AT
DIEPPE

OPERATION JUBILEE,
AUGUST 19, 1942

MARK ZUEHLKE

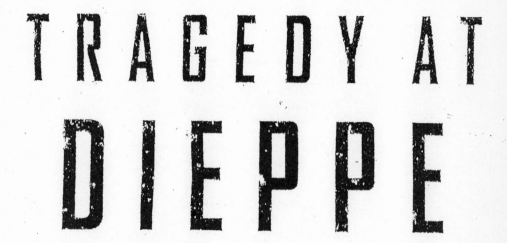

TRAGEDY AT DIEPPE

Douglas & McIntyre
D&M PUBLISHERS INC.
Vancouver/Toronto/Berkeley

Douglas & McIntyre
An imprint of D&M Publishers Inc.
2323 Quebec Street, Suite 201
Vancouver BC Canada V5T 4S7
www.douglas-mcintyre.com

Cataloguing data available from Library and Archives Canada
ISBN 978-1-55365-835-1 (cloth)
ISBN 978-1-55365-836-8 (ebook)

Editing by Kathy Vanderlinden
Jacket and text design by Setareh Ashrafologhalai
Jacket photograph: Library and Archives Canada/c-014160
Maps by C. Stuart Daniel/Starshell Maps
Photos used with permission from Library and Archives Canada
Printed and bound in Canada by Friesens
Distributed in the U.S. by Publishers Group West

We gratefully acknowledge the financial support of the Canada Council
for the Arts, the British Columbia Arts Council, the Province of British Columbia
through the Book Publishing Tax Credit, and the Government of Canada
through the Canada Book Fund for our publishing activities.

We were ready for Dieppe. We were well trained for Dieppe. Why shouldn't we have Dieppe? Why give it to someone else? I think whoever got it for the Canadians did absolutely right. Our attitude was, "Give us this show. Make it ours. Make it all Canadians. We want it."

—*Major Norman Ross, Queen's Own Cameron Highlanders of Canada*

The Canadians are 1st Class chaps; if anyone can pull it off, they will.

—*Lieutenant General Bernard Law Montgomery, July 1, 1942*

It is incomprehensible that it should be believed that a single Canadian Division should be able to overrun a German Infantry Regiment [equivalent to a Canadian Brigade] reinforced with artillery.

—*German 302nd Infantry Division after-action report on the Dieppe raid*

I am afraid that this operation will go down as one of the great failures of history.

—*Brigadier Church Mann to Brigadier Lucien Truscott aboard* HMS *Fernie*

[CONTENTS]

ACKNOWLEDGEMENTS

THE FOUNDATION UPON which each Canadian Battle Series book stands is extensive research. Along the way, many people pitch in to assist in this always enormous undertaking. Bruce Dodds, whose father was a 2nd Field Company, RCE, sapper at Dieppe, contributed a copy of Mountbatten's 1973 speech to Canadian veterans. During a whirlwind digital photography session at Library and Archives Canada (LAC) in Ottawa, Alan Boyce weighed in with his camera. The thousands of images collected that day would have been far fewer without his volunteering to help. Alan also saved the day later, when I realized the John Hughes-Hallett fonds file had slipped through the net, by going in and shooting hundreds more pages of documents. Johan van Doorn, my colleague in the Netherlands, remains a keystone in the research gathering. His skill at transforming the hundreds of files at various archives that are needed for each book into functional Excel spreadsheets is indispensable. He also, as always, brought his encyclopedic knowledge of World War II into play during readings of the manuscript and is a valued friend. From Newark, New Jersey, David Lippman provided material that fleshed out the American side of the story.

Again I am grateful to the staff at the various archives I consulted, who were always courteous and of great assistance. In the United Kingdom, the staff at Kew were amazing at providing files, sometimes within mere minutes of my filing a request. This was especially valuable, as my time there was shorter than I would have liked. In Ottawa, LAC staff were equally helpful and always sympathetic to an out-of-towner working on a tight budget and within a limited time frame. Steve Harris at the Directorate of Heritage and History, Department of National Defence, spent precious time discussing with me his perceptions of why things went right or mostly wrong during the Dieppe raid based on his having led many military tours of the beaches. The pages at DHH were also unfailingly diligent in retrieving files quickly and efficiently. At the Canadian War Museum, archivist Carol Reid trolled the interview collection to find everyone who had been involved in Dieppe. University of Victoria Special Collections staff were equally helpful in providing digital copies of interviews, recordings, and transcripts contained in the Reginald Roy Oral History Collection.

Scott McIntyre at D&M Publishers remains an unflagging supporter of the Canadian Battle Series and of Canadian military history in general. His commitment to ensuring that the entire series remains in print is laudable. Kathy Vanderlinden worked her usual magic in the tough substantive editor role. C. Stuart Daniel and I spent hours on the phone discussing how to create the so necessary maps, and I am as always grateful for his mapmaking skill and knowledge. Agent Carolyn Swayze not only keeps my writing career on track by handling the main financial and business details but also provides a sympathetic ear and oft wise counsel.

When my partner, Frances Backhouse, and I visited Dieppe, we were impressed by the small museum Mémorial du 19 Août 1942, housed in the former cinema that Royal Hamilton Light Infantry troops managed to occupy briefly during an incursion into the town. The staff there were extremely helpful in ensuring that we got everything possible out of our visit.

Finally, a huge thanks to Frances for her unhesitating support during the long and arduous writing of this book. She also shared the often sobering and sad moments of visiting the Dieppe beaches and overall battleground. But battleground touring is also a great pleasure for both of us. The Dieppe countryside can be lovely in good weather, and visiting the raid sites is a fascinating and richly rewarding educational experience. I recommend it highly.

NO SINGLE CANADIAN military action remains as well analyzed or as controversial as the August 19, 1942, assault on Dieppe. Operation Jubilee was indisputably a disaster. In a nine-hour battle, 807 Canadian troops were killed and 1,946 taken prisoner—more than during the eleven months from June 6, 1944, to the end of the war in May 1945. At least 568 of these prisoners were wounded. Seventy-two subsequently died in captivity, most from battle wounds. Of 586 wounded who returned to England, 28 subsequently died. Out of 4,963 Canadian soldiers involved, 3,367 became casualties. That is just shy of 68 per cent of the entire Canadian force. The majority who survived unscathed never got ashore.

British Army losses amounted to 18 officers and 157 other ranks, with 2 of these officers and 12 other ranks dying. Eleven officers and 117 other ranks were reported missing or captured. Fifty U.S. Rangers participating in the raid suffered 22 per cent losses—3 killed, 3 taken prisoner, and 5 wounded. As most of the Americans never made it ashore, the loss percentage among those that did was 73 per cent. Naval losses were also heavy, with 550 men killed or wounded—75 either killed or succumbing to wounds, 269 listed as either missing or captured. The Royal Air Force, fighting the single largest daytime air battle of the war, suffered its heaviest losses. A total of 106 aircraft were lost, 98 being fighters or reconnaissance aircraft. Sixty-seven airmen were listed killed or presumed dead. Among these were 10 Royal Canadian Air Force pilots.[1]

How could an operation have gone so terribly wrong? Who was at fault? Why had it even been mounted? And why had Canadians played the lead role and suffered such staggering losses? Was anything gained that could mitigate or justify the casualty toll? These were questions that arose immediately after August 19. They are still debated today.

When I turned to writing about Dieppe, I saw that the number of preceding books on the assault raised the question of whether a new book was required. But a closer look showed that most of these titles dated back several decades. And most authors had set out to argue a particular case within the numerous outstanding debates. Axes were being ground. Too often this led to a selective spotlighting of some military reports and participant accounts at the expense of others.

There was no shortage of historical material to draw upon. Hundreds of pages were generated during the planning of the attack. In the aftermath, a great effort was made to collect and preserve survivor recollections. Countless after-action reports examined the assault in general or concentrated on specific aspects: How had communication systems functioned? Was intelligence on German defences accurate? What lessons could be learned and applied to future amphibious operations? These and many other questions were examined in microscopic detail.

Given this bounty, I decided to focus on the historical record and draw from it my own conclusions. I believe this enabled me to examine the controversial questions with a largely unbiased eye.

It is difficult, though, for a Canadian to write about Dieppe and not be affected by the scope of the tragedy suffered in that single, bitter day. But it is important to remember that Dieppe is not purely a Canadian Army story. I included here a considerable number of non-Canadian experiences, so that Dieppe might be understood in its fuller context.

Unfortunately, few Dieppe veterans are still alive, and memories have greatly faded. But I found the personal "you are there" style that enriched the other books in the series was still achievable. The many accounts of soldiers, sailors, and airmen gathered in the aftermath of the assault ensured this. Ultimately, I could select only a sampling from literally hundreds of personal stories. Like the earlier books, this one is a tribute to those brave young men who went to war to make a better world.

Map 1

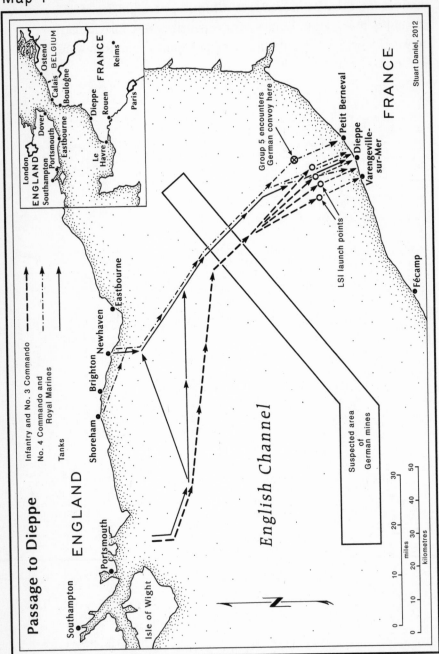

Passage to Dieppe

Stuart Daniel, 2012

Map 2

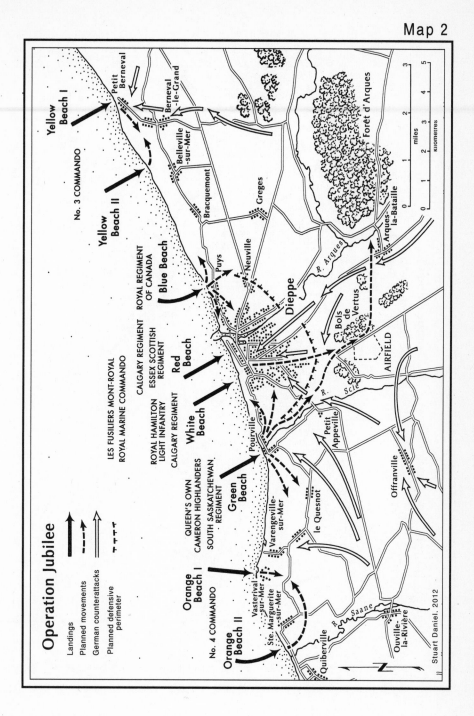

Operation Jubilee

Landings

Planned movements

German counterattacks

Planned defensive perimeter

Yellow Beach I

Yellow Beach II

No. 3 COMMANDO

Petit Berneval

Berneval-le-Grand

Belleville-sur-Mer

Bracquemont

Greges

Forêt d'Arques

Arques-la-Bataille

R. Arques

Puys

Neuville

Blue Beach

ROYAL REGIMENT OF CANADA

Dieppe

Bois de Vertus

AIRFIELD

R. Scie

Red Beach

CALGARY REGIMENT

ESSEX SCOTTISH REGIMENT

LES FUSILIERS MONT-ROYAL

ROYAL MARINE COMMANDO

ROYAL HAMILTON LIGHT INFANTRY

CALGARY REGIMENT

White Beach

QUEEN'S OWN CAMERON HIGHLANDERS

SOUTH SASKATCHEWAN REGIMENT

Green Beach

Pourville

Varengeville-sur-Mer

le Quesnot

Petit Appeville

Offranville

Orange Beach I

No. 4 COMMANDO

Orange Beach II

Vasterival-sur-Mer

Ste. Marguerite-sur-Mer

R. Saane

Quiberville

Ouville-la-Rivière

Stuart Daniel. 2012

N

miles

kilometres

0   1   2   3
0   1   2   3   4   5

Map 3

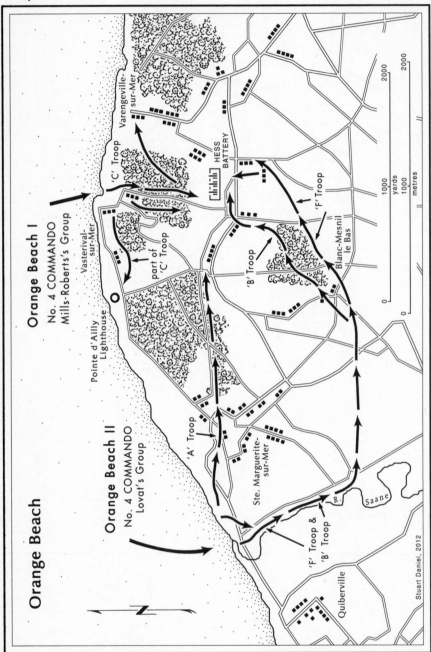

Map 4

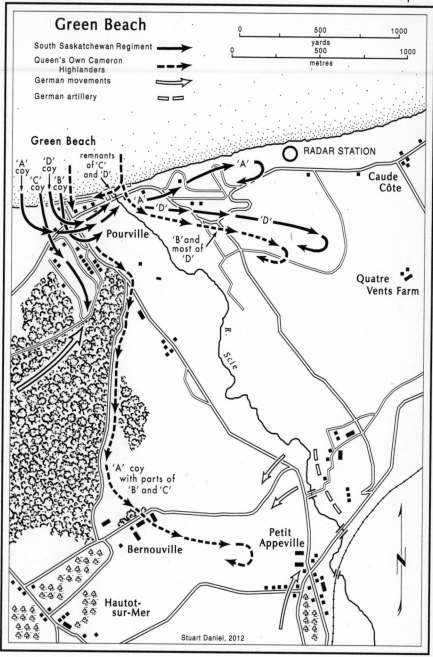

Green Beach

South Saskatchewan Regiment
Queen's Own Cameron Highlanders
German movements
German artillery

0 500 1000
yards
0 500 1000
metres

Green Beach

'A' coy
'D' coy
'C' coy
'B' coy
remnants of 'C' and 'D'

RADAR STATION

Caude Côte

'A'

'A'
'D'
'D'

Pourville

'B' and most of 'D'

Quatre Vents Farm

R. Scie

'A' coy with parts of 'B' and 'C'

Petit Appeville

Bernouville

Hautot-sur-Mer

Stuart Daniel, 2012

Map 5

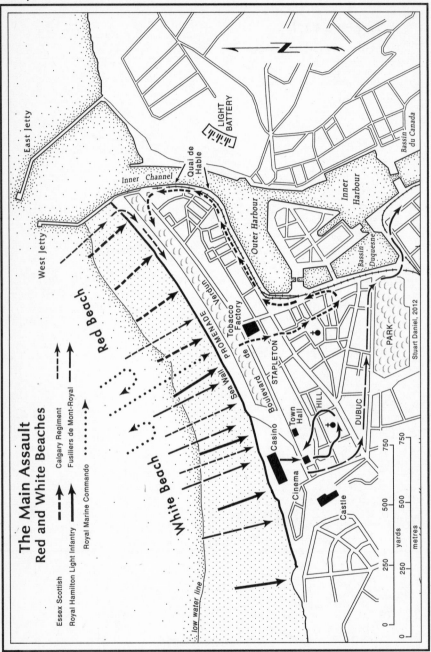

The Main Assault
Red and White Beaches

Essex Scottish
Royal Hamilton Light Infantry
Royal Marine Commando

Calgary Regiment
Fusiliers de Mont-Royal

Stuart Daniel, 2012

East Jetty

LIGHT
BATTERY

Quai de
Hable

Inner Channel

West Jetty

Red Beach

Inner
Harbour

Bassin
du Canada

Outer Harbour

Bassin
Duguesne

PARK

White Beach

Sea Wall

PROMENADE

Tobacco
Factory

Boulevard de Verdun

STAPLETON

HILL

DUBUC

Casino

Cinema

Town
Hall

Castle

low water line

0   250   500   750   yards

0   250   500   750   metres

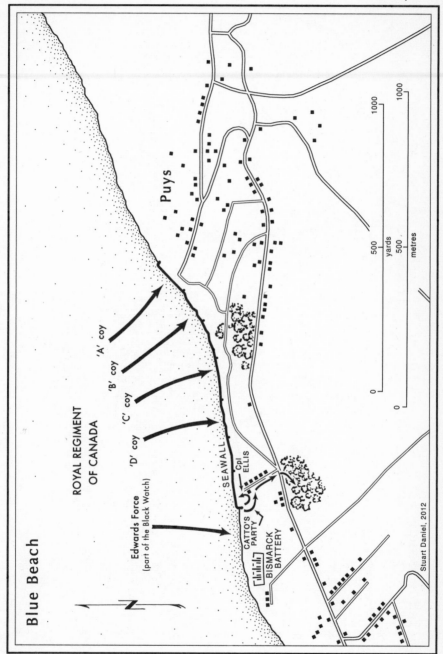

Map 6

Blue Beach

Puys

ROYAL REGIMENT
OF CANADA

'A' coy

'B' coy

'C' coy

'D' coy

Edwards Force
(part of the Black Watch)

SEAWALL

Cpl
ELLIS

CATTO'S
PARTY

BISMARCK
BATTERY

N

1000

1000

500

500

0

0

yards

metres

Stuart Daniel, 2012

Map 7

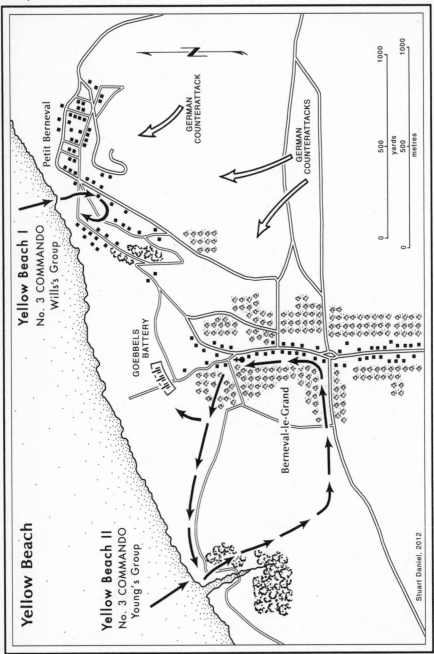

Yellow Beach

Yellow Beach I
No. 3 COMMANDO
Wills's Group

Yellow Beach II
No. 3 COMMANDO
Young's Group

Petit Berneval

GERMAN COUNTERATTACK

GERMAN COUNTERATTACKS

GOEBBELS BATTERY

Berneval-le-Grand

1000

500

0

yards

1000

500

0

metres

Stuart Daniel, 2012

A Crescendo of Activity

A T THE BEGINNING of 1942, the war that had raged since September 1939 expanded dramatically in response to two profound developments. First, Germany had invaded the Soviet Union on June 22, 1941. By December 7, German forces were within twenty-five miles of Moscow, and a Soviet defeat seemed likely. That same day, Japan attacked British, American, and Dutch possessions in the Pacific. The surprise aerial raid on Pearl Harbor in Hawaii jolted the United States out of neutrality and into the spreading conflict. In less than six months, the situation of Britain and its Commonwealth allies, including Canada, was transformed from a lone fight against the Axis powers to a joint venture with two of the world's mightiest nations.

Both the United States and the Soviet Union had stood on the sidelines since Germany's September 1939 invasion of Poland. When German troops invaded Norway and Denmark on April 9, 1940, neither nation responded. Denmark fell in a day, but British, French, and Free Polish forces reinforced the Norwegians. As the fight in Norway continued, the Germans expanded the war by invading Western Europe on May 10. Luxembourg, the Netherlands, and Belgium fell like dominoes. On June 25, France—Paris having fallen on June 14 and 400,000 of its troops having surrendered eight days later—capitulated. Allied forces had evacuated Norway on June 8 to

reinforce France, and the last Norwegian division surrendered two days later. Germany—allied with Italy, Hungary, and Romania—emerged as undisputed master of the European continent.

Only Great Britain, supported by the Commonwealth nations, remained standing. Germany seemed unbeatable. In North Africa, British forces suffered a string of defeats. April 1941 saw Greece's downfall, and Crete was lost the following month to German airborne invasion. A German amphibious and airborne assault on Britain remained likely, until Operation Barbarossa pulled too much German army strength away to the invasion of Russia.

Japan's strike against Malaysia, Singapore, Burma, and Hong Kong stretched the British virtually to the breaking point. When the Hong Kong garrison surrendered on December 25, 1,973 Canadian troops were lost there. Three hundred men from the Royal Rifles of Canada and Winnipeg Grenadiers were killed and the rest taken prisoner.

The Canadian presence in Hong Kong had come about as a last-minute response to a British appeal for reinforcement. The two battalions and a small command group had only arrived on November 16. Canada's army strength had been concentrated on England. By early 1942, four Canadian divisions—1st Infantry, 2nd Infantry, 3rd Infantry, and 4th Armoured—and 1st Canadian Army Tank Brigade were in England. All were organized within the Canadian Corps, which in early 1942 began expansion to form First Canadian Army. The 5th Canadian Armoured Division was also scheduled to soon arrive.

Now Britain was under increasing pressure from its new powerful allies to carry the war to the Germans via major amphibious assault on the European continent. Considering theirs was the only active front, the Soviets demanded that the western Allies open a second one. Soviet propaganda maintained that only they were fighting the Germans and doing so unaided. No thanks was offered Britain and Canada for stripping from their still meagre supply chain massive numbers of artillery pieces, tanks, trucks, planes, ammunition, and fuel for shipping by hazardous convoy to Soviet ports. In two major November 1941 speeches, Marshal Joseph Stalin ignored this assistance. Instead he claimed that German victories over the Soviet Army had occurred because "the absence of a second front in Europe enabled them to carry out their operations without any risk."[1]

Stalin's claim won sympathy in Britain and Canada—particularly among the largely socialist- or Communist-led trade unions, left-leaning intelligentsia, and popular press. A "Second Front NOW" movement was born that soon could no longer be ignored, especially by Prime Minister Winston Churchill's government. The slogan adorned countless factory walls. Large rallies drew thousands to venues such as Trafalgar Square, football parks, and large theatres in Manchester and Birmingham. The Canadian-born and -raised Lord Beaverbrook openly supported the movement through his newspaper empire.[2]

"Public opinion is shouting for the formation of a new Western Front to assist the Russians," Chief of the Imperial General Staff, General Sir Alan Brooke fretted in early 1942. "But they have no conception of the difficulties and dangers entailed. The prospects of success are small and dependent on a mass of unknowns, whilst the chances of disaster are great and dependent on a mass of well-established facts. Should Germany be getting the best of an attack on Russia, the pressure for invasion of France will be at its strongest, and yet this is just the most dangerous set of circumstances for us."[3]

On the heels of Pearl Harbor, Americans were quick to join the clamour for a second front. About two weeks after the surprise Japanese attack, President Franklin Roosevelt, Churchill, and the British and American Chiefs of Staff met in Washington to discuss mutual cooperation. Two key stratagems were decided during this Arcadia Conference. First, all American, British, and Commonwealth resources would be pooled under direction of a Combined Chiefs of Staff. Roosevelt and Churchill would provide political guidance, with Stalin offering input from, as it were, afar. This pooling was to ensure a common strategy implemented by a coherent Anglo-American command. The second decision affirmed an informal American and British "staff agreement" of March 1941 that should the two countries become allies, ultimate victory would rest on defeating

Germany first over any other Axis power. American confirmation of this point greatly relieved Churchill and the British Chiefs of Staff. Such was the anger in the United States over Pearl Harbor that they had feared Roosevelt would concentrate the American war effort against Japan. But General George C. Marshall, chair of the American Chiefs of Staff, had immediately stated that "Germany is still the prime enemy and her defeat is the key to victory. Once Germany is defeated, the collapse of Italy and the defeat of Japan must follow."[4]

This "Hitler First" stratagem left unanswered how to effectively make war on Germany. Having agreed to this approach, the Americans were hell-bent on starting immediately. Marshall particularly believed that the "decisive measure would be a blow directed across the Channel from the British Isles... and... that this should be struck at the earliest possible moment."[5]

Britain's Chiefs of Staff Committee agreed that a cross-channel assault would be required to defeat Germany. In late 1941, they had even drafted an invasion plan, code-named Operation Roundup. But the plan was meant to be a final step set in motion only after Germany began to collapse. As Hitler's armies fell back on Germany for a last stand, the British would land on the beaches west and east of Le Havre stretching from Deauville to Dieppe. Once control of a seventy- to hundred-mile-deep beachhead between Calais and the Seine was won, a northward advance would seize Antwerp and then penetrate Germany. Six infantry and six armoured divisions, along with six tank brigades and supporting troops, would comprise the invasion force. Only three naval vessels, including one battleship, would support the planned series of small-scale landings dispersed over a large front.[6] This version of Operation Roundup was a modest affair, and its timing little impressed the Americans during the Arcadia Conference.

They felt the British had given "only minor attention" to land operations in Europe and instead were relying on naval and air power to defeat Germany. Wars, the Americans chided their British counterparts, "cannot be finally won without the use of land armies."

The British little needed this obvious reminder. However, as one U.S. Army official historian later noted, "close to the scene of the war,

[they] tended to focus on the difficulties of the assault, and the tactical and logistical problems involved, while the Americans, some 3,000 miles away, found it easier to start with the large view of the strategic problem. British planners were deeply and continuously conscious that to attack northwest Europe armies had to get across an ugly piece of water called the Channel, that this crossing took boats and special equipment, that when the troops landed they had to storm fortifications and fight a German Army that had all Europe by the throat. Americans were aware of these problems only at second hand and at a distance. They worked from maps."[7]

Churchill proposed that instead of a cross-channel attack, the first step should be a joint Anglo-American invasion of French North Africa, controlled by the German-backed and -beholden Vichy regime. Resources were sufficient for such an invasion to occur in 1942. If successful, the Allies would control the Mediterranean—making it easier to transfer supplies to the Soviets via the Persian Gulf. It would also pull German forces away from both the embattled British Eighth Army in Libya and the even harder-pressed Soviets. It might also somewhat mollify Stalin's ever-louder demands for action by the western Allies.

When Arcadia wound up on January 14, the broad outlines of a western Allied strategy were agreed. Throughout 1942, German resistance would be worn down by increasing British and American air bombardment. The Russians would be assisted "by all available means." This would include operations aimed at gaining possession of the "whole North African coast." It was seen as unlikely that "in 1942 any large scale land offensive against Germany, except on the Russian front, will be possible." In 1943, however, the "way may be clear for a return to the continent across the Mediterranean, from Turkey into the Balkans, or by landings in Western Europe. Such operations will be the prelude to the final assault on Germany itself."[8]

Despite agreeing that North Africa would be the immediate target, Marshall and his planners did not abandon their belief that a cross-channel assault might remain feasible in 1942. In fact, they thought such an attack might prove essential to keeping the Soviets in the war. On March 10, 1942, First Canadian Army commander

Lieutenant General Andrew McNaughton met in Washington with Brigadier General Dwight D. Eisenhower—chief of the Operations Division of the War Department General Staff. Eisenhower warned McNaughton that Stalin might negotiate a separate peace with Germany unless the western Allies drew German forces away from the Russian front.[9] This was no idle concern, for the month before, Stalin had publicly declared a willingness for armistice discussions with Hitler.[10]

Eisenhower said "he had racked his mind to discover how we could present Germany with a second front, and that the more he thought it out the more firmly had he been driven to the conclusion that it would be possible to do so only by attacking Western Europe from the British Isles." McNaughton, who knew that his Canadians would certainly play a major role in any cross-channel operation, agreed that "the war could only be ended by the defeat of Hitler and the only way of doing so was to attack him from the West." He expressed his certainty "that an offensive would sooner or later have to be launched from the United Kingdom across the narrow seas." McNaughton added that the Canadian government had affirmed this point only the week before.

Rather than being in agreement, McNaughton and Eisenhower were talking at cross purposes. Eisenhower thought sooner, McNaughton later. Twenty days after this meeting, Marshall presented an argument to President Roosevelt for an invasion of northern France "as the theatre in which to stage the first great offensive of the United Powers." His plan envisioned a main operation in spring 1943 with a preceding diversionary attack against the French coast during the summer of 1942. This diversionary assault would only occur if the Soviet situation became desperate or the Germans in Western Europe were "critically weakened." Even in the absence of this diversion, Marshall wanted the British to establish "a preliminary active front this coming summer" with "constant raiding by small task forces at selected points along the entire coastline held by the enemy." On April 4, Marshall left for London to argue the American case. Accompanying him was Harry Hopkins, Roosevelt's most trusted civilian adviser.[11]

Marshall and Hopkins were polar opposites. The general was a tall, robust Virginian, who looked every bit the soldier and spoke his mind with little diplomacy. Hopkins, who suffered from hemochromatosis (excess iron) due to the cancer-necessitated removal of two-thirds of his stomach, was wizened, frail, and required regular blood transfusions. A chain-smoker, he dressed shabbily in clothes always rumpled. But Churchill, who had been won over by his plain-spoken, unassuming manner during an earlier visit in 1941, considered him a friend—not only personally but also of Britain.

Roosevelt had written Churchill on March 18 to set the tone for these discussions. "I am becoming more and more interested in the establishment of a new front this summer on the European continent... and even though losses will doubtless be great, such losses will be compensated by at least equal German losses and by compelling Germans to divert large forces of all kinds from Russian fronts."[12]

Churchill and his Chiefs of Staff received Marshall and Hopkins in the damp, smoky underground Cabinet War Room on Great George Street, close to Storey's Gate and St. James Park. The two Americans were quickly assured that the British were agreeable to the 1943 plans. This was merely an expansion of Operation Roundup, which the expected deployment of American troops to England over ensuing months made more feasible. But the American 1942 plans appalled the British. During Arcadia, a 1942 assault that Churchill suggested be code-named Operation Sledgehammer had been proposed. Since then the British had been studying how this might proceed. They saw Sledgehammer as far more modest than the American plan. The British envisioned "a limited-objective attack—something like a large-scale raid—the main purpose of which would be to tempt the German Air Force into a battle of destruction with the Royal Air Force under conditions favourable to the latter." Because of fighter ranges from England, the only feasible area for this operation was the Pas-de-Calais. Not coincidentally, this was precisely where German coastal defences were strongest.

Extensive scrutiny of Sledgehammer had disclosed by the beginning of April a string of obstacles. The coastal area selected had flat beaches ill suited to existing British landing craft, and there were too few exit points for vehicles and tanks to quickly and easily move inland. Area ports were also too small to supply the kind of force buildup required to hold a bridgehead against a determined German counterattack. While such an assault might lure the Luftwaffe into the RAF's gunsights, the problems this area presented were deemed insurmountable. A German counterattack would assuredly overrun the beachhead, resulting in great loss of men and equipment. Based on that grievous assessment, the British chiefs concluded that "establishment of a permanent bridgehead on the Continent would probably be impossible in 1942."

Marshall and Hopkins disagreed. The U.S. Joint Planning Staff proposal called for a major land attack across the English Channel that summer. While conceding that British and Canadian forces would have to carry out the initial assault, the Americans could rapidly reinforce the bridgehead with troops rushed to England. Marshall said such an assault could be made between July 15 and August 1. It would be preceded by a fifteen-day air attack that would draw large elements of the Luftwaffe away from the Russian front. The Allies would seek to establish air dominance over the Channel and at least one hundred kilometres inland between Dunkirk and Abbeville. While the air operations were going on, commandos would raid the Dutch, Belgian, and Normandy coastlines. Thirty days after air operations had begun, the major invasion would seize the high ground north of the Rivers Seine and Oise.[13]

Several days of often bitter argument ensued, with Marshall pressing the American line against the resistance of Brooke. Like Marshall, Brooke was a Great War veteran; he was also generally regarded as the man most responsible for bringing off the successful evacuation of British troops from Dunkirk in 1940. At one point, Brooke asked Marshall where he thought the soldiers should advance once they were ashore. "Do we go west, south, or east after landing?" To Brooke's astonishment, Marshall confessed that "he had not begun to think of it." This prompted Brooke to confide to his diary: "Marshall does not impress me by the ability of his brain... In many respects he is a very dangerous man whilst being a very charming one."[14] For his part, Marshall was equally unimpressed by Brooke's strategic sense.

Hopkins cautioned that Americans were demanding that their troops soon see combat. If there was no invasion in Europe, public opinion might well force the American effort to be largely directed against Japan.[15]

Ultimately, however, the British held the trump card—it would be their divisions that must carry out any 1942 invasion, and they were unwilling to commit them. On April 14, it was agreed that a 1942 landing in France would only be attempted if the Soviet Union was verging on collapse.[16]

With Sledgehammer relegated to the back burner, attention turned to Marshall's 1943 invasion scheme. This the British embraced enthusiastically, particularly when Marshall promised to deliver a million troops to the United Kingdom in the ensuing year. This proved to be a fateful turning point. Present at this meeting was Lord Louis Mountbatten, Chief of Combined Operations Command and the man recently placed in charge of planning and conducting all raiding operations against the European coast. When Marshall announced the numbers of men that he could deliver to England, Mountbatten realized that the "whole picture of combined operations against the Continent" was changing. "The plans, which we had been at present evolving, all fell short in one way or another for lack of essential resources. This would be all changed when the great flow of American forces began, and we should be enabled to plan that real return to the Continent, without which we could not hope to bring the war to a successful conclusion."[17]

Mountbatten was also heartened on the evening of April 14 when Marshall strongly advocated "repeated Commando-type raids all along the coast" in order to harass the Germans and give Allied troops experience. Combined Operations—which not only planned raiding operations but also increasingly directly controlled the army, air, and sea forces involved—would have a freer hand to expand the rate and size of its raids. This suited Mountbatten. At that very moment, Combined Operations staff was planning a raid far larger than any previously executed. Its target: the resort community of Dieppe.

Three days later, Churchill cabled Roosevelt to confirm that raiding would henceforth be more aggressive and on a larger scale. "The campaign of 1943 is straightforward, and we are starting joint plans and preparations at once. We may however feel compelled to act this year. Your plan visualised this, but put mid-September as the earliest date. Things may easily come to a head before then... Broadly speaking, our agreed programme is a crescendo of activity on the Continent, starting with an ever-increasing air offensive both by night and day and more frequent large-scale raids, in which United States troops will take part."

Soon thereafter, Churchill sent Prime Minister Mackenzie King a point-by-point outline of the agreed strategy. "Raiding operations," Churchill stated, would "be undertaken in 1942 on the largest scale which equipment will permit on a front from North Norway to the Bay of Biscay." The United Kingdom would serve as the base for "large scale operations in the spring of 1943 to destroy the German forces in Western Europe." Plans would "take advantage of any opportunity arising to capture in 1942 a bridgehead on the continent for an 'emergency' offensive if such should become necessary."[18]

On April 18, the British Chiefs of Staff confirmed the decisions agreed during the meetings with Marshall and Hopkins. A die was cast that would lead in little more than four months to several thousand Canadians meeting disaster on the beaches of Dieppe.

PART ONE

THE TWISTING PATH TO DIEPPE

1

A Boldly Imaginative Group

FOLLOWING THE ARCADIA Conference, Churchill gave Lord Mountbatten "special responsibility... to prepare for the invasion." The emphasis was to "devise the techniques of amphibious landings and to design and acquire the appurtenances and appliances needed for the invasion. I was to train vast numbers of soldiers, sailors and airmen to work as a single team in Combined Operations." Mountbatten would work with Commander-in-Chief, Home Forces, General Bernard Paget on "first plans for the return to the continent."[1]

Mountbatten had taken command of Combined Operations on October 27, 1941, receiving immediate promotion from captain to commodore first class. On March 18, 1942, Churchill advanced him to the rank of acting vice-admiral with the title Chief of Combined Operations.[2] A couple of weeks earlier, Churchill had also appointed Mountbatten to the British Chiefs of Staff Committee, carrying with it a place in the new Anglo-American Combined Chiefs of Staff Committee.[3]

Friends and family knew Mountbatten as "Dickie." His "pedigree practically drips with royal ermine," *Collier's Weekly* correspondent Quentin Reynolds gushed admiringly. His father had been the German-born Prince Louis of Battenberg, and his mother, Princess Victoria, was the daughter of Louis IV, Grand Duke of Hesse, and of

Princess Alice, the daughter of Queen Victoria. After immigrating to Britain, the family anglicized its name to Mountbatten. In 1922, the young lord married socialite Edwina Ashley, named for her god-father King Edward VII. During the pre-war years, Mountbatten and Edwina cut a glamorous path through the upper strata of British and American society. Reynolds observed that "they graced the late spots in London, they popularized pink champagne at Antibes, they gambled casually at Monte Carlo and often went half way round the world to keep engagements with their very great friend, Douglas Fairbanks, Sr.; Fred Astaire and other stage and film stars were their guests, and occasionally they varied the routine by dining with King George and Queen Mary."[4]

Born in 1900, Mountbatten had served in the Great War as a boy seaman and thereafter continued a naval career. In 1939, he held a captaincy and took command of the destroyer HMS *Kelly*. Reynolds thought Mountbatten looked the part of a hero. He "is tall, with pale-blue eyes and a wide mouth that smiles readily, but which can tighten into a thin, uncompromising, straight line" that Reynolds believed had become "a legend in the Royal Navy and among the people of Britain."[5]

Less enthralled commentators, including some Royal Navy officers, described his war career as "marked by fame, danger and folly in roughly equal amounts, with recklessness as its most significant characteristic."[6] But even his detractors admitted the man's courage. When a German mine badly damaged *Kelly* in the English Channel, he nursed it into port after a ninety-hour ordeal. His next command, HMS *Javelin*, was shortly torpedoed in a Channel fight. Again refusing to abandon ship, Mountbatten got her home and was awarded a Distinguished Service Order. Returning to the helm of *Kelly*, he participated in the doomed attempt to save Crete. During a fierce melee between British ships and Stuka dive-bombers, a bomb fatally pierced *Kelly*'s guts. Mountbatten ordered the crew to keep firing all guns, while he clung to the compass standard on the bridge until it was almost too late to abandon ship.[7]

To make room for Mountbatten, Churchill had fired the current Combined Operations director, Admiral of the Fleet Roger Keyes. Appointed on July 17, 1940, Keyes was given express instruction to move commando raiding towards larger-scale operations.[8] He dili-gently tried to do so, but fell afoul of constant resistance from both the army and navy to provide men, matériel, and logistical support for what many considered a pointless delivery of costly "pinprick" strikes against the Germans. Keyes was almost seventy. Churchill felt his often irascible nature caused undue friction with both supe-riors and subordinates. Mountbatten, he believed, had the leadership qualities, initiative, diplomatic skills, and ingenuity to enable Com-bined Operations to begin launching large-scale raids.

No sooner had the British escaped France at Dunkirk than they had turned to hit-and-run raids against German targets. Initially, these aimed to simply keep the Germans off balance and show that the Royal Navy could deliver small bands of soldiers anywhere along the European coast with impunity. This "showing of the colours" in desperate times greatly appealed to Churchill. He turned to Lieuten-ant Colonel Dudley Clarke, who had served alongside Arab guerillas during their campaigns in Palestine against the Turks in the Great War. Clarke suggested training small units of soldiers to wage irreg-ular warfare. He called the units commandos, a designation the Boers had given their irregular fighters during the South African War. Churchill, who had been a journalist in South Africa, enthusi-astically embraced the term and idea. The press quickly applied the word to the men, and it stuck. Commando units served within the Special Service Brigade, which was in turn controlled by Combined Operations.

The soldiers had to operate amphibiously, meaning "first and foremost... they must learn to co-operate with the Royal Navy. Schools for this purpose were established in various convenient places on the coast of Great Britain so that the men might become familiar with the ways of life, the customs, the habits and the out-look of sailors."[9]

Commando training was gruelling. "To get in and out of a small boat in all kinds of weather, to swim—if necessary in full equipment with firearms held above the water, to be familiar with all the porta-ble weapons of the soldier from the rifle and the tommy gun to the three-inch mortar and the anti-tank rifle, to be able to carry and use high explosives, to hunt tanks and their crews—here are some of the things that the Commando soldier must learn. To do so, however, is only to be proficient in the use of the tools of his trade of war. He must do more than this; he must master his mind as well as his body and become not only a specially trained soldier but a trained individual soldier. In other words, self-reliance and self-confidence form an integral, a vital part of his mental and moral makeup. To achieve these mutually dependent qualities the men, on entering the depot, are treated as far as possible as individuals. It is not for them to await orders from their officers or their NCO. They must do the sensible, obvious thing just because it is the sensible, obvious thing."

Physical training required forced marches over all types of terrain, scaling cliffs, and swimming or improvising bridges over rivers. One commando troop in training "once marched in fighting order 63 miles in 23 hours and 10 minutes, covering the first 33 miles in eight hours dead... Such marches are the rule, not the exception."[10]

These were the men and tasks Mountbatten had inherited in October 1941. When Churchill described his role as that of an adviser, Mountbatten had asked to return to active duty. "What could you hope to achieve there," Churchill replied, "except to be sunk in a bigger and more expensive ship next time?" During a private briefing, Churchill told Mountbatten that Combined Operations must start conducting more aggressive and larger raids, the main object being the "re-invasion of France." It would be up to Combined Operations to determine the bases from which the ultimate invasion would be launched, create training camps for the assault troops, and develop a proper inter-service structure in which the army, navy, and air force could work together seamlessly.

Although Mountbatten acceded to the task, he sought from Churchill expanded powers and authority. This led to his rapid promotion in rank and position within the Allied command.

The expansion of Mountbatten's authority displeased General Alan Brooke. On March 5, 1942, he wrote: "The title of Chief of Combined Operations was ... badly chosen, since every operation we were engaged in was a combined one. It was certainly not intended that he should direct combined strategy—his job was to evolve technique, policy and equipment for the employment of three Services in combined operations to effect landings against opposition."[11]

Brooke feared Mountbatten's close relationship with Churchill might fuel the prime minister's often unrealistic enthusiasm for raiding and lead to his insistence on an operation beyond the military's capability. Mountbatten was a regular weekend guest of Churchill's at Chequers, the prime minister's official country residence in Buckinghamshire. "Dickie's visits to Chequers," Brooke wrote, "were always dangerous moments and there was no knowing what discussions he might be led into and . . . let us in for." In March, such discussions inevitably revolved around calls for a second front to relieve pressure on the Russians.

Brooke agreed that some form of raid had to be mounted. At a March 10 Chiefs of Staff meeting—Mountbatten's first—discussion revolved around "the problem of assistance to Russia by operations in France, either large raid or lodgement. Decided only hope was to try and draw off air force from Russia and that for this purpose raid must be carried out on Calais front."

Investigating this possibility fell to Combined Operations Headquarters staff. On March 28, a difficult further meeting saw the chiefs "discussing ways and means of establishing new Western Front," Brooke wrote. "I had propounded theory that a Western Front . . . must force withdrawal of force from Russia. That it was impossible with the land force at our disposal to force the Germans to withdraw land forces from Russia, but that we might induce them to withdraw air forces. But to do this a landing must take place within our air umbrella, namely in vicinity of Calais or Boulogne. Mountbatten was still hankering after a landing near Cherbourg, where proper air support is not possible. Finally I think we convinced him sufficiently to make his visit to Chequers that evening safe."[12]

MOUNTBATTEN, MEANWHILE, HAD been reshaping Combined Operations to his liking. While publicly praising Keyes, Mountbatten quickly got rid of most senior staff. Mountbatten brought in forty-year-old Captain John Hughes-Hallett as his Naval Adviser because of the man's prior experience in preparing Britain's defences for a

German invasion. Slight of build, sharp-featured, and stylishly dapper, Hughes-Hallett became Mountbatten's most loyal subordinate and a close friend. "Jock," as Mountbatten called him, was as brash as his commander but also keenly intelligent, imaginative, and coldly practical.

Hughes-Hallett was quick to criticize what Combined Operations had achieved. "So far as I can make out the vision of COHQ [Combined Operations Headquarters] during the Keyes 'Regime' never went much beyond a bigger and better Zeebrugge-type raid. Moreover the Admiral and many of the older officers at COHQ had great difficulty in grasping the need for close co-ordination between all three Services." Launched on April 23, 1918, the Zeebrugge raid was intended to deny the key Belgian ports of Zeebrugge and Ostend to use by German submarines and light shipping. Keyes had masterminded the raid. Although largely a failure, the raid yielded a propaganda victory and won Keyes a knighthood. Hughes-Hallett believed this Great War experience led Keyes to focus Combined Operations entirely on "tiny raids, chiefly, I suppose, on account of their stimulating effect on morale. Nevertheless these operations achieved nothing, and a number of very gallant young officers... lost their lives to little avail."[13]

With Mountbatten often away attending to his higher responsibilities, actual operational planning fell to Hughes-Hallett. This was despite his being technically on equal footing with two other advisers representing the army and air force. Brigadier Charles Haydon was the Military Adviser and Group Captain A.H. Willetts the RAF Adviser. Hayden's purview included the commandos of the Special Service Brigade. Consequently he was "a fairly independent provider of raiding troops." Willetts, meanwhile, liaised between COHQ and RAF command levels. Hughes-Hallett took responsibility for "making outline plans for raids in consultation with the other advisers and keeping both the Admiralty and the Joint Planning Committee informed of what was in our minds at COHQ."[14]

Mountbatten and Hughes-Hallett inherited a headquarters they thought was "in a somewhat confused state. It was in part an Operations Headquarters responsible for planning and mounting raiding operations... in part a Government Department in miniature concerned with the provision of special craft and special weapons, and it also acted as a training authority for the personnel required for such operations." These differing agendas were all muddled together, with staff trying to do everything at once. Mountbatten began imposing order on the confusion. He separated "the operational and planning part of the work from the administrative, technical and training side. This separation," Hughes-Hallett believed, was "of crucial importance, as also was a certain tidying up of the administrative organization by separating training from the maintenance of material, and the procurement of new types of landing craft."[15]

In December 1941, Hughes-Hallett was recovering from jaundice and could only work a few hours each day.[16] So he was greatly impressed by how Mountbatten tackled his new command. A good thing, he believed, as COHQ still remained an unwieldy creation that left its head "grossly overloaded with work. Yet [Mountbatten] made an even greater contribution than getting COHQ more soundly organized. His boundless energy and enthusiasm infused a new spirit. In particular the operational planning side knew for the first time that their work was real and earnest: that the raids they were working on would in all probability be carried out."[17]

In early 1942, COHQ was a small outfit, with its offices in a maze-like network of underground rooms below a large modern stone building at 1a Richmond Terrace in Whitehall, London.[18] Each of the three advisers had a small staff, Hughes-Hallett's numbering just two other naval officers. These were Commander David Luce—soon a key planner—and Lieutenant Commander Ackroyd Norman Palliser de Costabadie, who had won a Distinguished Service Cross for evacuating one thousand troops at Dunkirk while commanding the motor gunboat HMS *Locust*.

Under Mountbatten, COHQ expanded breathtakingly. He inherited just twenty-three staff, including clerical help. Within a few months, Mountbatten brought the staff up to four hundred and joked that it was "the only lunatic asylum in the world run by its own inmates."[19]

Mountbatten was eager to start raiding. Everyone at COHQ "assumed that the main British effort, at least for the coming six months, would have to be confined to raids—chiefly cross channel—

but also against Norway and possibly on the French Atlantic coast."
But who would actually mount these raids? Mountbatten assumed
Combined Operations had the "exclusive right to do this work." Yet
General Bernard Paget, Commander-in-Chief, Home Forces, argued
what seemed to Hughes-Hallett to be "the extraordinary view that
the English South Coast and the French North Coast should be lik-
ened to a front line of two armies locked in trench warfare, with the
Channel as the no-man's land between them. From this it was
argued that the initiative for mounting raids should rest with the
Army Commanders whose areas faced a particular piece of enemy
coast. No raids took place under this arrangement, if only because all
the specialist craft needed to carry raiding troops came under COHQ,
which alone possessed the requisite three-Service Staff to ensure
close liaison with the RAF and Naval Commanders-in-Chief." Not
until March 1942 did Paget concede that "all raids," regardless of
location, would be under COHQ's auspices, and only then because
the Chiefs of Staff made it so by a formal directive.[20]

To get things going, Hughes-Hallett dusted off Keyes's plan to
raid the town of South Vaagso in Norway. The purpose was to
destroy military and economic targets there and on the nearby island
of Maloy. On December 27, after three weeks of hurried planning
and training, 626 commandos were landed by an amphibious force
composed of one heavy cruiser, four destroyers, and two Infantry
Assault Ships. The successful raid yielded only relatively light casualties of twenty men killed and fifty-seven wounded. No ships were
lost, but three supporting RAF aircraft and their crews failed to
return to base.[21]

Destruction of a radar station near the village of Bruneval, about
twelve miles northeast of Le Havre, came next. A small force of para-
troopers dropped near the station on the night of February 27–28.
Surprise was complete. The German guards and signallers were
overrun and many killed. After blowing up the station, the para-
troopers were evacuated off a nearby beach. Only one man was killed,
with seven wounded and another seven missing. The mission was
deemed a complete success due "not only to the valour of the troops,
but once more to careful planning and to the close co-operation of all
three Services."[22]

This was the last raid in which Hughes-Hallett could utilize plans developed under Keyes's tenure, so on January 21, he, Luce, and Lieutenant Commander de Costabadie "sat down to make tentative proposals for one raid every month" through to the end of August. That the navy should exclusively develop the target list made sense within COHQ's new culture, for there "was no use suggesting places which could not be reached by the appropriate landing craft or other vessels."[23]

For March, the planners targeted St. Nazaire. Operation Chariot quickly evolved from a simple raid into one designed to destroy the city's huge dry dock. Situated six miles up the River Loire, the dry dock in St. Nazaire's shipyard was Europe's largest—the only one of sufficient size to provide a safe haven for the German battleship *Tirpitz*. The British Admiralty lived in constant fear that this sister ship to the *Bismarck* would break out of Trondheim, Norway, where she had taken refuge on January 16, 1942. The 43,900-ton *Tirpitz*, with main armament of eight 38-centimetre guns mounted in four turrets, was more than capable of wreaking the same kind of havoc *Bismarck* had done in the spring of 1941 until her sinking on May 27. This was especially possible so long as St. Nazaire's dry dock offered shelter where she could undergo a major refit after a period at sea. The Admiralty wanted the dry dock destroyed so that *Tirpitz* could find safety only at German North Sea ports, like Wilhelmshaven or Kiel. Mountbatten and Hughes-Hallett seized the opportunity to stage the biggest raid to date.

IT WAS A daunting enterprise. St. Nazaire was an industrial town with a population of about fifty thousand. The port was home to a major German submarine base, where a series of massive submarine pens protected the U-boats from aerial bombardment. Nine of these pens were completed and five more were under construction. A large German garrison manned a network of coastal and estuary artillery batteries that made St. Nazaire one of the more heavily defended ports on the European coast.[24] To reach it, the raiders must navigate a narrow channel covered for its entire length by one or more of four batteries each containing three long-range guns. Inside the harbour, an interlocked network of strongpoints mounting light machine guns or Bofors anti-aircraft guns could sweep the water with fire.

The dry dock was huge—1,148 feet long, 54 feet high, and 35 feet thick, with access provided by 167-foot-wide gates. Hughes-Hallett decided the only way to render it unusable was to fill an expendable ship with explosives, ram her into the gates, and then blow her up. Meanwhile, a commando force would destroy the dock's pumps and power plants. He hoped to deny St. Nazaire's dry dock not only to *Tirpitz* but also to U-boats.[25]

An aging destroyer, *Campbeltown,* was selected for sacrifice. Stripped to the bone and with two of four funnels removed so that her night silhouette resembled that of German frigates, *Campbeltown* was crammed tightly with explosives. "An elaborate system of time fuses was arranged [inside], which made possible the blowing-up of five tons of explosives after allowing first for her impact with the lock and then for her scuttling."[26]

In charge of the naval side of the raid was Commander Robert Edward Dudley "Red" Ryder. Commanding the 268 commandos was Lieutenant Colonel Augustus Charles Newman. *Campbeltown* was under charge of Lieutenant Commander Stephen Halden Beattie.

At 1500 hours on March 26, a tiny fleet of fourteen motor launches (MLS) and *Campbeltown* sailed from Falmouth. Leading the way was a motor gun boat (MGB). In reserve was a motor torpedo boat (MTB) equipped with unproven delayed-action torpedoes. These would be used to breach the dry dock should *Campbeltown* fail to ram the gate.

With RAF bombers executing a diversionary raid, the little flotilla successfully entered the channel undiscovered. Fifteen minutes from where they were to begin a final run towards the dry dock, an Aldis lamp ashore flashed a challenge. A signalman on the MGB fired a series of flares known to be a recent German recognition signal. He then flashed the message in German that the fleet had two craft badly damaged by enemy action and requested permission to enter the harbour without delay. The subterfuge bought five minutes' grace before, suddenly, "every available searchlight concentrated on the estuary, floodlighting the entire Force." Commander Ryder later wrote, "Each boat, with her silvery white bow and stern wave was clearly visible, with the *Campbeltown* astern of us rising up above all the others. The glare of a disturbed enemy was on us."[27]

A torrent of fire killed or wounded half the men aboard the MLS, and most of the boats failed to land their commandos. Those who did get ashore were quickly caught in a close-quarters gun battle while trying to carry out their various demolition assignments. The MGB landed Lieutenant Colonel Newman and his headquarters party.

Pressing through a storm of shell, machine-gun, and Bofors fire that left many of her small crew dead or wounded and her upper deck aflame, *Campbeltown* slammed into the gates at 0134 hours. Beattie ordered the ship scuttled and abandoned, the surviving crew members descending to the dock via ladders placed against the hull by commandos. Although Beattie was taken prisoner, his handling of *Campbeltown* garnered a Victoria Cross.

The MTB's torpedoes, meanwhile, penetrated the foundations of the lock gate that provided access to the submarine pens. At 0230 hours, Ryder, realizing that there was "nothing we could do to help our gallant soldiers on shore," ordered the MGB to escape. For twenty-five minutes, dashing ahead at twenty-four knots, the MGB ran a gauntlet of fire. Able Seaman William Alfred Savage defiantly manned the MGB's badly exposed 2-pound quick-firing gun (nicknamed a pom-pom because of the distinctive sound that original models made when firing) until a last salvo fired by a coastal gun "straddled us in the dark at a range of about four miles." A shell splinter "struck and killed" Savage. He received a posthumous Victoria Cross that recognized not only his valour but also that "shown by many other unnamed [men] in MLS, [the] MGB, and MTB who gallantly carried out their duty in extremely exposed positions against enemy firing at close range." Ryder also received a VC, for conducting an escape the citation considered "almost a miracle."

Back at St. Nazaire, the commandos became separated into small groups fighting independently. The largest consisted of about fifty men, most of them slightly wounded, under Lieutenant Colonel Newman. Hoping to fight through to open country, the commandos pushed into the heart of the town. Dawn found them fighting up St. Nazaire's main street while dragging or carrying the wounded. Realizing there was no hope of escape, Newman finally surrendered.

The total remaining commando force numbered only 109, and 80 of these were wounded. A further 59 lay dead at the docks or in the town's streets. No man had more than three rounds of ammunition. Amazingly, five commandos succeeded in escaping to Spain and returned to England. The rest were taken prisoner.

In the morning, *Campbeltown* remained wedged into the dry dock. About forty senior officers and many curious German soldiers descended on its wreckage just before it blew up. About 400 Germans were killed, including all the officers. Then, at 1630 hours on March 30, the torpedoes began detonating. This caused a panic among the Germans guarding the area that resulted in their gunning down and killing about 280 French dock workers attempting to flee to safety. Between those killed by the explosions and others shot by their comrades, an estimated 300 to 400 additional Germans died.

St. Nazaire was deemed a success despite heavy losses to the raiders. Naval losses tallied 34 officers and 151 ratings killed or missing, from a force of 62 officers and 291 ratings.[28] A report on the operation concluded that "taking into consideration the extreme vulnerability of the coastal craft [MLS], neither the losses in men nor material can be considered excessive for the results achieved." The primary result was an important one. *Tirpitz* would never venture forth from Norwegian waters, her great power rendered impotent for lack of a safe harbour. The raid also "proved that it was possible for a comparatively small force to attack a heavily-defended port under cover of darkness by exploiting to the full the element of surprise."[29]

This was all that Mountbatten, Hughes-Hallett, and their planning staff needed to spur them towards larger, bolder operations. During the late-January planning phase, another French coastal town came into COHQ's crosshairs. "For June," Hughes-Hallett wrote, "we chose Dieppe, as by that time we expected to have sufficient landing craft to lift an entire division."

2

For the Sake of Raiding

A MAJOR REASON DIEPPE came to the fore of Combined Operations planning was an agreement by Captain Hughes-Hallett and Commander David Luce to forgo further raids in Norwegian waters. All too often, highly changeable weather and the sheer distance from Britain had resulted in cancellation or lengthy delay in mounting a raid. Mountbatten wanted a year of ambitious raiding—cancellations and delays would not suit. Although the English Channel was equally fickle weather-wise, distances were far shorter, meaning more raiding should be possible.

With great bustle and little consideration of actual practicalities, Hughes-Hallett, Luce, and Lieutenant Commander de Costabadie had selected their target during whirlwind discussions between January 21 and 23. "We were not so much concerned at this stage with the intrinsic value of objectives of a particular raid, but rather with the feasibility of reaching the place undetected," Hughes-Hallett wrote.[1] The raid on St. Nazaire, for example, had been proposed even before "the special objective against which it was finally directed—the great drydock—had been called to attention."[2] Other ideas seemed fanciful or downright foolish. Fanciful was Operation Blazing, a proposed raid on the most northerly of the Channel Islands—Alderney—by 2,150 men drawn mostly from the British Brigade of Guards supported by a few tanks. Foolish was an idea code-named Imperator. As Churchill described it, Imperator would "land on the Continent a division and armoured units to raid as effectively as possible during two or three days, and then ... re-embark as much as possible of the remnant of the force."[3] The raiders were to land at one captured port in Normandy, dash all the way to Paris, and then escape from another port on the coast. Whilst in Paris, they would shoot up the German headquarters at Hôtel de Crillon and rekindle the flame on the tomb of the Unknown Soldier at the Arc de Triomphe.[4] While some preparatory training was begun for Blazing on the Isle of Wight, Imperator remained a pipe dream that "excited serious doubts on high military levels." Still, both operations were booked into the Combined Operations schedule for 1942—Blazing for May, Imperator for August.[5]

These operations aside, COHQ planners were mostly eager to raid ports. Mountbatten stressed that "we really wanted to take a port because even if the invasion itself took place across open beaches, a sheltered port would be necessary immediately as weather statistics showed that one could not rely on more than four consecutive days fine enough to go on landing reinforcements, ammunition, vehicles and stores across open beaches. And if we could not do so the enemy could build up faster than us and fling us back into the sea."[6]

During the January discussions, Captain A.H. Willetts, the COHQ Air Adviser, recommended targeting only ports at the eastern end of the Channel. Anything farther west was beyond the range of fighters stationed in southern England. Brigadier Anthony Head, at this time representing the army, agreed to this limit because the troops would need to be at sea only briefly. This, he hoped, would leave them not too seasick to fight.[7] Boulogne and Calais were considered, but both towns were so large that a major multi-divisional raid would be required. Consensus at COHQ was that the first port raid should involve no more than an infantry division supported by some tanks and possibly several commando sections. There was also concern about inflicting excessive civilian casualties. A small port lessened civilian exposure.

After much consideration, Hughes-Hallett finally dropped a finger on Dieppe. "Right, let's take the old peacetime route—Newhaven to Dieppe and back. It's less than seventy miles away."[8] Hughes-Hallett later explained that Dieppe "was chosen for no particular reason originally except that it was a small seaport and we thought it would be interesting to do—to capture—a small seaport for a short time and then withdraw... It was not thought to be of any particular military importance... And it appeared... that it would be about the scale of objective that would be suitable for a divisional attack... But I must impress that we were raiding for the sake of raiding... There was no particular significance attachable to the places that were chosen."[9]

Dieppe was to be raided in June and then again in July because "we felt that a repeat raid... would achieve surprise and lead to the slaughter of specialist German engineers likely to be at work repairing and strengthening the fortifications" damaged during the earlier assault.

On January 23, Hughes-Hallett presented the list of operational targets to Mountbatten. He "agreed in principle" to them all and "asked for outline plans to be prepared."[10]

In short order Dieppe was described as "a worthwhile port in an opening in a long line of cliffs. It was near enough for air cover to be provided from airfields in the South of England, and to allow of the sea passage being made almost entirely under cover of the short summer darkness. It contained a small but first class port and facilities, and photo reconnaissance revealed many invasion barges and coastal craft, which could be removed and brought back to England by a 'cutting out' party, once the port had been captured."[11]

Although Dieppe was to be raided in June, the actual schedule was not brought to the attention of the Chiefs of Staff. Mountbatten instead pulled each proposed raid like a rabbit from a hat in whatever order seemed most likely to gain favour or keep Combined Operations at the centre of attention. Possibly this was because he had begun advocating an even bolder plan hatched during the late winter of 1941. On March 9, during a particularly rancorous meeting of the chiefs, Churchill demanded to know "whether an operation could be mounted against France at an early date in the event of this rather desperate action becoming necessary in order to keep Russia in the war." Everyone present, including Commander-in-Chief, Home Forces, General Bernard Paget, "reported that this simply could not be done." Mountbatten, however, said that he and his staff had concluded "it was possible... to mount an operation against the Cherbourg Peninsula." Mountbatten had a draft plan—mostly drawing on earlier planning by COHQ and various Home Army commanders—which was duly presented. It was immediately after this meeting that Churchill, appearing "delighted to find one Service authority that was prepared to recommend action," awarded Mountbatten his various promotions and cemented his presence as a full-fledged member of the Chiefs of Staff and Combined Chiefs of Staff committees.[12]

The scheme was incredibly ambitious. It envisioned not only invading and gaining control of the entire peninsula but holding it indefinitely. To foil German counterattacks, the marshes at the neck linking it to the bulk of Normandy would be flooded. Mountbatten threw most of his energy through the rest of March into the Cherbourg venture. Specifications were sent to the Admiralty for how to suitably equip a headquarters ship. A program for training landing craft crews was developed, as was one for RAF fighter squadrons in providing ground support to army units. A report was also drawn up on what was needed to ready ports in southern England for undertaking a major amphibious assault.[13]

Mountbatten's enthusiasm flew directly in the face of opposition from the rest of the Chiefs of Staff. Brooke had earlier flirted with the idea to the point that he had asked each commander of a region of the Home Army to develop an operational plan for a tactical exercise held at Camberley on December 13, 1941. All the commanders, save one, advanced a limited plan calling for brief occupation followed by rapid withdrawal. The lone dissenting voice had been South-Eastern Command's Major General Bernard Montgomery. He was also the only commander who presented his brief personally. Montgomery first pointed out the operation's hazardous nature before arguing that it would be better not to withdraw the troops but instead to flood the marshes. In this way, Montgomery provided the unreservedly brash Mountbatten with the base elements of his Cherbourg plan.[14]

Despite having instigated examination of this project, Brooke had by March lost all enthusiasm for it. And although Mountbatten continued to argue its viability, he simultaneously advanced other propositions that diverted attention from the Cherbourg venture, leaving his true commitment to the operation unclear. Had he strongly advocated it in the knowledge that such a venture would appeal to Churchill's love of a gamble? If so, it was a hand well played—as the rapid promotions proved.

Having gained the two coveted seats at the pinnacle of Allied decision making on the western front, Mountbatten was soon playing his self-appointed magician role to this august and largely captive audience. Brooke often quietly seethed during these sessions, in which Mountbatten "frequently wasted his own time and ours."[15] First out of the hat was a proposed raid on Bayonne in southwestern France. This was quickly set aside for the St. Nazaire raid, which won favour and was carried out. Spurred on by the success of this raid, Mountbatten directed Hughes-Hallett on April 4 to develop a detailed draft plan for the Dieppe raid.[16] Mountbatten had decided he should soon take this idea to the Chiefs of Staff, as it had more promise for being actualized than the Cherbourg scheme.

BY APRIL 14, the Dieppe raid plan had gained an operational identity—Rutter. After Hughes-Hallett briefly outlined the plan on that day at a COHQ meeting, it was "agreed that the project was attractive and worthwhile." The only refinement suggested was the possible use of "parachute troops in small groups for the purpose of cutting communications." The next step was for further examination by COHQ advisers and a representative from Home Forces to "define the object of the raid, state approximately the forces required, explain the way in which the forces would be employed, [and] enumerate the limiting factors." It was further agreed that "although the Advisers and Planners would have to go into considerable detail to test the practicability of the plan, the outline plan for submission to higher authority for approval should not be more than a broad outline."[17]

Even as Mountbatten prepared to propose the Dieppe raid to the Chiefs of Staff, he was at pains to keep the plan secret. This was a serious challenge, as the Anglo-American debate over the timing and fate of both Sledgehammer and Roundup were concurrently under way and still the source of intense wrangling. On the British side, the various commands involved in operational planning for these were numerous, with hundreds of personnel engaged. Mountbatten sought to keep the Dieppe raid tightly compartmentalized. No officers were allowed to attend planning meetings unless they possessed a special pass identifying them as having been cleared to know details of Operation Rutter.

But still the numbers in the know kept growing, and Hughes-Hallett considered "gossip... inevitable." He was not surprised when a Home Forces brigadier approached "one day and said he would like to have a word about our proposed raid on Dieppe." One plan the brigadier was examining involved initial, simultaneous attacks each of division strength on four or five small ports between Boulogne and St. Brieux. "He went on to say that each Divisional assault was to be based on identical tactics about which there was some division of opinion in the Home Forces Staff. However, the current idea was to deliver flank attacks, each of Brigade strength, while the third Brigade would be held back as a floating reserve ready to reinforce one of the flank attacks, or to deliver a frontal assault timed to synchronise with the approach of one or both of the flank brigades from the landward side of the seaport. 'Would it be possible,' he asked, 'so to plan the Dieppe raid, which was, after all, intended primarily to gain experience, that these tactics could be tested?'"

Although startled by the brigadier's level of knowledge regarding both the purpose and extent of the Dieppe raid, Hughes-Hallett said he was not in a position to make that decision. He would, however, take it to Charles Haydon—COHQ's Military Adviser—for discussion at their next planning meeting.

Even more than Hughes-Hallett, Major General Haydon was alarmed that "Dieppe should already—in the first half of April—be a matter of common knowledge to the big Staffs of the Combined Commanders." But both officers recognized that nothing could be done about it. Haydon, however, "felt that there were attractive features to putting the main weight of our assault on the flanks. The major problem and uncertainties of an invasion could be tested equally well by avoiding an initial frontal attack, and the risk to the troops if the landings were held up would be greatly lessened."

Accordingly, the initial Dieppe plan was developed along these lines.[18] Landings would take place at Quiberville to the west and Criel-sur-Mer to the east. Quiberville lay six miles from Dieppe, Criel-sur-Mer twelve miles distant. "These landings were to be supported by tanks," stated one Combined Operations report, "and were to be carried out by six battalions of infantry. The tanks landing at Quiberville would have only a short distance to go to the aerodrome of St. Aubin and the high ground to the southeast and west of the town, of which the capture would mean the ability to dominate Dieppe. On the other hand, to get through the tanks would have to cross the Rivers Saane and Scie and the bridges would therefore have to be seized and held by infantry. In the summer neither of these rivers are wide enough or deep enough to prove an insuperable tank obstacle.

"Tanks landing at Criel-sur-Mer would have been able to move parallel to the coast two or three miles inland and reach Dieppe within three-quarters of an hour, provided they could cover some 12 to 14 miles during that time period. Their progress might be delayed by a battalion of German infantry known to be in that neighbourhood."[19]

Although the operation centred on Dieppe, occupying the town was not a priority or even an objective. The emphasis instead was on seizing the airport—about two and a half miles inland from the beach fronting Dieppe—and heights overlooking the town. Damaging the airport and demonstrating that a landing force could isolate Dieppe was deemed sufficient experience in landing a force of divisional size, conducting limited operations against the Germans, and then spiriting the raiders safely back to sea.[20]

WHEN MOUNTBATTEN PRESENTED the broad outline to the Chiefs of Staff, it was approved subject to vetting by a Home Force commander appointed by General Paget. As the operation would surely be staged from ports in South-Eastern Command, Montgomery was the obvious choice. Montgomery requested a preliminary informal meeting "so that he and his staff could clear their minds on one or two points." The meeting convened in Hughes-Hallett's office at COHQ, with about nine officers attending.

COHQ staff had expected Montgomery to send only a representative, as the discussion was to "be of an exploratory nature." Consequently, Hughes-Hallett never considered asking Mountbatten to be present; Hughes-Hallett himself attended only because Charles Haydon suggested that he should chair, since it was the army part of the plan being scrutinized.

When Montgomery entered the room, therefore, everyone present was surprised. In 1942, Montgomery had not yet adopted his legendary outfit of tattered army sweater and black tanker beret. Instead, like any other British general, he wore the standard red cap and uniform of that rank. A lean whippet of a man, Montgomery was self-assured, possessing an acerbic tongue and a sharply critical nature. He had no use for Mountbatten and little more for Combined Operations. Mountbatten, he said once, was a "very gallant sailor. Had three ships sunk under him. *Three* ships sunk under him. [Pause.] Doesn't know how to fight a battle."[21]

"This is a COHQ plan," Montgomery told Hughes-Hallett, "so please take the chair." As this countered military protocol—whereby the senior officer present automatically has the chair—Hughes-Hallett politely demurred, while noting that Montgomery "needed little persuasion to take it himself.

"Coming directly to the point, he opened the meeting by saying that the Military part of the plan was 'the work of an amateur.'"[22] He then enquired as to whether the raid's duration could run for forty-eight hours.[23] Hughes-Hallett said the navy could support only fifteen hours ashore. Montgomery said that it would then be impossible for the flank brigades to work round and reach Dieppe from the landward side in time. This would still be true even if there was no German opposition. "He pointed out that the only way the town and seaport could be captured quickly was to deliver a frontal assault and take it by coup-de-main."[24]

Montgomery then asked if it would "be possible for the Navy to land the major part of a Division simultaneously on the sea front of the town with two or three Battalions on the beach at Pourville, some two or three miles to the south[west], together with another Battalion at Puys, about a mile to the north[west]."

Hughes-Hallett said a simultaneous landing "would hardly be practicable as there would be insufficient sea room with so many landing craft to form up in the dark without great risk of confusion. If, however, it was acceptable to have a 20 minute delay between the landings at the centre and on the flanks, then this would be possible from a Naval point of view."

Montgomery dismissed a twenty-minute interval as "too small to matter," Hughes-Hallett later wrote, and then asked that "we should re-plan the raid on these lines in conjunction with one or two members of his own staff."[25] At no time did Montgomery argue that the raid was simply ill conceived and should not be mounted. Even his authorized biographer, Nigel Hamilton, would later confess bafflement at his "approval of the outline plan." Did Montgomery, Hamilton asked, "seriously believe a Combined Operation using untried soldiers could successfully smash its way into the heart of Dieppe and beyond—to the airfield of Arques-la-Bataille—in a matter of hours, and then be successfully re-embarked on the following tide? Furthermore, [Montgomery's] own instructions relating to the defence of the South-East Army's coastline, with clear-cut orders on states of readiness of coastal batteries, the manning of radiolocation units, all-round wiring-in of strong points, and constant rehearsal of counter-attack operations, could hardly have left him in any doubt that his equally professional counterparts across the Channel would be similarly trained to repulse enemy raids."

Montgomery, Hamilton observed, had a "far more impetuous personality at heart than was commonly supposed." This was mitigated, even hidden, beneath the "self-imposed qualities of total professional discipline and the will to master all aspects of his profession." When "innate character acted in conjunction with self-conscious vocation, there arose a combination that would not only take him to the 'top of his profession' but bring him world-wide acclaim; but when such a conjunction did not occur—when rashness overtook studious mastery of tactical possibilities and impossibilities... the result was often failure."[26]

Over the next few days, this planning syndicate produced two alternative plans. The first precisely replicated Montgomery's proposal. There would be a frontal attack on Dieppe, supplemented by two flank attacks, at Puys and Pourville. Added into the mix were attacks by parachute and glider troops against two heavy batteries of coastal guns. One of these was situated near Petit Berneval, five miles east of Dieppe. The other battery was at Varengeville-sur-Mer, which lay four miles to the west of the port town.[27]

The second plan was an intervention attempt by Mountbatten and Hughes-Hallett, both of whom feared disaster if it came to a frontal attack on Dieppe. A modification of the original COHQ concept, this plan called for an infantry battalion supported by a battalion manning the new Churchill tanks—as yet untried in combat—to land at Quiberville. "They would go flat out for the local airfield and the heights just west of Dieppe itself," Mountbatten later wrote. "Whoever held those heights could command the Dieppe Front. Two battalions of infantry would land at Pourville, which was only two miles west of the harbour entrance at the mouth of a small river and support this pincer movement. Finally two battalions would be landed at Puys, a mile east of the harbour, leaving two more to remain afloat under the Land Force Commander's hand as a reserve."[28]

On April 18, a further meeting was held at COHQ, with Major General Haydon presiding. In addition to most COHQ planners, representatives from the general staff of Home Forces, the Home Forces planning section, and the Airborne Division attended. Although Hughes-Hallett was unable to attend, he had ensured that his view that "a frontal assault would be unduly hazardous" was on record. Despite this objection, the consensus of those attending was that "on balance there were advantages in taking the town by a frontal assault." As no minutes were written during this meeting, nobody could say afterwards how this consensus was reached.[29]

Three days later, Haydon chaired another meeting aimed at further developing the frontal-attack scheme. Unlike many COHQ meetings about Operation Rutter, this one was recorded in fairly extensive minutes. Originally, an initial assault wave of infantry and tanks was to have landed a half hour after nautical twilight, the period when the centre of the sun is between six and twelve degrees below the horizon. Bright stars are still visible in clear weather—a condition the raid depended on—and the horizon is coming into view. Yet it remains too dark on land to move about easily without artificial lighting. Nautical twilight in the early summer off the French coast would begin at just before 0600 hours, so the first flight of landing craft was to gain the beach in front of Dieppe at about 0630 hours.

Hughes-Hallett and Commander Luce, however, argued that landing tanks in the first flight would mean losing the element of surprise. The tanks would be carried to the beach by specially designed craft called Landing Craft Tank (LCT), which necessarily were larger and had a higher profile than the small craft used for landing infantry. German observers, the naval officers said, would easily spot the LCTs heading in about two hours before dawn. Attempting to approach the beach earlier, while it was still completely dark, risked the LCTs grounding on various obstacles "resulting in stranding and consequent confusion."

Accordingly, it was decided a first flight of infantry would land in front of Dieppe thirty minutes after nautical twilight. The moment they touched down would be designated Zero Hour. At the same time, a parachute battalion would drop near the Forêt d'Arques, about six miles inland from the beach. Glider troops would also be landed inland from the beaches on the flanks, while smaller groups of paratroops would descend to "deal with mobile batteries and any additional targets outside the port." There would be a "simultaneous air bombardment against the town and sea front."

The main landing force, consisting of one tank squadron and two infantry battalions, would land on the seafront forty-five minutes after Zero Hour. The rest of the tank force would follow sometime between Zero plus 120 minutes and 180 minutes. Engineers and other support troops "required for demolitions on the approaches to the town and in the town would accompany the forces" in the main and follow-on landings. No landing of tanks would occur at Pourville because this seemed "more difficult than was supposed at first."

Continuous fighter cover while the troops were ashore was considered vital. Fighter cover generally "would take the form of a moderate degree of cover throughout the hours of daylight with maximum intensity at certain hours when the danger to the naval force and small craft was greatest." These periods were estimated to be for about two hours after the follow-on tank landing and from the "time loading commences until dusk."

Offensive air bombardment was to "continue from Z+30 to Z+85 at high and low level. The high altitude attack will be against the town generally. The low level attack will concentrate against the sea front and beach defences.

"The withdrawal and re-embarkation would have to start with some of the tanks about 8 hours after zero. These would be followed by infantry. The maximum number of infantry would embark from the harbour itself rather than from the sea front."[30]

On April 25, Mountbatten chaired a meeting "to thrash out the pros and cons of the two plans."[31] He and the COHQ planners again opposed the frontal assault, pointing out "that so far as the main object of the raid was concerned, it really did not matter very much whether Dieppe was captured or not, and that this would make but little difference to the main purpose of the operation, namely, to gain experience." The representatives of the Home Forces (Montgomery not attending) however said it was their commander's view "that if we did not capture the town, the operation would be represented for ever afterwards as a failure."[32]

They argued that "if a force were landed as far from Dieppe as Quiberville, it would be difficult to achieve surprise against the town itself; while furthermore tanks put ashore there would have to cross two rivers (the Saane and the Scie) en route to Dieppe. This would necessitate arrangements for seizing the bridges to prevent their being demolished. In addition it was believed that Dieppe itself was probably held only by a 'single low-category battalion' [of about 1,400 men], though this was supported by a considerable number of guns."[33] Intelligence staff calculated it would "take five hours to reinforce the garrison and only after eight hours would the reinforcements be arriving in any considerable strength. At the end of fifteen hours the maximum number of enemy troops taking part in the defence... would not exceed 6,500 men."[34]

Hughes-Hallett and his fellow naval planners "still expressed doubt about the frontal assault, but not on naval grounds." To allay their concern, the army and air representatives emphasized that an air bombardment "of maximum intensity" would be put in immediately before the frontal assault, "and it was thought that the defence would be too confused by it and by subsequent attacks from low flying aircraft to be in a position to offer stout or prolonged resistance."

The Chiefs of Staff had earlier decided that ultimate authority for the army part of a divisional raiding plan rested with the Home Forces and, consequently, Montgomery. As Montgomery and his staff were set on the raid being anchored on a frontal assault, Mountbatten and Hughes-Hallett had no option but to give way.

Attention now turned to what troops would carry out the raid. Mountbatten wanted to use the Royal Marine Division, supported by commandos. Both formations, he felt, were "well trained for the job." Again the final decision was not his. Authority for selecting the troops rested with General Paget.[35]

AS THE PLAN now called for tanks to join the frontal assault on Dieppe, it was imperative to know whether they could surmount the seawall stretching from the western cliff in front of the beach to the harbour mouth. A Major Robinson serving with the clandestine Special Operations Executive, who had spent much time before the war visiting Dieppe, maintained that there were three ramps leading up from the beach onto the seawall. But aerial reconnaissance was unable to confirm this, as shadows from the adjacent tall cliffs rendered clear, detailed photography next to impossible.

The planners consequently turned to an unnamed person who had lived near Dieppe for more than twenty years. He assured them that "the shingle [pebbles] on the beach washes up to the top of the sea-wall and that there is direct access from the beach to the promenade over the top of the sea-wall which, in such cases, does not form an obstacle."

However, two aerial photographs taken the previous summer clearly showed an unramped "sea-wall at the western end of the beach near the casino." Undaunted, the planners concluded optimistically that "whilst this contradicts the reported statement, it may be, however, that in normal times the western end of the sea-wall is kept clear as being in front of the casino and probably the most frequented part of the beach, whereas the eastern part of the beach was more neglected and the shingle allowed to pile up against the sea-wall."[36]

That Dieppe—occupied by German troops, with its casino and all its beachfront hotels closed—was experiencing anything but normal times was not noted. So there was no allowance for the possibility that the Germans might consider the seawall a significant defensive feature they would do everything in their power to make as effective an obstacle as possible.

Information on the rivers within the operational area was equally scanty. All were described accurately as "slow flowing, meandering," and running along "flat-bottomed valleys with a slight fall towards the coast." Their banks were low, with flat grass meadows lying on either side. As none were navigable, there was "no information regarding their widths or depths." The Saane and Scie were believed to be no more than thirty feet wide at their mouths and unlikely to be more than six to eight feet deep. The Arques, which emptied into Dieppe harbour, was about sixty feet wide at its mouth.

"So far as the question of these rivers being tank obstacles is concerned, it is considered that this is entirely seasonal. It is known that the rivers Saane and Scie flood in the spring, but from aerial photographs the flooding appears to be near the mouth. It is not so much the depth or extent of the floods that would form an obstacle to tanks, but the resultant softness of the river banks which might quite well prove unable to bear any heavy loads. In summer and early autumn it is not considered that either the river Saane or Scie would be wide enough or deep enough to form tank obstacles. One feature in this respect is, however, worth noting and that is that on the river Scie from a point of about [2.5] miles upstream from its mouth to a point about 5 miles upstream there are no less than 10 waterfalls which may well consist of small dams and may thus mean that the river is deeper than would be expected from its natural features."

Photographs had revealed numerous footpaths leading down to the rivers at various points, and the analysts concluded that "fords may exist at these points. In many places footpaths bridge the rivers thus proving that they are narrow and easily bridged."[37]

Besides getting a feel for the terrain, the planners also sought to understand what enemy forces were present. As the raiders were expected to be ashore for fifteen hours, it was theoretically possible for German reinforcements to move to the Dieppe area from distances of one to two hundred miles away and present a threat. Where were these forces situated, and how soon could they reach the port once tactical surprise was lost? Presented with a series of questions in this regard on April 17, army intelligence responded a few days later.

"The only enemy armoured forces known to be in France are around Paris," the intelligence report stated. "They are believed to be equipped with only one to two hundred light French tanks. It is not believed that these could go into action at Dieppe within fifteen hours."

As for the Germans at Dieppe, they were reportedly a battalion from the 302nd Infantry Division equipped for coastal defence, which likely meant they were "short of mortars and anti-tank equipment. The troops are second-rate and are not mobile." It was also thought that the Dieppe regiment's Infantry Gun Company and Anti-Tank Company were in the area (meaning some presence of light artillery and anti-tank guns). Additionally, divisional troops providing a field artillery battery, and "considerable elements" of the "Anti-Tank and Engineer Battalions and of the Supply Unit" were believed to be close to or inside Dieppe. Mobile artillery batteries were certainly in the area, but their positions had not been located. These batteries might field 75-millimetre, 105-millimetre, or 150-millimetre guns. There were also definitely light anti-aircraft batteries armed with either 20-millimetre or 37-millimetre guns. Again, where these batteries were situated was unknown.

All told, the forces immediately available in the Dieppe area numbered about 1,400. During the first five hours, however, it could be expected that two battalions could arrive as reinforcements—one from the south and the other the west. Another two infantry companies could move in from coastal positions close by. There were also divisional troops that might advance from the suspected headquarters at Arques. Altogether these totalled about 2,500. Within eight hours of the raid beginning, further reinforcement of about 2,400 men could start flowing in from the Rouen area. By the fifteen-hour mark, as many as 6,500 Germans could be engaged at Dieppe.[38]

As the intelligence flowed in, it became increasingly clear to the COHQ planners that the "task was hazardous." But in the words of one Combined Operations report, "so is any operation of war." And Dieppe's "defences could... be taken as a fair sample of what the attackers [involved in the eventual cross-channel invasion] might have to meet at whatever point an assault was launched along the coast of Northern France."[39]

Having assembled an operational plan and gathered much intelligence—as dubious and vague as it might be—COHQ's staff were now ready to involve the naval, air, and, most importantly, army forces that would actually carry out the raid. Mountbatten and Hughes-Hallett were both surprised that instead of the combined force including the Royal Marine Division and supporting commandos they had suggested, a division of Canadians would form the raiding force's core. Neither man knew anything about the Canadians or their capabilities. But Mountbatten was told by General Alan Brooke that the Canadians desired "to be brought into a raiding operation as soon as possible."

Some other operation, perhaps, Mountbatten countered. The raid under consideration "was such a large and uncertain operation," he cautioned. "We were trying to find out things and even if successful in all our aims there would be nothing much to show for it to the outside world and we were bound to have heavy casualties... this was the very last operation on which untried and inexperienced Canadian troops should be used. They would not be able to cover themselves with glory however successful the operation and would be bound to suffer heavy casualties which would appear to be difficult to justify."

Mountbatten later recalled "going on and on at Brookie and asking not to have to take the Canadians. However he said that [Lieutenant General Harry] Crerar was absolutely adamant that they should be used and that the P.M. was prepared to accept them. I was over-ridden and I remember Brookie saying to me that now more than ever the land forces plan must be made by Home Forces themselves and the Canadians must be brought into the planning at once and take the final responsibility with Monty for the army plan."[40]

3

A Fantastic Conception

O N APRIL 27, 1 Canadian Corps commander Lieutenant General Harry Crerar was summoned to Montgomery's headquarters in Dover. "Crerar," Montgomery said in his direct manner, "you have been wanting action for a long time. Here's your chance." An infantry division supported by tanks was to raid a French port, and Montgomery believed the plan had "a lot of possibilities. The raid is yours, if you want it. If you accept, then the commander of the division you nominate will be responsible for producing a detailed plan in cooperation with Combined Ops, under the general authority of myself and Mountbatten. Do you want it?"

"You bet we want it," Crerar replied.

"Then you have it. The target is Dieppe."[1]

When Crerar nominated 2nd Canadian Infantry Division for the task, Montgomery agreed this was the best choice.[2] Having observed the division's performance during the three-day Exercise Beaver III, a mock invasion begun on April 22, Montgomery had concluded that 2nd Division's new commander, Major General John Hamilton Roberts, was "the best divisional commander in the [Canadian] Corps."[3]

This was actually faint praise, because Montgomery's opinion of the other Canadian divisional generals was largely negative. Major General George Pearkes, a Great War Victoria Cross winner, had assumed command of 1st Division upon Crerar's 1940 elevation to corps command. After Beaver III, Montgomery commented that Pearkes would "fight his division" to the last man, and "the last man would be killed all too soon."[4]

For its part, 3rd Canadian Infantry Division had only finished deploying to England at the end of September 1941 and was still finding its feet under another Great War veteran, Major General Basil Price. Although he had won both a Distinguished Service Order and Distinguished Conduct Medal during the last war, Price was proving a lacklustre divisional commander.[5]

Crerar's opinion of Roberts was mixed, and he had criticized the man's performance during Beaver III. Forward units, playing the defender role against 1st Division's invaders, had been deployed for passive defence rather than being readied to quickly switch over to offensive counterattacks at the first opportunity. Divisional staff work had been clumsy and rushed.[6] But Crerar would not let such concerns get in the way of securing the Dieppe raid for Canada. He had spent far too many months lobbying for precisely such an opportunity.

Montgomery cautioned Crerar to keep the offer confidential until he was able to present it to First Canadian Army commander Lieutenant General Andrew McNaughton. The last thing Montgomery wanted was any suggestion that he had gone behind the prickly senior Canadian officer's back to first secure Crerar's consent. This was purely a matter of protocol—both Crerar and Montgomery considered the deal now done. McNaughton, elevated to command of the newly minted First Canadian Army on April 6, was poorly positioned to refuse Montgomery. The previous September, McNaughton and Commander-in-Chief, Home Forces, General Bernard Paget had discussed Canadian troops participating in cross-channel raids against the French coast. The current offer could be considered a natural progression towards that objective. Since the Canadians had been shifted from Aldershot to Sussex, Paget had been sending small detachments for combined operations training at Chichester Harbour. McNaughton, meanwhile, had overseen the drafting of plans for Canadians to possibly participate in two minor raids during the winter, only to have each cancelled due to lack of landing craft.[7]

In truth, McNaughton was lukewarm on the idea of committing Canadians to raiding operations. During the Great War, he had proved a brilliant artillery officer with a fine scientific mind and ended the war as a brigadier and holder of a Distinguished Service Order. He was also as implacable a nationalist as Crerar, while strongly disagreeing on how Canada's role in the war should be conducted. Crerar was all for casting Canadians into battle at first opportunity. McNaughton was determined to keep the Canadian Army in England together and feared British desires to disperse it to suit their immediate needs.[8]

Although McNaughton had led the first Canadian contingent overseas in the fall of 1939, by 1942 he showed signs of having "grown increasingly distant from his army, which scarcely saw him." McNaughton's right-hand man, Brigadier Guy Simonds, viewed with dismay how the commander surrounded himself with a coterie of officers who were friends and allies but possessed only a modicum of ability. When such favourites failed to live up to the demands of their positions, McNaughton generally promoted them in rank and to jobs distant from operational command. Simonds considered this a "vicious practice" that diluted the army's efficiency.

McNaughton also increasingly seemed uninterested in the divisions being trained for battle. He "would not focus his mind on training and operational problems, and for a long time we were adrift," Simonds observed.[9]

EVEN WHILE STILL serving as Canada's Military Chief of Staff in Ottawa, Crerar had headed a cabal of officers that believed the army overseas needed some immediate limited combat experience to bolster its morale. McNaughton dismissed the idea that there was any problem or that sending some troops into combat would bolster overall morale.

During a March 1942 visit to Washington, McNaughton met President Franklin Roosevelt, who alluded to hearing rumours that the Canadians were experiencing morale issues due to "their long period of static employment." "I told him," McNaughton wrote, "that I had no particular anxiety on this score at the moment nor would I have for some months to come. I told him that this was because the force was rapidly growing, there were ample outlets for promotion, that we had been working the men very hard, that we were constantly changing the scene of our activities, that we had paid attention to education, etc., and most importantly that I thought our soldiers were a highly intelligent body of men, who recognized that they were only there for the purpose of making a definite contribution to the defeat of the Axis. They were just as well aware as I was of the wisdom of deferring action until a proper opportunity developed for their use, because what we wished to do was not to fight for the sake of fighting, but to bring the maximum possible continuing effect against the enemy."

McNaughton's overriding concern was to keep the army unified to fulfill this destiny. He explained to Roosevelt that the Canadian duty was to provide the Allied "foothold for an eventual attack on the Continent of Europe... There could be no question but that war could only be ended by the defeat of Hitler and the only way of doing so was to attack him from the West." McNaughton "never lost sight of this object and... had always been convinced that an offensive would sooner or later have to be launched from the United Kingdom across the narrow seas." His position precisely mirrored that of Prime Minister Mackenzie King and his cabinet.[10]

The invasion would be a massive combined operation on a scale never seen before. So McNaughton saw value in Canadian troops being trained to work alongside naval and air personnel in developing amphibious landing techniques and tactics for executing advances inland from a beachhead. But such training need not lead to participation in small raids.

McNaughton might well have fended off calls for Canadians to be committed to raiding had he not fallen ill due to fatigue and been forced to take sick leave on November 14, 1941.[11] When he returned to Canada for convalescence at the end of the year, Crerar was sent to take over 1 Canadian Corps in his absence. McNaughton would not return until the end of March 1942, and by that time Crerar was well advanced in undermining his superior's authority.[12]

The fifty-three-year-old Crerar had also served in the Great War as an artillery officer. Along the way he had developed a close friendship with then lieutenant colonel Alan Brooke, a Royal Artillery staff officer. He and Brooke "used to tramp the front line of battery positions together," often doing so under enemy fire. At war's end, Crerar was a lieutenant colonel, held a DSO, and had been Mentioned in Despatches. Continuing a career within the Permanent Forces after the war, Crerar had held a succession of senior staff appointments.[13]

These postings connected him well politically, but they also further developed Crerar's inherent aloofness, which masked a tendency towards shyness. He did not mix comfortably with the common soldier or his fellow officers, whether senior or subordinate. His insistence on strict discipline, proper dress, and adherence to military protocol helped little. His staff background gave him a near obsessive compulsion to generate detailed plans, background reports, and other documentation for the simplest operation. There was also the plain fact that Crerar did not have the dashing army officer look. As one observer noted, Crerar "cut an unwarlike figure; battledress was not kind to the middle-aged, especially those not blessed with trim figures."[14]

Crerar cared little for preserving the army for an eventual starring role in a decisive cross-channel invasion. He had been a key figure in encouraging the British request that Canada send troops to Hong Kong in the fall of 1941 and had personally selected the Winnipeg Grenadiers and Royal Rifles of Canada for the doomed venture.[15]

That disaster did nothing to dampen Crerar's determination to get the army fighting as soon as possible. That this intent was at odds with that of Prime Minister King was no deterrent. King's concern was to avoid high casualty rates that might force implementation of conscription for overseas service, rather than sending only volunteers. Although the National Mobilization Recruitment Act had been enacted in June 1940, those called up had to volunteer for overseas posting. Otherwise, they were assigned to defence duties in Canada. There was no appetite in Quebec for sending conscripts to fight against their will, but the English-speaking majority elsewhere generally favoured such deployment. King knew that committing conscripts to combat would fracture the nation's tenuous unity in the war effort. The longer the army was kept out of battle, the longer a manpower crisis could be averted. By late 1941, however, newspapers across the country were pressing for the army to get into the fight. The Second Front movement was also active, with massive rallies held in Toronto's Maple Leaf Gardens and even the Montreal Forum, the crowds demanding action to relieve the pressure on the Soviet Union. Newspaper editorials and the clamouring of opposition MPS fuelled the fire. "It seems an awful thing to say," mused a senior officer at Canadian Military Headquarters, "but the people of Canada are calling for blood."[16]

It was against this backdrop that Crerar took up corps command in England. It was a lofty responsibility for a man with no experience of divisional or even brigade command. To Crerar's credit, his inexperience was something he himself worried about.

Pearkes, who had been managing the corps in McNaughton's absence, was furious that Crerar got the posting instead of him. Soon asked to have a 1st Division battalion commander brief Crerar on a forthcoming exercise, Pearkes told the man to "make it simple. Imagine you are explaining to a man who has never commanded anything."[17]

Crerar recognized that there was much resentment of his posting among the Canadian headquarters staff. Many felt his promotion over them was unfair and unwarranted. Crerar was going to have to prove himself.

He found an unlikely ally in Montgomery. Polar opposites in personality and command approach, both men considered themselves consummate professionals in the art of soldiering. When the Canadians came under South-Eastern Command, Montgomery said he expected an "offensive" spirit and was going to impose a standardized training doctrine. McNaughton's loose, often unfocused training approach did not cut it. During his short tenure as corps commander, Pearkes had been irritated by Montgomery's direct interference in the Canadian training—particularly as it was accompanied by a patronizing and judgemental manner.

When Crerar asked someone on his new staff to describe Montgomery, the officer allowed that he was "an efficient little shit." Crerar would never use such language, but he did later admit that

Montgomery's idea of "an army with good morale was an army commanded by Monty." However, Crerar recognized Montgomery's professionalism and experience. During the early months of 1942, he was willing to allow Montgomery the lead in training the corps.[18]

The training to that point had lacked a sense of urgency or reality, and the troops had become increasingly "bored with make-believe exercises." Simonds had not hesitated to broach his concerns about the poor state of the Canadians' training as soon as they came under Montgomery's command. There was a rot running through the entire officer ranks, he confided to one of Montgomery's staff officers, that left serious weaknesses at the battalion and brigade command levels. He thought that few battalion commanders could effectively lead their men into battle, and only "four out of nine brigadiers could train their battalion commanders."

Crerar soon agreed, allowing that "McNaughton had sadly neglected training" and the corps was "in a 'hell of a state.'"[19] Montgomery immediately imposed his vision of how things should be done. A battle-training area sufficient for a brigade to operate within—a first for the Canadians—was set aside on the South Downs in Sussex. Realism was emphasized to replicate the intensity of battle. Montgomery also trained the troops from the bottom up—working them first through platoon-level tactics, then company tactics, and on upward until the time was deemed right for a divisional exercise. Montgomery issued one training instruction after another, all intended to forge the Canadians into a cohesive and effective fighting unit. He personally assessed the officers, letting Crerar know his opinion in no uncertain terms.[20] Some should be sacked, others demoted, a precious few retained or promoted.

Crerar accepted this and built upon it. He agreed—as did Simonds—to a broad-broom housecleaning of officers who were too old, too set in their ways, or incompetent. There was plenty of new, young blood at the lower levels of command or waiting in Canada for promotion.

SHORTLY AFTER HIS arrival in England, Crerar began sending an "avalanche of letters" to Brooke, Paget, and Montgomery, advocating the commitment of Canadian troops to combined operations raiding.[21] On February 5, he wrote Montgomery that the corps would receive a "great stimulus... if, in the near future, it succeeded in making a name for itself for its raiding activities." In early March, Crerar pressed the case personally to Brooke and Mountbatten. The latter agreed to "further combined training for Canadian troops," including a "large detachment" from 2nd Division in early April.[22]

On April 1, Crerar's effort bore some fruit. Combined Operations, he was informed, was "planning a raid [for] about the middle of April," and a small party of Canadians was invited. Operation Abercrombie was primarily a No. 4 Commando show under command of the flamboyant and eccentric Major Christopher Joseph Fraser, 17th Lord Lovat. The raid's target was Hardelot, a fishing village about six miles south of Boulogne. The commandos would land under cover of darkness, reconnoitre military defences on beaches to the north and south of the village, destroy a small searchlight post, capture prisoners, and gather documents and other information. Lovat's men would land on the northern beach, closest to the searchlight post. Eight Canadian officers and sixty-one other ranks drawn from the Carleton and York Regiment of 1st Division and commanded by Lieutenant Jack Ensor would go ashore on the south beach. Their task was to send fighting patrols to test defences and take prisoners. They were also to check out two large warehouses on the village's outskirts. If the Germans appeared to be using them for storage, they were to be destroyed.

After two cancellations due to weather, the operation got under way on the night of April 21–22. Despite perfect sea conditions, Lovat's men were landed a little off the designated beach. Three patrols sent out failed to reach the searchlight post. Lovat finally fired a recall flare, and the commandos withdrew without having taken any prisoners or achieved any other objectives. The commandos suffered no casualties.

Ensor's Canadians never reached shore. The morning of the operation, the naval commander of their flotilla of three vessels had fallen ill, and a very inexperienced young officer stepped in. Once the vessels were at sea, their compasses proved defective. Closing on the French coast, the command boat with Ensor aboard became separated from the other two. With the navigators unable to fix their positions either by starlight or by faulty compass, the vessels milled about until Lovat's recall flare was spotted. The flotilla returned to Dover. Despite some random, searching machine-gun fire from German defensive positions, there were no casualties. Operation Abercrombie, the Canadian Army official historian conceded later, "was pretty much of a fiasco."[23]

SO IT CAME as a relief to Crerar when, less than a week later, Montgomery asked if he wanted the Dieppe raid. On the morning of April 30, Montgomery next visited McNaughton. The Canadian general was just adjusting, somewhat uncomfortably, to his new role at the head of First Canadian Army. Expanding the Canadian corps into an army had been General Alan Brooke's idea and was proposed to McNaughton in January 1942. "I feel that you require a Force or Army Headquarters which will take over the running of all the war services, workshops, base organization, etc., and thus free the Corps Commander's hands for the job of commanding & training the fighting formations. That in itself is a full-time job." McNaughton did not want this primarily administrative position, but he could hardly refuse. And, of course, his elevation to First Canadian Army command entrenched Crerar as corps commander and the man who would direct any fighting.[24]

Montgomery told McNaughton that "he had been approached by Home Forces [Paget] with a proposal for a raid on Dieppe. Conditions of light and tide would be favourable for such operations during the week commencing" June 21. "The troops required were one infantry division to be selected from the South Eastern Command." To make McNaughton feel the Canadians were being offered an honour, Montgomery said he had been "pressed to agree to a composite British and Canadian force." Who was doing the pressing, he never clarified. Montgomery said he had stoutly declared "that it was essential to maintain unity of command and that in his opinion the Canadian troops were those best suited." Paget and his staff had "accepted this view." As an afterthought, Montgomery said he had already spoken to Crerar, who "had nominated [2nd Division] for the operation."

McNaughton was left with no recourse but to confirm the arrangements already made "subject to the details of the plan being satisfactory and receiving his approval." Montgomery would advise

Major General Roberts "that he might start work on planning." The division would take part in an exercise code-named Tiger as part of the preparations and then "move to the Isle of Wight for training."

A few hours before this meeting, Crerar had issued Training Instruction No. 9, which directed 2nd Division to begin combined operations training. Once 2nd Division's training was complete, the other divisions would be cycled through. In reality, this instruction was "simply security cover for training for Operation 'Rutter,'" one army report noted.[25] Crerar next invited Roberts to Canadian Military Headquarters in London, because "we haven't had a chance for an undisturbed chat in a long time."

The scope of Rutter far surpassed the limits of McNaughton's authority to commit troops without approval of the War Committee in Ottawa. So McNaughton sent a "Most Secret" cable to Chief of the General Staff, Lieutenant General Ken Stuart, reminding him that his authority was for "minor" operations only. "Plans are now being made which involve operations of a type indicated, but on a scale which cannot be classed as minor. I request therefore that my authority be widened by deletion of the term minor." Authority was quickly granted.[26]

That Rutter had evolved from a highly speculative Combined Operations scheme into an operation gathering a full head of steam worried the Chiefs of Staff. To clarify how future operations and the further development of Rutter would proceed, Paget issued a directive on May 5 regarding raiding. Because he was responsible to the British cabinet for "all raids on the Continent," Paget wrote, any future proposed raid must be submitted to him in outline form. He and Mountbatten would then decide whether the project warranted further study. Paget would select which command would provide troops and delegate the operation to the army commander concerned. This commander would "be at liberty to decide whether he would retain control himself or delegate not below a Divisional Commander." Only then would an outline plan be prepared by the Home Forces and COHQ planning staffs, with the participation of a staff officer "nominated by the Army, Corps, or Divisional commander concerned." Whichever level of commander had been delegated would "attend important meetings" and finalize details of the plan in consultation with Mountbatten. The outline plan would go to the Chiefs of Staff for approval. If given, force commanders would then be appointed, "and these with their staffs would work out the detailed plan in London."

Once the detailed plan was approved, any operation targeting France or the Low Countries would require the force involved to move to the Isle of Wight for concentrated training with the Royal Navy and Royal Air Force. During this phase, "military training and operational plans... would be under the supervision of the selected military officer, while combined training with other services would be under the CCO [Mountbatten]," represented by a naval officer on his staff.[27]

This directive was authored on Paget's behalf by Chief of the General Staff, British Home Forces Command, Lieutenant General J.G. des R. Swayne. On May 7, Swayne wrote McNaughton confirming use of Canadian troops in Rutter. Swayne said it was "desirable to keep to a minimum the number of officers who know of the details of the operation." He proposed sending information to McNaughton "from time to time personally, and if he desired any amplification at any time, the Planning Staff at GHQ would be at his disposal." Was McNaughton agreeable to this approach? Swayne added that "General Montgomery will be responsible for providing the Canadian Corps and the 2nd Canadian Division with such information as they require, since he is the General Officer Commanding-in-Chief selected by the Commander-in-Chief [Paget] to prepare the outline plan."

McNaughton replied the following day confirming his consent for selecting 2nd Division and attached troops to participate in Rutter. He agreed to "keep in touch with this matter by establishing close liaison with you." Lieutenant Colonel G.P. Henderson from First Canadian Army's operations general staff, he added, was delegated "to maintain contact with whoever you may indicate. LCol Henderson will keep me informed, and if the situation at any time so requires, I will get into direct touch with you."

McNaughton said he had instructed Crerar "to keep me fully posted from his end and as a matter of *information*, it being understood that all executive action in connection with the preparations would continue to follow the chain of command: GHQ Home

Forces—SECO [Montgomery's command]—1 Cdn Corps—2 Cdn Div." McNaughton closed by saying that Roberts, under Crerar, "has now been authorized to proceed with the preparation of plans."[28]

Little more than a week earlier, McNaughton had told Montgomery that if he approved of the plan, he would agree to commit Canadian troops. McNaughton now sidelined himself without any study of Rutter. In fact, the Canadians were now fully committed to executing the operation. Only the details remained to be worked out.

MAJOR GENERAL ROBERTS found Crerar's invitation for a "chat" in London ill timed. He had taken command of 2nd Division on November 7, 1941, but only in an acting role. Roberts had replaced sixty-one-year-old Major General Victor Wentworth Odlum, a Boer War and Great War veteran, whose relief due to advanced age and apparent incompetence Montgomery had effected. Odlum was to have been replaced by Crerar, but then came the expansion of the Canadian corps into an army. So Roberts had remained at 2nd Division's helm and been formally confirmed in his rank and position on April 6, 1942.

In the intervening months, he had tried to meld 2nd Division into a crack fighting unit and was at the time of Crerar's invitation engaged in weeding out brigade and battalion commanders that were too old, incompetent, or both. Their replacements were charged with conducting a similar sweeping out of company commanders and non-commissioned officers also too old or lacking as leaders. Roberts knew much work needed to be done before the division would be up to his admittedly demanding standard of competency.

Ham Roberts, as he was known, was fifty. Tall, broad-shouldered, heavily muscled, he looked every bit the soldier. He was blunt, serious, and a dedicated professional. As one observer put it, Roberts "refused to accept the excuse that a man's best is good enough, believing implicitly that excellence was always possible."[29]

During the Great War, then lieutenant Roberts had won a Military Cross while serving in the Royal Canadian Horse Artillery at the Somme. In June 1940, Lieutenant Colonel Roberts landed in France at the head of 1st Canadian Field Regiment as part of an ad hoc and reconstituted British Expeditionary Force intended to shore up French resistance. It was an ill-conceived venture. The French Army was collapsing, and it became evident that the British and Canadian troops landed at Brest should be evacuated before the Germans overran them. By the morning of June 16, Roberts's regiment was back in Brest, its twenty-four guns lined up on a congested quay for loading aboard a ship.

The following day, the increasingly panicked British general organizing the evacuation ordered all equipment not already loaded destroyed. Only men were now to be boarded. Roberts was incensed. The situation was not so dire that the guns could not be saved. As an artilleryman, he saw abandoning the guns as a disgrace. Rushing to the British headquarters in central Brest, according to the regiment's war diary, Roberts "fought hard for nearly two hours to save his guns." Twice ordered to destroy them, he each time argued until the order was countermanded. Finally, at 1415 hours, Roberts was given permission to load as many guns as possible before a 1600 sailing. He dashed back to the quay, and the regiment began lifting the 24-pounders onto the deck of the steamer HMS *Bellerophon*. With thirty minutes to spare, all the guns were soon aboard, so Roberts gathered up a dozen Bofors anti-aircraft guns, seven predictors, three Bren carriers, and several technical vehicles belonging to other units and added them to the roster. He reluctantly acceded to abandoning the regiment's tractors and ammunition limbers. At 1715 hours, *Bellerophon* and two other vessels sailed for Portsmouth. "Although there was evidently no enemy within 200 miles, the withdrawal was conducted as a rout," the 1st Field Regiment war diary recorded.[30] Roberts's career had been advanced by the gun rescue. Within a month he was promoted to brigadier.

Such rapid promotion was not unusual in the early war years. Inter-war cutbacks had ensured that the Canadian Army lacked the senior officer cadre required for the kind of major expansion undertaken between 1939 and 1941. Many captains and majors found themselves promoted at a dizzying rate. Experience was necessarily lacking. Roberts was but one case.

But his promotion to major general concerned even a fellow artilleryman, Lieutenant Colonel Stanley Todd, who commanded 2nd Division's 4th Field Regiment. Todd was a friend and considered

Roberts "a great soldier." But he also worried that Roberts had "been a gunner all his life." Even his "gunner friends ... were slightly concerned as to his welfare in commanding an infantry division when he had no experience of infantry except in training camps." Todd felt Roberts was consequently lacking in essential knowledge. Roberts had also never been on a staff course, so he had no background or experience to help him "understand what he was getting into."[31]

In London, Roberts found Crerar not at all in the mood for a simple "undisturbed chat." Crerar abruptly informed Roberts "that as his division had not yet participated in active operations, although it had been overseas for nearly two years, [Crerar] had selected [it] to carry out the operation." The division would be supported by a single 1st Canadian Army Tank Brigade battalion.

The outline plan, Crerar said, called for six infantry battalions, supported by one tank battalion, to carry out the raid. A proportion of engineers and specialized troops would be added during the detailed planning. Crerar assured Roberts that air "support was to be on a very large scale. Naval forces available were considered to be adequate. They included six 'Hunt' class destroyers with [4-inch] guns and the requisite number of landing craft."

Troops would be landed "on the flank beaches, and on the main beaches at Dieppe." There would be "adequate measures to deal with the batteries on the extreme flanks. The military intention was to seize and hold the town and vicinity while certain demolition tasks were carried out, thereafter re-embarking and returning to England."

Roberts realized there "was much to be done. No raid on such a large scale had been planned before."[32] He was thinking about racing back to his headquarters to start work, when Crerar said a suite had been reserved for him at the Mayfair Hotel. Roberts was to remain there until summoned by either Montgomery or Mountbatten for a more detailed briefing. The suite had been booked under an assumed name. He was not to use the phone and was to avoid going out for fear of being trailed by German spies. Roberts was spirited to the Mayfair Hotel and left impatiently pacing the suite for several days while awaiting the summons from on high.[33]

On May 8, he was temporarily released for a meeting with Montgomery at the War Office. Roberts was joined by his chief operations officer, Lieutenant Colonel C. Churchill "Church" Mann. Only now was Roberts shown a copy of the outline plan. When the meeting was over, Roberts returned to the Mayfair, while Mann reported to Combined Operations Headquarters. Here he was assigned a desk and told to collaborate with naval and air force planners on Operation Rutter's detailed plan. It was made clear, however, that Mann "carried the main burden of detailed planning on behalf of... Roberts, the Military Force Commander."[34]

Tall and sparely built, Mann was just thirty-six but recognized in the Canadian Army as "a quick-witted, versatile staff officer, an artist in operational planning whose briefings were models of articulate simplicity." Montgomery's personal liaison officer, Major Goronwy Rees, thought Mann "a brilliant staff officer, but what was more exceptional was that his mind had a wild and incalculable originality, and his contempt for normal military codes and conventions was extreme."

Mann, however, lacked operational experience. His staff officer talents had led to a rapid rise within the senior wartime ranks. Yet more than to anybody else, it fell to Mann to nail down how the army side of the raid would be conducted. Having a desk at COHQ was not of great help, for "the throng of wild, unconventional young officers of all three services" there "could give little assistance, for the simple reason that to date raiding had been confined to small-scale personal sideshows, and nothing of the magnitude of Rutter had ever been attempted."[35]

Mann was undaunted. He noted "that the Outline Plan was no more than its name implied, and a great deal of planning yet remained to be done." After an intense period of studying what plan there was, Mann focused especially on the proposal that the supporting tanks should be landed on the beach directly facing Dieppe. "Such a plan, on the face of it," he wrote, "is almost a fantastic conception of the place most suited to land a strong force of AFV [Armoured Fighting Vehicles]. It is, however, well worth evaluating with an unbiased mind."[36]

4

Of Considerable Difficulty

O N THE EVENING of May 8, Lieutenant Colonel Church Mann
got down to a careful study of Operation Rutter's outline plan.
The opening paragraph set out the raid's "object." The first sentence
read: "Intelligence reports indicate that Dieppe is not heavily
defended and that the beaches in the vicinity are suitable for landing
infantry and AFVs at some. It is also reported that there are 40 invasion barges in the harbour."

The raid's objectives entailed "destruction of defences in the
Dieppe area... installations at the aerodrome of Dieppe–St. Aubin,
directly south of the town, and of RDF [radio direction finding, or
radar] stations, power stations, dock and rail facilities and petrol
dumps. It is also proposed to remove for our own use invasion barges
believed to be in the harbour, to obtain secret documents from the
Divisional Headquarters believed to exist at Arques-la-Bataille, and
to capture prisoners."

To achieve these objectives it was "proposed to employ... a Naval
Force including about six small destroyers of the 'Hunt' class, the
shallow-draught gunboat 'Locust,' seven infantry landing ships, and
a great number of small craft." The Military Forces were to include
"two infantry brigades with Engineers; up to a battalion of Army tanks
and Airborne troops." Air support was to "consist of five squadrons of
support fighters, one squadron of fighter-bombers, and sufficient

bombers to produce extensive bombardments on selected areas and targets, to provide carrying aircraft for parachutes and tugs for gliders if possible." This meant "approximately 150 bomber sorties."[1]

By now the earlier sketchy intelligence on Dieppe and its surrounding topography had been significantly fleshed out. This was vital for Mann because, like most of the Canadians, he knew nothing about the town. It lay on the Normandy coast some sixty-seven miles from the port of Newhaven in Sussex. Before the war, cross-channel steamers had ferried British tourists over to play on the town's beaches and gamble at the casino. Some called Dieppe the "poor man's Monte Carlo," for the beach was cobble rather than sand, and the casino was hardly grand. A 1928 *Blue Guide* to Normandy listed its population at 24,658 and declared it "a seaport, fishing harbour, and fashionable watering-place."

Dieppe lay at the mouth of the River Arques within a valley less than a thousand yards wide. The river mouth had been improved by construction of jetties and basins to create a harbour described as "commodious and deep." Railway lines radiated from Dieppe outwards to Le Havre, Rouen, and Paris.

The coastline consisted "in the main of steep cliffs generally unscalable by landing parties. Immediately to the west of the town these reach a height of 91 metres, and there is a similar though less lofty headland to the east. Although the only really large gap in the cliff barrier is that at Dieppe itself, there is an accessible beach at Pourville, about 4,500 yards west of the harbour entrance, where the River Scie flows into the channel through a flat-bottomed valley similar to that of the Arques though not so broad. At Puits [actually Puys], about 2,000 yards east of the harbour entrance, there is a much narrower gap in the cliffs, occasioned by a gully which extends inland for about three miles in a generally easterly direction. In peacetime both Pourville and [Puys] are fashionable resorts, each possessing a number of hotels."

Dieppe was fronted seaside by a two-hundred-yard-wide promenade extending from the harbour entrance for almost a thousand yards to the western cliff face. A large white casino stood in the cliff's shadow. Perched on a step about halfway up the cliff was an old castle. Roughly halfway between the casino and the harbour mouth was "a large tobacco factory" with two tall chimneys. The harbour curved around the eastern half of Dieppe and consisted of several basins. Photographs had revealed that one basin appeared to have been recently filled for conversion to a park, though most maps showed it as still being water. The *Blue Guide* described the existence of caves on the eastern headland next to the harbour and on the western headland above the casino. These "Goves or Gobes," the guidebook claimed, were still "inhabited by a few survivors of the cave-dwelling age." The town's "fashionable hotels" were mostly on the Boulevard de Verdun, "which runs along the front of the town, and look out across the grassy Promenade and beach."

On the seaward edge of the promenade was "a wall which at most points rises not more than about two feet perpendicularly above the beach. The beach itself is composed of large 'shingle,' the stones being in some cases about the size of a man's fist. It is rough and irregular in contour."[2]

Separating the hotels and boarding houses from the promenade was a 150-foot-wide stretch of lawns and gardens. A second broad boulevard—Maréchal Foch—followed the curve of the harbour, and Dieppe's Old Town was contained between it and Boulevard de Verdun. Around the harbour's other flanks and bordering the railway and highway running inland, a newer section of the town had developed. Several narrow lanes switched up the chalk cliffs on either side of the valley to gain the headlands above. The airport of St. Aubin lay about three miles inland.

The assault plan was precisely as earlier set out by Montgomery. Two flank landings at Pourville and Puys would support the main frontal assault directly in front of Dieppe. Paratroops and glider-borne troops would land inland and farther out on the flanks to silence coastal gun batteries and create chaos. The main issue to Mann was the risky plan to land tanks in front of Dieppe. In pre-war years, Mann had been among a handful of Canadian officers studying the potential of mechanized warfare, so he was more aware of the strengths and weaknesses of tanks than most senior Canadian officers.[3] Clearly there were problems with tanks "attacking the enemy frontally," he wrote. Assuming the tanks could get off the beach, which he thought possible, there would be "the danger of failure to penetrate through Dieppe, after the heavy air bombardment" due to streets being blocked by rubble from destroyed buildings. Thinking about the layout of similar English coastal towns, however, Mann thought a similar attack stood good odds of success "providing the engineer tasks were suitably dealt with." Mann was cheered by the intelligence that Dieppe's garrison consisted of just two poor-quality infantry companies and some additional divisional troops.

Lack of serious opposition might mitigate the fact that the coastal terrain favoured the defence. As the outline plan recognized, between "Berneval to the east and Quiberville to the west of Dieppe, a distance of 11 miles, the coast consists of high cliffs ... The only considerable gap in the line of cliffs is that made by the valley of the River Arques at the mouth of which lies [Dieppe]. At the foot of the cliffs is a narrow strip of stone and boulders bordered by a fringe of rocks. The problem of landing on such a coast is, therefore, one of considerable difficulty."[4]

The difficulty of terrain elsewhere, Mann decided, further suggested Dieppe as the best spot for putting tanks ashore. There were fewer disadvantages to a frontal assault, in Mann's estimation, than advantages gained. Assuming the tanks landed successfully, they would be "in easy striking distance of the most appropriate objectives for their employment." Their arrival would attain complete "surprise" and "have a terrific moral effect on both Germans and French." They could easily support the infantry and engineers in this main assault. "Control and information," he added, "will be from front to rear, and difficulties of coordination to surmount obstacles, and deal with resistance would be the more easily met."

Mann decided that the outline plan had "the advantage of simplicity." It was also the best choice for using tanks in the withdrawal phase, as there would need to be a rearguard action inside Dieppe to protect the troops during the re-embarkation.

He looked with scepticism upon the alternatives of landing the tanks at either Quiberville or Pourville. The rivers between Quiberville and Dieppe, he felt, would limit the tanks to operating between the rivers Scie and Arques. They would not be able to gain Dieppe itself in time to affect the raid there. At Pourville there was the problem that intelligence maintained the existence of only "one exit (a one way track)." Pourville, he decided, might be useful for landing later flights of tanks, but not for the initial landing.

"In spite of an initial adverse reaction to the proposal to land AFV on Dieppe front," Mann concluded, "it seems to have a reasonable prospect of success, and offers the best opportunity to exploit the characteristics of AFV in this operation. If AFV were omitted from the operation it could still be very useful, but the likelihood of success in regard to the destruction of the aerodrome would be greatly reduced. In regard to the withdrawal phase, a proportion of AFV as part of the rear-guard will materially strengthen the rear-guard at a time when enemy re-enforcements may be deploying for counter-attack with the object of preventing our withdrawal. I am in favour of adopting the outline plan."[5]

ON MAY 11, Mountbatten met with the other Chiefs of Staff and submitted a simplified version of the outline plan for approval. In a covering letter, Mountbatten wrote, "Apart from the military objectives... this operation will be of great value as training for Operation Sledgehammer or any other major operation as far as the actual assault is concerned. It will not, however, throw light on the maintenance problem over the beaches." This problem of how to keep a stream of supply and reinforcement flowing across beaches rather than through a port with all the inherent cranes, jetties, and other paraphernalia for off-loading ships was a problem that bedevilled the naval planners at COHQ. Although they knew it must be addressed, the Dieppe raid would—despite the large number of troops involved—be of too short duration for resupply to be necessary. Experience in that would have to be gained elsewhere.

The outline plan advised the Chiefs of Staff that the earliest launch date of the raid would be the night of June 20–21 or "any of the six nights following." Buried in the details of the document—of considerable length in whatever form it was presented—was a suggested list of responsibilities to be imposed upon the three selected force commanders. The detailed plan and operation orders that the air, navy, and army force commanders developed were expected to conform to the outline plan. Further, the "approval of the Chief of Combined Operations, who will obtain the concurrence of the General Officer Commanding, South Eastern Command insofar as the Military Plan is concerned, and of the Commander-in-Chief, Portsmouth, insofar as the Naval Plan is concerned, is to be obtained for your detailed plan."[6]

Clearly lacking—a fact Montgomery later acknowledged but did not at the time attempt to rectify—was appointment of a task force commander, a "single operational commander who was solely responsible for the operation from start to finish."[7] Also missing was a single responsible headquarters through which the operation could be planned, administered, and then launched. Instead, there was a "Triumvirate," as one later commentator called it, consisting of three officers of roughly equal rank and "each with his own remit" and headquarters staff.[8] Major General Ham Roberts was required to clear his plans with Montgomery as South-Eastern Commander. The yet-to-be-named Naval Force officer would seek clearance from Admiral Sir William James, Commander-in-Chief, Portsmouth. Neither Montgomery nor James was empowered to override the other. How the lines of authority for the still undetermined air commander would run was unstated. The result was a committee that lacked a chair and had endless potential for buck passing.

Not that the Dieppe planning structure was unique. At this time, such triumvirates were common when mounting Combined Operations. These operations involved each service arm, so it seemed logical that all three should participate in planning and provide what expertise and personnel were required. But this also meant that each commander had divided loyalties. The welfare of his arm of service tended to override that of the operation. This natural tendency was to have serious repercussions on the Dieppe planning.

For the Chiefs of Staff, the proposed Dieppe raid was but one of a number of issues Mountbatten brought forward on May 11. Brooke noted that the day was "mainly concerned with various combined operations which Chief of Combined Operations is planning." Then, at noon, Churchill arrived to chair a meeting "to discuss the giving up of the attack on Alderney and raids planned as alternatives."

Dieppe was the paramount offering among those alternatives. Brooke recognized that this scheme was ambitious, but it would provide experience in landing modern technical equipment on open beaches and should force "the Germans to commit their air force to battle." On May 13, the Chiefs gave approval. Brooke wrote: "Main interest of morning's [Chiefs of Staff meeting] was examination of projected large-scale raid for vicinity of Dieppe. Little did I ever think in the old days of my regular journeys from Newhaven to Dieppe that I should have been planning as I was this morning."[9]

Immediately after the meeting, Mountbatten notified the three force commanders of their appointments and told them that the outline plan had been accepted as the basis for detailed planning. Already aware of his selection as Military Force Commander, Roberts was sprung from the Mayfair Hotel and allowed to return to 2nd Division's headquarters. Air Vice-Marshal Trafford Leigh-Mallory, who commanded No. 11 Fighter Group, was named Air Force Commander. The Naval Force Commander was to be Rear Admiral Tom Baillie-Grohman, who had to be rushed back to Britain from Cairo.

Of the three, Baillie-Grohman was the most experienced in combined operations. After serving for two years at the helm of the battleship *Ramillies,* he had been promoted to rear admiral and had taken command of the combined operations naval base in the Middle East. He organized the largest ever combined operations exercise, off the Suez Canal, in which a New Zealand division engaged in a three-day rehearsal. Baillie-Grohman had been planning an assault on the island of Rhodes in 1941 but had to scuttle this in order to deal with the sudden evacuation of the 55,000-strong British army in Greece. In the face of the rapidly advancing German army, under the overhead guns of the Luftwaffe, and operating in a foreign and chaotic country, Baillie-Grohman oversaw a largely successful rescue. It was a performance that earned him a Distinguished Service Order. The fifty-four-year-old Baillie-Grohman had a reputation for being intolerant of inefficiency by subordinates and, like Roberts, believed it possible for anyone to achieve excellence.[10]

Born in 1892, Leigh-Mallory served in the British Army during the Great War until he was wounded in the Second Battle of Ypres in the spring of 1915. Upon recovery from his wounds in January 1916, he volunteered for the Royal Flying Corps and became a pilot. By war's end he held a DSO and was promoted to vice air-marshal, one of the youngest. Noted as a quick-thinking and sound decision maker, Leigh-Mallory also had a reputation for using political connections to advance his career. During the Battle of Britain, he and Canadian acting squadron leader Douglas Bader advocated the so-called Big Wing approach to fighting the Luftwaffe. This entailed massed fighter formations attempting to bring German bomber groups to battle before they reached London or other targets. The tactic met with only limited success and received only lukewarm support from Air Chief-Marshal Sir Hugh Dowding, who headed Fighter Command. After the Battle of Britain, Leigh-Mallory used his influence to convince the newly appointed chief of the air staff, Air Chief-Marshal Charles Portal, to sack Dowding. Despite his ruthless tendencies, Leigh-Mallory was generally well regarded within the RAF.[11]

It would be some time before these three "strong, capable personalities" would meet.[12] Leigh-Mallory was busy running No. 11 Fighter Group from a headquarters in Uxbridge, near London. Baillie-Grohman must journey to Britain from the Middle East. He would not arrive and be formally appointed the Naval Force Commander until June 1. On May 13, meanwhile, Roberts was given a final briefing by Mountbatten at COHQ. He then left for 2nd Division's Sussex headquarters.[13]

THE SAME DAY Roberts departed London for Sussex, General Headquarters Home Forces authorized the transfer of the Canadian raiding force to the Isle of Wight. This two-day move would begin May 18. The new movement orders caught the division preparing for Exercise Tiger—a massive six-division mock "encounter battle" staged by South-Eastern Command that was to begin May 19 and run to May 30. All 1 Canadian Corps was to participate under Crerar's command. Two brigades of 3rd British Infantry Division were quickly substituted for the Canadians pulled from the exercise.

May 13 also saw conclusion of Exercise Beaver IV, in which 2nd Division had played the invader against an area between Bexhill and Beachy Head defended by 3rd Canadian Infantry Division. As had been true of Beaver III, the amphibious landing was assumed rather than attempted.[14] Beaver IV had started on May 10. The weather immediately broke. Heavy rains transformed the countryside into a muddy quagmire that hampered operations and left the troops sodden throughout an exercise that was "longer and more gruelling than its predecessors." The Royal Regiment of Canada's historian observed, however, that "the troops... remained amazingly cheerful in spite of abominable conditions." Late on May 13, the regiment returned to camp to find the area had been bombed by the Luftwaffe and reduced to a mess. It hardly mattered. On arrival, Lieutenant Colonel Hedley Basher was given "a warning order that [the regiment] would move to the Isle of Wight for intensive training in combined operations."[15]

Not all of 2nd Canadian Division was required. The divisional troops selected consisted of 4th Infantry Brigade, 6th Infantry Brigade, some light anti-aircraft and field artillery detachments (intended to man captured guns), a good number of engineers, plus divisional administrative units. Tanks were provided by the Calgary Regiment from 1st Canadian Army Tank Brigade. The regiments of 4th Brigade were the Royal Regiment of Canada, the Royal Hamilton Light Infantry, and the Essex Scottish. Those of 6th Brigade were Les Fusiliers Mont-Royal, the Queen's Own Cameron Highlanders, and the South Saskatchewan Regiment.[16]

Even these regiments would not move in their entirety to the Isle of Wight or be fully involved in the raid. The Royals left behind all transport personnel and certain other details.[17] Not all the battalions received warning orders to move on the same day. The Essex Scottish got the news on May 16. They were to send only 570 men of all ranks. The remainder of the battalion would remain behind as a "rear party," under administrative care of 5th Brigade.[18] Les Fusiliers Mont-Royal was still recovering from Beaver IV when its warning order was delivered on May 16. Battalion adjutant Captain C. Camaraire and a small advance party departed immediately to prepare for the battalion's arrival on the island.[19]

In all, about 4,900 divisional troops would be involved in the raiding force. All of 5th Brigade and—excepting the small field artillery detachment—the division's artillery and various other units would remain in Sussex. The 5th Brigade would participate in

Exercise Tiger under command of 3rd British Division. Code name for the move to the Isle of Wight was Simmer, which was also the name of the Canadian Operation Rutter training program.[20]

When Roberts returned to divisional headquarters on the evening of May 13, he found preparations for the move well in hand. Roberts considered his two designated infantry brigadiers highly competent, having brought them in to replace older officers. Brigadier William Southam was forty-one and a Toronto publisher. He had commanded 1st Division's 48th Highlanders of Canada regiment. On January 16, 1942, he replaced Brigadier J.P. Mackenzie at 6th Brigade. Mackenzie's removal was finessed by playing the upward promotion card. Promoted to major general, he was sent to serve as quartermaster general at National Defence Headquarters in Canada. Drawn from South Saskatchewan Regiment, Brigadier Sherwood Lett had taken the reins at 4th Brigade. The forty-seven-year-old had received a Military Cross in the Great War and a Rhodes scholarship in 1919. Most of his inter-war years were spent as a successful corporate and tax lawyer. He replaced Brigadier R.A. Fraser, who had requested a compassionate leave return to Canada. The leave was granted on the understanding that Fraser surrendered any return to brigade command.[21]

THREE OF THE six battalions in the two brigades had also undergone command changes. Lieutenant Colonel Paul Grenier, who had commanded Les Fusiliers Mont-Royal since 1937, was promoted to full colonel and returned to Canada to lead a reserve brigade. His replacement, Lieutenant Colonel Dollard "Joe" Ménard, had been a major with the Royal 22e Régiment. The Fusiliers also got a new second-in-command, Major René Painchaud, a member of the regiment, succeeding Major Maurice Forget, who had held this position since the battalion mobilized in October 1939.

Painchaud was well regarded by the Fusiliers, but Ménard was a stranger. When he took over on April 3, the troops at first called him "l'outsider" and made it clear they reserved judgement as to whether this soldier, who did not even hail from Montreal, deserved respect. None, however, could help but be impressed by his appearance. Ménard stood six-foot-two and, in the words of the Fusiliers' historian, had a *"splendide physique,"* broad shoulders, the muscles of an athlete, and a jutting jaw. His gaze was frank, and he soon won over his officers with a steady display of exceptional intelligence, concern for morale, and stubborn determination.[22]

Ménard loved action. After graduating from Royal Military College, he had been dismayed by the lack of it within the peacetime Canadian Army. Arranging a secondment to India in the late 1930s, he was commissioned into the 4/11 Sikh Regiment, then guarding the Khyber Pass. When war broke out, Ménard decided he must rejoin the Canadian Army. Resigning his commission, Ménard wrote the Defence Department in Ottawa requesting return to army strength. The government's reply was that he had freely gone to India and it was not up to Canada to fund his return. Furious at this perceived "Anglo-Saxon insult to a loyal French Canadian," Ménard set about making his own way back, despite being almost penniless. In Bombay, some British Army friends helped secure free passage to Hong Kong. There he found that the Commander of British Troops in China, headquartered in Hong Kong, was Major General Edward Grassett. Canadian-born and an RMC graduate, Grassett was also a personal friend of Ménard's father. Grassett got Ménard taken aboard a Royal Navy destroyer as a common sailor. By finagling transfers from one ship to another during a voyage that traversed the Panama Canal to finally reach Halifax, Ménard made his way home. Presenting himself in Ottawa, immaculately turned out in a full uniform adorned with Indian service medals, Ménard was quickly returned to army strength.[23]

Like the Fusiliers, the Queen's Own Cameron Highlanders also received a new and controversial commander. The thirty-nine-year-old Lieutenant Colonel Alfred Gostling had been a partner in a Winnipeg radio repair business before the war. Although the Camerons were a Winnipeg regiment, Gostling's regimental connection was to the Winnipeg Grenadiers. He came to the Camerons from a posting as adjutant and quartermaster general of 1st Infantry Division.[24]

Before his arrival, the Camerons had undergone a particularly brutal purge of senior officers. Lieutenant Colonel G.F. "Gil" Dudley, who had won both the Military Cross and Military Medal in the

Great War, was returned to Canada after suffering internal injuries in a training accident.[25] Several majors, all over the age of forty-five, were sacked—including the battalion second-in-command. One beneficiary of this cull was Major Norman Ross, who gained a promotion and company command, while also emerging as one of the battalion's most senior remaining officers. Ross thought the sacked officers "rightly should have gone. By this time the glamour of overseas service had worn off. They had out served their usefulness."

Gostling's imposition was of no concern to Ross. He believed none of the remaining officers were senior or experienced enough to warrant battalion command. Ross noted, however, that Gostling's imposition "sat a little harshly" on a couple of them. The new second-in-command, Major A.T. "Andy" Law, "was one of those who resented it very much."

Ross soon had his own causes for complaint. Gostling "might have been a brilliant staff officer," he said later, "but he didn't know how to command men." In one incident, Ross was travelling in a jeep at night and happened on a camouflage net lying alongside the road. He had it loaded aboard and then turned over to the base stores. The following morning, during an exercise in the same jeep, the order came to cover it with a camouflage net. Ross discovered there was none aboard, the one designated for the jeep having been unloaded along with the other. When the battalion adjutant asked about the jeep's camouflage net, Ross explained the accident. The adjutant soon returned, saying Gostling demanded a written explanation. Ross filed a written report. Gostling sent it back with a scribbled note attached: "Do not believe this."

"I resented this. He called me a goddamned liar. I thought to hell with you, buster. I did my job after that, just kept cool."[26]

Lieutenant Colonel Cecil Merritt was the new blood who took over the South Saskatchewan Regiment in March. Merritt was thirty-three. His maternal great-grandfather had been Prime Minister Charles Tupper. Merritt's father, Cecil Mack Merritt, had died on April 23, 1915, while serving as a captain in the 16th Battalion (Canadian Scottish). His uncle, Reggie Tucker, arranged for young Merritt to first attend University School in Victoria and then Royal Military College. He then took Merritt on as an apprentice in his law firm, resulting in his call to the bar in 1932. Merritt established a courtroom reputation for being direct and to the point.

Merritt was a big man—wide-shouldered, just over six feet, and weighing about two hundred pounds. He was an enthusiastic athlete, playing football at the Vancouver Athletic Club. Following in the footsteps of father and uncle, Merritt became a reservist in the Seaforth Highlanders of Canada. When the Seaforths mobilized on September 1, 1939, Merritt was promoted to major. Merritt had two siblings, a brother and sister. All three enlisted and were sent overseas. Before Merritt left, he said to his mother, Sophie, "I want you to know, mother, that I realize what you must feel about losing your family again."

"I don't want you to go," Sophie replied, "but I'd kick you out of the house if you didn't."[27]

Merritt was married and had two children. When the battalion entrained for Halifax on December 15, 1939, his wife, Grace's, parting words were: "Don't try to win medals, Cec. You just come home."[28]

During the next two years, Merritt held various staff and regimental appointments in Britain before attending the War Staff Course at Camberley in June 1941. He then joined the general staff of 3rd Infantry Division and remained there until being given the South Saskatchewan Regiment.[29]

Merritt hit it off poorly from the first. Lieutenant John Edmondson, 'D' Company's second-in-command, found him "a very autocratic, self-assured young man. He thought he knew how to do it. But I don't think he understood the prairie temperament... Don't think there was anything basically wrong with his knowledge, his ability to command or direct... [but] we had a custom in the regiment that we only said, 'Good morning, sir' and saluted the [battalion commander] once in the morning and that was it. [Merritt] expected everyone to jump to attention every time he walked in and out... He lacked, in my view, the man management skill to know how to get the best out of them."

Edmondson's appointment as 'D' Company's second-in-command had occurred just before Merritt's arrival. Yet during an administrative meeting, Merritt demanded he explain the loss of several bicycles six months before Edmondson had been posted to the company.

After several incidents of similar nature, Edmondson stormed back to 'D' Company headquarters and told Major John "Mac" MacTavish, "You can stuff this appointment. I want to go back and command my platoon." An older officer who had been with the regiment since the outbreak of hostilities, MacTavish was noted for his calm competence. Giving Edmondson his trademark quiet little grin, he said, "Just carry on." Edmondson sighed and decided to do his best.

Just before the regiment moved to the Isle of Wight, however, there was the "Soup and Tea Incident." During an exercise, the troops were each given a sandwich to carry with them for lunch. The weather was brutal, bucketing rain and chill temperatures leaving everyone soaked and frozen. So Merritt agreed that the other ranks should return to camp for some hot soup and tea in the mess. Officers, however, were told to remain outdoors and just eat the sandwich. Objections were raised, and Merritt conceded to letting the officers into their mess for some soup and tea. Soup finished, the officers were just pouring tea when Merritt stormed in and gave "everyone hell about what was going on with [the] training. And every officer picked up his cup of tea and walked out. It was just a sort of silent mutiny." Thereafter, "everybody disappeared as quickly as possible whenever he showed."[30]

The other three regiments in the two brigades were spared adapting to new, younger commanders prior to the move to the Isle of Wight. In a more orderly transition, Lieutenant Colonel A.S. Pearson—who had brought the Essex Scottish overseas—handed command to the younger Fred Jasperson. The new lieutenant colonel had been a lawyer in Windsor—the regiment's hometown. Lieutenant Colonel Ridley "Bob" Labatt, a stockbroker by trade, had commanded the Royal Hamilton Light Infantry since April 2, 1940. He followed in the footsteps of his father, who had led the regiment for almost two years in the Great War. Lieutenant Colonel G. Hedley Basher, meanwhile, had commanded the Royal Regiment of Canada since 1938.

In December 1941, Lieutenant Colonel G.R. Bradbrooke—who had won a Military Cross in the Great War—had been replaced at the Calgary Tank Regiment by Major John Gilby "Johnny" Andrews. Bradbrooke was promoted to brigadier and sent to the Middle East as a military observer. Bradbrooke had been a popular officer and had brought the "Red Deer plough jockeys" overseas. The handover, however, was congenial and seamless. The newly minted lieutenant colonel was thirty-three and had left a bank job to join the regular army in 1930, when he was commissioned as a lieutenant. In November 1936, he was one of five junior officer instructors appointed to the just-opened Canadian Tank School. When the tank school was redesignated in 1938 as the Canadian Armoured Vehicle Training Centre and established at Camp Borden in Ontario, Andrews was promoted to major. He went overseas as the brigade major of the Army Tank Brigade headquarters in June 1941. Many of the Calgarians had gone through the training school under Andrews's tutelage, and they felt it appropriate to be now commanded by "an officer who had been associated with the 'Fighting Vehicles' for the best part of his army career."[31]

5

Trial and Error

ON MAY 18, Major General Ham Roberts travelled with 2nd Infantry Division's headquarters staff by ferry from Southampton to the Isle of Wight and set up operation at Osborne House in the port town of Cowes. The sprawling three-storey Italianate villa overlooked the Solent and had been built as a holiday retreat for Queen Victoria. It was surrounded by 342 acres of meticulously maintained gardens. A yachting resort popular with members of the Royal Family, the Isle of Wight was now a training hub for Combined Operations. The 4th Brigade also arrived on May 18, with 6th Brigade arriving the day following. On the 20th, the Calgary Regiment arrived along with a large contingent of Royal Canadian Engineers.[1]

Close to Osborne House, Norris Castle became Brigadier William Southam's 6th Brigade's headquarters, while the South Saskatchewan Regiment set up tents on the grounds.[2] The Queen's Own Cameron Highlanders established a tent encampment at Wootton Creek—a small village of little more than a couple of shops and a pub around which a few houses clustered. Lieutenant Colonel Al Gostling and his senior staff requisitioned one building as a residence and another for the officers' mess.[3] Les Fusiliers Mont-Royal were in Whitefield Wood, just south of the old seaport of Ryde.

Lieutenant Colonel Joe Ménard had with him 570 officers and men, leaving the remaining 225 at a rest camp near Portsmouth.[4]

The 4th Brigade's quarters were on the island's western side. The Essex Scottish took over a Billy Butlin Holiday Camp. Quartered at nearby Freshwater, the Royal Regiment of Canada looked out upon the famous Needles rocks and adjacent lighthouse. The large three-storey Jacobean Northcourt Manor in Shorewell, once owned by Lord Byron, was home for the Royal Hamilton Light Infantry.[5] Officers and headquarters staff were housed in the manor and the troops under canvas on its fifteen-acre grounds.

To ensure that the tankers were close to their primary training area on the long beach fronting Osborne House, the Calgary Regiment was in another castle at Cowes. Lieutenant C.A. "Stoney" Richardson, the regiment's quartermaster, could hardly believe the "wonderful accommodation there... It was certainly a great place to stay and we enjoyed every minute of it."[6]

Engineers were to play a key role, particularly in the frontal assault on Dieppe. About 350 engineers had been drawn from a number of units. The 7th Field Company contributed the largest sapper element of about 150 men. Another 100 were drawn from 2nd Field Company, about 65 from 11th Field Company, and 25 from 1st Field Park Company. Much smaller details were drawn from 2nd Road Construction Company and the Mechanical Equipment Company. A total of 12 officers commanded the various engineering units.

Overall command rested with Lieutenant Colonel Frank Barnes, appointed senior engineer officer.[7] Born in Britain, Barnes had served as a Royal Engineer during the Great War in postings to East Africa, India, and Persia. Discharged in 1919, he immigrated to Canada and joined the militia as an engineering lieutenant in 1927. By 1939, he was a militia lieutenant colonel and retained that rank upon being accepted into the regular army. In order to go overseas, however, he reverted to the rank of major and became second-in-command of 2nd Battalion, Royal Canadian Engineers. He arrived in Britain in September 1940. That December, he was re-promoted to lieutenant colonel and command of the RCE Reinforcement Depot. He remained at this posting until taking command of 2nd Infantry Division's engineers.[8] His second-in-command for Rutter was Major Bert Sucharov, who had been cooling his heels in a reinforcement unit. Sucharov was thirty-three and had graduated with an engineering degree from the University of Manitoba in 1937.[9] He was a flamboyant character, sporting a large moustache and arming himself with two pistols in holsters that would do a western gun-fighter proud.[10]

Other, smaller groups of specialized troops augmented the engineers. Ten officers and 116 men from the Royal Canadian Medical Corps supplemented the brigade and battalion regular medical staffs. Five officers and 120 Toronto Scottish (MG) Regiment personnel, all specially trained to operate and fire belt-fed medium machine guns, were to perform anti-aircraft gunnery roles aboard the various landing craft. Forty men from the Canadian Provost Corps were there, along with a few soldiers posted from the Service, Ordnance, and Intelligence Corps and "miscellaneous small units and detachments," plus "a few brave men of the Inter-Allied Commando—mostly native German speakers assigned to specialist intelligence gathering."

Security was extremely tight. The Isle of Wight had been selected as a Combined Operations training area because it could be sealed off from the outside world. Just twenty-three miles by thirteen miles, the island was also a microcosm of British countryside. Lush meadows sloped to broad beaches or came up abruptly to the edge of sheer chalk cliffs that plunged to the sea. The sandy beaches were ideal for amphibious landing training. No civilians who did not have permanent homes or businesses on the island had been allowed to remain. The population had shrunk from 85,000 before the war to just 10,000.[11] In addition to the Canadians, there were about 5,000 sailors, airmen, and assorted groups of various nationalities. Some of these were to join what was being called Simmerforce, while others were there to assist in the training or were awaiting instruction about their future fates.

Once the Canadians arrived, nobody else was allowed on the island unless bearing papers assigning them to Simmerforce. Leaving the island was possible only with personal approval from Roberts, Rear-Admiral Baillie Grohman, or a senior security officer.[12] "Officers and men," noted the Royal Hamilton Light Infantry official historian, "received a series of lectures on security, and a strict unit censorship was put into effect."[13] All communications from the island were closely monitored and censored.[14]

Baillie-Grohman had established the naval headquarters in Cowes Castle, the former home of the Royal Yacht Squadron. According to naval custom, whereby land-based headquarters are considered "stone frigates," the castle was renamed HMS *Vectis*. Baillie-Grohman massed a small fleet of landing craft and larger ships in the Solent, which had been emptied of pleasure boats.[15] Present here were the vessels of 1st and 2nd Canadian Landing Craft Flotillas. Each flotilla had a flotilla officer, seven boat officers, twelve coxswains, twenty-four seamen and a dozen stoker drivers—fifty-six men in total. These Canadian sailors were part of an overall commitment of Royal Canadian Navy and Royal Canadian Navy Volunteer Reserve personnel to Combined Operations that totalled fifty officers and three hundred ratings.[16]

EVERYONE PLUNGED INTO intensive "preliminary training designed to harden the men and otherwise prepare them for the arduous work ahead." Infantry tasks included "embarkation and beaching, assault courses, unarmed combat, training in the use of bangalore torpedoes, speed marches," and much physical exercise.[17] South Saskatchewan Regiment's Lieutenant John Edmondson found it "hard training, physically demanding—route marches, PT, running, climbing up and down walls, up fences. You had a toggle rope to use in emergencies. March five miles in fifty-five minutes and then climb a hundred foot cliff with a seventy-five pound box of ammunition strapped across your back."[18]

In the first week, the Royals engaged in "obstacle courses, bayonet fighting, unarmed combat, cliff climbing, firing from the hip, embarking and disembarking from landing craft, demolition practice, and river crossings by breeches buoy [circular lifebuoy attached to a form of zip line]." Despite the elaborate security measures, German observation planes must have taken some note. On the night of May 24, the Royals underwent an air raid by several German planes. Fortunately, the bombing produced no casualties.[19]

Although consensus among the troops was that they were putting out all they could, those overseeing the training were unimpressed by the first week's effort. On May 28, a divisional training report noted: "Although the condition of the men is reasonably good, the assault courses and speed marches have shown that there is a great improvement to be made in this direction. In the speed marches units are able to do five miles in 45 mins but took from 1½ hrs to 2 hrs to do the remaining 6 miles. In the Assault courses [troops] were able to complete the course, but were, in many cases, unable to fight or fire effectively when finished."[20]

The Sasks had been told that "these commandos would teach us all about combined op training," Edmondson recalled. "I would say that other than a couple of techniques about how to get over a beach wall and how to get out of an assault craft in nineteen seconds, they didn't teach us anything. Most of the stuff we were already knowledgeable about ourselves... A lot of the things we did, we developed by trial and error."

Training-related casualties were always a danger. During one landing exercise, the Sasks piled out of boats on the island's south coast. As they charged across the beach, an umpire shouted that the men were in the middle of a minefield sown to meet the feared German invasion. Everyone stopped in his tracks, but they were already in its midst. "We were as safe going ahead as coming back, so we went through." Nobody tripped a mine.[21]

Each day, the tempo intensified. As soon as the Rileys "mastered the elementary technique of amphibious attack [they] went on to train under more difficult conditions, such as landing under smoke, and to practice... beach consolidation and withdrawal manoeuvres. There was also a series of demonstrations of tank firepower, and training in co-operation with armoured units. At the same time, the Rileys were required to train in speed marches. Day after day the men tramped the roads... in battle order, perfecting their performance until they could meet the required standard of covering 11 miles in two hours with the first five miles covered in 45 minutes. By this time, after more than two years of training, the physical condition of the whole unit was at a peak."[22]

The Calgary tankers had brought fifty-eight shiny new Churchills to the island. There were two variants, one mounting a 6-pounder gun and the other a much lighter 2-pounder. Both types had a five-man crew. Secondary armament consisted of two 7.92-millimetre Besa machine guns. The Churchills were heavy, weighing 87,360 pounds, as compared with the later Shermans at 69,700 pounds. They were powered by a Bedford twin 6-cylinder gasoline engine capable of a top speed of 15.5 miles per hour. Armour was relatively thin—102 millimetres at the thickest and only 16 millimetres in some spots.[23]

Most tank training took place on the long beach in front of Osborne House, which had been much loved by Queen Victoria. Her old bathhouse was regularly pressed into service as a rain shelter. On this great stretch of white sand, the Calgaries practised embarking and disembarking from Landing Craft Tank (LCT). Basically a flat-bottomed barge of just less than 190 feet in length with a drop ramp at the front and a wheelhouse at the back, each LCT could carry six Churchills; it also had a twelve-man crew and light armament of either two single-barrelled Oerlikon 20-millimetre cannons or two single-barrelled Bofors 40-millimetre guns.

"We had never done this with the landing craft before, where the ramps dropped down and we drove off into the water. We did this dozens and dozens of times," Lieutenant Stoney Richardson wrote. "Our tanks were all waterproofed... We did landings, first of all, with the tanks' hatches open, then we closed down and disembarked further out. Then we turned around and had to do it all over again at night, loading and unloading at night."

Every day the tankers tackled a seawall that the engineers had built on the beach. It was "our business... to either crash over the top of it or crash through it and go on and fan out to take the higher ground beyond." As to the purpose behind surmounting the wall, the tankers, like everyone except the senior Canadian commanders, remained in the dark.

"We did a lot of range practice to train gunners and, of course, we were doing all kinds of experiments with water-proofing. We had some funny things happen with our water-proofing. Some of it was most successful, some was very poorly done until we learned better how to do it. It was all tested in a large pool at the castle. The tanks were water-proofed and then were driven into this swimming pool where there was a ramp. Some tanks were good and there were some that leaked very badly."[24]

In addition to repairing the seawall after each day of tanker training, the engineers learned a multitude of new skills. They learned to make special demolition charges and "suitable carrying packs for the explosives and tools. The performance of the Churchill tank on sand, shingle and mud beaches had to be determined and some type of beach track selected, developed and tested to match the capabilities of the tank... Also convenient means of getting the Churchills over sea-walls, from two to seven feet high, had to be found."

The engineers realized they were preparing for a "first operation of its type and, for all practical purposes, much work had to be done from scratch. Owing to the limited number of sappers available, every effort had to be made to teach every man all the various types of jobs. It was evident that the engineer parties would be small and would have to operate almost independently. There could be little or no duplication or reinforcement after the assault was launched, so that even a single casualty might put a particular group out of action if the men were not versatile."

Much emphasis was placed on the engineers being able to get "in and out of landing craft and across various natures of mined and wired beaches with an assortment of vehicles." It was discovered that chespaling—flexible roll fencing similar to wood slat snow fencing but made with tough split slats of chestnut—could be laid to provide traction for crossing shingle or sand that might otherwise disable tanks. The engineers soon realized that placing the chespaling into position under fire would require the tankers to do it themselves. A device was rigged that enabled the chespaling to be rolled and attached to the tank's front. The crew inside could then trigger a release that would unfurl the roll out ahead of the tank and then jettison it. This device could also be used to surmount a seawall of up to twenty-eight inches high. For anything higher, the engineers had to construct timber crib ramps.[25] During training, engineer Major Bert Sucharov observed that a "well trained squad of 30 men... made the record time of 5 minutes in building [a timber crib ramp] for a 6 [foot] wall... carrying timber from a dump 30 yards away." Using twelve-foot lengths of timber and railway sleepers, the engineers would hammer together a ramp with steps varying in tread width from one to two feet, which the tank could then ascend to surmount the seawall.[26]

From the sidelines, Captain John Hughes-Hallett uneasily watched these efforts to breach seawalls. He thought the army's ideas were "primitive." Clearly it was "important that gaps should be blown through which tanks could pass, but the army's technique for achieving this depended upon the troops manhandling 'Bangalore Torpedoes' which would be carried in tank landing craft and lugged ashore up to the seawall. It seemed to me that the soldiers entrusted with this task would be sitting ducks. We therefore urged that some well armoured, but obsolescent heavy tanks should be filled with explosives and driven up the beach to the seawall where the soldiers could jump out and take cover while they were blown up." This suggestion from the Combined Operations naval planners was dismissed without any real consideration. Hughes-Hallett was left with the impression that Major General Roberts and his staff feared that pressing for special equipment might lead to the raid's cancellation. Roberts was well aware that this fate befell more combined operation raiding plans than not.[27]

In truth, the engineers were experimenting with more advanced charges than the simple bangalore torpedo—a long pipe filled with explosive, intended more for clearing a path through barbed wire than for breaching a seawall. The engineers created sixty-pound conical charges that could be set against the wall on small crosses of timber. Three such charges set three feet apart were found capable of creating a 13.6-foot-wide breach—more than adequate for passage of a 9.5-foot-wide Churchill tank. Emplacing such a string of charges and readying them for detonation required two to three minutes' work by a nine-man team. Several similar techniques were devised using lighter, thirty-three pound explosive loads, two of which were carried by one engineer and then hooked together and hung from the top of the wall before detonation. In all cases, it was assumed that the engineers placing the charges would be protected by covering fire from infantry and tanks. Once the breach was created, it was determined that a tank could get through in about a minute.[28]

Breaching seawalls was not the only engineering concern. The men had to devise techniques for creating paths through minefields. Two types of "snakes" were designed. The first "consisted of sections of pipe loaded with explosives which, when coupled together, could be pushed as a unit ahead of a tank across a minefield. The subsequent detonation would clear a path through the field." Lieutenant T.B. Doherty of 11th Field Company devised a variant nicknamed a "sausage." This entailed rolling plastic explosive into a long sausage charge of either seventy-five or one hundred feet in length. Primers were placed at each end of the charge and within it at distances of twenty feet. The charge was then wrapped in waterproof fabric and threaded through a heavy canvas fire hose. The hose was coiled on a wooden frame fitted with four carrying handles so it could be lugged into position by engineers. Each sausage weighed between 200 and 250 pounds.[29]

All unit training repeatedly returned to surmounting seawalls. Before the war, Lieutenant Edmondson had been on a gymnastics team. Learning of this, Lieutenant Colonel Cecil Merritt said to him, "You know something about climbing walls and falling on your head." He pointed to a sixteen-foot seawall. "I want you to teach people how to get up and down these walls."

"What the hell do I know about getting up and down beach walls?" Edmondson fumed. All he could really teach the men was how to roll and tumble if they had to jump over something. "Why not just use scaling ladders?" Edmondson asked at repeated briefings. "They're as old as warfare." Merritt finally told him to shut up and be quiet.[30]

By early June, Major Norman Ross thought his Camerons "had never been fitter." They were also adept at getting in and out of the R-Boats (R for "raid"). This early version of the Landing Craft Assault (LCA) had no ramp in front. Instead, the troops jumped over the side. Of plywood construction with armoured bulkheads, the thirty-four-foot boats had very shallow draft and could normally carry about twenty-five men. Twelve men would be under the gunwale, with the rest in the stern. "We were landing on beaches, jumping out into waist deep water, and then running ashore."[31]

They also trained aboard Landing Craft Mechanical Mark 1 (LCM) vessels. First launched in 1920, the LCMs were relatively crude landing craft designed to carry one medium tank, 26.8 tons of cargo, or up to one hundred men. Displacing thirty-five tons, they were forty-five feet long by fourteen feet wide, with a four-foot draft. Crewed by six men, the LCM was powered by two Chrysler hundred-horsepower petrol engines and armed with two .303-calibre Lewis medium machine guns. Each LCM was commanded by a coxswain.

Ottawa-born Norm Bowen held this rank aboard one LCM in a Canadian flotilla. The "big thing," he recalled, was that "we had to learn to handle these bloody craft. You had a great big solid door in front of you and you are on the deck. How the hell can you see where you are going? . . . We used to open the hatch and climb up and sit on the top and steer with our feet. Because you had to see over the door or at least the side of it and the only thing you could see at night is the phosphorous from the propeller [of the vessel] ahead of you. It was a damn antiquated thing." The ramp door at the front was about eight feet high and armoured. The soldiers crammed into the LCM were equally blind, surrounded by sides higher than their heads. This caused problems for Bowen and the other coxswains because inevitably the infantry officer would try to climb up the side to see where they were. "I would tell him to get down. And he'd demand, Who the hell am I to tell him anything? I would have to explain, that on this ship, I am the captain and, 'If you don't get down, I'll have you thrown down.'" A humble Canadian sailor, Bowen found this kind of conflict a "bit embarrassing at times."[32]

As the training became more advanced, the Camerons were loaded in boats one evening and spent the night circling the island to reach a dawn landing point. They stormed ashore, scaled a cliff, and carried out a simulated attack against headland targets. Attack successful, they then marched back to Wootton Creek. Everyone was looking forward to a hot meal when Lieutenant Colonel Gostling announced an inspection. Gostling carried this out in reverse order, meaning Ross's 'A' Company was last in line. Ross began experiencing a growing sense of "trepidation," as he heard "rough screams" coming from where Gostling was farther up the line. Eventually the battalion commander reached 'A' Company and closely inspected each rifle. "And he couldn't find anything wrong. I could tell he was mad as hell at that, but he was quiet." Finally, Gostling found a rifle that failed inspection, "and he started screaming at [the man] and then suddenly walked away."

All the battalion officers were summoned to a briefing, where Gostling "read the riot act. We'd just come out of salt water, just off an operation, really there had been no time to clean up rifles or anything else... Well, of course, this was ridiculous... But this was the type of commander he was."

Ross did his best to avoid Gostling thereafter and thought the other company commanders did likewise. The "paradox" in the training that perplexed him, however, was that most of it was at a company level. There were virtually no battalion-scale exercises and nothing at all at brigade or divisional level.[33] Ross was unaware of the simple reason for this. Those overseeing the training had realized there was simply insufficient time to train the men on a battalion scale without "sacrificing" other "valuable training" that required individual company tasks. Instead, on June 10, the division would be subjected to a full-dress rehearsal raid on the south English coast in cooperation with the navy and air force assets assigned to Operation Rutter.[34]

Such was the intensity of training and the sense of urgency surrounding it that the Canadians on the Isle of Wight could not help but sense they were being prepared for something big. And the nature of the training in these first days of June—with its emphasis on amphibious landings and surmounting seawalls—made the whole affair all the more mysterious.[35]

MEANWHILE, ON JUNE 5, a meeting of critical import had convened at Combined Operations Headquarters. Neither Mountbatten nor Hughes-Hallett attended. Both were then in Washington, sent by Churchill to convince the Americans "once and for all that nothing but harm would come from an attempted major operation in 1942, and that in consequence there was no prospect of such an operation being undertaken." Although the British had decided any 1942 amphibious cross-channel operation entailing multiple divisions was doomed to fail, the Americans kept advocating its resurrection. Churchill consequently had decided to send Mountbatten, Hughes-Hallett, and some of the St. Nazaire raid veterans to convince the Americans that Sledgehammer must be abandoned.

Mountbatten preceded Hughes-Hallett, flying in General Dwight Eisenhower's private plane and arriving on June 3. Hughes-Hallett and the other Combined Operations officers departed on June 1 but took a circuitous route, first through neutral Eire, then by flying boat via Newfoundland to Baltimore, and then to the American capital by train.

Churchill believed Mountbatten could charm the Americans out of Operation Sledgehammer, while Hughes-Hallett would be in the background to underscore his arguments with detailed information. Once Sledgehammer was buried, Mountbatten would advocate an invasion later that year of North Africa.

Several long meetings with "senior American staff officers" ensued, during which the two British naval officers explained "the logistics and our reasoning." These led to a final two- to three-hour meeting with the U.S. Combined Chiefs of Staff wherein Mountbatten argued there were insufficient landing craft for any major cross-channel assault in the summer of 1942. By late 1942 or early 1943, the picture might change, but at this point there were simply too few craft for a major venture. Mountbatten and Hughes-Hallett got the "impression . . . that we had at length convinced them."[36]

In reality, the Combined Chiefs remained unpersuaded that Sledgehammer was a bust. To those staunch proponents of a Second Front Now, such as Colonel Albert Wedemeyer, Mountbatten was a threat. Suddenly thrust into their midst was "an extremely articulate Britisher endeavoring to raise bogies about the hazards of a cross-channel operation." And to cap their worst fears, Mountbatten left the meeting with the Combined Chiefs to dine with President Roosevelt. For six hours, in a meeting that spilled over into the early hours of the following morning, Mountbatten had Roosevelt's undivided attention. Mountbatten convincingly argued that a North African invasion offered a sound alternative to Sledgehammer, that ambitious raiding in 1942—including the grand foray against Dieppe—could keep the Germans off balance, and that a cross-channel invasion was likely feasible in 1943. Pressed by Roosevelt, he conceded that Sledgehammer might be resurrected in 1942 if the Germans proved unexpectedly weak or if the Soviet Union needed to be rescued from collapse by a major offensive action on the western front. Mountbatten considered the dinner a stunning success—one that played perfectly to Roosevelt's weakness for British royalty and his personal affection for Mountbatten.[37]

Mountbatten told Hughes-Hallett "he felt quite sure that Mr. Roosevelt had at last accepted the British point of view." Hughes-Hallett departed Washington the next day for London and arrived there on June 9. Mountbatten stayed behind for another couple of days in order to "watch some army exercises." Upon reaching London, Hughes-Hallett reported to Churchill's private secretary on the success of the mission. Almost immediately, however, "it turned out that our impressions were quite wrong, and that the Americans remained wholly unconvinced by our arguments. The Prime Minister pulled our legs about this, saying that it was not unusual for Ambassadors to fail in their missions, but they usually knew they had failed."[38]

Three days later, Churchill announced to Chief of the Imperial General Staff, General Sir Alan Brooke that they would immediately leave for Washington. Roosevelt, he said, "was getting a little off the rails, and some good talks as regards Western Front were required." On June 17, they set off by air on the two-day flight. They would not return until June 28, but as a result of their journey they felt sure Sledgehammer would finally be buried. And while the buildup of American forces in Great Britain would be assured, equally the first major amphibious operation would be directed on North Africa.[39] In the meantime, the British would continue with combined operations raiding.

Churchill and Brooke's personal intervention won what Mountbatten's visit had not. They now had time to prepare while the Americans built up strength in Britain, and a shift of focus away from immediate cross-channel operations and towards North Africa promised relief to their embattled forces there. It was uncertain whether the diplomacy of Mountbatten and Hughes-Hallett had achieved anything besides ensuring that both men were absent from preparations for Operation Rutter at a time when momentous decisions were being made.

ON JUNE 5, Lieutenant General Bernard Montgomery, as commander of the South-East Command, chaired a meeting at Richmond Terrace. Representing Combined Operations was its vice-chief, Major General Charles Haydon. Rear Admiral Baillie-Grohman attended as Naval Force Commander, Major General Roberts as Military Force Commander, and Air Vice-Marshal Leigh-Mallory as Air Force Commander. Everyone had a bevy of staff officers along. For his part, Roberts relied on Lieutenant Colonel Church Mann to explain the military plan, while Lieutenant A.H.L. Butler set out the naval plan and Leigh-Mallory personally spoke for the RAF.

Until now, the Naval and Military Force Commanders had had little opportunity to work with the RAF, so they were anxious to tie things down. Smokescreens were considered vital to conceal the landings, and they wondered if RAF could do this. If not, was Leigh-Mallory open to the navy laying thick smokescreens? Leigh-Mallory, according to the minutes, "pointed out that it was difficult for aircraft to lay smoke accurately on a narrow beach and that in any case the use of smoke would interfere with attack by Cannon Hurricanes [fighters tasked with strafing the beaches]." After some discussion, it was "agreed not to use smoke by aircraft on beaches but to rely on the attack by four squadrons of Cannon Hurricanes to cover the landing." Some LCTS would be "equipped with mortars and would be prepared to lay their own screens if the situation made this necessary."

It was quickly agreed that a small naval demonstration somewhere near Boulogne between the hours of 0250 and 0550 on the day of the assault—which was still set for June 20—might "take the enemy's attention off the [invasion] convoy." Leigh-Mallory at this point fretted that over the course of the raid, the vessels would be standing off Dieppe and the nearby beaches for about six hours and "subject to attack by German fighters and fighter-bombers," and it might "not be possible for him to reinforce the two fighter squadrons in the vicinity of Dieppe before the German attack had been launched." Pondering this, Montgomery stressed "the importance of doing everything possible to increase the Anti-Aircraft defence of ships and vessels to overcome these attacks during the period of occupation." Montgomery promised "extra Bofors guns" if Combined Operations could provide ships to mount them on. Also agreed was provision of "sufficient ammunition on all ships in view of the high expenditure rate which was to be anticipated."

Leigh-Mallory then dropped a bombshell. A major premise regarding support for the raid had rested on Dieppe being heavily bombed by RAF Bomber Command the night before.[40] Leigh-Mallory now opined that "bombing of the port itself during the night of the assault would not be the most profitable way to use bombers and might only result in putting the enemy on alert."[41] He added that high-level "bombing with very large bombs at night is not accurate enough to expect to destroy prepared positions such as existed at Dieppe." The only alternative would be to conduct day bombing, which would require "prolonged training" for the bomber crews. With the scheduled assault just fifteen days away, this was not an option. Leigh-Mallory also believed, and Lieutenant Colonel Church Mann agreed, that heavy bombing would cause "a good many fires" and "it would be unlikely that our engineer programme could be carried out; and also of course, a good deal of risk would arise in endeavouring to get the tanks through a burning town." Everyone worried about the effect on the French population if they were heavily bombed.[42]

Roberts accepted Leigh-Mallory's assertion that Bomber Command could not guarantee any degree of accuracy. As land commander, of course, he could insist that the air bombardment was essential to the raid's chances. He recognized, however, that to do so would likely "see the operation cancelled, which he badly wanted to avoid." In any event, he later said, "my prime concern was the heavy batteries on the headlands flanking the beaches. If they could be neutralized, there was a good chance of the element of surprise compensating for lack of fire-power. I had reason to believe that the Air Force and the Navy would take care of those guns."[43]

To somewhat compensate for the withdrawn air bombardment, Leigh-Mallory proposed to bomb Boulogne with seventy planes as a diversion. Strikes against Luftwaffe airfields at Crécy and Abbeville would also be launched between 0230 and 0400 hours. He figured these strikes would divert the radar defences at Dieppe away from the assault forces coming in from the sea and might "at least for some hours... put out of action" two airfields, "which the enemy would wish to use during the day of operation."

In the absence of heavy bombing, "cannon fighters should attack the beach defences and the high ground on either side of Dieppe [targeting the heavy batteries causing Roberts's concern] as the first flight of landing craft were coming in to land. It was also agreed that air action would be taken against German Headquarters in Arques at 0440 [hours]."

Haydon then asked the three force commanders "to state their requirements for any special equipment which might be in short supply." Baillie-Grohman was the only officer to weigh in, worrying about offshore obstacles hobbling his vessels. He asked for "three shallow diving suits and experts to use them," plus "six large wire cutters for removing wire or other obstacles from propellers."

Neither Roberts nor Mann requested anything to replace the now stripped-away air bombardment support. Baillie-Grohman also offered no objection to its loss.

The meeting was about to break up when Lieutenant Colonel A.G. Walch, representing the British airborne division tasked with supporting the seaborne landing by an earlier air drop, arrived to say that he was to meet with Roberts "at an early date, in order that the whole plan might be explained to him in full detail." To this point, just fifteen days before the scheduled raid date, there had been no coordination between the seaborne raiding forces and the airborne elements.

As a last item, Commander Red Ryder, hero of St. Nazaire, pointed out that there would be insufficient fuel aboard the raid ships to fill "the enemy invasion craft which it was hoped would be captured. If these craft were found with empty tanks they would have to be towed back and special arrangements were being made to meet this contingency."[44]

Cancelling heavy bombing of Dieppe was a staggering decision. This was the only real fire support that had been laid on for the raid. Naval support was restricted to a handful of destroyers and gunboats. Yet nobody protested. In his memoirs, Montgomery would claim that he would "not... have agreed" to "elimination of any preliminary bombing of the defences from the air." Yet he chaired the meeting and was no shrinking violet in making his opinion known.[45] In fact, the Dieppe raid had ceased to really be a Combined Operations plan. It was now largely a Montgomery plan, wherein the main thrust would be delivered frontally against Dieppe and there would be no major air support. Instead, the raiders would have to rely on surprise. And that would require an excellent level of training across the three services, so that the plan unfolded like clockwork. Within a week of the June 5 meeting, the first test of that level of training would occur with a full-dress rehearsal code-named Exercise Yukon. Yet, to maintain secrecy, no officers below the rank of battalion commander knew the exercise's true purpose. Despite the enlarged scale of training, most junior officers and all the troops were led to believe it was simply another in the unceasing string of exercises in which they regularly participated.

6

These Are Anxious Days

UPON RETURNING FROM Washington, Captain John Hughes-Hallett embarked upon an unusual mission. With the Dieppe raid just ten days away, Hughes-Hallett secretly embedded himself within the ranks of the Queen's Own Cameron Highlanders. His guise was that of a clerical clerk from Combined Operations Headquarters who had been sent for infantry training. His plan was not only to participate in Exercise Yukon but also "to witness the Dieppe raid by landing with" the Camerons. "This was not just idle curiosity, although I was certainly interested to see what a raid looked like from a soldier's point of view. The truth was that I had always been a little uneasy about planning hazardous operations backed up by no personal experience and no sharing of the risks."

Hughes-Hallett had hatched this scheme prior to going to Washington and had sought permission from Major General Ham Roberts. He selected the Camerons because they would be neither first to land nor last to leave. "I have never believed in taking undue risks," he later explained. Roberts consented with the proviso that Hughes-Hallett join Exercise Yukon to ensure he was capable of keeping up with the Camerons during a seven-mile round trip under the weight of full equipment. His guise as a private and clerk was dictated by security concerns. If captured, it was unlikely the Germans would bother interrogating someone of lowly rank, and

Hughes-Hallett might avoid being identified as a valuable intelligence asset.

On June 10, Hughes-Hallett met with a British intelligence agent at a London flat. "Here I was dressed up as a private soldier and taught how private soldiers spoke to Corporals, and how they behaved in the presence of an Officer, and so forth. I was also given bogus papers which had been prepared by the War Office."

At Portsmouth, he caught a boat to the Isle of Wight and was soon delivered to the Camerons' tent encampment at Wootton Creek. His first impression was how informal the Canadians were in terms of rank and behaviour. The battalion assigned him to No. 16 Platoon of Captain John Runcie's 'D' Company. His tent contained nine other men. Rather than being from the same platoon section, they were instead placed together because they were all under the age of twenty-six. Men in the platoon over twenty-six were housed in other tents. The naval officer was pleased to be mistaken for a younger man. But he *did* look younger than the older men in the regiment. Most hailed from Winnipeg or the surrounding countryside, and "a number of them earning their living as hunters and trappers were aged by their tough life. They were naturally very fit and displayed a complete indifference to all outward forms of discipline. The Section Commanders were the key men. My own Section was commanded by Lance Corporal Bender—a [twenty-two] year old farmer for whom I quickly acquired a deep admiration and respect."[1]

The Camerons accepted Hughes-Hallett into their fold but not without reservations. One soldier soon approached Major Norman Ross. "There's something queer about that British guy," he said. "You know any common soldier who wears silk underwear? And he buys us drinks in the pub." Ross was bemused. Canadian soldiers were paid more than their British counterparts, a fact that gave them an edge dating local women. Rare was the British soldier who stood a Canadian a drink.[2]

Exercise Yukon was to commence the following day. The plan was for 2nd Canadian Infantry Division to assault the south English coast at West Bay, with local defence forces posing as the enemy. The Canadians were to destroy objectives in both West Bay and Bridport, then attack an inland airport, and finish by advancing three miles inland to Bradpole to capture a divisional headquarters. Re-embarking at West Bay, the Canadians would sail back to the Isle of Wight.

The Dorset area selected for the exercise in many ways resembled that of Dieppe. The inland airport was about the same distance from the coast as the one at St. Aubin, and Bradpole about as far in as the suspected German headquarters at Arques-la-Bataille. Thirty minutes after the Canadian assault began, three companies of 1st Battalion of the 1st British Parachute Brigade would drop on the flanks and eliminate mock coastal gun batteries.

For the South Saskatchewan Regiment, the shingle beach at the mouth of the Bride River at Burton Bradstock mirrored Pourville. The Royal Regiment of Canada would set down on a narrow beach west of West Bay. An hour after these battalions landed, the Royal Hamilton Light Infantry and Essex Scottish would strike directly at the mouth of West Bay harbour, with Calgary Tanks supporting. Simultaneous to this landing, the Queen's Own Cameron Highlanders would pass through the Sasks and advance to the airport and headquarters at Bradpole. Les Fusiliers Mont-Royal would remain as a floating reserve off West Bay, finally landing to provide rearguard cover for the re-embarkation.[3]

The exercise was considered so important that General Bernard Paget, Lieutenant General Bernard Montgomery, Lieutenant General Andrew McNaughton, and Lieutenant General Harry Crerar all would be on hand to observe the dawn landings.

EXERCISE YUKON BEGAN on the night of June 11–12 with the Canadians boarding vessels and putting to sea. Most of the infantry were to be landed in LCMS launched from various passenger liners converted into Landing Ship Infantry, Medium—LSI(M). Some, however, crossed to the Devon coast in small R-Boats. Lieutenant Colonel Cecil Merritt's company headquarters and some Sask elements were aboard the Dutch liner *Princess Beatrix,* a ship specially assigned to Combined Operations for transporting commandos on raids. The rest of the regiment was either aboard another LSI(M) or in R-Boats. The moment the ships cleared the Isle of Wight, they were caught in a gale.

When the larger vessels were about four miles offshore, they released their LCMs into the churning seas. A Combined Operations planner, Major Walter Skrine, was lowered from *Princess Beatrix* in the same LCM carrying Merritt and his headquarters. Waves were breaking over the eight-foot bow ramp, drenching the men with salt water. Around him, men were cursing and shouting as one wave after another sent spray showering over them. "Too much talking," Skrine primly noted with a pencil.

The lack of noise discipline was only a minor concern—far worse was the fact that soon half the regiment's LCMs were missing. The whole regiment was to sail towards the coast in a tidy line-abreast formation. Those LCMs that were visible slogged shoreward in total disarray. Searchlights stabbed the darkness as shore defenders tried to catch the approaching craft in their beams. Smoke-laying motor gunboats were to have blinded these lights, but there were large gaps in the screen.

Merritt had expressed a dislike for many aspects of the exercise.[4] It particularly galled him that he was not allowed to apprise his company commanders that this was a rehearsal for a true raid. How could the company commanders take things seriously when it seemed they were engaged in just another in a seemingly endless series of exercises? "Is your company battle worthy?" he asked one Sask company commander. "Oh yes, sir!" the man answered. But after some questioning, Merritt expressed doubts. The officer asked defensively, "What do you mean by that?"

"Are you ready to go into action tomorrow against the Germans?" The officer demurred. There were "a few things I'd like to do" first, he said.

"When are you going to do them?" Merritt snapped. If only he could put this man in the true picture. Then he would recognize the gravity of things and act on them. But he must keep his officers in the dark.[5]

Nor had he been allowed to decide what companies sailed in which vessels or how the troops were distributed among the landing craft. On *Princess Beatrix* he was left isolated and unable to consult at the last minute with any company commanders. He also had been given no chance to meet the Naval Force Commanders charged with providing support fire to his battalion. Denied air photographs of the beach, he could not know whether the navy was delivering him to the right place. Skrine agreed with all these concerns. In his report afterwards, Skrine suggested that all officers should be trained in using stereoscopes to study air photographs so they could plan their attacks on enemy defences with this knowledge at hand. As the Sasks closed on the beach, it was obvious the flank defences had not been blinded by smoke. Yet so much smoke drifted to their front that nobody could see the beach until they were right up on it. Looking around, Skrine saw that all the landing craft were now present. It was still a motley approach and fifteen minutes behind schedule.

The ramps dropped. Merritt and his men rushed ashore, Skrine gamely following. Ashore, the Sasks milled about. Merritt and the other officers were uncertain of their location. Several buildings were visible, which was odd. The beach had reportedly been clear of buildings. "If all concerned had studied the photos and maps before-hand it would have obviated the confusion and doubt on our arrival," he wrote.

Skrine thought Merritt took too long deciding what to do. "If landed on wrong beach," he noted, "leading [battalion commanders] must act quickly. Suggest the best plan is to go ahead inland if there is any beach exit. When daylight comes, they will soon find out where they are." Another problem cropped up immediately. Nobody in the regiment "knew how minefield gaps were marked. They were expecting a [Royal Engineer] man to be standing there and show them." A reasonable assumption, perhaps, had any engineers been with the regiment's leading assault wave. But there were no engineers with the battalion. Nobody had mine detectors. There was insufficient tape to mark gaps that were cleared, and the "worry about mines and the effect of an uncomfortable crossing in R-craft left officers and men in no state to get on with the job of pushing inland."[6]

The Sasks were not alone in confusion. Chaos reigned throughout Yukon. Major P.E.R. Wright with 2nd Division's general staff found no established system for organizing non-brigade units on the beaches. This led to the location of the engineer headquarters being totally unknown to anybody else. Its whereabouts remained a mystery not even solved by later analysis. Yukon unravelled because there had been no divisional-level training. Each battalion operated separately and in ignorance of how it fit into the overall scheme. The two brigadiers exerted little control. Isolated aboard separate destroyers, each lacked adequate wireless links to their battalions ashore. Major General Ham Roberts and his divisional headquarters aboard the destroyer and fleet command vessel, HMS *Calpe,* had even less idea of what was developing once the operation was under way. As Major Wright put it: "Although [communications equipment] provided was the best that we have ever had, information... was practically nil." The brigade headquarters failed to use the secure net to pass information to divisional headquarters. After the exercise, Wright suggested creating an administrative headquarters to function as an "information bureau." Its personnel would be aware of unit locations, where stores were dumped, who was headed where and when—and use wireless and runners to disseminate this information to whoever needed it.[7]

Combined Operations' shortcomings were illuminated, but not recognized, during Yukon's unravelling. Previous operations had entailed small numbers of men landed at night or at dawn to carry out "murder and run" operations. A few demolitions of defensive or strategically important positions, perhaps, but the routine was largely to get in, kill or capture a few Germans, seize whatever documents could be grabbed, and then get out quickly. St. Nazaire had been the exception, but it was an operation still being studied. The inherent hit-and-run nature of commando raids fostered a careless approach. As veteran No. 3 Commando raider Major Peter Young wrote: "Describe a typical World War II landing operation? Well, it would be pitch dark, with no lights permitted. There would be a sea running, so most people would be sea sick. It would take twice as long as we thought it would to get the chaps into the landing craft and then half the landing craft would disappear in the dark and never be seen again. When the rest of us embarked, we would bounce around for a while and then be landed on the wrong beach and while we were working out where we actually were we would be shelled by the Royal Navy... and that was on a good day."[8]

While this was the kind of piratical, make-it-up-on-the-fly operation Combined Operations thrived on, the Dieppe raid was an entirely different beast. It was a raid in force that required a high organizational level because of the sheer number of troops, naval ships, and air resources involved. Planning for cooperation between naval and army forces involved in the landings, however, was not developed much beyond the norm for a raid by fifty men or less. This contributed significantly to Yukon's confusion.

AS PLANNED, the Camerons had stood offshore while the Sasks secured the beach. But this meant taking a beating in the rough seas. Aboard the LCM carrying Major Norman Ross and 'A' Company, even the naval crew were vomiting. Hardly a soldier had not been sick at least once during the night crossing. As the gunwales were higher than their heads, the men had to lever up them to puke overboard. During one of Ross's many trips, "I caught my upper lip and bashed it and it puffed up. There I was seasick, puffed lip, rain running down the back of my bloody neck. And I didn't care where we were going or how we got there. I just wanted to get off that vessel. Daybreak came and of the whole division we could see about three ships, period." Soon a destroyer gathered these vessels "up like a mother hen" and herded them to where the rest of the Camerons were formed off the beach where the Sasks had landed. "We hadn't had anything to eat since the night before, so we decided to open up our boxes and have something to eat before going ashore. Of course it was beans or some damn thing and sour. Everyone took new turns over the side."[9]

The Camerons were landed on the same "wrong beach, because the [naval crews] saw [the Saskatchewan] landing craft ahead of them," Skrine reported.[10] "The bloody navy," Ross groused, "put us out about three miles from the proper place and we had to march... along the beach. Sand would have been bad, but we were on stones like golf balls... You march on that and you're just sliding. For three miles we went along, feeling miserable. It was hot by this time. The weather cleared up."[11]

Skrine thought the Camerons should have pushed inland from the wrong beach, rather than waste time following the seashore to the correct insertion point. When they did start inland, he found the pace "extremely slow... Is the role of this battalion to push on to its objective and by-pass opposition or to wait until opposition en route is overcome? I suggest it is better for this battalion to detail a small [detachment] to occupy the opposition, while the main body swings round it and makes for the aerodrome with all speed." Tanks, he felt, would normally come up behind the infantry and "liquidate this opposition in due course."

As the Camerons closed on the airfield, Skrine saw they were entirely unaware of the Calgary tanks standing about five hundred yards distant. Nor were the tankers aware of the infantry. Each operated in isolation from the other. Do "Canadian infantry and tanks practice talking to each other on No. 18 sets?" he wondered. The tanks, of course, had not landed with the Camerons. Instead, they had set down on the main beaches about a mile west of where the Camerons were to have landed.

Not noted in the exercise was the fact that these beaches were sand and occasionally pebble rather than cobble, as would be the case at Dieppe. In fact, all beaches on which the tankers had trained were mostly sand. There had been no concerted effort to test tank landing on a beach similar to Dieppe's. Although the Calgarians and Camerons were to have married up near the airport, this never happened. Skrine decided this was because the LCTs landed the tanks "in the wrong order." Once ashore, the tankers waited for those who were supposed to land first to arrive and complete their allotted beach-clearing tasks. "All tank squadrons and troop leaders," Skrine recommended, "must be in the picture so that squadron tasks may be interchangeable in an emergency."[12]

The Royal Regiment also "landed two miles to the west of their proposed landing beach." Thundering ashore, the lead companies overran a group of British soldiers completely bewildered by the sudden appearance of men on their beach. "Didn't you know we were coming?" Lieutenant Sterling Ryerson demanded. "No, we didn't know anything," a man answered. Ryerson was in high dudgeon, determined to rectify this lack of defensive vigilance. Somebody summoned the British company's sergeant from where he had been sleeping soundly. "What would you have done if we'd been Germans?"

Ryerson exclaimed and then roundly berated the man. "Are you going to report me, Sir?" the sergeant asked. "No," Ryerson replied. "But, for Christ's sake man, wake up. We could have been Germans."

The Royals were still at least two miles from their correct beach. "We'll have to double... to the correct landing place," Ryerson told his platoon. Private John "Jack" Abernathy Poolton and the rest of the men never hesitated. "There wasn't a guy," he recalled, "who would say the hell with that. I'm not gonna double no Goddamn three miles. This is how dedicated we were. We doubled the three miles because we wanted to be good soldiers. We wanted to be trained. We wanted to be fit. We wanted to do as we were told and that's why we did it. I was carrying the two-inch mortar."[13]

WHEN IT SPUTTERED to a close, Yukon was unanimously declared a fiasco. A post-mortem convened on June 14 back on the Isle of Wight in a Newport drill hall. Roberts presided. When it was suggested that the troops had been overburdened by ammunition loads and other stores, he countered that it was "in the best interests" of all to carry as much as possible so long as it did not interfere "with the fighting power of the men and the loading of ships."

Someone asked whether "plans could be made to ensure landing of craft on right beaches." Roberts replied that "this could not be done and there may be a repetition of craft landing on the wrong beaches such as in Yukon at any time."

Roberts was more concerned about the bunching up that had occurred in front of the single gap leading off the main beach where tanks, Essex Scottish, and Rileys had landed. "This should be avoided," he cautioned, "as it tends to make a very vulnerable target for machine guns." It was also noted that far too many infantry landing craft had stayed on the beach. Once the troops were off-loaded, the craft should move a short distance offshore until it was time for re-embarkation.[14]

None of the three force commanders, including Roberts, were sufficiently discouraged by Yukon to suggest that the Dieppe raid— still scheduled for the week commencing June 21—be postponed. Mountbatten, however, had missed Yukon because he was en route from the United States. After studying the reports and talking to various sources, he decided it was "necessary to postpone the operation... until a further exercise could be held."

This decision did not sit well with Lieutenant General McNaughton's First Canadian Army headquarters' delegate, Lieutenant Colonel G.P. Henderson. He noted in a memo to McNaughton that Mountbatten—having not witnessed the exercise—"felt he could not... assess the responsibility for the errors." This prompted Mountbatten's desire to have the entire force stage another Yukon-scale exercise under his personal watch. Henderson feared that delaying the raid raised "considerable risk of loss of security." Also, "the men were trained up to a high pitch and there was danger of them going stale." Mountbatten was not swayed, insisting that "further rehearsals were essential." After meeting with Roberts and securing his agreement, Mountbatten proposed pushing the Dieppe raid back to early July.

The following afternoon, Mountbatten, Montgomery, and the three Dieppe force commanders met at Combined Operations Headquarters in London. They agreed that "a second full scale exercise should be held on June 22–23," with the raid following "on the first favourable date between 3–4 July and 8–9 July." This second exercise was code-named Yukon II.[15]

Mountbatten had further cause to delay Operation Rutter. His foray to Washington had absented him from the meeting that cancelled the pre-raid air bombardment. Although the force commanders and Montgomery had agreed to this on June 5, Roberts and Baillie-Grohman had since had second thoughts. Roberts's only option would have been to demand some equivalent alternative support or withdraw the Canadians from the operation. He had no intention of doing either. Even had he done so, Crerar would likely have just replaced him with another more amenable Canadian general.

Baillie-Grohman, however, knew of one possible substitute for the lost bombers. If he could get a capital ship—either an 8-inch cruiser or a battleship—detailed to the raid, it would be possible to provide devastating and precise bombardment from the sea. When the rear admiral put the request to Admiral Sir William James, Commander-in-Chief, Portsmouth, he was sharply rebuffed. James made clear he had no intention of risking a capital ship in the Channel during daytime.[16] Fresh in mind was the disaster that had befallen two British capital ships on December 10, 1941, off the east coast of Malaya. During that one day, the battleship HMS *Prince of Wales* and the 15-inch gun battle cruiser HMS *Repulse* had been attacked by swarms of Japanese bombers and torpedo planes. In barely more than an hour, both ships were sunk, with great loss of life. James feared the same fate would befall any capital ship exposing itself to attack by the Luftwaffe in the Channel.

Despite the possible risks, Mountbatten also wanted a capital ship. Hoping to bypass James, he met with the First Sea Lord, Admiral of the Fleet Sir Dudley Pound. The *Prince of Wales* and *Repulse* had lacked air cover, their only protection being evasive manoeuvring and naval anti-aircraft fire. Any capital ship standing off Dieppe could be provided with dense air cover by RAF fighters. Pound was unsympathetic. He countered that fire from a battleship or cruiser would "merely increase the debris which the army wished to avoid." Mountbatten wrote later that Pound closed his argument by saying: "Battleships by daylight off the French coast! You must be mad, Dickie." Mountbatten reported that his parting volley was, "Sir, when the actual invasion comes all your available battleships and cruisers will be used."[17] Disappointed by the rebuff, Mountbatten was still no readier than his force commanders to see Operation Rutter cancelled, so he accepted the loss of capital ship support.

Exercise Yukon 11, running from June 22 to 24, was launched against the same terrain as before. Mountbatten, Paget, McNaughton, Montgomery, Crerar, and Hughes-Hallett—restored to his proper authority—observed the troops landing at dawn on June 23. Although the Essex Scottish's landing craft lost direction, they still managed to land on the right beach—though badly behind schedule.[18] The Camerons were put ashore a thousand yards east of their beach. Caustically, the regiment's war diarist noted that even as the navy became lost, "every Private could tell we were headed for the wrong beach!"[19] The Royals fared better. Their war diarist recorded that "on this occasion the landing was effected at the proper beach, and all went smoothly and according to plan."[20]

Canadian Press correspondent Ross Munro was with the Essex Scottish as their vessels wandered six miles off in the wrong direction. The resulting delay in landing was such that the Calgary Tanks went ashore ahead of the infantry. Had this been the real thing, Munro realized, such an error would have been disastrous. Seeing McNaughton standing with other senior officers on the beach, Munro walked over. McNaughton "looked extremely worried." Turning to Munro, he said, "These are anxious days. There is great peril when the Navy does not land our men on the right beaches at the right time."[21]

Paget, Montgomery, and Hughes-Hallett had been standing on the beach when suddenly "a Canadian soldier took careful aim and fired a smoke rocket at us. Monty took cover with great agility," Hughes-Hallett wrote, "but I made the mistake of supposing it would be easy to step aside as the rocket approached. Unfortunately these rockets weave in their flight, and this one secured a direct hit on my chin, fortunately without breaking the bone. Nevertheless it was extremely painful and I was grateful to accept the offer of a lift back to London in General Paget's personal train."

Montgomery was also aboard and took the opportunity to offer Hughes-Hallett some advice on directing "a great battle, such... as will take place at Dieppe." A battle commander, Montgomery said, "feels very lonely and gets a deep conviction that defeat is inevitable. That is the time when great strength of mind is needed. All you must do... is to trust the plan and let the battle win itself. The strength of mind required is simply to do nothing and refrain from dithering."[22]

7

What a Blow!

ALTHOUGH YUKON II was more successful than its predecessor, both Paget and McNaughton believed the naval errors must be rectified. In a June 23 memo, McNaughton expressed concern that there had been a "lack of precision in place and time in bringing the landing craft to the particular beaches to which they had been directed in the plans." Also, smoke cover had been insufficient. Clearly it was up to the navy to rectify these problems, he said. McNaughton asked Montgomery to ensure they did. His closing signature was "Senior Combatant Officer, Canadian Army in the United Kingdom."

On July 1, Montgomery reported to McNaughton that he had gone to the Isle of Wight the previous day and spent it discussing issues of concern with the force commanders. He was satisfied that steps had been taken to resolve the problems. These included provision of three special radar vessels to act as guides and also the detailing to the force of two officers who knew the Dieppe area well and could "lead the flank parties in." Montgomery was "satisfied that the operation as planned is a possible one and has good prospects of success, given:— (a) Favourable weather. (b) Average luck. (c) That the Navy put us ashore roughly in the right places, and the right times." The truly essential ingredient for success, he emphasized, was "confidence... I am now satisfied that... the Force Commanders, Staffs, and

Regimental Officers have confidence in the combined plan and in the successful outcome of the operation. I say, 'now,' because there was a moment when certain senior officers began to waver about lack of confidence on the part of the troops—which statements were quite untrue. They really lacked confidence in themselves."[1]

Montgomery had identified this lack of confidence from reports arising out of a June 27 meeting in Osborne House's ballroom. About three hundred officers were present, descending in rank from Roberts to the infantry and tank commanders. Major Norman Ross of the Camerons, the Rileys' Captain Denis Whitaker, and the Sasks' Lieutenant John Edmondson were all present. Ross had gathered with others around a large sand table model that showed "the beaches, the river, the hills, the town, and the buildings. Everything was there," exactly to scale. "It showed all the [German] slit trenches, their wire fortifications, the barbed wire tangles. They were all outlined and traced in." Ross considered the degree of intelligence work "well done."[2]

Roberts opened the meeting. "We have waited over two years to go into battle against the Germans. The time has now come. We are going in."[3] The air in the large room was stifling, wreathed with cigarette smoke. All windows had been blacked out, and armed sentries guarded the entrances. Ross Munro listened, as Roberts stood behind "the big plaster model of a stretch of coastline and port." Roberts "launched right into his talk without preliminaries and in short, clipped sentences, told them how the force would raid this target, and he specified the tasks of each battalion and unit."[4] Other than saying the port was French, Roberts carefully avoided identifying it. But suddenly someone gasped, "Good God! It's Dieppe!" Furious at this security breach, Roberts warned everyone that no word of this was to go beyond the briefing room. He neither confirmed nor denied it was Dieppe.[5] Lieutenant Colonel Church Mann interrupted to warn the officers that "other ranks are not to be informed [of the operation or its objective] until on board ship."[6]

The entire operation would be completed over a "two tide" duration, ending within twelve to fifteen hours of first landings. The general mood, Whitaker noted, was enthusiastic.[7] "None of us felt that we wanted anything more than we were getting. We had every-thing, in my opinion, necessary to do the job as assigned to us and do it successfully," Ross said. "We were in full confidence and with-out any apprehension whatsoever."[8] Such was the prevailing optimism that it was hard to credit Montgomery's concerns. Far the opposite seemed on show.

Not everyone, however, was swept up by the prevailing mood, and at least a couple of officers expressed serious reservations. An Essex Scottish officer, Lieutenant Art Hueston, remembered his days of training at Camp Borden after being called up for service. One of the "first principles of war" taught was that "you never go into a defile, which is a valley. So the first thing we are doing is we are going into a defile if I ever saw one and I thought this is crazy. But that's the way it was and you don't get a chance to debate."[9] So Hueston kept silent.

Roberts insisted the operation would go smoothly. From some-where in the room a voice offered that it would prove "a piece of cake." Whitaker was sure Roberts said this, the moment frozen in his mind because his good friend Essex Scottish Lieutenant Jack Prince leaned over and whispered, "A funny fucking piece of cake!"[10] Munro, who had been thinking that the operation "looked like a good thing," had no idea who offered the "piece of cake" comment. He thought instead about the expected estimate of Canadian casual-ties—five hundred killed, wounded, or missing at the raid's end. "Everyone left that room with a feeling of high elation. Here was the big job at last; all this training was now to be put to use as the real thing of a daring operation."[11]

ALTHOUGH SOME LEADERS were mildly wavering over the wisdom of Dieppe, the most serious expression of concern came from Prime Minister Churchill. On June 30, Churchill convened a conference in the Cabinet Room at 10 Downing Street. Five men joined the prime minister. They were Mountbatten; Hughes-Hallett; General Alan Brooke; Churchill's Chief of Staff, General Hastings Ismay; and Sec-retary to the Chiefs of Staff, Major General L.C. Hollis. Mrs. Churchill hovered in the background throughout the meeting, bus-ily arranging flowers. Churchill was in one of his "black dog" moods, and for good reason. On June 21, Tobruk had fallen to the Germans, and 25,000 British and Commonwealth soldiers had been taken prisoner. This disaster in Africa had prompted a parliamentary censure of Churchill's war management. It was against this dark background that Churchill asked for "one final review of the outlook for the Dieppe raid and [to] decide whether... it was prudent to go on with it."

During the discussion, Churchill suddenly turned to Hughes-Hallett. "Can you guarantee success?" he snapped. Before the startled naval captain could respond, Brooke interrupted and told him not to reply. "If he, or anyone else, could guarantee success," Brooke said, "there would indeed be no object in doing the operation. It is just because no one has the slightest idea what the outcome will be that the operation is necessary."

Churchill growled "that this was not a moment that he wanted to be taught by adversity."

"In that case," Brooke replied hotly, "you must abandon the idea of invading France because no responsible general will be associated with any planning for invasion until we have an operation at least the size of the Dieppe raid behind us to study and base our plan upon."

Chastened, Churchill said that if this was Brooke's considered view, then the raid "must go forward."[12] Still, he fretted. Would the Canadians fight well? Did he have to worry about another calamity like Tobruk and thousands more men lost as prisoners? Turning on the charm, Mountbatten asked Hughes-Hallett to share his experiences as a "private" with the Queen's Own Cameron Highlanders. As Hughes-Hallett spun his tale, Churchill smiled delightedly. The men he had served so briefly with, Hughes-Hallett concluded, would "fight like hell."[13]

LIEUTENANT GENERAL HARRY Crerar never doubted his Canadians were keen to advance towards the sound of the guns. Learning of Montgomery's concerns, Crerar had immediately rushed to the Isle of Wight on July 2. The following day, he submitted a report to McNaughton. "I spent yesterday with Roberts. He and his Brigadiers expressed full confidence in being able to carry out their tasks—given a break in luck. There was previously some doubt as to the ability of the Navy to touch them down on the right beaches. That has now pretty well disappeared, although I told Roberts that 100% accuracy should never be expected in any human endeavour, and that some error might be expected, and should be then solved by rapid thinking and decision. I agree that the plan is sound, and most carefully worked out. I should have no hesitation in tackling it, if in Roberts' place."

But Crerar was concerned that, once launched, "the operation can only be influenced by Air Power." For this reason, Montgomery, Mountbatten, and RAF Air Vice-Marshal Leigh-Mallory would all be "together" at 11 Fighter Group HQ in Uxbridge in order to jointly decide on alterations to the air plan.[14] Crerar agreed with this scheme. But ever quick to defend Canadian independence, he considered that either he or McNaughton "should have been included in this group."

McNaughton agreed and immediately telephoned Chief of the General Staff, British Home Forces Command, Lieutenant General J.G. des R. Swayne to press the case for "the presence of a Canadian officer at Fighter Group HQ." He followed up with a letter to Swayne's superior, General Bernard Paget. "It is my view that, having regard to the particular Canadian responsibility in this matter to maintain the proper channel of command to the Canadian units involved... Crerar should be with the group of Senior Officers of the three services at Fighter Group who appear to be charged with the exercise of command in this operation."

Swayne responded on July 4. He had taken the matter up with Paget, who said there was "no room for any more at the Group Headquarters." Besides, Paget thought, "it would be wrong for General Crerar to go there. There can only be one man in command of the operation... and Montgomery will see to it that he keeps Harry Crerar in hourly touch with the situation."

Crerar, meanwhile, had taken the matter directly to Montgomery by telephone on July 4. This led to a personal visit to Montgomery's headquarters. "I opened by informing that he was making a mistake in attempting to treat the problem of command of Canadian troops as a simple military issue, capable of solution along strictly British channels of command when, in fact, it was a complicated problem, and one involving national policies and Imperial Constitutional relations."

While agreeing that the Canadians were under Montgomery's command, Crerar said this "did not for one moment imply that I could be divested of my personal responsibility through . . . McNaughton to the Canadian Government in respect to the manner in which those troops were committed to actual operations." No agreement between Montgomery, Paget, and Mountbatten, or even the Chiefs of Staff Committee, "could affect this constitutional position." Crerar asked Montgomery to consider the United Kingdom's situation in the Great War when Field Marshal Douglas Haig and the British Expeditionary Force fell under overall command of the French Field Marshal Ferdinand Foch. Was there not a demand to be present in the headquarters where decisions were being made that could cost the lives of British troops?

Crerar made it plain that Paget's suggestion that there was "no room" was mere blowing of smoke and "obviously failed to take into account the really important factor which I had previously explained to him concerning separate Canadian responsibility." If the decision were not reversed, he said, it would be "raised to the highest political levels," and Paget and Montgomery would be overruled.

Montgomery, who could in such confrontations be either irritable and inflexible or politely accommodating, took the latter tack. The conversation was "most frank and friendly," Crerar admitted after. At its end, Montgomery said he intended to "ring up" McNaughton and suggest he join the command group for "the course of the intended operation." Crerar was also welcome in a headquarters suddenly bursting with room. "He thanked me for my frankness and for the explanation which I had given which had put a different light on the question at issue." After Crerar left, Montgomery did call McNaughton.

This short brouhaha concluded with a note from McNaughton to Paget describing the change. As for himself, McNaughton wrote, "I am not particularly concerned . . . although for obvious reasons, I would like to see this end of the work at first hand. I do, however, think that Crerar should be present because the Canadian troops taking part are under his command and he therefore should not be excluded."[15] In the end, only Crerar joined the command group.

FAST APPROACHING WAS the time for Crerar's Canadians to fight. On July 1, a bevy of war correspondents joined the Canadian force on the Isle of Wight. Previously, Ross Munro had been the only one inside the security zone. "I guess the job is imminent," he scribbled in a diary. At midnight, the correspondents crowded into a tiny room on the top floor of Osborne House. Perched on the back of a chair, with the large plaster model before him, Lieutenant Colonel Church Mann briefed them. "In typical breezy fashion, Mann gave us all a crystal-clear understanding of the plan. He made a big hit with the correspondents with his clear-cut approach and his good humour, which persisted even at midnight after weeks of night-and-day work, planning this show."[16]

For security purposes, preparations for boarding ships was conducted under the guise that this was but another exercise—Klondike 1. To maintain the illusion of normalcy, each Canadian infantry brigade staged a sports event on Dominion Day. The Essex Scottish delighted in their softball and volleyball victories.

On July 2, the Essex moved by ferry to Yarmouth and boarded ships there.[17] Over the course of the next twenty-four hours, some five thousand soldiers and three thousand sailors took station on ships anchored off ports in the Solent strait running between the Isle of Wight and mainland England. The raid was to occur on July 4.

During the move, there had been much grousing among the men about having to participate in yet another exercise. The general feeling was that everyone was fully trained. "Nobody had any fat on them. We were primed and ready," Major Ross remembered.[18] After first crossing to Portsmouth, the Camerons caught a train to Newhaven harbour. Ross's 'A' Company, along with 'B' and 'C' Companies, boarded the *Golden Eagle*, an old cross-channel paddlewheeler ferry. The battalion's headquarters and 'D' Company loaded onto a similar vessel, *Aristocrat*.[19] Slipping aboard and rejoining 'D' Company's No. 16 Platoon was Captain Hughes-Hallett, again disguised as a British private and determined to go raiding.[20]

Elsewhere, the Rileys were distributed on the morning of July 2 onto several ships. 'C' and 'D' Companies boarded *Queen Emma*, 'A' Company was on *Jeannie Deans*, and 'B' Company, less one platoon, loaded onto LCT4. Lieutenant Colonel Bob Labatt and the headquarters embarked on LCT5. "Landing exercises were becoming monotonous," the regimental historian later wrote.[21] As the commander of No. 4 Platoon, tasked with protecting Labatt's headquarters, Captain Whitaker was on LCT5. The men, he noted, "sweated, swore, and gambled on the role of the dice and the upswing of the barometer. A southwest wind was blowing."[22] Until that wind moderated, the fleet would not sail. But the forecast was for improvement, so the raid was expected to proceed on the night of July 3–4.

Once the vessels were loaded and "sealed, steps were at once taken to put all ranks in the picture." Lieutenant Colonel Hedley Basher informed his Royals aboard *Princess Josephine Charlotte* and *Princess Astrid* "that the so-called exercise was, in fact, an actual operation against the enemy." Elsewhere, other battalion and unit commanders did likewise. In the afternoon, Major General Roberts visited each vessel.[23]

Maps were distributed that detailed the Dieppe coastline and interior. Company and platoon commanders briefed men on their specific roles. The role each battalion was to undertake accorded with those rehearsed during Yukon I and II. A few refinements were introduced. Major Ross learned that his Cameron 'A' Company was to look for specific "books, manuals, and codebooks" when it seized the divisional headquarters beyond the airfield. "They were all described by size and colour. This one being red, another brown. We were to clear them all out."[24]

Hughes-Hallett noted the "great enthusiasm" among the troops. "They spent the evening studying maps ... and writing out their wills on special printed forms."[25] Mountbatten visited all vessels on July 3, announcing each time that the raiders would sail that night to be in position to strike at 0430 hours on July 4.[26]

When the winds persisted, word passed that the operation would be postponed for twenty-four hours. "As the operation was largely dependent on paratroops and a very large scale of air support, the weather required must be ideal," the war diarist for the Royals observed.[27] The paratroops and glider-borne troops, of course, were to take out the coastal gun batteries on the flanks of the main landing beaches. The raid could not proceed if there was risk of these troops being blown far off course. Expectation remained that the winds would be moderate.

The morning after the initial postponement, the Camerons aboard *Aristocrat* had transferred to the *Royal Eagle*. Another Thames paddle-wheeler, the vessel already had two companies of Les Fusiliers Mont-Royal on board. Conditions were extremely cramped, but this was the case on most every vessel. To avoid attracting attention from possible spies ashore, the men on the larger vessels were largely confined below decks. Tarpaulins were slung over the open decks of the LCTS to conceal the "cargo of tanks, carriers, and sweltering soldiers." Meals were cobbled together from compo ration boxes—a selection of "hard tack, cans of stew, bacon (mostly grease), and margarine (just like rock); as well as tea, hard candies, powdered milk and eggs, and tins of Woodbine cigarettes." Water was in short supply.[28]

On the morning of July 5, Roberts, Baillie-Grohman, their staffs, and Air Commodore Adrian Trevor Cole—representing Leigh-Mallory—conferred. The forecast called for forty-eight hours of continuing unsettled weather. That meant the raid was unlikely to happen before July 8. The plan called for the raiders to remain ashore through the day's two tides, but this would mean no withdrawal until 1700 hours. The prospect of keeping the troops ashore for just over twelve hours was worrisome. Only an estimated eight hours' travel time from Dieppe, the German 10th Panzer Division was stationed at Amiens. There was little doubt that this division's tanks and well-trained panzer grenadiers would pour down upon the beaches well before the embarkation of troops could be completed. Disaster was assured.

So the plan would have to change. The raid would now be a one-tide operation, with everyone withdrawn by 1100 hours. Roberts thought all the planned demolitions could be carried out "under the new short timetable, as practice had increased the speeds attained by the engineers." Some later stages were "somewhat abridged" to fit with the new timing.[29] A key modification cancelled the planned advance by elements of the Calgary Tanks to join the Camerons' assault on the airfield and headquarters at Arques. There was insufficient time for tanks to push through Dieppe and to Arques before they would need to be re-embarked. Under the new schedule, the last tanks were to be lifted off by 1000 hours. Moving the final departure time to 1100 hours, it was thought, would give "less time to the enemy to develop a counterattack and rendered interference by the Panzer Division at Amiens much less probable." The LCTs carrying the third and fourth flights of tanks ashore would remain at beachside and begin lifting the first Churchills off the beach at 0800 hours.[30] The modified plan was dubbed Rutter II. This was a last-ditch effort. The raid would happen on July 8 or not at all. Tide conditions for July 9 and 10 were deemed unsuitable.

Aboard the vessels, circumstances were deteriorating. Everyone was so crowded that it was often impossible to move more than a few steps. The rolling boats caused seasickness; the heads were plugged and overrunning. The air stank of vomit, feces, urine, and sweat.[31] Still, the Camerons' war diarist noted that the men "took it without more than good natured wisecracks... The spirit of all ranks was high and morale had never reached such a peak."[32]

To offer some relief, Roberts issued orders on July 5 for Exercise XLAX. Beginning the morning of July 6, the troops were taken ashore in groups to carry out "conditioning marches" along routes carefully "planned to avoid Canadian camps and towns as far as possible."

So many vessels standing in the Solent could not escape German detection for such a long period. Not surprisingly, at about 0615 hours on the morning of July 4, four Luftwaffe Focke-Wulfe 190s swooped down on vessels off Yarmouth Roads. Each plane dropped a 500-kilogram bomb. *Princess Astrid* and *Princess Josephine Charlotte* were both struck.[33] The bombs, however, sliced clear through each ship before exploding. Only four of the Royals on board the two ships were injured, and their wounds were minor. *Princess Josephine Charlotte* was so badly damaged, however, that the men were put ashore on the Isle of Wight and sent marching to Cowes for re-embarkation on HMS *Glengyle*.[34]

The Royals were still tromping along when a despatch rider roared up with orders turning them back from Cowes. There had been no improvement in the weather. In the mid-morning of July 7, Baillie-Grohman—who, as the senior naval officer, had final say—cancelled the raid.

From the dock next to the ships bearing the Camerons, a man called over a loudhailer for Captain Hughes-Hallett to make himself known. Major Ross was startled when "who steps forward but this British private." Without ceremony, Hughes-Hallett was whisked off in a car.[35]

"The heartbreaking news comes at 10:30 A.M.," Ross Munro wrote in his diary. "God, what a blow to these troops! Men break down and cry on the troop decks, they take the disappointment so hard. In the wardroom the officers drink innumerable double scotches (at eight cents a glass—navy prices). 'Let us hate,' is the toast. I have never been more depressed in my life. Here was the opportunity for which Canadian troops had waited so long and it has been fouled by weather."[36]

PART TWO

REBIRTH

8

A Brainwave

THREE DAYS AFTER Rutter's cancellation, the Canadians were all returned to camps on the English mainland. On July 10, Major General Ham Roberts circulated a message cautioning everyone "to say nothing about this operation which we had hoped to carry out, because if you do not there is always the possibility that we may be able to do it again at a later date."[1] The Canadians had abandoned the Isle of Wight with haste. Lieutenant Colonel Bob Labatt was one of the last to leave. The Rileys commander found Osborne House deserted. Just the day before, Royal Marine sentries had guarded the entrances, and pretty Wrens worked tirelessly at secretarial duties behind locked doors. Now those doors hung open, and "Rutter papers stamped 'Cancelled' were scattered everywhere. There was no doubt that the raid was off for good."[2]

With so many thousands apprised, Lieutenant General Bernard Montgomery thought it "impossible to maintain security."[3] The raid must soon be "a common subject of conversation in billets and pubs."[4] He "recommended to the powers that be that the operation be off for all time."[5]

"The decision... must have been a bitter disappointment to all commanders, regimental officers, and other ranks," Montgomery consoled Lieutenant General Harry Crerar. "The raiding force had been trained up to a high standard of efficiency, and I have no doubt whatever that, given average luck and weather, the operation would have been carried through with all that élan and dash which has always been so typical of the Canadian troops." Montgomery asked Crerar to convey to Major General Ham Roberts his "appreciation of the good work done, and his regrets that the operation had to be cancelled."[6]

He was not truly disappointed. Despite Montgomery's previous supporting and pivotal role in planning the Dieppe raid, it had always been of peripheral importance to him—perhaps even a "distracting operation," as biographer Nigel Hamilton put it. In Montgomery's "heart of hearts," Hamilton believed, he had "written off" the raid and was now grateful to no longer be responsible for it.[7] "I considered the operation was cancelled and ... turned my attention to other matters," Montgomery wrote.[8]

Montgomery's main concern, even during the lead-up to Rutter, had been ensuring that all South-Eastern Command was fighting-fit. As 2nd Division trained for Rutter, the other Canadian and British divisions had continued to learn how to fight coherently at army scale. With Rutter consigned to the dustbin, Montgomery continued on this track without pause.[9]

Meanwhile, at Combined Operations Headquarters the mood was initially funereal. First the Alderney raid had been scrubbed, now Dieppe. "Abandonment of these two raids," Hughes-Hallett thought, "was rightly felt to be tantamount to a defeat."[10] Mountbatten and Hughes-Hallett presided over "a post mortem" to "discuss the experience gained during training."[11] An angry Hughes-Hallett demanded a formal inquiry "by some outside authority into the question of whether there was a defect in the method of planning and whether the recent cancellations of operations had been justified."[12] Before leaving the meeting, Mountbatten airily dismissed this notion. He was currently distracted by the demands of stardom, for Noël Coward was in the process of filming *In Which We Serve*. Loosely based on Mountbatten's loss of HMS *Kelly* off Crete, the film was intended as propaganda, but Coward had encountered stumbling blocks within both the military and government that jeopardized its completion. Mountbatten had personally intervened, serving as primary consultant and also smoothing the political waters. This was but one of many concurrent demands that forced Mountbatten to compartmentalize tasks—including the Dieppe raid.[13]

After Mountbatten's departure, only Hughes-Hallett, the three force commanders, Major General Charles Haydon, and a couple of headquarters staff officers remained. Discussion revolved around an apparently insoluble dilemma. Operation Rutter had been considered essential tactically to provide lessons for the ultimate invasion of the Continent and politically to appease Russian and American demands for a major cross-channel operation. "The government," Hughes-Hallett pointed out, "would probably expect a divisional operation to be mounted that summer; and there appeared to be no other possibility so good as the Dieppe operation." There was a "ready-made plan . . . and a force had already been trained."

But Rutter's security was blown. Everybody acknowledged this. It must be assumed that German intelligence would learn of it and recognize a restaging was under way the moment troops moved to concentration points close to the ports. Ever quick thinking, Hughes-Hallett suddenly saw the solution. The operation could "be re-mounted," he suggested, "without preliminary concentration, and therefore without danger of the Germans discovering what was afoot." If Roberts "was prepared to undertake the operation without further combined training," Rutter could be revived.[14]

The troops would move directly from their camps and billets to the ports for embarkation, and the ships would only arrive in time to load them aboard and set sail that same evening.[15] It was a formidable proposition that would require split-second timing and precise organization to ensure that everyone loaded correctly and with the equipment required to complete particular missions. But Hughes-Hallett knew it could be done. There just needed to be "the united determination of the Chief of Combined Operations and his subordinates to drive on, unless told otherwise by superior authority."[16] Roberts, now nursing second thoughts about Rutter, gave Hughes-Hallett a mixed response. He agreed that no other division was trained to execute the raid.[17] But he was unwilling to immediately commit to a restaging on Hughes-Hallett's terms.

Mountbatten considered the idea "a brainwave, so unusual and daring that I decided nothing should be put on paper."[18] If the Germans suspected that Rutter was being restaged, it would meet with disaster. His next task was to sell the idea to the Chiefs of Staff and Prime Minister Churchill.

Rutter's cancellation had put Churchill in a bad position. The British had promised President Roosevelt and Stalin serious cross-channel raiding in 1942. Now the summer would pass with no such action. The Americans still hoped to force the British to launch Operation Sledgehammer. Stalin was sending cables bitterly complaining to Churchill of the failure to relieve any pressure from his front. Churchill wanted an attack somewhere. "Like a terrier momentarily released from the grip of a more powerful dog, his one idea was to fly back at the enemy's throat," General Alan Brooke noted. Churchill demanded that the Chiefs of Staff "consider yet another plan for invading Norway... and proposed that the operation should be entrusted to the Canadians." Churchill thought perhaps Lieutenant General McNaughton, "with his more flexible and fertile brain... would find a way out when the Chiefs of Staff had failed." To nip this notion in the bud, Brooke invited McNaughton to his office on July 9 to discuss the issue privately, as he "did not want him afterwards to imagine that we were suggesting the Canadians should undertake an operation which we considered impracticable."[19]

Mountbatten, meanwhile, pitched restaging Rutter to the Chiefs. "Candidly all were startled and at first argued against it on security grounds. I persuaded them that if they considered a reconnaissance in Force was still necessary in the summer of 1942 then there was absolutely no alternative target that could be got ready in time."[20]

Churchill was intrigued. "In discussion with Admiral Mountbatten," he wrote, "it became clear that time did not permit a new large-scale operation to be mounted during the summer, but that Dieppe could be remounted... within a month, provided extraordinary steps were taken to ensure secrecy. For this reason no records were kept."[21]

EVEN AS MOUNTBATTEN secured approval for Rutter's rebirth, resistance was rising within the ranks. On July 9, Baillie-Grohman submitted a critique that he had written and Leigh-Mallory and Roberts had endorsed. In their planning, he asserted, Combined Operations staff had failed to conduct a proper military appreciation. Such appreciations identify an operation's aim, factors either hindering or abetting achieving this aim, and detailed steps required to succeed. "This is not a criticism of the planners in any way," Baillie-Grohman wrote, even as he itemized how Combined Operations had failed to produce appreciations specific to the needs of the army, navy, and air force components. This lack "made it far more difficult for us to get into the planning picture. There was... nothing to guide us on certain points."

Always a reluctant player, Baillie-Grohman felt that the absence of large-scale aerial or naval bombardment beforehand guaranteed failure.[22] He had convinced the other two force commanders to seek a return to the planning board that accorded with military conventions. The memo sent Hughes-Hallett into a rage. The "preoccupation of the Admiral with the need for 'appreciations' and all that sort of rot," he thundered, directly opposed how Combined Operations operated.[23]

On July 11, Hughes-Hallett faced down the three force commanders at Richmond Terrace. Despite being junior, he seized the offensive—threatening Baillie-Grohman and Roberts with an official inquiry into the reasons for Rutter's cancellation. Leigh-Mallory, who cared only to draw the Luftwaffe into a duel over Dieppe, staunchly supported his counterparts. But Hughes-Hallett was not to be drawn into this talk of appreciations.[24]

Events snowballed. Baillie-Grohman, realizing his concerns would be ignored, requested a reposting. He was immediately invited by Admiral Bertram Ramsay to join his staff, which was engaged in preliminary planning for a large-scale invasion of the Continent. Baillie-Grohman went happily.[25]

Roberts, meanwhile, remained torn. He wanted the operation reexamined according to accepted military doctrine. Yet he did not want the Canadians shouldered aside due to perceived lack of aggressive desire. With Baillie-Grohman gone, Leigh-Mallory stepped away from the squabble and let events unfold as they would. He either got his air duel with the Luftwaffe or not.

After two days of consultation with his divisional staff, Roberts agreed to continue. Hughes-Hallett thought "he was [not only] quite prepared to undertake the operation... [but] in fact gave the impression of being anxious to do so."[26] Lieutenant Colonel Church Mann wrote later that Roberts and he concluded "the [British] Government [had] decided that it was necessary to carry out an operation at once and obviously the only operation which could be mounted on short notice was the raid on Dieppe.

"It was therefore decided that this operation should again take place using the same troops and the same staffs, and that, since these troops were already completely trained and informed as to the particular tasks, it would not be necessary to assemble them beforehand but that they could be embarked together with their stores and equipment from their normal accommodation areas.

"The most detailed arrangements would of course [be] required in order to embark the necessary stores in the right ships and craft and a large scale movement exercise [would need to be] arranged with five ports as ultimate destinations." Despite this quartermaster's nightmare, Mann was confident. It just required masterful staff work at divisional, brigade, battalion, and other involved unit levels to identify what was required, where it was currently stored, and how it could be moved to the correct vessels.[27]

"I could have refused," Roberts later said, "but it wouldn't have done any good [as] somebody else would have taken it on."[28] Roberts also did not have authority to withdraw. He was first answerable to I Canadian Corps commander Lieutenant General Harry Crerar and then to First Canadian Army's Lieutenant General Andrew McNaughton. Neither man would countenance the Canadians being cut out of a Dieppe raid.

MOUNTBATTEN, MEANWHILE, FENDED off the recurring anxiety expressed by the Chiefs of Staff and Churchill over the security issue. Although the Luftwaffe had obviously detected the gathering of the ships and finally attacked them, he argued that there "was no suggestion that they knew... the actual mission of the force. And if by some unsuspected chance they had stumbled on Dieppe as our target, they would never for a moment think we should be so idiotic as to remount the operation on the same target."[29] This was Mountbatten at his silken best. The circular logic yielded the desired result. Because remounting the raid was a preposterous idea, the security issue could be set aside. Only someone exceedingly bold would take such an action. Mountbatten and Hughes-Hallett were, of course, nothing if not bold.

The new operation was wrapped in the tightest security. A very limited number of people were let in on the secret, and each was briefed only when their involvement became essential. Mountbatten told McNaughton on July 14 that just twenty people were privy to the rebirth. These included Churchill and the Combined Chiefs of Staff—but not Brooke's immediate subordinate, Lieutenant General Archibald Nye. McNaughton, Crerar, Church Mann, and the force commanders knew. At Combined Operations, only Mountbatten and Hughes-Hallett were apprised. At South-Eastern Command, Montgomery and his personal representative to Combined Operations, Major Goronwy Rees, were aware. Leigh-Mallory and his immediate boss, Air Marshal Sholto Douglas, were the only RAF personnel informed. The newly arrived American commander in Britain, General Dwight D. Eisenhower, was informed but sworn to strict secrecy. His inclusion was intended to assuage bruised American feelings over Sledgehammer's cancellation.[30] Not even Britain's First Sea Lord Dudley Pound was briefed.[31] Major Walter Skrine, who had played a pivotal role in analyzing the training for Operation Rutter, was also excluded from the need-to-know list.[32]

This exceedingly tight security enabled Mountbatten and Hughes-Hallett to cherry-pick who joined the debate over restaging the raid. Mountbatten was determined that there would be no naysayers. When Montgomery learned the raid might be revived, he immediately wrote Commander-in-Chief, Home Forces, General Bernard Paget to say that "if it was desirable to raid the Continent, then the objective should not be Dieppe."[33] Paget, who was privy to the discussion, set about easing Montgomery out of the command chain. Montgomery, who had already burned every paper in his office regarding Rutter, accepted his exclusion without complaint.[34]

McNaughton wrote Montgomery asking that Major Rees, "who had been a valuable member of the Planning Staff for 'Rutter,' might remain with the group to provide continuity in the intelligence work." Montgomery replied: "Now that you have taken over responsibility, I suggest it is best that I should cut right clear; it is not suitable or desirable that I should have a representative in the party who reported direct to me on what was on... It might lead to trouble."[35]

ON JULY 14, the new command structure began to take shape by way of a directive setting out operational basics and providing a new code name—Jubilee. It was a circumspect document, giving no hint of the target. Rather there would be "an emergency operation" using the same forces. "The locality and form of the new operation are being chosen so as to ensure that the training of individuals of lower formations will be as similar as possible to that which was given for Rutter." As Baillie-Grohman and the senior staff of his department had all departed, Mountbatten announced that Combined Operations would provide the naval staff.[36]

McNaughton learned that day from Crerar that 2nd Division would "probably re-commence... training." As with Rutter, McNaughton immediately sent Lieutenant Colonel G.P. Henderson to represent him at 2nd Division headquarters.[37] On July 13, Church Mann had been promoted to brigadier general staff at 1 Canadian Corps. Within days, Roberts requested his return as the chief planner.[38] Crerar consented, and Mann was soon behind a desk close to Roberts, who had little patience for the minutiae of paperwork and detailed planning.

On Thursday, July 16, the force commanders met in second-floor rooms set aside for the planning at Richmond Terrace. Roberts and Leigh-Mallory were joined by Hughes-Hallett and Mountbatten. For the other two force commanders, this was the first word that Hughes-Hallett would command naval forces. Mountbatten explained that there was too little time for a new officer of flag rank to be included in the operation.[39]

Discussion turned to how the original plan might be changed or improved. Of particular concern was the use of paratroops. The likelihood of their dispersion by winds had scuttled Rutter. It was decided to eliminate this unpredictable element. Hughes-Hallett reported on his recent visit to Admiral Sir William James, Naval Commander-in-Chief, Portsmouth. "It had been virtually decided," he had informed James, "to re-mount the Dieppe raid with slight modification to the plan." The raid would likely occur "on or about August 18." James provided some good news. He could offer the addition of two ships, one being the passenger ferry HMS *Invicta,* which had just completed Landing Ship, Infantry conversion on June 3. *Invicta* could carry six Landing Craft Assault and about 250 troops. The LCAS were the new variant of the old R-Boat. Although still plywood hulled, they were slightly larger and capable of carrying about thirty-five men. More importantly, a drop ramp had been added to the front, so the troops no longer had to leap over the bow and sides. Hughes-Hallett immediately recognized that the addition of these two vessels and their LCAS meant he could substitute commandos for the airborne troops.[40]

The airborne troops' primary purpose had been silencing the powerful coastal batteries at Varengeville to the west and Berneval to the east of Dieppe. Both batteries posed a serious threat to the invasion ships and might also shell the troops ashore. This role could, everyone agreed, be fulfilled by two independent commando units. No. 3 Commando would knock out the Berneval battery and No. 4 Commando the battery at Varengeville.[41] Although the two commando leaders would be "responsible to [Roberts] for their plans," they would prepare these themselves.[42]

To maintain security, the three force commanders decided that the "troops should be kept in ignorance of what was required of them until the last moment and not be briefed until a few hours before sailing." This would avoid having troops confined to ships for several days, resulting in much unnecessary physical and psychological discomfort.[43] The briefing "should not be until the operation is definitely about to take place." Senior naval and military commanders would have to be informed earlier so they could make necessary arrangements and plans. But they were only to "be warned in the strictest confidence that an emergency operation is being planned for August and may be ordered to take place at short notice. They will be informed that the same personnel will participate as in the case of 'Rutter,' although the objectives will be different."

This latter provision proved unworkable. When Brigadier Church Mann began outlining the plan to brigade and battalion officers, he never offered "any suggestion... that the objective would be different and the briefing was done on the exact and original model of Dieppe."

Discussion returned to supporting the raid with a heavy air bombardment. Because of tide considerations, two windows were available for the operation: one between August 18 and 23, and another between September 1 and 7. "In neither period," Leigh-Mallory explained, "is the state of the moon satisfactory from the point of view of night bombing." He "stressed the fact that accurate bombing of the houses on the sea front could not possibly be guaranteed. If bombing is to be carried out at all, it should be timed to take place as... close as possible to the time of landing." Alternatively, he suggested, "it might be better to dispense with the bombing, and to rely entirely on supporting fire from the destroyers."[44]

Roberts did not like losing the heavy bombing support, but he consented because he feared "that the destruction caused by such an attack would make the passage to tanks through Dieppe difficult if not impossible." It was also felt, he wrote, "that a large scale attack, probably inaccurately placed, would merely serve to place the enemy on the alert. At all stages it was insisted that bombing could only be carried out by night and [as a result] inaccuracy, rather than accuracy, was guaranteed."[45]

This meeting was followed by another at 1800 hours involving only Mountbatten, McNaughton, and Roberts. McNaughton summarized the basic details of the revived plan and instructed Roberts "to proceed with plans and preparations... at once." This was mere formality, and the three men quickly turned to their primary task— establishing a senior chain of command. Mountbatten said that during Rutter it seemed that Admiral James in Portsmouth "was not in the best position to act as Supreme Commander and discharge the responsibility of despatching the expedition." He proposed assuming this role himself. McNaughton said the decision was for Paget to make. This was not what Mountbatten wanted to

top · Canadian infantrymen carry out an amphibious landing exercise near Seaford, England, on May 8, 1942. Such training little prepared the troops for the reality ahead. C.E. Nye photo. LAC PA–144598.

bottom · Chief of Combined Operations Vice-Admiral Lord Louis Mountbatten (right) was determined to conduct major raids against the Germans in the summer of 1942. Photo in the author's possession.

top · The Calgary Regiment stands on parade, July 1942, before going to Dieppe. The Churchill tanks have not yet been waterproofed. Photographer unknown. LAC PA-116274.

bottom · Brigadier Church Mann (left) and Lieutenant General Harry Crerar (centre) were both keen to ensure that Canadian troops formed the backbone of the Dieppe raiding force. This photo was taken in February 1945. The RAF officer on the right is Air Marshal E.C. Hudleston. Ken Bell photo. LAC PA-145766.

top right · Major General John Hamilton Roberts believed that if he tried to withdraw 2nd Division from the Dieppe raid, his Canadian superiors would replace him with someone willing to carry out the operation. Photographer unknown. LAC PA-153351.

bottom right · Ships en route to Dieppe as part of Operation Jubilee, August 19, 1942. Photo in the author's possession.

top · ML230 was one of the escort vessels for the R-Boats of Group 7, which carried the Queen's Own Cameron Highlanders to Green Beach. Four of the R-Boats are seen here just as they start the run towards shore. Photographer unknown. LAC PA–113247.

bottom · Sailors on guard aboard a destroyer standing off the long chalk cliffs that line the coast around Dieppe. The small beaches are not visible at this distance offshore. Photo in the author's possession.

top right · This photo of Canadians inspecting one of the pillboxes on the eastern flank of Blue Beach at Puys was taken in 1944. The obstacles dotting the length of the beach were not present in 1942. From the pillbox, it is easy to see how its guns would have dominated the entire beach. Ken Bell photo. LAC PA–134448.

bottom right · LCMs cast off from one of the landing ships and head towards shore. Photo in the author's possession.

top left · Pourville and Green Beach were clearly visible from the eastern headland. German batteries positioned here inflicted heavy casualties on the South Saskatchewans and the Queen's Own Cameron Highlanders. Ken Bell photo. LAC PA–137299.

bottom left · The smoke in this aerial view of Dieppe is coming from the burning tobacco factory. Photo in the author's possession.

above · An LCA carrying members of No. 4 Commando comes alongside a landing ship crowded with Canadian troops, returning from their successful raid on the coastal battery at Vasterival-sur-Mer. Frank Royal photo. LAC PA–113245.

HMS *Calpe* lays a smokescreen off Dieppe. Photographer unknown. LAC PA–116291.

hear, but it was also true. When asked, Paget required that the "decision whether the operation was to take place would be made" by Mountbatten, James, "and the Force Commanders in consultation." This differed from Rutter only in the elimination of Montgomery.

Although Montgomery was excluded, McNaughton was determined to make this a certainty. McNaughton announced that he would ask Paget "to agree to General Crerar being named as the responsible military officer to coordinate and if this were done I would arm him with appropriate authority as regards the use of Canadian troops." Further, "the detailed proposals for the Operation when prepared would be subject to my approval in the same way as [Paget] and Chiefs of Staff Committee had approval for operations of British troops."[46] Jubilee was suddenly becoming a Canadian plan, albeit one whose essentials still derived from the Rutter operational plan.

That evening, McNaughton telephoned Paget's office and requested a meeting, which took place on the night of July 17. Paget agreed that the chain of command would run from him to McNaughton, then to Crerar, and then Roberts. Crerar "would be the responsible military officer" under the same terms previously held by Montgomery. Paget would formally notify Montgomery that he was written out. For an operation playing out as rapidly as Jubilee, the formalities took a surprising ten days to conclude. Not until July 27 did McNaughton formally notify Crerar that he was now the "responsible military officer for operation *Jubilee,* and I direct that you place yourself in contact with CCO [Mountbatten] to concert plans therefor." He authorized using elements of 2nd Division and the Calgary Tank Regiment.

On July 28, a Tuesday, Crerar notified Mountbatten "that he was at his disposal for a meeting," which took place two days later.[47]

Mountbatten had been busy tying down Combined Chiefs of Staff authorization. His approach was oblique. On July 20, Mountbatten had requested that Hughes-Hallett be appointed Naval Commander for "the next large-scale raiding operation." The minutes of this meeting provide approval only "by inference," as the official Canadian military historian later put it. He added, however, that the "absence of more specific approval in the record is probably the result of determination to take extreme security precautions in connection with the revived operation."[48]

The first formal meeting of the force commanders to openly discuss Operation Jubilee occurred the next day at Richmond Terrace. Mountbatten chaired. In addition to the three force commanders, the two new commando leaders, Lieutenant Colonel Lord Lovat and Lieutenant Colonel John Durnford-Slater, attended. The number of officers being brought into the picture was expanding. Lieutenant Colonel G.P. Henderson from 2nd Division; Air Commodore G. Harcourt-Smith of No. 11 Group, RAF; Commander David Luce and three other naval staff from Combined Operations; and a secretary were present.

At Mountbatten's urging, it was agreed that the three force commanders would "prepare and sign a combined plan," which he would then "forward to the Chiefs of Staff Committee for approval." Roberts emphasized that he would be acting under direct orders from Crerar.

A new element Mountbatten introduced was the inclusion of fifty American rangers. Durnford-Slater said he "could very usefully employ about 20 of them."[49] American interest in commando operations had led to Brigadier Lucien Truscott and a small team being posted to Combined Operations on May 17, 1942. Nine days later, the tall Texan had written the American Chief of Staff, General George Marshall, suggesting that formation of a purely American unit for raiding be adapted to U.S. tables of organization and equipment. He suggested calling them rangers, after a band of irregulars who had fought during the French-Indian Wars under command of Major Robert Rogers and had been known as Rogers' Rangers. The 1st U.S. Ranger Battalion was activated on June 19, 1942, at Carrickfergus, Northern Ireland, under command of Major Bill Darby. It consisted of 29 officers and 575 men.[50]

On July 11, Eisenhower had reported to Marshall that the British recognized "our keenness to participate" in what he understood would be "raids on an increasing scale in size and intensity." He was "very hopeful that not only our 1st Ranger Battalion, but other units... can gain this experience during the summer." On July 25,

Truscott ordered 1st Ranger Battalion to report to the commando headquarters in Scotland and begin combined operations training. When the Americans learned that only fifty rangers were to be mixed in with British commandos for the raid, President Roosevelt expressed their dissatisfaction. "For reasons of politics and prestige," he wanted a U.S. "military contingent" to participate in the assault. But the British General Staff refused, stating that "the few American units in Britain at that time were green troops." The offer to "take along a token number of Rangers to gain combat experience" was a sop to U.S. prestige.[51]

Much of the raid planning covered well-travelled ground. Putting in a "synchronised attack," where everybody hit the beaches at once, was impossible. Some landings, such as those of the commandos, had to take place at night. In other cases, the ships involved were too slow and ponderous to carry out a landing except in daylight. Again Leigh-Mallory was pressed to see if bombers could neutralize the artillery batteries on either of Dieppe's immediate flanks while the commandos silenced the more distant ones at Varengeville and Berneval. He agreed to try. Hughes-Hallett said the navy would look into providing support fire against these guns. It was suggested that perhaps the air force could blind these guns with smoke. Everyone agreed that it was "preferable that Jubilee town [Dieppe] should be submitted to naval fire and not be bombed by RAF."

Leigh-Mallory worried that the air force would be stretched too thin by now having to support the commandos. Lovat said that "air support though not essential, would definitely be an advantage in [his] attack." A Spitfire squadron was promised to support the commandos, and bombers would attack the outer coastal batteries, "providing that the light made this a reasonable target."

Mountbatten said he was obtaining meteorological data for the chosen period. The best day for a two-tide operation was agreed to be August 18, 19, or 20. A one-tide raid might happen on either the 22nd or 23rd.

Hughes-Hallett, meanwhile, was still seeking heavier bomber support for the raid. Could not the "troublesome batteries" be silenced by putting a force of twelve Stirling bombers in the air over

Beachy Head and then calling them in once the targets could be pin-pointed? Leigh-Mallory took the idea to Bomber Command, only to be rebuffed. "The Stirlings would inevitably be shot down," was the reason given. Leigh-Mallory thought "that adequate fighter protection could have been arranged for these Stirlings," but there was nothing more he could do.

Then, in a meeting attended by Crerar, Leigh-Mallory voiced his most dire thoughts. Was the military plan practicable? "Are you speaking as an airman?" Crerar wondered. Leigh-Mallory replied that he spoke "as a last-war Western Front subaltern." He feared "that the troops would be pinned down in the very beginning and would never get going again."[52]

9

Fraught with Alarming Warnings

INTRODUCTION OF THE commandos brought into the scheme two officers seasoned in combat and combined operations. Thirty-one-year-old Lord Lovat—"Shimi" to his friends—had joined the commandos in 1940 and first raided in March 1941 against targets on the Lofoten Islands, off Norway's northern coast. In April 1942, he won a Military Cross at Hardelot. Promotion to lieutenant colonel and command of No. 4 Commando soon followed.[1] The thirty-three-year-old Lieutenant Colonel John Frederick "Torchy" Durnford-Slater was so nicknamed because of his red hair. As a founding member, he had recruited the first troops to form No. 3 Commando. By the summer of 1942, he was a veteran raider.[2]

In late July, Special Service Brigade's Brigadier Bob Laycock had shown up at the training base where Lovat was leading mock combat exercises. "Can you climb cliffs?" Laycock demanded, because a "big raid was on." Lovat turned to troop leader Captain Robert Dawson. Educated in Switzerland, Dawson had rock climbed since his youth and was No. 4 Commando's mountaineering expert. Dawson said he had sixty men "who could scale anything with a reasonable surface, provided there was no overhang."

Lovat and Durnford-Slater caught a night train to London while their respective commandos were to move within forty-eight hours to Weymouth in southern England. "There was no time to spare," Laycock warned the two officers. "The job was on."[3]

The two commanders hated Richmond Terrace. It was not unusual to be kept waiting for hours, even days, for an appointment of little consequence. So Durnford-Slater, whom Lovat considered "a go-ahead fellow," led the way past the gatekeepers without a sideways glance and burst in unannounced upon Major General Charles Haydon. Unperturbed, Haydon locked the door and disconnected the telephone for security reasons before outlining the operation and what was expected of the commandos. Haydon said he "did not like the overall plan," but the commandos' job was to destroy two batteries before the main landing could occur. It was Haydon who had proposed using Nos. 3 and 4 Commandos, and "he had staked his reputation that we would succeed."

Haydon arranged for them to study air photographs and models of the target area. Soon Lovat and Durnford-Slater returned to his office. They wanted some changes. First, the commandos would land before daylight. Second, each commando would be independent, "fighting its own way in." They would maintain wireless contact with the Military Force Commander and only report when their jobs were complete.

Haydon agreed and briefed them on the shipping arrangements. Lovat's men would be on the LSI *Prince Albert* and then board its LCAS. Durnford-Slater's commando, however, would have to make the crossing aboard the small and vulnerable R-Boats.

Lovat said the Canadian battalions were landing too late. A daylight attack, presumably on Dieppe, was asking for trouble. Haydon blanched. "And why the devil do you settle on Dieppe, may I ask?" he bellowed. There had been rumours that such an operation had been staged last month and then cancelled, Lovat said. But the best evidence was in the photos studied. Each was backed by a label reading: "*Les Falaises de Vasterival près Dieppe.*" Haydon swore both men to secrecy.[4]

Lovat and Durnford-Slater first met the rest of Jubilee's senior officers at the July 21 meeting. Major General Ham Roberts, Lovat found, was "a nice fellow but very thick; he sat there looking very bovine and solid." Roberts expressed no concerns about the operational plan. The only negative voice was Leigh-Mallory's. Although Lovat had concerns about the operation overall, he never doubted that No. 4 Commando would succeed. Developing his plan independently, Lovat was not to be distracted by things beyond his influence.[5]

No. 4 Commando established itself at Weymouth and No. 3 Commando at nearby Seaford. While the rest of Jubilee force was scattered and unaware that the Dieppe raid was back in play, these two commandos set about training for it. Lovat picked Weymouth in order to conduct mock raids at nearby Lulworth Cove, a property once owned by a great-uncle. "Here we trained tirelessly in eight rehearsals, working night and day from *Albert*'s landing-craft... The boat crews were good and trained with a will as No. 4 Commando wound up to concert pitch. Every soldier would meet the events of the day like a trained athlete off his mark to the crack of a starting pistol. We were playing for high stakes. All knew it." Lovat considered he had "the cutting edge," which was intelligence. "Usually a battle is fought at short notice, with little or no plan of action. Here the data had been sorted out and sifted like a jigsaw puzzle. We had an admirable model prepared to scale by RAF intelligence. We knew the range and the distance to be covered." The men tirelessly examined "every fold and feature... on the ground." Guns were repeatedly live-fire tested, as everyone "blazed ammunition on short-range practices." The 2-inch mortar men were soon dropping eighteen out of twenty rounds within a twenty-five-foot square from a range of two hundred yards. They practised throwing rolled rabbit netting—a wire mesh blanket—over barbed-wire aprons and rolling over the obstructions. Assigned specific spots in the landing craft, each man was soon able to be out and away precisely as required. Officers exchanged roles so each could seamlessly replace anybody wounded or killed. Then one landing craft or another would be declared sunk, and the entire force had to adjust to compensate for the losses. The withdrawal to the beach and re-embarkation were repeatedly rehearsed. Men carried others on stretchers while pursued by fierce opposition, covering their withdrawal with heavy screens of smoke.

Timing, timing, became a Lovat mantra. They would hit the beach at 0450 hours, ten minutes before the end of nautical twilight. "Those ten minutes, I believed, were vital." The covering darkness would help the commandos get off the beach without being lashed by German machine guns. Unable to see, the "jittery" gunners would "shoot high." It was what men did. But once they could see targets, the fire would become deadly.[6]

Despite their late entry, the two commandos would be ready. Even the introduction of American rangers caused no hiccups. Four men joined No. 4 Commando. Under command of Captain Roy A. Murray, forty rangers were divvied up within No. 3 Commando.[7] Six other rangers would be posted to Canadian units as observers at the last minute.[8]

WHILE THE COMMANDOS trained in full awareness, the Canadians nursed disappointment over Rutter's cancellation. On July 19, the Royals learned their long-time commander, Lieutenant Colonel Hedley Basher, was being eased out by promotion to No. 1 Canadian Divisional Reinforcement Unit. The good news was that the regiment's second-in-command, Major Doug Catto, was promoted to lieutenant colonel and assumed command of the regiment. A Great War artilleryman, Catto had worked as a Toronto architect during the inter-war years. He had been with the regiment a long time and "enjoyed the confidence of all ranks," the regiment's historian wrote.[9]

Deliberately kept in the dark about the raid's revival, the troops began a series of training exercises like those that had preceded assignment to combined operations. At Billinghurst, the Royal Hamilton Light Infantry spent July 21 through 24 engaged in Exercise Lenin. Although used to exercises involving machine guns firing on fixed lines, they were perplexed at having to undergo the same form of fire from the 6-pound guns of Churchill tanks. Lenin over, the battalion moved to Arundel Castle on the Duke of Norfolk's huge Sussex estate. Billeted in tents, the men spent their days being bused out into the countryside in order to march back to camp. This, the regimental historian later learned, was all "part of Combined Operations' elaborate plan to avoid arousing suspicion of the revival of Rutter."[10]

Periods of leave were granted on a rotational basis. Consequently, many men and officers of the Queen's Own Cameron Highlanders were on leave when Lieutenant Colonel Al Gostling held a parade on

July 27 to explain future tasks. He promised only more rigorous training. The following day, a divisional sporting match was held. Major General Roberts presided over the event, and Lieutenant General McNaughton's wife handed out awards to winning teams. None went to the luckless Camerons, who had lost in every category.[11]

Roberts shunted regularly from divisional headquarters to Combined Operations for meetings, fine-tuning Jubilee. It was decided that not only No. 3 Commando would make the crossing in their small landing craft—the Camerons would also embark at Newhaven in landing craft, while Les Fusiliers Mont-Royal would do likewise at the small port of Shoreham, in Sussex. Neither Canadian battalion would cross in R-Boats, however. Instead, they were equipped with the newer LCAS. This decision was made to enable greater dispersion of the battalions to various ports than if all were assigned to the larger LSIS.[12]

As soon as Captain Hughes-Hallett resolved one channel-crossing problem, another cropped up. Towards the end of July, naval intelligence reported that a German minefield had been laid in the middle of the channel. Roughly shaped like a hockey stick, it lay between the Pas-de-Calais and the Baie de Seine. The raiding force would have to sail through it to reach Dieppe. Normally, minesweepers would go out during daytime, clear paths through the field, and mark these with buoys. Doing so now might warn the Germans. The two minesweeping flotillas—the 9th and 13th—must then precede the raiding convoy by only a short distance. Each flotilla's eight ships would create a passage about a quarter mile wide. Their operational speed was about eight knots. Careful timing would be required to ensure the job was complete before they were overrun by the main ships—now comprising eight destroyers and nine LSIS—which would barrel along at speeds of sixteen to nineteen knots. "There was no margin of time, or indeed, of sea room," Hughes-Hallett later wrote. Another puzzle was how to ensure that the leading ships found their assigned passage entrances in the darkness of night "with dead accuracy."[13]

Navigational radar technology was in its infancy. But after some trial and error, it was decided to situate a motor launch at the entrance of each passage. Using Type 78 directional finding beacons, the launches' locations would be transmitted in Morse code on a frequency received by ships fitted with Types 286 and 290 radio directional finders. The ships leading the various force convoys would pick up the signals when they were within five to seven miles' range. Inside the passage itself, buoys mounted with flashing lights would mark the outside boundaries.[14]

For several nights in early August, Hughes-Hallett took the LSIS to sea from Southampton harbour to rehearse "passing through a dummy minefield. This was difficult and complicated, as it involved getting the ships out of Southampton and getting them back in again, both during the short hours of a single summer night. This was successfully done, but not without arguments with the Southampton port authorities, who had never heard of such goings-on."[15]

OPERATION JUBILEE'S FINAL plan, meanwhile, had been finished on July 31 and distributed to the small coterie in the know. It was a massive document, almost three hundred pages long. Its three parts set out the naval plan as drafted by Hughes-Hallett and his staff, a military plan generated primarily by Brigadier Church Mann and his 2nd Division planners, and a less detailed air plan worked up by Leigh-Mallory's RAF team at Uxbridge. Each section was supported by many supplementary documents. With regard to the military plan, Mann continued to disseminate ever more detailed instructions to the relevant officers as the scheduled launch date neared. These covered such matters as allocation of weapons and other equipment, intelligence reports on enemy strength, analysis of tidal action on the beaches, and other minutiae running to hundreds more pages. No detail was too small to warrant consideration. Nobody involved could afterwards recall a more thoroughly documented operational plan.

One instruction issued by Mann to 3rd Canadian Light Anti-Aircraft Regiment's Lieutenant Colonel B. Russell Kerr, for example, ordered him to assemble a party of 113 men and officers under command of Major C.R. Ostrander. It then instructed that five specific soldiers—Bombardier M.W. Phillips, Gunner R.A. Antille, Gunner R. Donaldson, Gunner A.N. McKenzie, and Gunner A.V. Drake, along with two others, "but not Gnrs. Stewart or Fry"—would travel to Dieppe aboard LCT13. Once on board, each man would be given a pistol.[16] Considering the thousands of personnel involved, Mann's extent of personal oversight was astonishing.

With Jubilee fast approaching, the number of officers informed began to increase on August 1. First let in on the secret were 4th Canadian Infantry Brigade's Brigadier Sherwood Lett, 6th Brigade's Bill Southam, and Lieutenant Colonel Johnny Andrews of the Calgary Tank Regiment. Roberts warned the three men that an emergency operation might be imminent. Everyone tasked to Rutter would raid against the same objectives. Mann then pulled aside a cover to expose the same plaster model of Dieppe. Lett's heart sank. The naval problems with exercises Yukon I and II in landing at the right spot and on time had convinced him such a raid was sure to be costly. "When the fact that the actual Dieppe operation was on again sank in, I knew at once that we were for it."

All three officers responded negatively to there being no heavy aerial bombardment. Roberts and Mann offered assurances that the element of surprise would enable them to overwhelm the German beach defences. Nobody was convinced. The only ray of hope was the promise that it would be a one-tide operation of about five hours' duration. Such a hit-and-run operation might succeed without too heavy loss. Still, the officers considered the scheme overly risky.[17] Their agreement was not, however, being sought.

Sustaining the veil of secrecy while at the same time ensuring that the necessary preparations were carried out required a delicate dance. It was the kind of dance Mann was ably suited for. On August 4, a divisional training summary set out the month's exercises. There would be three: Foothold, Popsy, and Stranglehold.[18] On August 7, Exercise Foothold would entail "the invasion of Britain," with 2nd Division securing a bridgehead between Littlehampton and Arundel. Eight destroyers would be in support. The best dates were between August 21 and 23, with the 21st favoured.

The order was unusually concise—just two pages. Roberts explained this brevity as resulting from his loss of Church Mann "to a higher formation. I propose, therefore, to leave the working out of these plans in detail to the [brigade] commanders." Mann, of course, was an almost constant presence at divisional headquarters, but one totally engaged in keeping Jubilee steaming along. Foothold also provided a neat cover within which the actual forces for Jubilee could be organized.[19] To the soldiers and officers preparing for Foothold, it seemed they engaged in nothing more serious than yet another staged invasion—something they could do almost in their sleep.

Except for the changes introduced towards the end of July, Jubilee was Rutter reborn. And that plan had been constructed by Combined Operations with significant alterations made by Montgomery—who was no longer involved. On August 7, he had been appointed to command the land forces of Operation Torch, the new code name for the North African invasion, which was set for October. This was to be a joint Anglo-American affair, with Eisenhower in overall command. Sledgehammer was now formally scrubbed. In the meantime, Churchill and Alan Brooke had gone to Cairo on July 31 and were then to proceed to Moscow for discussions with Stalin. During meetings in Cairo on August 4, the senior British staff there agreed to Brooke and Churchill's recommendation that Montgomery switch from command of Operation Torch to heading up Eighth Army and its defence of Egypt.[20] Montgomery duly arrived in Cairo on August 12.

By that time, Churchill and Brooke were en route to Moscow, where they received a stormy reception. Stalin remained adamant there should be a major offensive across the Channel to force the Germans to draw divisions away from the Russian front. Churchill could only offer the Dieppe raid and Operation Torch as substitutes capable of achieving the same end. Worrying that the raid on Dieppe might again be cancelled, he signalled his Chief of Staff, General Hastings Ismay, on August 15. "What is the position about renewal of Rutter?" the cable pleaded. Ismay replied quickly. "Jubilee, which is renewed Rutter in all essential features, is due to be carried out First Light 18 August. If weather unfavourable 18th August, operation can be launched any subsequent day up to 24th August inclusive." Churchill assured Stalin there would be a "reconnaissance in force" against Dieppe.[21]

BACK IN SOUTHERN England, the brigadiers, battalion commanders, and company commanders assembled on August 14 in the senior officers' mess at 2nd Divisional headquarters at 0930 hours. Roberts announced that the raid was back on and would take place between August 18 and 22. Full operation orders and instructions were issued down to the company commanders.[22] While most were excited by the prospect of action, a few were dismayed. Essex Scottish captain Walter McGregor was dumbfounded that anybody would conceive of raiding the same port as set out in Operation Rutter after some 5,500 men had been on leave throughout England.[23] Lieutenant Colonel Doug Catto argued that the plan was "fraught with alarming warnings of possible disaster." He was particularly concerned about his regiment's attack at Puys. Before Catto could finish his protests, Mann wheeled on him and barked, "If you want to keep your command, keep your mouth shut."[24] Whatever dissent might have stirred in the room beforehand was silenced.

At 1130 hours, the 6th Brigade's battalion and company commanders were given the opportunity to study the model—each battalion was allowed forty minutes. Then the officers spent the afternoon carefully going over the plan, which largely involved refreshing themselves on the role they were to have played in Rutter.[25]

Other than the addition of commandos to replace the airborne troops, little had changed. As in the original scheme, there would be six assaults consisting of two outer flank attacks, two inner flank attacks, and the main attack delivered directly against Dieppe and its harbour.

The four flank attacks were to begin at 0450 hours, British Summer Time. The "success of these flank landings would depend very largely upon the achievement of surprise, and upon the landing craft touching down while it was still sufficiently dark to make it difficult for enemy gunners who might be on the alert to see their targets," as one army report put it. "No arrangements, therefore, were made for naval fire support on these beaches in the first phase."

At 0520 hours, half an hour after the beginning of nautical twilight, two 4th Brigade battalions would land at Dieppe. The Essex Scottish would attack the eastern half (Red Beach) and the Royal

Hamilton Light Infantry the western half (White Beach). Simultaneously, the first wave of Calgary Tank Regiment tanks, consisting of three troops, would set down. More waves of tanks would follow in close sequence.

Royal Canadian engineers would land on the heels of the two assaulting battalions and assist the tanks in crossing the beach and getting through or over the esplanade seawall. They would also detect and clear minefields, as well as destroy heavy obstructions known to be blocking the streets facing the beach.

Once the tanks crossed the esplanade, they would press through Dieppe "and assist in clearing German gun positions south of the town and in capturing the entrenched position west of Les Quatre Vents Farm (Four Winds Farm), which was about one and a half miles inland from Green Beach at Pourville. The tanks would then link up with the Queen's Own Cameron Highlanders advancing from Green Beach and support their attacks on the airfield and divisional headquarters.

The Rileys were to push out of Dieppe towards Quatre Vents Farm and join up with the South Saskatchewan Regiment, which would have led the way onto Green Beach. These two battalions would clear German resistance to the southwest of Dieppe. The Essex Scottish, meanwhile, would seize Dieppe's harbour and capture several armed trawlers. Assisted by tanks and a detachment of No. 40 Royal Marines' 'A' Commando, who were to be landed by Motor Gunboat *Locust* and several French *chasseurs* (wooden submarine chasers similar to motor torpedo boats), the Essex would clear the area southeast of Dieppe and link up with the Royal Regiment of Canada—coming in from Blue Beach at Puys.

This would conclude establishment of a perimeter around Dieppe. While the Camerons and supporting tanks operated outside of it against the airfield and headquarters, engineering parties within would wreak destruction on dock facilities, bridges, railway installations, a railroad tunnel, and other targets, in accordance with a tight script. Brigadier Mann thought it "doubtful if any programme for the destruction of objectives of a similar nature has ever been so completely and scientifically prepared. Personnel had been sent on special courses to study the destruction of particular objectives, the stores had been especially prepared, and the parties rehearsed in their duties."

There was even a "well arranged train wreck, which was a saboteur's dream. A number of cars were to be derailed well inside the tunnel, and then a train with a good load of explosives was to be sent in with open throttle." The tunnel was southwest of Dieppe, immediately east of Petit Appeville. Its destruction would disrupt rail movement from Dieppe to Le Havre or Rouen for "a very considerable time." Other demolitions would render the harbour "largely useless for a long period."

A detailed withdrawal plan existed. All the troops ashore, save those of Nos. 3 and 4 Commandos, who had their own re-embarkation schemes, would fall back upon Dieppe. Withdrawal was to be carefully coordinated, lasting several hours and requiring the battalions to withdraw to specific pre-set defensive lines. There were thirteen of these. Once one was reached, a coded signal alerted Leigh-Mallory at Uxbridge that he was free to direct bombers to strike outside this zone. The thirteenth line, for example, would be reached at three hours and thirty minutes during a two-tide operation. This zone would be practically on top of the buildings facing the esplanade, and the coded signal was "Obliterate."[26]

Les Fusiliers Mont-Royal, remaining off Dieppe during the assault, would land to provide a rearguard covering the re-embarkation of assault forces on the western side of Dieppe's beach. On the eastern side, the Essex Scottish would perform the same duty. Once all other troops were at sea, the rearguard battalions would re-embark and the raid come to a close.[27]

One aspect of the plan that bothered many was the delayed timing for the landing at Dieppe. With the flank attacks occurring thirty minutes prior, the garrison troops inside the town were sure to be alerted by the time the Rileys and Essex Scottish reached the beach. Why could the landings here not be concurrent with those on the flanks?

It was a question Hughes-Hallett had explained repeatedly to the other force commanders. "Simultaneous attacks all along the front at

Dieppe were impracticable for naval reasons," he said. There was simply not enough sea room for all ships and craft to shoulder in together. The vessels, jockeying to avoid each other in such a confined area, would be thrown into chaos. "Moreover the differences between ships' speeds constituted a serious obstacle. In order to put in the main attack at the same time as the flank attacks it would have been necessary to sail the LSIS from Southampton half an hour earlier than [scheduled]; and in that event they would inevitably [be] spotted by the Germans' routine evening air reconnaissance as they left the harbour." So the frontal attack had to come later, even though this meant loss of surprise.[28]

LIKE THE MILITARY plan, the naval plan was highly complex, minutely detailed, and reliant on a timetable that must unroll with unfailing precision for the raid to succeed. Excluding the sixteen minesweepers, which would clear the two passages through the minefield, the Naval Force consisted of 252 ships and craft. As one Canadian Army report stated, "to move this great number of vessels across the Channel without detection by the enemy, without mishap, and on a timetable, was a most difficult and complicated task."

The force would sail in thirteen distinct groups. Comprising the first four groups were the LSIS and their small armed escorts. Group 5 was made up of No. 3 Commando's R-Boats and escorts. Les Fusiliers Mont-Royal were carried in the R-Boats and escorts of Group 6, while Group 7 consisted of the R-Boats carrying the Camerons and escorts. LCTS and escorts formed Groups 8 through 12, and the seven French *chasseurs* and the sloop HMS *Alresford* comprised Group 13. Escorts for the LSIS consisted of five destroyers, one being HMS *Calpe*. Hughes-Hallett and Roberts would be aboard this ship, which was fitted out with special communications equipment to serve as the raid's headquarters. A duplicate headquarters existed aboard the destroyer HMS *Fernie*, which would provide escort for the LCTS and small landing craft flotillas. Brigadier Mann would be on *Fernie*, ready to take over command should Roberts be killed or incapacitated by wounds. If Mann fell, command passed to 6th Brigade's Southam and then to 4th Brigade's Lett. Were all the generals down, McNaughton's staff representative, Lieutenant Colonel G.P. Henderson, would take charge.[29] On the naval side, Commander David Luce would take over from Hughes-Hallett. Luce would be replaced by Commander H.V.P. McClintock, then Commander Red Ryder, and finally Commander G.T. Lambert.

"During the passage across the channel," Hughes-Hallett's orders stated, "there are a large number of ships manoeuvring close to each other at varying speeds. It is of the utmost importance that Commanding Officers and in particular Senior Officers of groups in company and Senior officers of detached groups keep to their proper routes and timing by accurate navigation, not only so that the landing may be carried out according to plan, but also to avoid ships and groups meeting at night... Attention is drawn to the necessity of accurate station keeping. In order to prevent ships straggling with the possibility of becoming detached, senior officers of groups are to keep their groups closed up as much as possible at all times."

Once through the minefield, six of the destroyers would provide flank protection, with two to eastward and four westward. As the main force closed on the shore, these destroyers would dash back and rejoin it. Once the LSIS lowered and released their assault landing craft, they were to turn about for England to avoid being targeted by the German bombers expected to attack the Naval Force at first light.

After supporting the Essex landing on Red Beach, *Locust* and the *chasseurs* would enter the harbour and unload the Royal Marine commandos and engineering demolition parties. Some commandos would work with these vessels as a "cutting out force" to take control of a number of barges standing at the docks. These had been intended for use by the Germans during their planned invasion of Britain. As many as possible would be towed out to sea and back to England. Those unable to be taken under tow would by destroyed, along with any other ships that could not be pirated away.

Any landing craft en route to Dieppe that lost speed for one reason or another was to be abandoned by its group. Under no circumstances were group leaders to cease maintaining the speed required by the timetable—even if they encountered enemy forces. The group commanders were to "take drastic avoiding action if contact is made with enemy forces or to avoid contact if the enemy are known to be in the vicinity. But the proper course must be resumed as soon as it is considered safe to do so as timely arrival of groups, particularly the early ones, is vital to the operation."

Wireless silence was to be maintained until the Essex Scottish and Rileys began landing in front of Dieppe. The only exceptions were if someone discovered the force had been spotted by German ships, if an LSI commander realized his landing craft were going to be more than fifteen minutes late reaching the beach, or if the senior officer commanding Group 5 determined that, because of delays or casualties, the landings on the Yellow beaches were "seriously compromised."

"In an operation of this complexity," Hughes-Hallett warned, "there is a great danger of signal congestion causing breakdown of communications. It is for this reason that the operational orders are prepared in much greater detail than would be necessary in normal operations."[30]

Whereas the plan for the passage and initial landing was set out in minute detail, this was impossible for the re-embarkation of troops and withdrawal across the Channel. A plan "could not be rigidly laid down because the tactical situation during the re-embarkation of troops cannot accurately be forecasted." But Hughes-Hallett did offer a general guide. "The intention is that all tanks and the majority of the troops are re-embarked from Red and/or White beaches ... The time at which withdrawal is to begin, and the speed at which it will take place is governed, as far as the Navy is concerned, by the times when the tide is suitable (i.e. rising)."

If the raid took place between August 18 and 21, withdrawal would be carried out on a two-tide basis. On either the 22nd or 23rd, it would be on a one-tide basis. During the two tides, there would be a low-tide period when water levels at the beaches would prevent practicable re-embarkation of tanks and troops.

The order to begin withdrawal—"Vanquish"—would be given jointly by Hughes-Hallett and Roberts. They would issue a start time for the withdrawal to begin, designated as "W."[31] Assuming a two-tide operation, the withdrawal would begin thirty minutes after "W" was announced, with the Royals being first to re-embark. Other battalions and units would follow in stages, with the last—the beach party and signals personnel—lifted free three hours and forty-five minutes after "W."[32]

These general orders were supplemented with specific orders governing the actions of naval beach parties, the commanders of the various landing craft, the destroyer captains, and anybody else with a commanding role. There were instructions detailing how and when smoke might be laid and how bombardments would be called for by shore-based forward observation officers. Wherever possible, Hughes-Hallett and his planners had removed any requirement to act on personal initiative. There was a script for everyone to follow, and if it was accorded to faithfully, all should be well.

By comparison, the RAF plan was distinctly concise. This was partly due to the inevitably fluid nature of air support likely to be required. Leigh-Mallory had at his disposal a formidable force. Forty-six Spitfire squadrons and ten squadrons of Hurricanes provided the fighter cover. There were two squadrons of Hurricanes converted into fighter-bombers, three squadrons of Boston bombers, and two squadrons of Blenheim bombers—sixty-three squadrons in all.[33] The Royal Canadian Air Force provided six of the fighter squadrons and two army cooperation squadrons (equipped with fighter-bombers). There were also one New Zealand, five Polish, two Czech, two Norwegian, one French, and one Belgian squadron. The rest were all RAF.[34]

Leigh-Mallory's pilots and crews faced a daunting task, for they would be required to operate "most intensively throughout the day from dawn until late afternoon." With the entire raid playing out over a single day, there would be "a far heavier strain... on the air forces than would [be] the case had our occupation of Dieppe been more prolonged." Air support by bombers and fighter-bombers would take the form of either attacks on targets or creation of smoke-screens. The latter would be generated by Bostons and Blenheims dropping one-hundred-pound phosphorous smoke bombs from elevations of just fifty feet. Leigh-Mallory expected all Luftwaffe forces within range would be sent against the raiding force, so he wanted to maintain a constant rotating fighter cover over the entire area to protect the ships, his bombers, and the troops on the ground. His ability to communicate quickly and effectively with scores of squadrons based throughout southern England was critical. For this reason, he would remain at Group 11's Uxbridge headquarters and personally direct the deployment of the squadrons based on reports sent by air force officers aboard *Calpe*, by Roberts, or by Hughes-Hallett.

Ever the most cautious of the force command triad, Leigh-Mallory expected that the "attacks from the sea ... under the supporting fire of destroyers only" would be met by "strong and well organised shore defences." He must accordingly make "every effort to provide maximum air support and air cover during the initial assault" and then continue doing so until all forces had safely withdrawn to England.[35]

10

Our Historic Task

SANDWICHED BETWEEN Captain John Hughes-Hallett's naval section and Brigadier Church Mann's military section of the overall Operation Jubilee plan was a single crudely sketched map of the Dieppe area. The map was titled "110 INF DIV," and a subtitle identified it as presenting the "order of battle" for 110th Infantry Division. Various flags and circles indicated divisional and regimental headquarters and the disposition of units.[1] This map was illustrative of a colossal British intelligence error resulting from a German deception plan.

In July, German intelligence discovered that British agents, largely operating out of Switzerland, were attempting to use French Resistance cells to determine the strength and nature of coastal defences. Information was sought for almost the entire coastal area, but there was a clear focus on Dieppe.[2] To disrupt these efforts, German Army Command in the West (OB West) sowed false information regarding Dieppe's defences. The previous February, the *Abwehr* (German military intelligence) had captured a Special Operations Executive radio operator in Paris. Forced to serve the Germans or suffer torture and death, the operator agreed to be turned. In mid-July, he reported to British intelligence that a new infantry division had taken over Dieppe's defences. Its vehicle identification markers resembled a white church topped by a small tower. The radio operator used the term "nave." Using German insignia catalogues, British intelligence officers matched the description to 110th Infantry Division. As "nave" could be interpreted as either a church or a ship, the fact that the 110th Division's "totem"—as the Germans called these insignia—was a white Viking ship fit.[3] The British took the bait, and on August 1, intelligence reports were changed to remove 302nd Infantry Division from the Dieppe area in favour of 110th Infantry Division. In fact, the 110th was still on the Russian front.[4]

A Combined Operations intelligence report issued on August 7 stated that the 110th Division had arrived in France on June 11. The report provided detailed operational history of the unit since its formation in December 1940 and traced its service on the Russian front. The division had repeatedly "suffered heavy casualties." The report stated that the 110th Division was believed to have relieved the 302nd Division but cautioned that "this cannot be regarded as absolutely certain." Even if it were true, the 110th would "almost certainly have the same dispositions as the old [division]." These included a forward headquarters at Arques-la-Bataille. As to its "fighting value," the report concluded that it was "potentially a high-quality field force. It has evidently suffered severely on the Eastern Front, but has been in France long enough to have received at least a large proportion of personnel and material. However, no reports of any such replacements have been received."[5]

Appendix A of the military plan for Jubilee was duly adjusted—without any of the qualifiers offered by the intelligence section—to show the 110th as having taken over the Dieppe area. It was described as a "first line division" sent to France "to rest and refit ... Whilst the division may not be up to full strength, it has a good fighting record." The division's fighting strength rested on three infantry regiments, but only one was directly defending the beaches targeted for Jubilee, the appendix claimed. During the first three hours of the raid, the opposing strength would be limited to about 1,700 men. This included the defending infantry regiment, about 500 troops attached to divisional headquarters, a company of infantry east of the River Arques, and some artillery and engineer troops. But within three hours, German reinforcements would begin arriving from elsewhere with increasing rapidity and in ever greater numbers.[6]

A point of significant concern remained the proximity of 10th Panzer Division, believed to be near Amiens on the River Somme. But the intelligence report said this division was "now considered ... on the point of departure."[7] This led to the military plan being slightly modified to reflect the possibility that this division's mechanized reconnaissance unit, reported in July as stationed at Abbeville to the west of Amiens and about thirty-five miles from Dieppe, might be gone. If not, however, the reconnaissance troops, riding aboard their armoured cars and motorcycles, could reach the beaches within three hours of the first landings.[8]

In reality, of course, 302nd Division and 10th Panzer Division were still in place. The former had about twice the manpower of the 110th Division estimate. But at least the assessment of how it was deployed closely mirrored the truth. Overall information on German forces was quite highly and accurately detailed—the product of hundreds of photo reconnaissance flights carried out from early 1942 through to the launch of Jubilee.

THE 302ND DIVISION, first raised in November 1940, had deployed to Dieppe in April 1941. It inherited fifteen French 75-millimetre guns that seriously bolstered its artillery. The division assumed responsibility for a fifty-five-mile front stretching from just east of Veules-les-Roses to the River Somme.[9]

Generalleutnant Konrad Haase commanded the 302nd. Tall and broad-shouldered, the fifty-three-year-old Haase wore round-lensed glasses perched solidly on a prominent nose.[10] On November 26, 1940, he was tasked with raising the 302nd Infantry Division, formed as a French occupation unit. Designated a static unit, it was not fully mobile. The division was created by drafts taken from two other infantry divisions. Initially, the division was well staffed and equipped. By spring of 1942, however, many of the division's best men had been sent to the Russian front. They were replaced with new recruits and so-called ethnic German foreign nationals, such as Poles and Hungarians.[11]

Haase was competent and always determined to do his duty. He spent most of April carefully studying the division's defensive sector. On April 12, he described the division's task as being the "prevention of a landing from the sea and air." The "focal point of the defence lies at Dieppe." Haase turned to considering how a British attack might develop. On April 25, he wrote that "Dieppe will not be attacked directly by the enemy, but rather by landing attempts at nearby points and the formation of a bridgehead." He envisioned the same flanking strategy Mountbatten and Captain John Hughes-Hallett had proposed in the early planning of Operation Rutter. Haase set about identifying where such landings would occur and then establishing positions that could defend them.[12]

There was no slackness in the division's execution of its duties. On August 28, 1941, Haase issued an order demanding "Total Commitment" from his men to defending their coastline. "Each officer, NCO, and man must know that the Division is 'defending,' that is, that the position must be held to the last shot." Troops manning defensive positions on any given day were to be in "constant readiness for action, that is, they are prepared to repulse an attack at any time." During this early stage of readiness, designated the division's "normal condition," positions would be occupied only during daylight hours." The next stage was "increased readiness for action." Sentries would be reinforced, patrols stepped up, all observation posts, gun positions, and other defensive works manned day and night. Reserves would be on alert. The last phase of readiness was "highest degree of readiness for action." At this stage, all prepared defences were fully occupied "for defence in expectation of an imminent or identified attack."

The division's conduct of battle was "to be such that attempted enemy landings lead to defeat and destruction of the enemy, if at all possible even *before* the landing... The main line of resistance—that is the coastal strip—must be firmly in the possession of the troops at the conclusion of the fighting; and enemy troops that had reached the mainland must have been destroyed." This was not mere rhetoric. Haase's defensive plans were based on defeating an attack right on the beach. Every potential landing spot was to be heavily defended by strongpoints. The troops within each strongpoint were to consider themselves an independent battle group capable of mounting all-round defence.

The division's Operation Order No. 29 ran to eighteen pages and detailed precisely how the defences would be constructed. More importantly, it set out a strict doctrine for the division's response to attack. A regular training regimen tested the division's tactics through mock drills. By August 1942, Haase's preparations were well developed. The quality of his troops may have deteriorated due to losses of men sent to the Russian front. But those in place were still relatively well trained and had no doubt that they were expected to man positions with determination, to "the last shot."[13]

HAASE'S DEFENSIVE DOCTRINE reflected overall German strategy for European coastal defence. Prior to the end of 1941, the Germans had hoped for a quick and decisive victory over the Soviets. By December, however, Germany had been thrown onto the defensive and it was clear the campaign would be long and costly. With the United States entering the war, probability of an Anglo-American invasion in Western Europe became a true threat. The German high command began seriously considering how to meet such an invasion. On December 14, Hitler's chief of staff, Generalfeldmarschall Wilhelm Keitel, stated that the Führer had decided that coastal regions of the Arctic Ocean, North Sea, and Atlantic Ocean "controlled by us are ultimately to be built into a 'new West Wall,' in order that we can repel with certainty any landing attempts, even by the strongest enemy forces, with the smallest possible number of permanently assigned field troops."

Keitel acknowledged that the sucking drain of Russia on troop strength and matériel "compels us to restrict construction." Therefore, first emphasis was placed on building field fortifications and strengthening strongpoints wherever invasion seemed most likely. After Norway, Hitler considered the Franco-Belgian coast most threatened. He wanted special focus on "the areas along the central part of the Channel coast from the Scheldt to the region west of the Seine Estuary."

In the Dieppe sector, the first three months of 1942 had not seen a flurry of defensive construction. For the divisional commanders in each coastal sector, "launching... a vast coordinated programme of construction would require much planning, and problems of organization and procurement would have to be solved before the lowest echelons could swing into action." Haase concentrated on evolving his tactical defence scheme. He also had to train the recruits sent to replace three large drafts of experienced soldiers lost to the Russian front.[14]

Haase realized the length and nature of the coastline made establishing a continuous defensive line impossible. He lacked the necessary troops. Nor was it essential to have men guarding every foot of coast. The long stretches of cliffs were largely unassailable. Where steep ravines cut through the cliffs to the sea, most had no usable beach before them or provided poor routes inland. Consequently, Haase concentrated his defences on logical focal points, "around the ports where landings were possible or probable. With the weak forces under... command," he wrote, "we knowingly didn't defend every ravine." This meant accepting the chance that small commando raids might gain the headlands and cause damage. But Haase decided this risk must be taken.

"Our main strategy is to be as strong as possible near the ports... on which our strongpoints are based, so that an attack from land and sea can be beaten off. Besides that, it is important to have as many mobile reserves as possible in order to be able to support strongpoints and initiate immediate counter-attacks against enemy troops that may have landed in between these strongpoints. It is all the more important to withhold strong reserves as in any large scale assault the enemy will certainly launch a simultaneous air and sea attack against our coastal defences: the air attack consisting of strong airborne and parachute forces."

Dieppe was the pivotal strongpoint. He deployed here the headquarters of 571st Infantry Regiment and two of its battalions. The division's engineer battalion was also headquartered in the town, along with two engineer companies. Eight artillery pieces guarded the beach. There were also nine anti-tank guns, including one French tank that had been concreted into the harbour's west mole. Two other anti-tank guns were mounted at the corners of the casino.

These weapons were all manned by infantry. Adding more punch to the defences were two batteries of 3rd Battalion, 302nd Artillery Regiment, armed with light howitzers. Another two batteries of this battalion's artillerymen were in Dieppe but acting only as porters of equipment and supplies. The 265th Heavy Infantry Howitzer Battery was also in place.

Dieppe's anti-aircraft defences were strong—one heavy battery of 75-millimetre guns, a section each of 50-millimetre and 37-millimetre guns, and two sections of 20-millimetre guns.

In addition to the divisional troops, Haase could call upon about two hundred men from different naval units and Dieppe's sixty-man German police force.[15] There was also a naval unit designated an "experimental company." It was robustly armed with five 37-millimetre anti-tank guns and three light machine guns.[16]

Dieppe's Naval Force also maintained a defensive screen of three harbour protection boats, which stood offshore every night. These *Hafenschutzboots* were typically captured fishing trawlers modified for coastal defence by mounting a light artillery piece or heavy machine gun on the bow.[17]

BY AUGUST 1942, 302nd Division had transformed its defensive frontage into a very tough nut. Mid-August brought a report that it had sown 8,923 Teller mines, 6,359 *Schützenmines* (S-mines), and 274 explosive charges described as "miscellaneous."[18] The pressure-activated Teller anti-tank mines were shaped like a covered cooking pan about two and a half inches deep by fifteen inches across. When a tank tread came into contact with the mine, the plunger-style trigger buried under the ground surface ignited the high explosives within. Although insufficiently powerful to destroy a tank, a single Teller could break a track and immobilize it. S-mines were anti-personnel mines. They typically consisted of a canister loaded with 350 ball bearings attached by a spring to an igniting prong. Step on the prong and the spring snapped the canister about three feet into the air before it exploded. The ball bearings would shred the torso of the man who stepped on the mine and likely wound others within close range. Mines were most thickly sown on potential landing beaches and up the length of ravines that might access the head-lands. But minefields were also laid farther inland to intercept movement of enemy forces beyond the beaches.

All of the Dieppe *Stützpunktgruppe* (Group of Strongpoints) was surrounded to landward by a continuous barbed-wire obstacle that wrapped out on the eastern flank to encompass Puys. Berneval was protected inside its own defensive perimeter. The heights immedi-ately east of Pourville lay within the Dieppe wire, but the village and facing beach did not. These were more lightly protected by wire and mines on and around the beach.

As the Canadian Army historian later put it, the Dieppe front was "very strong in artillery."[19] The coastal battery at Varengeville, designated No. 813 Coastal Battery, was particularly powerful. Lieutenant Colonel Lovat's No. 4 Commando was to take this bat-tery. It consisted of six 150-millimetre Krupp guns, each capable of firing a 113.5-pound round to a maximum range of 25,000 yards. Its ammunition consisted of about two thousand percussion-fused high-explosive shells. The battery was manned by two officers com-manding about ninety-three men. Each gun had a ten-man crew. Firing of the guns was usually under direction of a battery sergeant. The two officers, meanwhile, were set up in an observation post on the clifftop about 1,500 yards northwest of the guns and next to Pointe d'Ailly Lighthouse. A concrete bastion, this observation post had a convex front facing the sea in which a two-foot-long observa-tion slit had been cut. From here the officers would direct the battery's fire onto targets. The battery had at least one pre-desig-nated firing target. This was the sea to the front of Dieppe, about 8,500 yards distant. On command, the battery could bring fire upon this area almost immediately. In the event of attack by parachut-ists—fully expected in Haase's defensive scheme—the battery was so organized that the gun crews could be reduced to four men and the rest quickly sent to man an all-round defense.[20]

On Dieppe's opposite flank, at Berneval, the 2/770 Coastal Bat-tery would fall to No. 3 Commando. It possessed four 105-millimetre guns and three 170-millimetre guns. This battery was defended by 127 battery troops, with a field picket of ten men from No. 1

Company of the 302nd Division's 570 Infantry Regiment guarding the approach off the beach at Petit Berneval. The battery was also protected by two 20-millimetre anti-aircraft guns. A nearby radar station was manned by 114 Luftwaffe personnel, who were well positioned to reinforce the battery.

To the northwest of Arques-la-Bataille and roughly parallel to the airfield, No. 265 Coastal Battery contained four 150-millimetre howitzers. This battery was to be wiped out by the Queen's Own Cameron Highlanders as part of their push against the airfield and divisional headquarters at Arques-la-Bataille. It stood about four miles inland from Dieppe on high ground, which enabled it to easily fire on the beach and out to sea. It could also bring Pourville under fire. Four other coastal batteries more distant from Dieppe could range on the landing beaches.

In addition to the coastal batteries, 302nd Division had established four batteries of its own. Each was armed with four 100-millimetre Czech field howitzers. Battery 'B' was just inland of Puys and was to be eliminated by the Royal Regiment of Canada after it won the beach there. On roughly the same line from the coast, Battery '8' lay just over a mile inland. No raiding troops were tasked with eliminating this battery. Battery '7' stood inside the Dieppe wire just to the west of Quatre Vents Farm and less than a mile east of Pourville. It was to be knocked out by the South Saskatchewan Regiment. Also inside the Dieppe wire was Battery 'A,' situated about two miles southeast of Pourville and one and a half miles southwest of Dieppe. This battery was also not specifically targeted.

Running along the headland extending from east of Pourville to the cliff overlooking Dieppe, eight 75-millimetre guns were stationed. Anti-aircraft guns manned by Luftwaffe troops were numerous, with the 302nd Division's sector alone containing thirty.

Haase had also concentrated on exploiting the defensive advantage of the terrain. Both the River Scie at Pourville and the Saane at Quiberville had been dammed where they flowed into the sea. This caused flooding upstream for about two miles and created marshy areas about 250 feet wide. These, it was hoped, would provide some anti-tank protection.

The ravines cutting through the cliff faces were "covered with wire entanglements and booby traps to the depth to which, judging from the beach, an ascent by a landing enemy would have been feasible," Haase later wrote. "The valleys of Dieppe, Pourville, and Quiberville are lined on both banks with dominating heights on which were installed defence works and heavy infantry weapons, including beach defence guns. Stretches of the beach between the heights on both sides of the valleys are protected against tanks as follows: near Dieppe in conjunction with the port entrance, and at the two valleys in conjunction with the flooded area, by means of anti-tank obstacles, dragon's teeth, anti-tank walls, anti-tank minefields, anti-tank ditches. Specifically in Dieppe all approaches from the beach to the interior of the city are sealed off by strong concrete walls."[21] Although in some cases a small gap was left, most walls entirely closed off the streets. Each roadblock was about eight feet high and three to four feet thick. On the town side, roadblocks were sloped to create a fire step. British aerial reconnaissance failed to detect that most roadblocks had an anti-tank gun sited behind them. To avoid detection, these guns were emplaced after dark and then pulled into cover at daybreak.[22] Several old caves in the west cliff upon which the castle stood were used to hide guns. One cave, about nine feet wide by twelve feet deep, concealed a 75-millimetre gun. The ammunition, consisting of 150 rounds, was stacked in boxes against the cave's rear wall.[23] Other caves in both the west and east cliff faces concealed machine-gun positions and other light artillery.

The Dieppe strongpoint was protected by all-round obstacles, such as wire barriers, gun positions, and concrete command posts. Not expecting a frontal assault on Dieppe, the Germans emphasized landward defences as much as those on the beach. All approaches into town were as "thoroughly covered" as those leading off the promenade, as protection "against parachute landings."[24] By mid-August, the division had completed about 60 per cent of its construction plan.[25]

ALTHOUGH THE GERMANS had gathered no concrete intelligence about the staging and subsequent cancellation of Operation Rutter, by mid-July they believed that a strong raid or even cross-channel invasion was imminent. This fear was based on logical calculation rather than intelligence gathering. Moon and tide information indicated that the periods of July 23 to August 3, August 10 to 19, and August 25 to September 1 were feasible for such operations. After that, conditions would be less favourable.

On July 3, Commander-in-Chief, West, Generalfeldmarschall Gerd von Rundstedt began whipping the troops to a fever pitch to meet the threat. "It is our historic task to prevent at all costs the creation of a 'Second Front,'" he warned. All strongpoint and defensive area commanders were sworn to defend their positions to the death. On July 6, Haase summoned all the division's officers down to the rank of captain. Before these witnesses, Haase pledged to defend Dieppe to his last breath.[26]

The Germans became increasingly anxious about the expected attack. On July 10, LXXXI Corps—of which the 302nd Infantry Division was a part—authorized "an immediate and drastic increase" in established divisional strength. Each rifle company was bolstered by two light mortar sections. A heavy mortar platoon consisting of six 12-centimetre mortars was added to every machine-gun company.[27] These mortars were most effective at ranges between 2,200 and 3,800 yards, but had a maximum range of 6,500 yards. When fitted with percussion fuses, the shell shattered on explosion into splinters that flew horizontally to cover a large area.[28]

The division's regiments were each supplemented by one light-infantry gun platoon armed with two light guns. Regimental infantry anti-tank platoons were strengthened to anti-tank company size. Two platoons within these companies were armed with 37-millimetre anti-tank guns and two other platoons with 50-millimetre anti-tank guns. Each artillery battalion was increased by a third battery. One of these batteries was armed with four 80-millimetre field guns. The other two each received four light field howitzers. Substantial increases were also made in signal, supply, and medical personnel.[29]

A month later, on August 8, the commander of Fifteenth Army, Generaloberst Kurt Haase (no relation to Konrad Haase), issued a veritable call to arms that was distributed throughout the ranks of 302nd Division. "Various reports suggest that owing to the DESPER-ATE position of the Russians—the Anglo-Americans will soon be forced TO TAKE SOME KIND OF ACTION IN THE WEST... I have repeatedly given the troops this news, and request you to REPEAT my orders AGAIN AND AGAIN in order to ensure that these thoughts BECOME AN OBSESSION and that they DO NOT EXPECT ANY-THING ELSE!

"The troops must realize that it will be a VERY STICKY BUSINESS!" He went on to describe how they would face attack from bombs, naval guns, commandos, assault boats, airborne troops, and hostile citizens. Sabotage and murder could be expected. "STEADY NERVES will be required if we do not want to GO UNDER!

"FEAR DOES NOT EXIST! When the hail of smoke pours down upon the troops, they must wipe their eyes and ears and grasp their weapons firmer than ever and defend themselves as never before! HE OR WE! That's the slogan for all!!

"I have looked into YOUR EYES! You are GERMAN MEN! You will willingly and bravely DO YOUR DUTY! And THUS REMAIN VICTORI-OUS! Long live our PEOPLE, our COUNTRY, OUR FÜHRER ADOLF HITLER!"[30]

Ten days later, on August 18, 302nd Division was at a high state of readiness as the sun set over the English Channel. All personnel were to man their normal duty stations fully dressed. Clothes were to remain on when sleeping, and equipment was to be kept close at hand.[31] In the past few days, the men had been repeatedly told there would be an English invasion by August 20 because Russia "had threatened she would otherwise throw in the sponge."[32] Yet the repetitive routine of garrison duty made it difficult to remain constantly vigilant. Every night, from 2200 hours to 0600 hours, most men were on sentry duty, with two hours on followed by two hours off. At 0600 hours, they stood down and slept until 0930. The next hour was spent bathing and eating breakfast. From 1030 to 1130, weapons were cleaned. At noon, a two-hour dinner period began. Then, from 1400 to 1730 hours, the troops laboured on defensive construction. At 1730 hours, a free period began that lasted until 2200 hours. This was the pattern. One day blended unchangeably into the next.[33]

Although OB West had issued an alert for the entire coast, and von Rundstedt considered the weather forecast for August 18–19 "suitable for enemy raiding operations," his Luftwaffe counterparts differed. The prediction of fine morning weather followed by thick overcast in the afternoon convinced the headquarters of Luftwaffe No. 3 Air Fleet that enemy action was unlikely. As the Luftwaffe operated independent of OB West, there was nothing von Rundstedt could do to override its commanders. And they decided to grant a twenty-four-hour leave to one of every three pilots. Most passed the night of August 18–19 in a village forty miles from Dieppe with women from the LN-Helferinnen (Women's Auxiliary Air Signals Corps). In the afternoon of August 18, a gaggle of correspondents, film cameramen, and photographers descended to record the activities. This was part of a propaganda tour intended to encourage more Aryan women to join the corps by showing the happy times they could have helping dashing pilots relax. After dinner, a large dance ensued, with the women in evening gowns and the pilots wearing white dinner jackets or their white summer mess tunics. The party was still in full flight at dawn.[34]

The night was warm. Despite all warnings, the soldiers of 302nd Division felt no sense of urgency. German air reconnaissance in the early part of the night reported activity around British ports "was, if anything, less than normal." At 0130 hours on August 19, sentries returning to the Varengeville battery "undressed and went to sleep" in disregard of their orders to remain fully clothed. They expected to wake to another dawn as repetitive as those that had preceded it during their many months of duty near Dieppe.[35]

11

The Die Was Cast

ACROSS SUSSEX, 2ND Canadian Infantry Division spent early August enmeshed in preparations for exercises serving as covers for Operation Jubilee. It was a time of unusual orders. All infantrymen now conducted every exercise loaded down with "all the items that would normally be carried on an actual operation. Each man carried three grenades, 150 [rounds] .303, special bombs, 200 [rounds] .450 if equipped with the light automatic and extra .303 for [light machine guns]," the Royal Regiment's war diarist noted.[1]

Although battalion and company commanders knew better, the junior officers and men were told on August 10 that these preparations were for a combined-operation demonstration in conjunction with the Calgary Tank Regiment. Such was the level of authenticity, the tankers were instructed to waterproof their Churchills.[2] Not everyone was fooled. When Essex Scottish's Company Sergeant Major Cornelius Stapleton saw that the exercise involved only those battalion members originally detailed to Operation Rutter, he suspected the raid was back on. He nursed the suspicion in silence.[3]

The demonstration was code-named Popsy and was to be proceeded by a movement exercise to designated positions called Ford 1. There would also be a Ford 11 and Ford 111. These exercises would last "for a month commencing 15 Aug 42," the divisional war diary recorded.[4] August 15 was a Saturday. The officers down to the company commanders spent this weekend ostensibly planning Ford 1, first at divisional headquarters and then at their respective brigade and battalion headquarters. For the men, meanwhile, the weekend was largely free of extra duties. After Sunday morning's church parade, the Royals' diarist wrote, "the rest of the day was observed as a holiday."

On Monday morning, umpires arrived at the Royals' headquarters to oversee Popsy and were assigned two rooms. Ford 1, Lieutenant Colonel Bob Labatt announced, would begin on Tuesday, August 18.[5]

Later, the many unusual occurrences during the week leading up to August 19 would be recognized as preliminaries to staging the raid. For Les Fusiliers Mont-Royal, one clue was the premature recall on August 14 of Captain Robert Hainault and thirty men from an anti-tank-gun course. All weekend, more officers returned abruptly from leave or courses. On Sunday, Lieutenant Pierre Loranger, off serving as a 3-inch mortar instructor at the Rowlands Castle Battle Drill Course, returned. He was accompanied by Lieutenant M. Ranger, who had been taking the course.[6]

It was the same for all regiments. "A few eyebrows went up" among the troops of the Royal Hamilton Light Infantry, its regimental history reported, when on Monday, Major N.A. "Norry" Waldron returned unexpectedly from a posting at the divisional reinforcement unit. A spare, short, bespectacled man, with a Groucho Marx–style moustache, Waldron was the regiment's toughest training officer. Although he yelled at the men almost incessantly, Waldron always personally demonstrated each task with a perfection not easily matched. His return could only foretell that Popsy was going to be a tough one.[7] Waldron was not the only officer returned unexpectedly that day. Captain A.C. "Tony" Hill showed up. More surprisingly, Captain John Currie, Lieutenant Colonel Bob Labatt's brother-in-law, was yanked from a course on becoming a company commander. Lieutenant T.R. McCoy hurried back from an intelligence course.[8]

Requiring more time to move their Churchills to LCTs at Gosport harbour, four troops of the Calgary Tank Regiment's 'C' Squadron and two of 'B' Squadron loaded onto tank transporters and started out from billets at Seaford on Sunday evening at 1900 hours. They did so even though the decision to launch Operation Jubilee would not be finalized until the morning of August 18, the Tuesday.[9]

The waterproofing of the tanks was mostly complete, and operating them in seawater was possible at depths of six feet. Louvre extensions—long, box-shaped stacks—were attached to air vents. Two angled extensions to the exhaust pipes thrust up well above the turret. A crossbar connecting the two pipes added stabilizing strength to prevent bending or breaking due to the drag caused by moving through water. Once ashore, electrically triggered cordite charges would blow most of the waterproofing materials and louvre extensions clear of the tank. Not considered an operational impediment, the extended exhausts stayed in place. Tank waterproofing was still experimental, and tanks so treated had never previously gone into battle. There was, however, no fallback plan should the waterproofing fail and the tanks founder underwater.[10]

Development of the waterproofing had been supervised by the regiment's technical adjutant, Captain Bill Payne, and his quartermaster sergeant, Joe Freeman. Prior to Rutter, they had used a swimming pool on the Isle of Wight to test and improve techniques. The job had been exasperating. Payne finally declared to anybody who would listen that tank hulls could only be fully waterproofed during construction. The most they could hope to achieve now was reducing leakage to a slow trickle or seep. Since by mid-August the waterproofing had been installed for more than a month, Payne's new anxiety was that the materials might have deteriorated.[11]

On Monday, that part of the regiment selected for movement to the closer harbour of Newhaven concluded its final preparations. Trucks were loaded with ammunition and the tanks given last inspections. Personnel were instructed on when to leave billets and meet assigned transport. At 2000 hours, the last tanks of 'B' and 'C' Squadrons and all of 'A' Squadron clattered off under their own power for Newhaven and were soon loaded onto LCTs. They were promptly followed by the other regimental vehicles that would be going to Dieppe and the trucks loaded with ammunition. By midnight, the quays next to the LCTs were hubs of activity, with ammunition, tanks, carriers, scout cars, and blitz-buggies (early-model jeeps) all being slung aboard.[12]

Eighteen LCTs were required to carry the fifty-eight tanks, eleven Daimler scout cars, and fifteen blitz-buggies. Although manned by Calgary tankers, two of the blitz-buggies were equipped as ambulances, and most others were to be under divisional control. Several scout cars were similarly designated to serve brigade and divisional headquarters.[13]

The loading process was complete by 0630 hours. Then the tankers slung hammocks on deck and rested until noon. After eating their emergency "iron" rations, the tank crews completed last-minute waterproofing, cleaned guns, and carried out routine tank maintenance. They were in the midst of this when Lieutenant Colonel Johnny Andrews spread word that the exercise was in fact "an actual operation against Dieppe, a strongly fortified town on the French coast. Excitement ran high as all ranks prepared their vehicles and equipment for the coming engagement," the Calgary war diarist wrote. "By 2100 hours, all vehicles were ready and crews were waiting impatiently for the landing craft to leave harbour."[14]

ALTHOUGH THE TANKERS moved in advance of the other raiding troops, they learned at the same time as everyone else that the exercise was really a raid. In fact, the final decision to launch Operation Jubilee was not made until the next day—August 18. After consulting with Major General Ham Roberts, Air Vice-Marshal Leigh-Mallory, and Captain John Hughes-Hallett, Commander-in-Chief, Portsmouth, Admiral Sir William James issued this order at 1002 hours. It was not an easy decision. Originally, the force commanders had favoured initiating the operation on August 17 so that it would take place the following day. But poor weather forecasts had led to a twenty-four-hour push-back. The forecast remained questionable, but if the raid was to proceed, mobilization of troops to embarkation points must begin. And the two minesweeping flotillas had to stage near Beachy Head to move ahead of the convoy into the minefield. Accordingly, 9th Minesweeping Flotilla sailed at 1215 hours from Portsmouth and 13th Minesweeping Flotilla at 1545.[15]

Confident that weather would not scrub the raid, Hughes-Hallett wrote two formal letters to Mountbatten. The first, which he authored alone, outlined Combined Operations' need for a dedicated navy.

Naval vessels for previous combined operations had to be borrowed from other commands. The LCTs, for example, came from an administrative LCT command based at Troon in South Ayrshire, Scotland. Because of the secrecy surrounding Jubilee, the LCT commander was unaware of the purpose to which his vessels were assigned. Consequently, he nearly derailed the operation by issuing orders that would relieve half the LCT commanding officers and their first lieutenants. Hughes-Hallett's frantic intervention got the order cancelled, but it had been a struggle to do so while maintaining operational secrecy.

This was not the only calamity narrowly avoided at the last minute. Hughes-Hallett had secured two obsolescent motor gunboat flotillas because of their "unusually large smoke-laying capability." These would "protect landing craft lying offshore from ... enemy fire." On August 16, the young captain in overall command of these flotillas arrived unannounced at Fort Southwick—a small fort overlooking Portsmouth from Portsdown Hill that served as the local Combined Operations Headquarters for the Dieppe raid. The officer said he was under orders from his boss at Coastal Forces Depot in Gosport "to return [the flotillas] at once so that the smoke making apparatus could be dismantled and removed." Again, Hughes-Hallett acted quickly to have this order overruled.

These two outside threats to Jubilee's naval plan had convinced him that Combined Operations required its own dedicated navy consisting of sufficient landing craft to carry an entire brigade group. It would also require dedicated "escort craft and destroyers, its own navigational craft to act as guides to landing craft flotillas, and its own headquarters ship. The primary role of the force should be training, and it should be expanded steadily as the date for the invasion [of France] approached until it was large enough to lift the whole of the British Army units which were to be committed to the assault. A secondary role would be to carry out cross Channel raids from time to time as opportunity offered. Above all, this Naval Assault Force should be commanded through the normal naval chain of command."

His second letter was written after consultation with Major General Ham Roberts. This was a final and critical stage for

Hughes-Hallett because it answered the tricky question of how many ships and landing craft would have to be lost before he would scrub the operation. Although the decision to abandon a combined operation technically had to be made jointly by the military and naval commanders, Hughes-Hallett also made it plain that "the executive action which has to be taken is purely naval, is usually irreversible, and therefore needs to be decided upon in advance because there may be no time for consultation when the crisis comes."[16]

He decided that the loss of certain numbers and combinations of LSIS would prompt cancellation. If both LSIS carrying the South Saskatchewan Regiment were lost, there could be no landing at Pourville or subsequent capture of the western headland. This left the main force landing in front of Dieppe threatened from that flank. Consequently, loss of these two ships meant cancellation. The Royal Hamilton Light Infantry would be aboard a single LSI and would land on White Beach at Dieppe. Roberts believed that the loss of this regiment could be counterbalanced by the troops on the LCTS landing in concert with the tanks. So that loss would not trigger a cancellation. Nor would the loss of either of the LSIS carrying the Essex Scottish into Red Beach next to Dieppe's harbour, because 'A' Commando of the Royal Marines could attack alone. If, however, the Essex Scottish LSIS and the one carrying the Royal Marines were all lost, the operation must be abandoned. Roberts advised that loss of one or even both LSIS carrying the Royals to Blue Beach in front of Puys would not, from "a purely military view," jeopardize the rest of the raid. But Hughes-Hallett felt this would leave the German guns and troops on the eastern headland dominating the harbour entrance and its inner basins. So he declared his intention to cancel if these two LSIS were lost.

"I wish to place on record," Hughes-Hallett said in closing, "that the foregoing conclusions would have been profoundly modified had it been possible to have a number of bombers to call in the area from dawn onwards with a view to making low-flying daylight attacks on enemy batteries in the event of an emergency."[17] Hughes-Hallett had not ceased campaigning to reverse the decision against using bombers. Even during a final planning meeting on August 17, he had pressed for commitment of heavy bombers. But Roberts was wedded to the idea that "the destruction... it would cause would make the passage of tanks through Dieppe very difficult, if not impossible, and the decision not to carry out such a bombardment was therefore maintained."[18]

With these letters filed, Hughes-Hallett joined Commander David Luce for a three-hour walk on Portsdown Hill. The two men carefully reviewed "the entire operation in our minds trying to imagine and anticipate all the contingencies that might arise."[19]

WITHIN MINUTES OF the order initiating Jubilee, all the Canadian battalions were preparing to move towards embarkation ports. Security remained extremely tight. In another testament to Brigadier Church Mann's exceptional organizational skills, this process had been meticulously orchestrated to avoid delays or traffic jams. Inevitably, however, the last-minute nature of the operation's launch led to some glitches.

The 3rd Canadian Light Anti-Aircraft Regiment, for example, provided 10 officers and 236 other ranks for various tasks. Although the gunners were trained to operate Bofors anti-aircraft guns, they were equipped with unfamiliar Bren guns.[20] The Brens were brand new and covered in grease. Lacking cleaning material, the gunners had to borrow fuel from the Calgary tankers and use strips of cloth torn from their own shirts as cleaning rags.[21]

The Canadian engineers assigned to Jubilee were mostly the same men earlier designated to Rutter. They were divvied up according to assigned tasks and distributed aboard ten LCTs, Motor Gunboat *Locust*, and the LSIS *Glengyle*, *Prince Charles*, and *Prince Leopold*. Although some loaded at Gosport, the majority boarded LCTs at Newhaven.[22] The engineers numbered 666 in all. Ninety-three were tasked to beach and assault parties, 240 to demolition parties, and 333 to engineer groups. Those engineers arriving at Newhaven found their necessary stores well organized and ready, thanks to the efficient work of twenty-one men from 7th Field Company, who had assembled everything at Warnford Park and moved it to the harbour.

But transferring the stores onto the LCTs proved a nightmare. "Great difficulty was experienced by the sappers in carrying their equipment, plus their heavy packs, in having to climb down a vertical ladder on the side of the dock and then moving across the 4 LCTs berthed alongside the dock. Towards the end of the embarkation a gang plank was used, but the descent was very steep and the gang plank very narrow and very difficult for the men to carry their packs on board by that method," 2nd Division's chief engineer, Lieutenant Colonel Frank Barnes, reported.[23]

Things started out well on August 18 for the Queen's Own Cameron Highlanders. Just after 1000 hours, they were notified to be ready to board seventeen trucks and move to Newhaven beginning at 1420.[24] The Camerons involved numbered 488. They were joined by three signallers from the Royal Canadian Signals Corps, a member of the divisional field security section, a Special Operations Executive agent, four artillery forward observation officers (FOOs), a Royal Air Force observation officer, a single member of the press, and a U.S. Ranger. This rounded the total number of personnel to 500. The Camerons were organized into a flight designated Group 6 and loaded aboard a mix of 25 R-Boats and the larger LCMS. Group 6 was further subdivided into divisions consisting of five craft each. The number of personnel loaded onto each craft was carefully detailed.

Major Norman Ross led 'A' Company out of the battalion's tent camp on schedule to meet the trucks rolling along the road. Only the previous day, he had gone personally to fetch a platoon commander, Lieutenant Bill Goodall, back from a course. When the instructors asked why a lieutenant was being dragged off by a major, Ross curtly replied that the officer's presence was required at battalion. He was painfully aware of how compromised security might be. God knew who had blathered in the wrong ear over a beer somewhere, but there was nothing to be done. Good friends, Ross and Goodall spent the drive back to camp catching up on personal news. Goodall was twenty-eight and married, and Ross considered him a steady hand.

Not until the truck convoy reached Newhaven at about 1700 hours did Ross learn what vessels they would use for the channel crossing. He had feared it would be the creaky coastal paddlewheeler from Rutter. Although the LCAS and LCMS before him were much smaller, they were quick and manoeuvrable. They could also go straight into the beach at Pourville without the men having to first transfer from a large vessel to the landing craft.[25] They found much of their equipment was waiting at Newhaven. But the gremlins were loose again. Instead of being neatly organized and labelled, it had been unceremoniously dumped into a large pile. Many crates, some full of explosives, were unlabelled.[26] Included in the stack were 30 Sten guns each with five magazines, 13 Smith & Wesson .38 calibre pistols with holsters, 8,000 rounds of .303 ammunition, 240 rounds of .38-calibre bullets for the pistols, 200 No. 5 smoke generators, 100 incendiary hand bombs, 1,460 detonators to arm the battalion's No. 36 hand grenades, 500 Mae West flotation devices, 70 wire cutters, 12 medical compresses, 5 scaling ladders, 150 toggle ropes, 24 grappling hooks, 25 bicycles, one signals handcart, 10 Union Jacks, 50 sandbags, 4 stretchers, and 20 bangalore torpedoes.[27]

By prior arrangement, the navy provided the troops with dinner. It was poor: a greasy stew with gristly meat and some strong tea most of the men found undrinkable.[28] While the Camerons ate, naval personnel divvied up the additional equipment among the various landing craft. Dinner over, the most junior officers, NCOs, and other ranks were "briefed in the part they were to play in this great raid," as one Cameron report later put it. Major A.T. "Andy" Law then gathered company commanders together to ensure all the necessary supplies were aboard.[29]

The only Cameron who had ever fired a Sten gun was Lieutenant Colonel Al Gostling. Each man assigned one was personally instructed by Gostling in how to load and fire it. Designed for rapid production, the Sten had just forty-seven parts, which were stamped out of metal like cookies from dough—the parts were then welded, sweated, or riveted together. From the tip of its stubby barrel to the end of the metal shoulder butt, it was just thirty inches long. The Sten fired 9-millimetre ammunition fed from a 32-round magazine fitted at a right angle to the barrel on its left-hand side. Each gun was still packed in grease, which had to be cleaned off.[30]

As August 18 unfolded, more Canadian and British troops were on the move. Lord Lovat and No. 4 Commando left Weymouth in "a kind of vanishing act." Warned on Monday afternoon that they would depart the next morning on a two-day exercise, the men paraded on the waterfront at 0500 hours with their light packs. Taken into the country, they spent "a hard day weapon training." Meanwhile, No. 4 Commando's quartermaster transferred the heavy weapons, ammunition, Mae Wests, iron rations, and explosives onto the LSI *Prince Albert* at Weymouth. The vessel then sailed to Southampton, where the still unaware commandos—228 strong—unloaded from trucks and boarded. Waiting for No. 4 Commando was an RAF observer and five U.S. Rangers. Watches were zeroed as the men boarded. Major Derek Mills-Roberts had a watch on each wrist. "There was to be split-second timing in the fighter sorties that strafed the enemy at tree-top height next day." Two watches ensured he would know precisely when the fighters should arrive.[31]

The South Saskatchewan Regiment, meanwhile, had departed at 1145 hours "for an unknown destination. No-one knew where they were going until they arrived at Southampton Port... at about 1530 hours." The battalion boarded two LSIS—*Princess Beatrix* and *Invicta*. Then company commanders advised their men "that the scheme Ford 1 was the real thing, a raid on France, and that there would be no umpires or blanks fired. Every officer and other rank cheered with joy knowing at last the time had come when they could get a crack at the Hun.

"About 1930 hours tea was served to all ranks. Immediately after, all ranks started to prepare their weapons... All ranks showed the highest of spirits, there was no sign of fright in any man. A look of happiness seemed to be gleaming from all faces knowing that at last the hour had finally arrived to give the Hun some of their own medicine... Officers, NCOS, and other ranks were studying maps of Dieppe and Pourville... so as to make sure of the landing at the proper place and of their objectives which they had to destroy," the war diarist wrote.[32]

Lieutenant John Edmondson had guessed earlier that the raid was back on. Everything about the way the exercises were organized, particularly the insistence on full battle kit, was suspicious. As 'D' Company's second-in-command, he was responsible for its supplies and equipment. Seeing that he was to load the company's G1098 stores, which was a reserve of ammunition normally carried only during an actual operation, Edmondson asked the company commander, Major Mac MacTavish, "Does everything we do and everything we take have to be completely man worthy and operational?" MacTavish looked at Edmondson consideringly. "Then that little grin came on his face and he said, 'Yes.' So I knew."

At the dock, the Sasks found that the two ships had been camouflaged with fake stacks and other accoutrements to make them look like freighters to German reconnaissance planes. Nets concealed the troops.[33]

Twenty Sten guns had been delivered to *Princess Beatrix* and ten to *Invicta*. Edmondson was with the 274 Sasks aboard *Princess Beatrix*, while another 210 were on *Invicta*.[34] When the men broke open the Sten gun cases and found the weapons packed in grease, "we had to try and clean them," Edmondson later recalled. "Weren't allowed to test fire them, so we had no idea whether they were working properly."[35] Some of the more weapon-savvy men eyed these new submachine guns warily. When fitted into the breach, six rivets held the front of the magazine in place. Some rivets protruded too far into the magazine and might cause a jam. The functionality of these guns would not be known until the battle began.[36]

Hundreds of No. 36 grenades had to be primed with detonators. Aboard *Invicta*, a man in Lieutenant Leonard Kempton's No. 14 Platoon of 'C' Company had a grenade suddenly explode. Out of the platoon's thirty men, seventeen were wounded. Sergeant M. Lehman was impressed to see that this calamity failed to "worry Mr. Kempton. In fact it made him that much more determined and he had us load up with just that much more ammunition to take the place of that the men who were left behind would have carried. The boys were glad to get it and Mr. Kempton carried more than any of us as he was an officer that would not ask you to do anything he would not do himself."[37]

Princess Beatrix had twenty-six non-Sask passengers. Most of these were beach-party and other support personnel. Also on board were a Canadian sergeant from the intelligence corps named Roy Hawkins and RAF Flight Sergeant Jack Nissenthall.[38] The twenty-one-year-old Hawkins hailed from Fort McMurray, Alberta. Nissenthall, a twenty-three-year-old Jewish Cockney from London's East End, was a radar technician. Getting him to the radar station on the eastern headland overlooking Pourville was the job of the Saskatchewan's 'A' Company, commanded by Captain Murray Osten. Because Nissenthall was privy to British radar technology secrets, a special detail of ten men served as his personal guard. Their instructions were to "provide adequate protection as an RDF expert must under no circumstances fall into enemy hands."[39]

Nissenthall was to gather information on German radar directional finding techniques while Hawkins looted documents and files. Nissenthall had become known to the Sasks during Rutter's preparations; Hawkins was new. His mission, he told Nissenthall, was to protect him. When Nissenthall pointed out that he already had ten minders, Hawkins shrugged. "Now you've eleven." Both men knew what this meant. If things went sour, Hawkins was to ensure Nissenthall was not captured. So it might come to killing him. Each man carried a green cyanide pill in their regulation Evaders Pack.[40] But confidence ran high. The radar station gambit was going to be an adventure.

Nissenthall's mission was not the only caper afoot. Various attached 30th Commando intelligence specialists were to scour a Dieppe harbourfront hotel for possible Ultra-related codes and equipment. La Maison Blanche was "believed to be a white house" used as an officer's mess. Papers from there were deemed worthwhile. The airfield at St. Aubin would be searched for "papers, pamphlets, code books, and signal papers." Signal equipment should be carried off. At the last moment, it was recognized that the divisional headquarters at Arques-la-Bataille—still identified as 110th Infantry Division's— might have moved. (In fact, 302nd Division had relocated its headquarters to Envermeu, about eight miles inland from Dieppe.) If the headquarters was still in place, the Camerons capturing it were to collect "secret files, pamphlets, order of battle, code books." Almost every battalion had at least one specialist attached, with a list of specific tasks. One three-man group landing at Red Beach in front of Dieppe was to loot an identified wireless transmission station of its "wireless plan, three-letter codes, [and] instruction pamphlets," all within ninety minutes. In the next thirty minutes, they would scour the hundred-room Grand Hôtel for military papers. In continuing thirty-minute phases concluding three hours and thirty minutes after they landed, the three men were to have scoured the forty-room Hôtel Bellevue, the seventy-two room Hôtel Étrangers, and the Maritime command headquarters. This last target was to be stripped of "military passes, R.T.O's papers, Movement control, instructions and tables, etc."[41]

BECAUSE THE ESSEX Scottish and Royal Hamilton Light Infantry would lead the charge against Dieppe, the two battalions deployed eighty-two men each onto the LCTs carrying the Calgary Tanks that were to land in the first armoured flight. This meant dispersing Essex personnel by truck to vessels at Portsmouth, Southampton, and Newhaven. At Portsmouth, 'A' and 'D' Companies embarked on HMS *Prince Charles,* while 'B' and 'C' Companies and the battalion headquarters loaded onto HMS *Prince Leopold* at Southampton.[42] A total of 455 Essex Scottish boarded these ships. Meanwhile, two groups of thirty-five loaded onto two LCTs carrying tanks. Another three men would accompany the tanks from a third LCT slated to land a few minutes later.[43]

Despite orders to clean weapons and load up with a heavy issue of ammunition before leaving camp, secrecy was so well maintained that "the men had no inkling" the raid was reborn. "There was no excitement evinced," the regiment's war diarist wrote.[44]

Once aboard the two LSIs, junior officers and the other ranks were "informed that they were there for the purpose of attacking Dieppe." Captain Don MacRae observed that this "announcement was greeted with high spirits and considerable eagerness to get on with the job. Pistols, Sten guns, ammunition, hand grenades and hand incendiaries were turned over to the unit and... issued to the appropriate personnel. New air photographs of Dieppe taken 16 August were made available and the troops got down to intensive study of the plan of attack. As most of the troops had been completely in the picture from the first attempt [Rutter] it was more or less a case of review. By 2300 hours... arrangements were all ready and the troops bedded down for some sleep."[45]

The Royal Hamilton Light Infantry's 31 officers and 551 men had been alerted at 1400 hours that they were to parade in full battle order to meet twenty-eight three-ton lorries in just two hours. The column proceeded from Arundel Castle via Chichester to Southampton, a forty-two-mile journey. On a motorcycle, Captain Denis Whitaker guided the convoy as it rolled along at a steady fifteen miles per hour. No stops were permitted. Standing dockside was HMS *Glengyle*, the battalion's Rutter vessel. Walking up the gangplank, Whitaker wondered if "Dieppe had been revived." A few minutes later he learned that it had and that his platoon would be providing protection for the battalion headquarters.

Unlike the Camerons, the Rileys had experience with Sten guns from Rutter training. They had found the Sten "recalcitrant" and easily jammed by the protruding rivets. Filing these down had rendered them more reliable. When Rutter ended, the Rileys had turned in these guns and now "glared helplessly at their replacements... still in crates, packed in heavy grease." There was no way, working in darkness, to adequately prepare them in time for the landings. Whitaker had another concern. About 5 to 10 per cent of the men were new reinforcements. They were going into an amphibious assault with no training.[46]

They also had a stowaway. Padre Captain John Foote "just packed up and went along with the rest of them," despite orders that chaplains were to remain behind. "I always intended to go. From the time I went into the army, whatever the men were doing I did. I don't think I would have been a very popular padre if I had stayed on shore and greeted them when they came back."[47]

Les Fusiliers Mont-Royal arrived at Shoreham at 1600 hours on August 18. Instead of immediately boarding their small landing craft, the men were assembled in a requisitioned schoolhouse by Lieutenant Colonel Joe Ménard, who informed them that the raid was on. Then Padre Major Armand Sabourin gave absolution and led them in prayer. At 1645, companies gathered in separate classrooms and were briefed by their commanders. Padre Sabourin then administered communion and said "au revoir."[48] Dinner was served on white tablecloths, with Wrens serving as waitresses. How all this was orchestrated was never detailed, but this lavish send-off certainly contrasted with the boarding procedures of the other battalions. Ménard and his quartermasters ran things their own way and often off regulation. Private Ray Geoffrion later recalled it "as a most delicious meal." The men boarded their LCAS and LCMS singing.[49]

The Royal Regiment of Canada moved in three groups to three ports. To bolster this regiment's strength, three Black Watch platoons and a mortar detachment were attached. Together, the Royals and Black Watch comprised the full strength that would attack Puys.[50]

At Southampton, the Black Watch troops boarded the HMS *Duke of Wellington*. After Private Harry Smith primed a grenade, he put it aside to take an issue of forks and spoons. Picking up the same grenade, he tried priming it again.[51] This set the fuse burning. When he tried to chuck it out an open porthole, the grenade struck the bulkhead and bounced back.[52] In the ensuing explosion twenty-six-year-old Private Emile Phillipe Williams was killed.[53] Eighteen other men were wounded.[54]

Canadian Press correspondent Ross Munro boarded the LSI *Queen Emma* at 1900 hours. He was one of a score of Canadian, British, and American journalists scattered throughout the ships. Munro thought that few of the Royals he found aboard seemed to be "in as confident a mood" as they had been during preparations for Rutter. "The rush to the port and the mass of detail, which had to be crammed again in a few hours, left everyone rather ragged." A lot of officers seemed "puzzled" as to "why the raid had been decided upon so suddenly. They would have liked more time to adjust themselves." Munro agreed. Going over the aerial photographs, studying the maps, and reading the plan details, Munro was surprised how much he had forgotten. "I found misgivings growing in my mind. This seemed somewhat haphazard, compared with the serene way in which the cancelled raid was mounted."[55]

AT 1600 HOURS, the man most responsible for how Operation Jubilee was coming together had risen from a long nap. Captain John Hughes-Hallett then met the other two force commanders, Major General Ham Roberts and Vice-Air Marshal Trafford Leigh-Mallory, in an office at Fort Southwick. The Portsmouth admiral Sir William James and Mountbatten were also in attendance.

It was the moment of truth. Weather forecasts remained dubious. Admiralty and Air Ministry meteorologists, Captain John Hughes-Hallett thought, "were every bit as gloomy as the Old Testament Prophets." But Hughes-Hallett and Leigh-Mallory "pressed hard for a decision to sail that evening." They argued that the meteorological officer at the Fleet Air Arm base at Lee-on-Solent, Lieutenant Ronald Bell, offered a differing forecast. Considered an expert on local weather, Bell predicted "a pocket of fine weather in the central channel ... that would last until the late afternoon of August 19." Although Bell was alone in this prediction, Hughes-Hallett chose to believe him. Leigh-Mallory said Bell's forecasts could be trusted. After some discussion, all agreed that Operation Jubilee would proceed.

Just before Hughes-Hallett left Fort Southwick, he received a last message from the Admiralty director of operations "begging me not to sail ... on account of the weather. However, the die was cast, and ... General [Roberts] and I, with our respective staffs, embarked in HMS *Calpe* at 7:45 p.m. August 18 and sailed at 8 p.m. It was a perfect evening."[56]

As *Calpe* put to sea, Lieutenant General Harry Crerar signalled Roberts from Canadian Army headquarters. Roberts received the message standing next to Hughes-Hallett on the bridge. "Good luck and give him the works," Crerar said. Roberts replied, "Thanks, we will."[57]

12

The Most Remarkable Thing

"THIS IS RATHER a historic occasion," Captain John Hughes-Hallett told *Collier's Weekly* correspondent Quentin Reynolds on HMS *Calpe*'s bridge. "This is the greatest invasion of its kind ever attempted in modern warfare. We have every type of smaller ship with us from transports to motor-torpedo boats." In the gathering gloom of nightfall, Reynolds saw boats "as far as the eye could pierce... There were fat transports, heavy bellied, with the small invasion barges which were on their decks, behind protruding coverings of protective burlap. There were the long tank landing craft, low in the water, and occasionally the sleek form of a destroyer slithered by on its way to her post."[1]

A total of 245 vessels had departed from five different ports. On board were about 6,100 soldiers. Of these, 4,963 were Canadian and about 1,075 British. There were also 50 U.S. Rangers and 20 men of No. 10 (Inter-Allied) Commando, 15 of these being French and the other 5 German anti-Nazis.[2]

Reynolds was the only journalist aboard *Calpe*, a plum posting granted personally by Mountbatten. Such was Reynolds's level of access that Hughes-Hallett presented him with a copy of the entire Jubilee plan before shooing him below because the bridge was too crowded. "I was the luckiest guy in the world... This script was foolproof; it couldn't miss. And what a show it would be! In addition to the show I'd see, I even knew now what the rest of the audience didn't know, and wouldn't know. I knew all of the offstage directions."[3]

As Reynolds poured over the plan, *Calpe* led one group of vessels through the most southwesterly of the passages cleared of mines by the 9th and 13th Minesweeping Flotillas. Each flotilla's eight minesweepers had slipped away from the English coast just before midnight. By 0051 hours, the two lanes were cleared and their flanks marked with lighted buoys.[4]

When Reynolds visited the wardroom, he found Major General Ham Roberts relaxing in the company of Air Commodore Adrian Trevor Cole, "a lean and affable Australian." The forty-seven-year-old Cole represented Vice Air-Marshal Trafford.[5]

Reynolds was surprised at how calm the officers were. "The tension had gone, and we all had a drink and, except for the uniforms, this might have been the smoking room of a small ocean liner and we a group of business men on a holiday... Roberts was not a general who stood too much on dignity. Like a good soldier he was relaxed now. Tomorrow would be a tough day, but to worry about it now would only be to borrow trouble. The entire plan was made. Now Roberts only had to carry it out and his part in the program would not begin until just before daybreak."

Much to the journalist's surprise, Roberts asked if he would like to join him on the beach at about 0830 hours "if things are going according to plan." To "actually set foot on enemy soil would be the best story of all," Reynolds thought, and he quickly accepted.[6]

Soon Reynolds rejoined Hughes-Hallett and Commander David Luce on the bridge. Reynolds asked what it felt like to command this great fleet. The two men "agreed... that the experience of literally watching hundreds of ships and craft as far as the eye could see wherever we looked, and knowing that all were under our command and committed to the greatest amphibious operation since Gallipoli, had a certain dream-like quality."[7]

Mustering so many vessels capable of greatly differing top speeds and manoeuvrability required a complex timetable, with vessels sailing at different times and following various routes in order to reach their assigned passage through the minefield on schedule and in the right order. Although the craft carrying troops were organized into thirteen groups, most of the supporting destroyers and gunboats operated independently. Given their speed and agility, the destroyers were both protecting the groups and acting as shepherds to keep them on course and schedule.[8]

Each group had at least one protective support ship. Landing Craft Flak, Large 6, for example, escorted a group of LCTS. The LCFS were LCTS converted into floating gun platforms by anchoring top decks onto their sides. They literally bristled with gun turrets, mounting four double 2-pounder guns and ten double-barrelled 20-millimetre Oerlikons. In addition to firing against enemy aircraft, the 2-pounders could be directed against naval or land targets. The LCFS had a normal complement of sixteen sailors and sixty marines, the latter manning the guns. Lieutenant W.K. Rogers commanded the marine contingent on LCF6, which had arrived off Newhaven at 2000 hours to meet up with its LCT group. During the two hours spent cruising off the harbour while awaiting the appearance of the LCTS, Rogers briefed his marines that their job this night was to escort a raiding force to Dieppe. "There was a spontaneous cheer!" he wrote.

The LCF would also serve as an amphibious field-dressing station during the raid. A medical officer and two stretcher-bearers were aboard. They had brought with them a large stock of stretchers and cases of medical supplies.

It was almost dark before Rogers saw the LCTS emerge out of the murky gloom of Newhaven harbour. The LCF's commander flashed a light signalling the LCTS to form on him. Then LCF6 led the group off. Rogers detailed half his marines to be on duty at any given time; the other half were allowed to sleep "on deck around their guns." As the group entered its assigned minefield passage, he noted how well it was marked by the buoy lights.[9]

CALPE HAD LINGERED outside Portsmouth harbour until Hughes-Hallett was certain the main units were away. Then the destroyer dashed at full speed to take the van. *Calpe* led four other destroyers and the LSIS towards the western passage. The duplicate headquarters ship, HMS *Fernie,* guided the landing craft groups and LCTS through the eastern channel.[10] Once *Calpe* was out front, its speed was cut to eighteen knots. "I felt a deep sense of relief that at last the entire force was safely at sea, and without apparently having been detected." Lying down in the captain's sea cabin, Hughes-Hallett reflected "that perhaps the most remarkable thing about the operation was that it had actually been launched despite so much obstruction and so much frustration that had dogged Combined Operations since early April 1942."[11]

Aboard *Queen Emma* with Royal Regiment's headquarters and two rifle companies, correspondent Ross Munro also pondered the extraordinary fact of the raid's remounting, which left him "confused and baffled." Munro joined the officers in the wardroom for dinner "as the last sunshine poured through the open portholes." The food was good, and the Royals "were in good spirits... Looking around the table you would never have thought that they were facing the biggest test of their lives. They joked and bantered across the tables and renewed old friendships with the naval officers whom they had known in 'practice Dieppe' training days."

Dinner over, Lieutenant Colonel Doug Catto spread maps, photos, and orders across a table illuminated by a "weird blue blackout light." He and the company commanders worked through everything, ensuring each knew his appointed role. "In every cabin on the ship other officers were running over their orders and scanning their maps once again. It was the same on the troop decks. Platoon commanders, company commanders, sergeants, corporals, and privates were going over the details of the plan and their part in the attack.

"Weapons and ammunition were checked and then the soldiers just lay down on the decks or on their own kit and dozed. Through the darkness the *Queen Emma* pounded to the rendezvous with the other ships of the fleet."[12]

Back on *Calpe*'s bridge, Hughes-Hallett thought *Queen Emma* was actually "proceeding at an excessive speed." So fast, in fact, that *Calpe* and the other destroyers had to race to catch up. At 0016 hours, *Calpe* pulled abeam of the charging LSI and flashed a signal to her commander, Captain G.L.D. Gibbs, "that she was ahead of station and instructing her to reduce to 18 knots." The destroyers then lined up to enter the western passage. Hughes-Hallett began fretting they were off course, but just two minutes before *Calpe* was to enter the passageway, the navigator spotted the buoys and motor launch marking the entrance. The destroyers sailed smoothly into the passage.[13]

Not so the *Queen Emma*. With *Prince Albert, Princess Beatrix, Invicta,* and *Princess Astrid* all doggedly following, she set off on her own heading and plunged into the eastern passageway—racing past the groups of LCTs and landing craft already in the passage. Nobody aboard the *Queen Emma* contingent realized they were off course. Ross Munro "could vaguely distinguish ships around us" as he was carried through the minefield.[14]

Finally, *Queen Emma* and the other LSIS passed the destroyer *Fernie* just as it emerged from the passage. *Calpe,* meanwhile, had stopped just beyond the minefield and was able to get Gibbs's attention with a signal lamp. Once the wayward ships were back on station, Hughes-Hallett sent them off under the protective and navigational watch of the destroyers towards their landing craft launch points about ten miles from the coast. *Calpe* lingered at the passageway exit until Group 4, consisting of HMS *Glengyle* escorted by the destroyer *Brocklesby* and Polish destroyer *Slazak,* emerged at 0210 hours. Joining this group, *Calpe* proceeded to *Glengyle*'s drop point.[15]

Queen Emma's captain was not the only one to lose his way. The gunboat *Locust,* unable to keep up with her assigned LSIS, lost contact shortly after leaving Portsmouth. Accompanied by ML291, *Locust* was unable to locate either passageway. Resorting to dead reckoning, Commander Red Ryder sailed directly into the minefield on a bearing aimed at bringing him to where *Glengyle* was to discharge her landing craft.[16] That neither craft struck a mine was later credited to their shallow draft.[17]

Aboard *Calpe,* an officer on the bridge pointed to where a lighthouse's beam flashed. Good news, he told Reynolds. The lighthouse would not be operating if the Germans knew of the raid, because it provided a perfect marker against which the ships could check their locations.[18]

Everything seemed to be unfolding as planned. The LSIS and other groups of landing craft were all in position and on time to begin the final runs towards the beaches. By 0305, the troops from the LSIS were aboard the LCAS and LCMS and had been lowered to the sea. At

0340 hours, six flotillas of landing craft would lead the way towards the beaches. MGB312 and SBG9 were protecting the No. 4 Commando LCAS, bound for Orange Beach I and II. The South Saskatchewan Regiment's LCAS and LCMS, heading for Green Beach at Pourville, were guarded by MGB317 and SGB6. The Royals bound for White Beach at Dieppe were watched over by MGB326, while ML291 supported the Essex Scottish headed for adjacent Red Beach. Those Royals moving towards Blue Beach at Puys were under care of MGB316 and SGB8. On the far-eastern flank, No. 3 Commando's R-Boats headed in with SGB5, ML346, and LCF(L)I supporting.

Not far behind the assault formations, the flotilla of LCAS bearing the Royal Marine contingent from *Duke of Wellington* was inbound— absent the delayed *Locust* and accompanying ML291. Following even farther behind and separated by several miles were the LCT formations bearing the Calgary Tanks and engineers towards White and Red Beaches, the LCAS and LCMS carrying the Camerons towards Green Beach, and the sloop *Alresford* accompanied by the seven French *chasseurs* headed for Dieppe's harbour. The destroyers *Garth*, *Bleasdale*, *Albrighton,* and *Berkeley* swept out to the westward flank to guard against possible attack by enemy ships from that direction, while *Slazak* and *Brocklesby* did the same to the east.[19]

Aboard *Queen Emma*, the Royals had climbed into their landing craft, with Munro boarding one of the large LCMS. "Nobody spoke. Silence was the strict order but as our boat... jammed with about 80 soldiers, pushed off from the *Emma,* a veteran sailor leaned over and in a stage whisper said: 'Cheerio, lads, all the best; give the bastards a walloping.' Then we were drifting off into the darkness and our coxswain peered through the night to link up with the rest of our assault flotilla... Eyes were accustomed to the darkness now and we could discern practically all our little craft; the sea was glossy with starlight.

"The boats plunged along, curling up white foam at their bows and leaving a phosphorescent wake that stood out like diamonds on black velvet."[20]

To the east, the darkness suddenly shattered "brilliantly in a riot of dazzling green and bright-red streaks that arched the sky, flashing vividly against the black velvet of the night." On *Calpe*,

Hughes-Hallett and Reynolds stood on the bridge "stunned. These were tracer bullets, hundreds of them, and they came from our left. What had happened? To the left were the Royals and No. 3 Commando. Were they the targets?"[21]

THIRTY MINUTES AFTER Group 5, bearing No. 3 Commando, had departed Newhaven at 2030 hours, a small German convoy left Boulogne for Dieppe. It consisted of five coastal freighters protected by two sub-chasers, UJ-1411 and UJ-1404, and Motor Launch 4014. UJ-1411 was commanded by Oberleutnant S. Wurmbach, the convoy leader.[22] His vessel was a converted 331-ton whaler built in 1936.[23] Capable of twelve knots, it mounted a 37-millimetre dual-purpose gun, four 20-millimetre cannons, and several 12.7-millimetre machine guns. UJ-1404, a converted deep-sea trawler, was similarly armed. The convoy proceeded at a leisurely six knots. Although its sailing had been detected by an Ultra signal intercept that was deciphered by 0316, Portsmouth's naval commander-in-chief, Admiral Sir William James, was not informed.[24]

Despite this lapse, James was alerted to the convoy's existence by coastal radar detection. He sent two warnings signals to *Calpe*—the first at 1327 hours and the second at 1444. Neither signal was received by *Calpe*.[25] Both, however, reached *Fernie*—the secondary headquarters—but no action was taken, presumably because it was assumed that *Calpe* had received the signals. Nor was the signal forwarded to *Slazak* and *Brocklesby*, the two destroyers positioned to protect the flank towards which the convoy sailed.[26]

Unaware that Group 5 was on a collision course with the German convoy, Commander Derek Wyburd aboard SGB5 (HMS *Grey Owl*) faced a litany of other problems. Group 5 was divided into two flotillas travelling side by side. A slight headwind had forced him to increase speed to 9.75 knots, which he realized "was just more than the [R-Boats] could make comfortably. A number of them dropped back, and at one time it was only possible to see 15 through binoculars and the order became slightly disorganized."[27] Twenty-three R-Boats had started out. Each carried about eighteen commandos, their fighting gear, and a limited amount of specialized equipment that included two bangalore torpedoes, a couple of 2-inch mortars, and a single

3-inch mortar. The R-Boats' normal top cruising speed was 9.5 knots. Lacking sufficient fuel capacity to make the crossing and back, each boat carried sixteen two-gallon petrol cans for refuelling. Their crew consisted of four sailors, an officer, and three ratings. Armament was provided by either one or two 7.62-millimetre Lewis light machine guns.

The pace proved too demanding for four of the R-Boats. Defeated by engine trouble, their crews turned about for Newhaven. The rest steamed on, ML346 doing its best to chivvy them into order and catch up to *Grey Owl*. ML346 was lightly armed with a 3-pounder gun and single 20-millimetre cannon. LCF(L)1 mounted twin 102-millimetre dual-purpose guns and three 20-millimetre Oerlikon rapid-fire anti-aircraft guns. One troop of commandos was on board, the intention being that they would land as a second wave on Yellow Beach 1.[28] Wyburd's *Grey Owl* was more robustly armed. It mounted a 3-pounder gun amidships, two single 6-pounder guns in powered turrets (one each in bow and stern), two twin 20-millimetre Oerlikons in powered turrets either side of the bridge, and two 21-inch torpedo tubes abreast of the funnel.[29] In addition to Wyburd and *Grey Owl*'s crew of three officers and twenty-four ratings, Lieutenant Colonel John Durnford-Slater, most of the commando's signallers, several liaison officers, and the U.S. Ranger Captain Roy Murray were aboard. All told, the troops in Group 5 numbered 374, of which 325 were from No. 3 Commando. Forty were U.S. Rangers, five Free French were from No. 10 (Inter-Allied Commando), and an officer and three other ranks came from a special signals unit to establish a radio link with RAF No. 11 Fighter Group's headquarters in Uxbridge.[30]

Wyburd's situation kept worsening. Not only were many R-Boats lost to sight but the SGB's navigational system was "working erratically, and... I was not sure of my position to within three miles." At 0345 hours, Wyburd could see only seventeen R-Boats. He could only hope the rest were nearby.

Two minutes later, about seven miles off the French coast, Wyburd spotted a "shape... on the port bow."[31] A star shell arced into the sky. Sub-Lieutenant David Lewis, a Royal Canadian Navy Volunteer Reserve (RCNVR) officer who was to serve as beach master on Yellow Beach, was aboard R-Boat15. To his starboard, the star shell "lit the

whole fleet in a horrible quivering semi-daylight. Our boat was leading the starboard column. It was immediately enveloped in the hottest
tracer fire I have ever seen. The air was filled with the whine of rico-
chets and the bangs of exploding shells. While after every burst of the
streaking balls of fire came the clatter of Oerlikons."

The commandos aboard his boat "threw off their blankets, fumbled for tin hats and weapons. The flak was lying but a few feet ahead
and a few astern. Some was right above us." Everybody was shouting,
"E-Boats," thinking that they were under attack by German motor
torpedo boats.

Aboard R-Boat42, Sub-Lieutenant Clifford Davis Wallace of Montreal was shot in the back of the head and instantly killed, while
Lieutenant Commander Charles L. Corke was badly wounded. A bullet punched through the windscreen and killed the coxswain. Corke
ordered a commando to grab the wheel and steer towards the coast.[32]
Five other R-Boats followed. Corke, whose wound would prove fatal,
guided the little party towards Yellow Beach 1.[33]

Wyburd initially thought the fire came from the covering destroyers, but quickly realized it was enemy fire. Mistakenly believing his
fragile flotilla under attack by E-Boats, Wyburd fell back on a contingency plan and ordered Grey Owl to maintain course and speed with
the intention of "fighting our way through." To radically alter course
would surely throw his already straggling formation into confusion
and make an orderly landing impossible. For the next ten minutes,
Grey Owl churned on at 9.5 knots in a straight line, presenting a
main target to the Germans. "She was hit a very large number of
times," he wrote. "All guns were put out of action; all wireless sets
were hit; boiler and engine room received several hits (there were
five direct hits on the one boiler). Approximately 40% of those on
board became casualties, although fortunately only one man was
killed. At the end of this ten minutes it was evident that my plan to
get through had failed. sGB5 can only be described as in a shambles."
Realizing most of the R-Boats had scattered, Wyburd ordered Grey
Owl turned away from the enemy and limped off at 5 knots, with five
landing craft tagging along.[34] As all navigational equipment had
been shot away, Wyburd had no idea of his precise location. He told

Durnford-Slater, who had been slightly wounded by shell splinters, that there was little chance they could find the beach. Even if they did, it would be after daylight. Durnford-Slater looked out at the R-Boats and judged he had about sixty men there and possibly two boatloads of signallers and other people on board *Grey Owl*. The two officers decided, Durnford-Slater wrote, "to proceed towards the beaches of Dieppe to report to the Force Commander, as a daylight landing from R-Boats with the very limited force available and no naval support was not considered practicable."[35] En route to Dieppe, *Grey Owl* lost power. Durnford-Slater and Wyburd transferred to an R-Boat and carried on, instructing the other four to tow *Grey Owl* back to Newhaven.[36]

As they set off, Wyburd saw LCFI still "energetically continuing the action."[37] Under command of Australian lieutenant F.M. Foggitt, LCFI slashed away at the German craft with heavy gunfire that left UJ-1404 burning. Despite all the officers and many of the crew of LCFI being wounded, she continued fighting until 0450 hours. Realizing that Zero Hour for the landings was nigh, Foggitt steered clear of the action and, with three R-Boats trailing behind, sailed towards Dieppe. Lieutenant Alexander Fear's MI346 had also kept fighting, partly due to his confused attempts to marry up with either *Grey Owl* or LCFI. Each time Fear closed on what he took to be one of these ships, it proved to be a German sub-chaser. Finally, he broke off the engagement, linked up with the six R-Boats under Corke's command, and guided them towards Yellow Beach I.

The swirl of vessels caught in the surreal light of star shells had left the Germans equally confused. UJ-4014's captain had initially believed this was just "one of the usual [speed]-boat skirmishes" common to Channel actions. All the R-Boats dashing every which way were misidentified as being British motor torpedo boats. "Then UJ-4014 brought under fire a clearly visible target that was a long, rather heavily armed vessel. A noticeable feature was that this vessel had its bridge superstructure very far aft." He was engaging LCFI.

In the fury of the moment, both sides overestimated the destruction they caused. Lieutenant Foggitt claimed not only UJ-1404 sunk but possibly also two other small armed trawlers. The German convoy commander reported exchanging fire with "numerous gun boats and E-boats." At least two enemy boats, he said, were engaged with "rapid fire from all weapons" and sank after exploding. He also reported ramming a large landing craft with about fifty troops aboard and seeing "many of the embarked soldiers down in the propeller wake" of his rampaging ship. It is probable this was actually the R-Boat being driven by commando Corporal Tom Gerrard, who was steering it while lying prone. Seeing a German boat steaming towards him with obvious intent to ram, Gerrard managed to jam the boat into reverse and narrowly avoided the collision.

In fact, no R-Boats were sunk. Although only seven continued towards the Yellow Beaches, the others all remained afloat. Badly scattered, some with naval crew all dead or wounded, each made its way to safety. Some headed west to be picked up by ships of the main raiding force. When a shell killed the naval crew aboard his R-Boat, Sergeant Clive Collins took the helm. The craft's compass was shattered, so he sailed for England by guiding on a prismatic pocket compass and limped into Newhaven harbour at 1000 hours.[38]

R-Boat15, commanded by Lieutenant H.T. "Henry" Buckee, meanwhile, had initially sought cover under *Grey Owl*'s stern. But he and Sub-Lieutenant Lewis knew their orders "were to land the troops at all costs or the operations would be a bloody failure. At full speed we tore away from the lashing beams of flak. Another star shell went off on our port side, but it was distant. Still unhit, except by shrapnel," the boat "belted all alone for the French coast."

Crouching as low as they could, none of the commandos aboard were hit, despite the fact that Major Peter Young, their commander, saw that the "canopy... was full of holes." As soon as the R-Boat was clear of the German fire, Young saw that "we were now alone." Buckee, who believed *Grey Owl* to be disabled and floating adrift, said that undoubtedly some of the others would find the beaches despite Wyburd being unable to guide them in.[39] It was 0420 hours, and thirty minutes before the commandos were to land. The coast ahead "was perfectly quiet in spite of all this firing at sea." Buckee and Young agreed they should try to find Yellow Beach 11. They hoped to "fall in with other... boats scattered during the fighting, but none came."[40] Locating the beach proved fairly easy, as the light-house near Dieppe still flashed its beam seaward. By that light they were able to see "the cliffs quite clearly and a black patch which Buckee said was the gully at Yellow [11]. I thought it was Yellow 1, but Buckee insisted that he was right."

The two men kept pondering what to do, with Lewis listening in. "It seemed suicidal to go ashore. But they must," Young and Buckee agreed. "It might mean the loss of twenty men. But who could tell how many would be lost if they did not keep the six-inch batteries on the cliff above Berneval from firing at our heavy ships."[41]

"There you are," Buckee said. "There's your beach."

"What do we do now?" Young asked.

"My orders are to land even if there's only one boat."

Young was not about to show timidity. After quickly conferring with his second-in-command, Captain John Selwyn, he said, "Those are my orders too. We are to land whatever happens, even if we have to swim." Buckee offered to land his sailors to bolster the small party, but Young refused. He also told Buckee to flee if the R-Boat was fired upon. The commandos would withdraw overland to join the Canadians at Dieppe.[42]

THE SUDDEN FLURRY of tracer fire east of the main fleet confused everybody aboard *Calpe*. Someone shouted that it was the Polish destroyer firing. Red and green tracer rose lazily into the air, accompanied by the "sharp bark" of anti-aircraft guns firing. "It was a beautiful display of fireworks... They flamed incredible distances across the sky and then melted into the darkness." A radar station had mistaken the ships for aircraft, somebody else declared. "They haven't spotted us."[43]

On *Fernie*, Brigadier Church Mann thought he had "ring side seats for a considerable naval battle about two miles to the north east... It was like watching a demonstration of tracer firing punctuated with the flash and crash of [4-inch] guns from both sides and although it was a thrilling and spectacular display, it filled us with foreboding as we all realized that the chance of our effecting surprise was greatly diminished."[44]

Most everyone in the Dieppe raiding force thought that the element of surprise was lost. Yet 302nd Infantry Division issued no alarm or orders for defences to be manned. This was largely due to the German convoy commander's failure to recognize that he had encountered more than a normal coastal interception force, which he reported to Naval Group Command West. Not until 0545, long after it no longer mattered, did the naval command pass a signal to OB West that at "0450 [hours] our convoy attacked by surface craft 4 km off Dieppe. No further details yet available. In the opinion of Naval Group Command customary attack on convoy."[45]

Even later, with the Dieppe raid under way, Fifteenth Army headquarters reported to OB West it had received a report from LXXXI Corps headquarters that "English fast units attacked our convoy at 0500 hrs 20 km off Dieppe. Troops in higher state of alert, Navy and Air Force have been informed." In a lengthy after-action report on the raid, Generalfeldmarschall Gerd von Rundstedt noted, "As appeared later, this convoy had run into the first wave of English landing craft and partly upset the time plan and beaching of the English, having at least the effect of delaying them."[46]

The Dieppe port commandant was alerted by signallers at 0450 hours that "a naval engagement was in progress about 4 nautical miles on the bearing of 352 [degrees]." He passed the report to the naval signals officer at Le Havre and also the Luftwaffe local Air Reporting Centre. "It was assumed that [the engagement] was a matter of a fight between the expected convoy... and enemy naval forces." The commandant ordered only that it be further observed, even though the "fighting was more severe than normal." No further action was taken beyond noting that the engagement seemed to "terminate towards 0525 hours." The three harbour protection boats standing offshore of Dieppe were neither recalled nor warned to be extra vigilant. Tugboat 32 also stood outside Dieppe harbour. A pilot aboard waited to guide the convoy into dock.[47]

More locally, the offshore engagement did alert a field picket at Berneval, which reported hearing the naval battle at 0345 hours. Two minutes later, the Luftwaffe crew at the radar station on the eastern edge of Berneval manned their points of resistance, which overlooked Yellow 1. These actions were reported to 302nd divisional headquarters, which merely logged them as part of an escalating number of reports that some naval action was occurring. "The divisional order for all troops to move to action stations was not issued until 0501 hours, by which time landing craft had been sighted off both Pourville and Puys some thirty minutes earlier. The 571st Infantry Regiment reacted only a minute earlier, as British troops were seen landing at Pourville. [In the division's log, all times are given an hour later than recorded here. There was a one-hour difference in British and German time-keeping practices. For simplicity, British times are given.]"[48]

As the Canadian Army official historian later wrote: "All in all, we seem forced to the conclusion that the convoy encounter did *not* result in a general loss of the element of surprise. It did seriously impair our chances of success in the eastern sector off which the fight took place. To this extent it had an effect upon the operation as a whole." But he was unable to accurately assess how or to what degree.

For his part, Hughes-Hallett decided he must assume that the operation was compromised. Reynolds watched as he discussed the situation via talking tube with Roberts, who remained below. He struck Reynolds as being icily calm.[49] But his mind raced. It seemed obvious that Group 5 had become mixed up in some firefight. But why had Wyburd not broken radio silence and reported?

Why, too, had the destroyers *Slazak* and *Brocklesby* not joined the fight? No guns heavier than their 4-inchers had been fired. The senior destroyer commander was the Polish Captain Romuald Tyminski. Although he had seen guns firing five miles distant, no enemy ships were detected by his radar. Consequently, Tyminski decided No. 5 Group was being fired on by shore batteries. To investigate would only betray the destroyers' presence to the enemy, so he ordered them to maintain their patrol track. As a result it was not until 0500 hours that the vessels passed the area where the engagement had occurred. Thirty minutes later, *Brocklesby* encountered the still-burning UJ-1404, sank her with shellfire, and rescued twenty-five German sailors.

Hughes-Hallett later declared Tyminski's decision an "error of judgement," because "the sole reason for his patrol was to provide support for vessels engaged in the landing in the event of a contingency such as this." Tyminski's failure to rush towards the fight convinced Hughes-Hallett that all detached naval units during combined operations should thereafter be under command of British naval officers.[50]

At the time, however, Hughes-Hallett's thoughts were focused on what to do now that surprise seemed lost. Should he abort the raid? Could he do so when landing craft were already moving towards the beaches, particularly those of No. 4 Commando bound for the Orange Beaches near Varengeville? In England, such a brush between a coastal convoy and unknown vessels would likely result in coastal defence batteries being put on alert but not the infantry battalions charged with beach defences. Hughes-Hallett decided to leave the raid in play, gambling that the Germans defending the beaches would not be alerted.[51] This irrevocable decision taken, the raid on Dieppe continued.

PART THREE

THE RAID

13

Good Luck to All of You

LIEUTENANT COLONEL Bob Labatt blinked rapidly as a light flashed on in the captain's cabin of *Glengyle* at 0200 hours. The Royal Hamilton Light Infantry commander had been vainly trying to sleep for a few hours. "Breakfast in ten minutes," the steward said. "Captain won't be there." An "enormous waxed paper packet of white bread sandwiches" went into Labatt's haversack. "No need to fight on an empty stomach, sir, and I've put in something extra to eat on the way home. Weather's fine."

Labatt shaved and enjoyed a warm soak in the tiled tub before donning his uniform. He found a table set with stiff white linen and silver cutlery. Mouth-watering aromas came from an electric chafing dish. His adjutant, Captain Herb Poag, joined him. The battalion second-in-command, Major Frederick Wilkinson, Poag said, had already breakfasted and was checking the LCMs. "The steward brought in our porridge and large mugs of coffee," Labatt would later recall. "Then we helped ourselves to bacon, eggs, and kidneys. Hot toast, butter, and marmalade completed the... meal."

"Sleep well?" Poag asked. The forty-six-year-old had been a Riley in the Great War until invalided out by wounds, then re-enlisted in 1939, serving as quartermaster and then as adjutant. His steady organizational hand had endeared him to the men. Labatt considered him a trustworthy confidante.

"Not a wink," Labatt said. Instead, he had been replaying the events since *Glengyle* sailed, recalling the happy expressions when the men learned this was the real thing. The "issue of maps and photos, the talk to the officers, the briefing of all ranks, the issue of special equipment—Stens, demolitions charges, grapnels, ladders, smoke, bangalores, and Mae Wests. The ticklish business of arming [No.] 36 grenades in the dark. No casualties, thank God, in spite of a lot of detonators spilled on the steel deck in the stygian blackness." All this Labatt had taken in stride. The anxiety he could not shed arose from doubts as to the wisdom of mounting the raid so secretively. Certainly his officers knew their "job thoroughly, but [there was] no time to satisfy myself about the men. It seemed fantastic. Units were being launched into an involved operation. The success of which depended on two factors—one, surprise—two, the thorough knowledge by each man of the several operations to be carried out by his sub-unit and his particular job in each. Yet no time had been made available for him to study his task. It should have been." Breakfast finished, Labatt fetched his fighting kit. "Don't forget your Mae West," he reminded Poag. "I won't. I don't trust boats and I hate water except in whisky," the adjutant replied.

Labatt struggled into his battle kit. "Skeleton web, Colt .45, two extra mags, water bottle, prismatic compass, maps in oiled silk and field message book in left leg pocket; pencils, pen, torch, cigarettes, chocolate, wallet and escape kit in breast pockets. In the haversack, sandwiches, more chocolate and cigarettes, message pads, Sten mags, two No. 36 grenades and 1 smoke canister. Binoculars around the neck, Mae West around the chest, Sten gun in hand and there I was—the 1942 amphibious soldier."

Winches rattled as Labatt hurried deckside. The LCMS were already slung out, and the smaller LCAS hung flush to the boat deck for loading. When the winches stopped, the silence seemed total despite "hundreds of soldiers... pouring up from the mess decks to... allotted boat stations... Their silence was uncanny... Everything was at peace, everything seemed to be going according to plan. Perhaps I had been wrong, we would achieve surprise." Labatt found Captain Donald Stuart McGrath on the bridge, illuminated by the dim glow of the binnacle. A small man with a big beard, McGrath wore a beret, enormous sweater, corduroy trousers tucked into sea boots, and a Mae West. He was from Jamaica and always put Labatt in mind of a pirate.

"Bloody awful, look," McGrath said with a grimace and a finger jabbed eastward. Labatt turned, and his "spirits did a nose dive... The darkness was flecked with bright incessant sparkles. Here and there a dull red glow appeared and faded and over all arched the long lazy streaks of tracer." Probable, McGrath said, that No. 3 Commando was "catching hell" from E-boats. Although worried, Labatt decided the Germans would fixate on the commandos in their R-Boats and "take it for the usual type of commando raid." So long as they did not come farther west, the E-Boats posed no direct threat to the Royal Regiment's landing on Blue Beach at Puys. His spirits rose.

No sense worrying further. *Glengyle* was ten miles offshore and, facing Dieppe, a good five miles west of the commandos. It was time to start the two-hour run to White Beach. "I'll have a drink with you tonight," McGrath called as Labatt left. "Good luck to all of you."

Labatt found flotilla leader Lieutenant Commander Lowe standing next to his LCA. "How about landing us on the right beach for a change?" Labatt chuckled. "Ouch," Lowe replied. "There will be no mistake this time. We know where we are." Labatt took his spot portside on a bench against the gunwale. To his right, a signaller had a wireless set keyed to 4th Brigade's net. Poag sat to his left. Captain Denis Whitaker and the protective platoon faced forward in front of the ramp. Aft was the reduced shore battalion headquarters, a small number of signallers, intelligence personnel, and Wilkinson with "a duplicate set up" on a second LCA. If Labatt's group was lost, Wilkinson should be able to smoothly assume command. Lowe was starboard, standing at the controls. Labatt talked with him over the heads of men sitting low on the centre benches. "I had my fingers on everything going on in the craft and if necessary could take control instantly without climbing about."

Gongs rang, "electric motors hummed and we sank smoothly into the night. Waterborne we hung onto the sides until the other craft were lowered. Looking up and towards the bridge, I realized for the first time the immense size of the ship. Lowe was talking quietly into a telephone swung on the end of a line. He finished and the phone disappeared heavenwards. We were to move forward while they lowered the [LCMS] from each side of the ship. We had gone about 300 yards when I heard McGrath's voice roaring from the bridge. 'Let go those bloody boats.'" A small boat raced up. "That you, Lowe?" a voice called. Lowe acknowledged. "Move off, you are complete," the voice snapped. A small bell in the engine room rang and the LCA moved off at a steady six knots. "The craft was absolutely silent... For better or for worse we were well and truly launched. Next stop France."[1]

AT 0445 HOURS, five minutes ahead of schedule, R-Boat15 with Major Peter Young's commando contingent edged ashore fifty yards right of the sharp gully that ran from Yellow Beach 11 up to the headland. Landing off to the side might keep any Germans manning a machine-gun position in the gully from detecting them.[2]

From the R-Boat, Canadian sub-lieutenant David Lewis watched the commandos slide silently over the sides and dash up the shelving beach to crouch against the cliff. With their darkened faces and hands, these first Dieppe raiders to land were virtually invisible despite the rapidly brightening sky. Lewis was to have overseen a beach defence party, but there were too few commandos for Young to leave any behind. Lieutenant Henry Buckee's small naval crew would remain aboard and linger off the beach as long as possible. As the boat pulled away, the commandos crouched in a tight circle next to the gully for a hurried confab. Then they "vanished up the gully."[3]

The twenty commandos consisted of men from Young's headquarters troop and Captain John Selwyn's No. 3 Troop. Lieutenant "Buck" Ruxton was the only other officer. The group was lightly armed. Young carried an American M1 Garand automatic rifle—a gift from the U.S. Rangers. Nine men were armed with Lee-Enfield rifles. Selwyn, Ruxton, and four others had Thompson submachine guns. One carried a Bren. They also had one 2-inch mortar and a 3-inch mortar. The signaller carried a rifle and a No. 18 wireless set.[4]

Barbed wire choked the gully. When Young asked Selwyn for a bangalore torpedo, he learned the R-Boat had carried none. Nor did anybody have wire cutters. Irritated by Selwyn's poor preparations, Young started climbing the left-hand side of the gully, only to lose his balance and topple onto Selwyn. The captain observed that they were achieving nothing and perhaps should just go back to England. Although Young had entertained similar thoughts, Selwyn's suggesting them was infuriating. Emitting "a sort of surly growl," he started up the right-hand side of the gully.

Young found that the Germans had hammered iron stakes into the cliff and wrapped the barbed wire around them to string across the gully. He used the stakes as handholds to climb the cliff but often had to grasp strands of wire, too. The closely clustered but "fairly blunt" barbs pierced his hands and left shallow cuts. Behind him, driver J. Cunningham, a Royal Army Service Corps trucker turned commando, collected the toggle ropes they'd brought. Each was six feet long, with a loop on one end and a wooden toggle on the other. Cunningham quickly strung these together and threw an end to Young. Unfurling the line as he went, Young carried the rope as he climbed. He made good progress for the first twelve feet. Then the Garand fell off his shoulder, causing him to swing perilously away from the cliff face. "If I fall now, I shall never get up," Young thought, but managed to maintain a foothold and grasp the wire with one steadying hand. Soon exiting the gulley, he faced a sign announcing in German and French that it was mined. Obviously, ascending the side rather than the centre of the gully had saved his life.

The rest of the commandos made the climb assisted by the toggle-rope line. At 0510 hours, one of the first to gain the headland reported seeing five R-Boats headed for Yellow 1 Beach. Young was anxious to get moving, but it took forty-five minutes from touchdown on the beach for everyone to finish the climb. They had abandoned the 3-inch mortar. Even dismantled, it was too heavy and awkward. Somehow the signaller had managed to carry the heavy wireless set up "but could not get in touch with any of our other parties."[5]

It was light now. Young led the way to a small wood at 0530 hours. Noticing that some of the men looked uneasy, Young gave them a short pep talk. "Young soldiers will follow their commanders out of the innocence of their hearts," Young liked to say. Assuming a confident air, he declared this was a mission worthy of telling their children. "Young was flamboyant," Gunner Stephen Saggers observed, "but he was a bloke you could have confidence in."[6] In fact, Young was optimistic. With R-Boats sighted closing on Yellow 1, he expected reinforcements would soon bolster his small force. And for now he would do what commandos did in adverse situations—get to the objective and cause havoc.

WHILE YOUNG'S FORCE landed unopposed, the commandos coming into Yellow 1 at 0510 hours landed in broad daylight and in the sight of Germans looking down from the cliff to the narrow strip of shingle beach. Just nine minutes before, 302nd Division headquarters had sounded Action Stations. Off-duty troops piled out of beds, grabbed weapons, and ran to their assigned positions. But the situation remained murky, the German commanders unsure where attacks were falling and in what strength.

Aboard one R-Boat, Captain Richard Wills—the senior officer present—thought the small force could still land and assault the coastal battery. But it would clearly be a close-run thing. A small church and large white house on top of the three-hundred-foot cliff served as a marker for the beach and gully that constituted Yellow 1. Through binoculars, Sergeant Wally Dungate saw about ten Germans watching from the cliff edge and realized surprise was lost.

Lieutenant Alexander Fear's ML346 hovered protectively, its 3-pounder gun and 20-millimetre Oerlikon cannon tracking the Germans. As the five R-Boats touched down and the commandos spilled ashore, the Germans opened up with a single machine gun and rifles. Private Norman Harrison, the first man off, died instantly when a bullet struck him between the eyes. Commandos scrambled raggedly across the loose shale to the shelter of the cliff face.[7]

Aboard LCP42, the dying Lieutenant Commander Charles L. Corke still commanded. His other naval personnel were either dead or wounded. A commando had steered the craft in. As the bullet-riddled boat sank, Corke ensured all the wounded were shifted to another R-Boat. Refusing to put anybody at risk moving him, Corke remained aboard as the boat foundered offshore.[8] As the other four R-Boats sped seaward, they were passed by another heading towards the beach. After its commandos piled out, the boat was raked by machine-gun fire and sunk just off the beach. The commandos on Yellow Beach 1 now numbered 117, alive or dead.[9] Offshore, Fear had ML346's guns target the large white house where a machine-gun post seemed to be sited.

As had been the case at Yellow 11, the gully was blocked by large barbed-wire tangles. The commandos had no scaling ladders or ban-galore torpedoes. They could only queue behind a couple of men clearing a path with wire cutters. Precious time was lost that allowed a coast patrol from 572nd Infantry Regiment and a few Luftwaffe personnel from the gun battery to reinforce the small picket line.

When the wire was breached, the commandos quickly gained the heights and the scattered buildings of Petit Berneval. Corporal "Banger" Halls charged towards a machine gun firing from the right, throwing grenades as he dashed forward and silencing it single-handedly without suffering a scratch. Then he ran to assist Captain Wills, who fell with a grenade fragment in the neck. Losing con-sciousness, Wills urged Halls "to get on with the battle." Wills was later taken prisoner.[10]

Once the commandos left the cliff edge, ML346 could no longer provide supporting fire. As Lieutenant Fear turned seaward, a vessel suddenly hove into view that he realized was German. Perceiving that the ship mounted two or more guns amidships, he ordered the helmsman to close "at full speed." As ML346 charged with all guns blazing, Fear realized at the last minute he had mistaken the valves and oil pipes on the deck of a fuel tanker for 105-millimetre guns. In fact, *Franz*—part of the convoy that had encountered Group 5—was armed with a single 20-millimetre gun. As soon as this gun was knocked out, its crew leapt overboard in fear of being burned to death when the fuel aboard exploded.[11] *Franz* ran aground without igniting, and Fear had a boarding party fetch its ensign as a trophy. ML346 then hovered offshore of Yellow 1, hoping to help the com-mandos evacuate.[12]

In Petit Berneval, meanwhile, the commandos were meeting escalating resistance as the coastal battery code-named Goebbels dispatched more troops in small detachments of eight to a dozen men. Fifteen Germans from the nearby radar station also rushed towards the fighting. It was 0600 hours.[13]

IN THE WOOD, Major Peter Young and his small party had heard the gunfire from Yellow 1 at 0545 hours. Having no idea what was happening there, Young "decided that our best course was to go into Berneval-le-Grand and try to join the 5 boat-loads who had landed there." If, however, the battery fired, Young would "attack [it] at once" and alone. The commandos moved along a cart track to a junction with the road running from Berneval to Dieppe. As they gathered in the wheat alongside the road, a French youth peddled past on a bicycle. Captain John Selwyn stopped him. Young asked the strength of Goebbels Battery, which the boy estimated at about two hundred. He then let the boy go, "as he was obviously very frightened and unlikely to betray us." Young ordered Lieutenant Ruxton to cover the rest of the party with the 2-inch-mortar team as they entered Berneval. Suddenly, six Spitfires streaked overhead, one strafing the battery. After entering the village, two men shinnied up telephone poles and cut the wires running to Dieppe. They filtered cautiously forward, wary of an ambush, until several civilians reported the Germans were all on the village's other side. Trusting this information, Young double-timed his men for a hundred yards up the main street to the church. As they went, Young counted about ninety civilians. These included three men pushing a wounded woman in a handcart. A civilian fireman wearing a bronze helmet stood next to a burning house. Most of the civilians seemed friendly. They waved before going inside and shutting their doors.

As the commandos passed the church, they were fired on by a light machine gun. Then two German infantrymen dashed across the road to take cover in a hedge. Lieutenant Ruxton returned their fire with his Thompson submachine gun. A sharp firefight ensued until the light machine gun ceased firing and it appeared the Germans had retreated. Young placed the Bren gunner and a couple of snipers in the church's steeple, which overlooked the gun battery.

Taking the other men, Young set out to outflank any German positions guarding the road near the battery by moving through an orchard adjacent to the church. In the orchard, the men discovered an aircraft undercarriage camouflaged to resemble a small gun. "Here we came under a desultory fire from concealed riflemen, whom we could not discover. They fired many rounds, but hit nobody and probably could not see us very well." A light machine gun loosed several bursts towards the commandos, who were unable to pinpoint its location. Carrying on into a cornfield, they attempted to close on the battery, which was firing one gun in an apparent attempt to range in on a target out at sea. Young sensed the gun crew lacked any fire direction from an artillery observer. So much smoke wrapped around the battery that he figured the gunners were firing practically blind. Looking towards Dieppe, Young saw nothing but more smoke obscuring the town. Only fleeting images of an occasional ship proved that the main raiding force had arrived.

Creeping closer, the commandos situated two of the guns. Approaching from the flank, Selwyn and a few men closed to within two hundred yards of them, while Young's party brought them under fire from the cornfield. Ruxton engaged with the mortar until Young realized the guns were more dummies and ordered a ceasefire. Leading his group into another field, "we started a hot fire at the smoke and flashes where the guns appeared to be. Groups of riflemen were still firing at us from the edge of the orchards... but they showed a marked tendency to fire over our heads."

Suddenly, one coastal gun ponderously fired four rounds directly at the commandos. Small explosions also erupted close by, probably from grenades. One man was nicked in the ear. But the coastal gun's fire proved pointless—its barrel was unable to depress sufficiently. Instead, each shell lumbered overhead and exploded a mile distant. "Every time the guns fired we gave a volley of small arms at the black and yellow fumes which appeared." It was about 0745 hours. Although each man had carried approximately a hundred rounds, ammunition was running low, and Young decided they had done all that was possible. He ordered Selwyn to withdraw his men back to the cliff. If LCP15 was still waiting, he should fire three white Verey lights and Young would quickly fall back. Selwyn was to get Lieutenant Buckee's attention and prepare for embarkation.

After Selwyn's party left, Young began disengaging his small force. As they withdrew towards the cliff, Germans manning a flat-topped concrete observation post opened fire with a machine gun. The commando's Bren gunner shot back at a range of five hundred yards, and two Germans on the roof "vanished." Three Verey lights soared up from Yellow 11 Beach, and Young's men hurried back, "wriggling the first few yards for we were under fire... Two or three riflemen followed us at a respectful distance and another sniped at us from the Dieppe side of the gully."[14]

Selwyn had found LCP15 lingering just off the beach. Buckee had held close by, despite occasional bursts of machine-gun fire from the heights. Now seeing four men on the beach, Buckee and Sub-Lieutenant David Lewis were uncertain whether they were commandos or Germans. Buckee decided to go in anyway. Only as the R-Boat grounded did Lewis recognize them as commandos. The tide had ebbed, leaving the beach "very badly ribbed with rocks," he wrote. "We pulled several men in over the side and the boat seemed to stick fast fore and aft."[15]

Young's commandos streamed onto the beach and piled aboard. Scrambling down the gully, the lance corporal in charge of the 3-inch mortar tripped a mine. He was moving so fast the blast failed to tear away his foot, but fragments lacerated his ankle. Hobbling onto the beach, he hastily set up the 3-inch mortar there. Chucking out rounds, he covered the withdrawal of the rest until he ran out of ammunition. The mortar crew then dragged the weapon out to the boat.[16]

Its 126-pound weight rendered the R-Boat truly stuck. Buckee ordered the commandos to throw it and most of their guns overboard to lighten the load. Snipers were shooting downward from the cliffs into the boat. The coxswain cried out as a bullet pierced his leg. Other bullets tore through the overhead cover, and the fuel tank was holed eight times. Lewis realized the commandos "were fagged out" by the long run to the beach. He alternated between firing a rifle at the snipers and hauling exhausted men over the gunwale.[17] Three commandos remained on the beach covering the descent down the gully of Young and Ruxton, who had covered the retreat of the others. Buckee started cursing at the three to get aboard.

Young, Ruxton, and the Bren gunner dashed into the water, grabbing hold of lines cast out behind the retreating R-Boat. Three hundred yards from shore, Buckee paused so they could be dragged aboard. Bullets showered around the boat, but few struck home. Someone grabbed the Bren gun and fired at the cliffs. Ruxton fetched up a rifle and joined in. The gun battery punched out shells "still at a slow rate and wide."[18] LCP15 gunned away, streaming covering smoke. Lewis was amazed that they had recovered "every man we put ashore."[19] The R-Boat joined ML346, and the two craft made for Newhaven. It was 0820 hours. No further sounds of fighting came from Yellow 1 Beach.[20] Major Young and Lieutenant Buckee were both awarded the Distinguished Service Order. Although unable to silence the coastal battery, the attack by Young's intrepid band threw the battery's garrison into disarray, and for the duration of the raid the battery fired only occasionally and without effect.

HAVING FOUGHT THEIR way into Petit Berneval by 0700 hours, the commandos from Yellow 1 Beach had been halted by the arrival of 3rd Company of 570th Infantry Regiment. More Germans, consisting of the division's Cyclist Squadron and 302nd Engineer Battalion's 3rd Company, were rapidly closing from the south. The engineers were in trucks and under orders to "overthrow enemy landed near Berneval."[21]

The commandos quickly broke into small groups to escape the intense fire, and Captain Geoffrey Osmond realized they would never reach the battery. Withdrawing to the beach was the only option.

Machine-gun fire pinned nineteen-year-old American ranger Lieutenant Edwin Loustalot and a small clutch of commandos close to the path leading to the beach. The German gun covered a wide field between the commandos and the path. To escape, the gun must be silenced. Standing, Loustalot signalled the commandos to follow him. He charged the gun, binoculars slung around his neck bouncing wildly. Several commandos followed, firing from the hip. Suddenly, a long burst slammed into Loustalot, and he dropped. Two more commandos also fell dead or wounded. But the commandos' fire caused the German gun to quiet abruptly.

When one commando checked Loustalot, he found the man's midsection drenched in blood, the binoculars smashed by bullets, and the officer clearly dead. Loustalot was the first American soldier killed in the European land war. The commandos ran for the gully.

Ranger Walter Bresnahan hesitated, dropping to a knee beside the fallen officer. Then a fresh rattle of German gunfire nearby sent him scurrying for the beach.

Two rangers, Private Edwin Furru and Sergeant Albert Jacobson, encountered each other descending the gully. Twenty feet short of the beach they paused and shared a cigarette, then walked out onto the gravel and saw three stranded R-Boats. The two Americans ran for the cover of a cave in the cliff face. About a dozen men already hunkered in its cover, staring seaward and hoping for the arrival of the other two boats. It was about 0800. There would be no rescue.[22]

An hour earlier, responding to a white Verey light that was the pre-arranged signal for withdrawal, Lieutenant Dennis Stephens had led the R-Boats in. It was low tide, and the boats weaved through a network of iron stakes driven into the seabed to create obstacles for any boat landing. LCP157 was first ashore, its crew finding only the two-man naval beach party, which had spent the last two hours "at the base of the cliff avoiding grenades which were lobbed over at them from the top of the cliff." A coastal gun battery shell had also punched into the cliff about forty feet above their heads and "covered them with debris."[23] Taking the two men aboard, LCP157 began backing away, only to be impaled on an iron stake. LCP1 attempted to help and grounded on the rocky beach. When the coxswain managed to wrest it free, he steered well out to sea. Meanwhile, LCP85 came alongside LCP157 to lift its crew and the beach party. German gunfire quickly set the abandoned boat on fire. The crew of LCP81, badly holed during the earlier sea battle, was also taken off and the boat was left to sink. Exposed by the ebbing tide from its earlier watery grave, LCP42 still held the bodies of Lieutenant Commander Corke and a couple of other naval personnel. After lingering offshore under fire until 0730 hours, Stephens assumed the commando force lost and headed the two remaining R-Boats for England.

Seeing the three lost boats, the commandos realized their situation was dire. With bayonets, they pinned a Union Jack—to have been raised over the captured gun battery—to the cliff face, hoping that naval forces offshore would come to investigate. Discovering that the beach party had left its wireless set behind, a commando tried raising friendly forces, but the set was hit by gunfire. To escape the German fire and grenades showering the beach, everyone crowded into small caves. Hundreds of Germans lined the cliff face, chucking grenades or shooting. Others could be heard descending the gully. When these were twenty yards from the beach, Captain Osmond ordered a surrender.[24] Some men tried to creep away along the beach, but the Germans had it covered with machine guns. Lieutenant W. Druce tried this and ended up hiding with about twenty-two men in a cave until a patrol found them at 1500 hours. Druce surrendered the group, some of whom were wounded.[25]

Thirteen of the 117 troops landed at Yellow 1 were killed in the fighting, another eleven were missing and believed dead, and six died later of wounds. The rest were taken prisoner. In addition to Lieutenant Loustalot, one other fatality was not a member of No. 3 Commando. This was French Sergeant S. Moutalier of No. 10 (Inter-Allied) Commando.[26] The only man to escape was Corporal Alexander Sinclair, who swam out to sea and was eventually rescued by a passing Allied ship.[27]

14

Smash and Grab

ABOARD HMS *Prince Albert*, No. 4 Commando's 252 men had by 0300 hours finished eating and making final preparations for the raid on Hess Battery, which stood to the southwest of Varengeville-sur-Mer. Thirty-four-year-old Major Derek Mills-Roberts, commanding the party bound for Orange 1 Beach, noted his men's "quiet concentration" as they readied ammunition, cleaned weapons, applied greasepaint to hands and faces, and donned the woollen caps this commando wore instead of helmets. The battle was expected to be short, so "it was all weapons and ammunition with no trimmings."[1] Just before boarding the landing craft, they crowded into the wardroom to hear Lieutenant Colonel Lord Lovat's final words. Disliking greasepaint, Lovat had the only unblackened face. He wore an old beloved sweater with his name stitched across it and comfortable corduroy pants. His favoured Winchester repeater sporting rifle—with which he was deadly accurate—was slung over a shoulder.[2]

They embarked, he said, on an "operation of prime importance." If the guns were not destroyed, "the battery would wreak havoc among the ships of the main convoy." Lovat reminded them that "the German soldier was not at his best at night, and that here lay our advantage in the first part of the operation."

Orange I Beach was a little sixty-yard-wide stretch directly below the headland on which the gun battery was situated about a half mile inland. After the briefing, Lovat took Mills-Roberts aside. "D'you think you'll find your crack in the cliffs, Derek?"

"Yes," Mills-Roberts replied. "No need to worry." Mills-Roberts was actually very worried about finding this small target in the dark.[3] He could only trust in the navigational skill of the boat commander, a man he trusted, Lieutenant Commander Hugh Mulleneux. Aboard MGB312, Mulleneux would guide the entire force to a point two miles off the coast. The LCMS would then split. Three landing craft carrying eighty-eight men under Mills-Roberts would head for Orange I behind Mulleneux. In four other LCMS, Lovat and 164 men would run into Orange II supported by Lieutenant Peter Scott's SGB9 (HMS *Grey Goose*). Orange II was larger—about three hundred yards wide. It lay just east of Quiberville, next to the River Saane's mouth. Lovat's force would advance along the river's eastern bank for about a mile before cutting cross-country a mile and a half to attack the battery from the south.

Five U.S. Rangers and two Free French commandos had joined No. 4 Commando. One French commando accompanied each party as a guide and translator. Two rangers were bound for Orange I, the other three Orange II. At 0330 hours, Corporal Frank Koons climbed into an LCM destined for Orange I. The soft-spoken Iowa native rechecked his weapons—rifle, 260 rounds, three No. 36 grenades, and a smoke grenade.[4]

The boats were loaded well beyond "stipulated weight" due to all the munitions—particularly mortar rounds—and explosives. Mills-Roberts worried that the davits might jam while lowering the LCMS, but the convoy was soon afloat and away. *Prince Albert* turned sharply about and made for England. All the LSIS were racing to gain harbour before dawn exposed them to the Luftwaffe.[5]

"The sea was a little choppy and it was very dark," Koons wrote. "We moved off at once and everything was so comfortable that I fell asleep...and dozed...till some spray...woke me up."[6] Mills-Roberts napped too until wakened by the sound of gunfire and tracer flash well off to the left. It was about 0350 hours, and he realized some part of the raiding force had been discovered.[7]

Almost dead ahead, a light flashed three times and again twenty seconds later. After five minutes, the light ceased, only to start up with rhythmic regularity five minutes later. Mulleneux realized the beam of light originated from the eighty-foot-high octagonal tower of Pointe d'Ailly Lighthouse, which perched on a headland 250 feet above the sea. Almost precisely midway between the Orange Beaches, the lighthouse provided an excellent navigational marker. Its silhouette was starkly visible through binoculars on clear nights to about five miles offshore.[8] A naval contingent of seventy-seven Germans manned the lighthouse, and nearby Hess Battery had an observation post connected by communications cable to the battery fire control centre. Having no direct seaward view, the guns were dependent on the observers near the lighthouse to provide firing coordinates.

Mills-Roberts, warily watching the lighthouse beam sweep the sea, observed that he and his men were "like thieves in an alley when the policeman shines his torch." He was grateful that the low-riding boats would be difficult to spot. As planned, at 0342 hours, the boats divided into two groups. "Good luck," Lovat whispered across the water to Mills-Roberts.[9]

Eight minutes later, the darkened silhouettes of three ships appeared between Lovat's group and shore. Lieutenant Scott had the small flotilla swerve hard to one side to avoid a meeting. They had chanced upon a coastal convoy, and Lovat realized the lighthouse beam had been turned on to help guide it. The convoy chugged past, the landing craft unseen.

Just before 0430, Lovat's group split again as an LCM carrying 'A' Troop under command of Lieutenant A.S.S. "Fairy" Veasey surged ahead. Suddenly, at 0443 hours, the lighthouse's beam went out and several star shells arced skyward. Surprise lost, Lovat shouted for the LCMS to make for the shore at full speed. Veasey's boat, meanwhile, set down precisely as dictated in Lovat's plan at 0450 hours. Almost immediately, three RAF fighter-bombers swept in from seaward and up the River Saane valley. German anti-aircraft and machine-gun positions around the beach opened fire, all their attention concentrated on the aircraft. This diversion was to buy the commandos a few more undiscovered minutes.[10]

LIEUTENANT VEASEY'S 'A' Troop raced across the beach and towards two concrete pillboxes overlooking the beach from a low cliff. They were to knock these out and then advance through woods in a direct line to close on the battery from the western flank. Veasey's commandos belted up to the cliff, and those in the lead slammed a couple of tubular scaling ladders in place. Surprise was complete. One pillbox proved unoccupied. The Germans in the other died without firing a shot. Preparing an all-round perimeter defence, Veasey's men were ready to cover the second flight of landing craft. Veasey sent Trooper William Finney to cut a nearby telegraph line connecting Quiberville to the hamlet of Ste. Marguerite just west of the lighthouse.[11] As Finney began climbing a pole, a German machine gun opened up. Clinging to the pole, ignoring the splinters being ripped from it by bullets, Finney calmly snipped the line with cutters. "Finney bore a charmed life and got down again uninjured," his Military Medal citation concluded.[12]

The second flight landed just three minutes behind Veasey's man. Machine-gun fire laced the beach. Most of the commandos hit the dirt in front of a great tangle of barbed wire that blocked passage up the river's eastern bank. Although most of the fire was passing well overhead, Lovat knew that would soon change. His men were "like herrings in a barrel." Suddenly, a mortar bomb killed a section of 'B' Troop.[13] A shell fragment struck its commander, Captain Gordon Webb, in the right shoulder, rendering the arm useless.[14] Shouldering his rifle, Webb gripped a pistol in his left hand.

Having ranged in perfectly with their first round, the mortar crew could have slaughtered Lovat's men. Instead, they went after the withdrawing LCMs. As these were fleeing at high speed and streaming smokescreens, chances of hitting one were slight. The wire barrier in front of Lovat was fifteen to twenty-five feet wide, and the commandos were too close now to use bangalore torpedoes to blast it apart without endangering themselves. Luckily, the mortar shell had catapulted the men into action. Those previously appointed to form wiring parties began throwing rabbit netting onto the wire to create a bridge. When the five-man wiring party was killed by machine-gun fire, six others took over. Everyone knew "it was better to go forward than to remain lying on the beach to be picked off by the mortar at leisure."

Men crossed the wire on the rabbit-netting bridge and moved rapidly inland under continuing heavy machine-gun fire coming from positions near Ste. Marguerite. Most of the fire remained high, and soon the commandos were sprinting up the river's edge. This was dead ground that the Germans could not fire on directly from their fixed positions. By 0435 hours, the sprinting commandos had crossed 1,600 yards of open, boggy country. Their time on the beach had been two minutes, but it had seemed much longer.

Lovat had known this hard run lay ahead and that it must be done quickly for the raid to succeed. So every day at Weymouth, No. 4 Commando had donned all their equipment and gone running before breakfast. Length and speed increased daily until they were "covering one mile at top speed."[15]

THE COMMANDOS BOUND for Orange 1 Beach were still headed for shore when a star shell rose from a semaphore tower next to the lighthouse. Major Mills-Roberts shouted for his LCM commander to head for the beach at top speed. Just three minutes behind schedule, at 0453 hours, the three craft touched down precisely where they were supposed to. Mills-Roberts jumped ashore without getting wet feet.[16] Corporal Koons was less fortunate. He went into hip-high water and waded forty yards to the beach.[17]

Two narrow gullies led to the top of the cliff. Mills-Roberts sent Lieutenant David Style with a subsection of 'C' Troop to see if the left one was passable. Style discovered it "was full of complicated wire in depth" about thirty-five yards in. Although he then found the right-hand gully similarly blocked, the wire here was not as thick. Still, it took two bangalore torpedoes to clear a path wide enough for men to pass through in single file. Mills-Roberts feared things were taking too long, but there was no recourse. The white chalk cliffs were too sheer to scale. It was the gully or nothing. If the torpedo explosions had been heard, it would have taken only a couple of Germans and a machine gun to prevent their exiting the gully. Fortunately, each time a torpedo detonated, its sound was masked by RAF fighters strafing the battery and lighthouse.

The plan was for Mills-Roberts to attack the battery head on and draw its defenders onto 'C' Troop. This would leave the guns exposed to capture and destruction by Lovat's larger force. To bring the battery under fire from a distance, 'C' Troop was heavily armed with a 2-inch mortar, a 3-inch mortar, a Boys anti-tank gun that fired a 14.3-millimetre armour-piercing round, several Bren guns, and two grenade-launching rifles. Moving up the sides of the gully, the commandos avoided the well-worn path in the centre. It was surely mined. Coming into Vasterival-sur-Mer, an area of luxurious seaside villas, Mills-Roberts ordered Style to take his section and clear the houses left of the road leading to the battery. Captain Robert Dawson's section did the same to the right.[18]

Although most villas proved deserted, an old Frenchman wearing nightclothes was spotted in a garden as Mills-Roberts passed by. When two commandos pointed their guns at him, a young girl asked flatly, "Are you going to shoot Papa?" After announcing that they were British soldiers, Mills-Roberts had the two commandos escort the old man to his house. It was 0540 hours, and the plan called for 'C' Troop to engage the battery no later than 0615. Lovat would then attack at 0628. Time was wasting.[19]

While 'C' Troop's main force made for the battery, a small subsection under Lieutenant E.L.K.A. Carr peeled off westward—its job was to protect 'C' Troop's right flank from the Germans at the lighthouse. They were also to locate and sever the communication cable linking the observation post to the battery.[20]

Mills-Roberts dashed with the mortar detachment, signallers, and his personal runners through a wood and paused on its fringe. Ahead, the battery fired a salvo. Mills-Roberts heard the gunnery commander shout a command. He could only assume the battery was firing on the main landing force. It was urgent to stop this. Spotting a small salient of woods extending towards the battery, Mills-Roberts led his men into it. They stopped in front of a barbed-wire obstacle that seemed to encircle the battery. Mills-Roberts decided he did not have to breach the obstacle. A runner was sent to tell Style and Dawson to finish clearing the villas and get "forward at once to prepare to open fire on the battery." At 0550 hours, twenty-five minutes early, 'C' Troop had everything ready except the mortars. These were still being carried into range. Mills-Roberts ordered the other heavy weapons to start firing from where he had positioned them around a large house alongside the road. Another Bren fired from scrub at the tip of the salient. Soon the 2-inch mortar arrived and started firing from a room inside the house. Its first round fell short, but the second struck a munitions magazine "and a blinding flash resulted, which silenced the guns at 0607 hours. [This action may have also coincided with Lieutenant Carr's cutting the communication line and effectively blinding the gunners.] At this point the battery was being engaged by small-arms fire and all efforts to fight the fire were heavily sniped. I ordered the Bren gun in the scrub patch... to fire bursts at the flames and I was sniping figures around the main conflagration." Mills-Roberts heard the cries of Germans caught in the terrific blast of the cordite and shells detonated by the mortar round. Signallers had managed to string a telephone line back to the beach, allowing Mills-Roberts to check with an observer posted there on whether the guns' rounds had struck any of the main landing force. The observer reported all shells had fallen harmlessly into the sea and well short of the vessels sailing towards Dieppe.

By now the 3-inch mortar was in action and firing a mix of explosive and smoke rounds. The blanketing smoke further confused the German defenders. Next to the battery guns stood a tower mounted with anti-aircraft guns that the Germans depressed to fire on the commandos. As 20-millimetre rounds sizzled into the salient, Mills-Roberts and his men slithered frantically to escape the line of fire. Gunner Thomas McDonough cracked off sixty rounds from the Boys gun in rapid succession, which finally silenced the anti-aircraft guns.[21]

Snipers were at work. The most deadly sniper was Corporal Richard Mann. Face and hands painted green to blend with foliage, Mann lay in low bush 150 yards from the battery and picked off several Germans with precise fire.[22]

Corporal Koons found a horse stable, "a splendid spot for sniping... I fired through a slit in the brick wall. I was standing up to do so and the wall gave me very good cover... I fired quite a number of rounds at any stray Germans who sometimes appeared and I am pretty sure I got one of them."[23]

The commandos held the initiative. Their fire—particularly that of the Bren gunners—silenced a light machine gun on the roof of a building next to the battery and two other machine-gun positions set behind the perimeter wire. But a lot of small-arms and mortar fire still came at them.[24]

Mills-Roberts was "desperately anxious to know how Lovat's main assault force were getting on." Attempts at wireless contact had proven fruitless. If no main attack had developed by 0630, his instructions were to assault the battery. Chances of success were slight. Although "we were getting away with it better than expected," 'C' Troop had casualties, and ammunition was running low. Suddenly, the mortar fire intensified. Mills-Roberts glanced at his watch. The second hand was approaching 0628, when a strafing run by cannon-firing fighters was scheduled. Two minutes after that, he would have to attack.[25]

AT 0605 HOURS, just thirty-five minutes after landing at Orange 11, Lovat's men reached the western edge of the woods that were to cover their approach on the coastal battery. A "heavy volume of small arms fire" told Lovat that Mills-Roberts was heavily engaged. Then a sudden, terrific series of explosions was heard, and he knew a devastating hit had been scored on the battery's munitions. When the 3-inch mortar's "heavy crump" joined the chorus, Lovat's spirits soared.[26]

The commandos found the wood "exceedingly thick and dense." All the countryside seemed more thickly wooded than indicated by the aerial photos, maps, or scale models. But that was fine. It provided "numerous covering lines of approach to enable trained men to do their evil stuff."[27]

Lovat's force split inside the wood to carry out a pincer assault. Captain Webb's 'B' Troop approached from the left and 'F' Troop, under Captain Roger Pettiward, the right. Lovat, meanwhile, advanced his headquarters through the wood to an orchard edged up against the battery's wire perimeter. The signallers immediately set up and contacted Mills-Roberts, who "gave a heartening situation report." Lieutenant Veasey's 'A' Troop were contacted next. Veasey's troops "were covering the western flank of the battery"; they had put a second flak tower out of action and eliminated several defensive positions behind the wire. Having arrived at the battery perimeter just after first light, they had since inflicted heavy casualties on the gunners "and subsequently during attempts by the gun crews to beat out the flames started by [the] mortar bomb. Some of the men were using a house that provided a vantage into the battery perimeter for cover."[28]

Pettiward's men, meanwhile, surprised a platoon of about thirty-five infantrymen next to a farmhouse, who were being organized by an officer "for what was clearly to be a counterattack on Mills-Roberts." 'F' Troop killed these Germans with point-blank fire.[29] At 0610 hours, 'B' Troop's Webb reported having exited the wood and "worked forward across orchards and small enclosures" to a final assault position. Bangalore torpedoes ferreted into the wire were ready to ignite at Lovat's signal. A minute later, 'F' Troop reported ready. They had been under accurate fire from a sniper on the flak tower, but Gunner McDonough had silenced that threat. More snipers—including the battery commander—fired from windows of the battery headquarters and other buildings to their left.

Precisely at 0628, a dozen Spitfires of 129 Squadron careened in with guns firing. But they were also dodging several German Focke-Wulfe 190 fighters attacking from above, so their fire was erratic. A burst slammed the house being used by 'A' Troop, and one of the commandos was seriously wounded. The 3-inch mortar, which 'C' Troop had been firing, chucked out ten smoke rounds, and then its crew shut down for fear of hitting Lovat's assaulting force. As soon as the mortar quit, Lovat checked his watch—0630 hours. He signalled the attack by firing three Verey lights.[30]

THE VEREY LIGHTS appeared none too soon for Mills-Roberts, who wanted to get on with his next task. All No. 4 Commando was to evacuate from Yellow 1. 'C' Troop was to establish a defensive line around the gully and cover the withdrawal of the others. Just as Mills-Roberts ordered his men to start falling back on the gully, an 80-millimetre mortar found the range. One round exploded in a tree

Mills-Roberts was standing under, and a large branch crashed down beside him. Private William Owen Garthwaite, the troop's medical orderly, was killed. Lieutenant David Style suffered a bad leg wound but continued leading his section. This included the 2-inch-mortar crew and the Bren gunners, who kept the forward German positions under fire to prevent their disrupting 'C' Troop's withdrawal.

Once everyone passed Style's men, they fell back as well. With most of 'C' Troop concentrated around the entrance to the gully, Mills-Roberts sent a patrol forward to secure the road running from it to the battery. Except for a few snipers, it was found to be clear and so could be used to bring out No. 4 Commando's wounded. Accompanied by his runner, Mills-Roberts walked up the road towards the battery to personally contact Lovat.[31]

'B' AND 'F' Troops charged the battery at 0615 hours with bayonets fixed. "It was a stupendous charge," Lovat wrote, "in many cases over ground swept by machine-gun fire, through a barbed wire entanglement, over running strong points and finally ending on the gun sites themselves."[32]

'F' Troop went in "yelling like banshees." 'B' Troop came on just seconds later, Captain Webb running with a pistol in his left hand and right arm flapping uselessly. "Razor sharp, Sheffield steel tore the guts out of Varengeville battery," Lieutenant Donald Gilchrist wrote. "Screams, smoke, the smell of burning cordite. Mad moments soon over." A commando in 'B' Troop fell wounded, and the German who shot him dashed out of a barn, jumped up, and crashed his boots down upon the commando's face. Gilchrist and three others raised their weapons, but a corporal signalled them to hold fire, aimed his rifle and squeezed the trigger. The German fell, clutching his stomach "as if trying to claw the bullet out. He tried to scream, but couldn't. Four pairs of eyes in faces blackened for action stared at his suffering. They were eyes of stone. No gloating, no pity for an enemy who knew no code and had no compassion. We doubled across the yard to where the two wounded lay side by side. For our comrade—morphine. For the beast—a bayonet thrust."[33]

'F' Troop charged straight into fierce fire that toppled several men. A grenade killed Pettiward, and Lieutenant John Alexander

Macdonald, the troop's other officer, was mortally wounded. Captain Pat Porteous, a liaison officer, rushed to steady the men and keep them advancing. A slug tore through his right hand and arm. Seeing the German who had shot him, Porteous switched his pistol to his left hand and fired a fatal bullet. Nearby, Sergeant Major Bill Stockdale was down with part of a foot blown away by a grenade. Porteous rushed a German closing on the sergeant, wrestled his rifle away, and stabbed him to death with its fixed bayonet. Rallying 'F' Troop's survivors, Porteous led them in a charge that secured the battery's guns. Shot through the thigh, he fell, bleeding heavily beside one gun. Struggling to his feet, Porteous retained command until all enemy resistance in the battery ended. As several commandos started rigging the guns with explosives, Porteous, bleeding heavily, finally fell unconscious.

Porteous would be awarded a Victoria Cross for his "brilliant leadership and tenacious devotion to duty." He dismissed it all as "just luck."[34]

There had been much luck in No. 4 Commando's assault. But there had also been fighting skill and the ability to precisely implement a simple tactical plan. Lovat had seen the task clearly. "In and out—smash and grab," he described it. That's exactly how the raid played out. Two hours after the initial landing, five coastal guns were blown, "charges being placed to destroy both breach blocks and barrels." But there were supposed to be six guns. Finally, Lance Corporal J.C. Skerry found the sixth in a position well off from the rest. Stuffing the barrel and breach with plastic explosive, he blew the gun.[35] Sergeant Jimmy McKay had seen to stuffing charges into the other five gun barrels. "They fit like a glove—just like a glove," he told Gilchrist.[36]

At about 0715, the "subterranean stores and ammunition dumps were blown sky high... The gun sites were in a remarkable state. Burnt and mangled bodies were piled behind two of the sandbag dugout works which surrounded the guns... Many Germans had been badly burnt when the cordite had been set alight in the early stages of the operation."[37] The commandos gathered their dead comrades and laid them beside the "now useless guns... Before they left, the Union Jack was run up over the British dead."[38]

The commandos started withdrawing as soon as Mills-Roberts told Lovat the road was open. Stretcher cases were carried out with the walking wounded in company. There being too few stretchers, some men were put on doors torn from hinges. Four German prisoners were put to carrying stretchers. Before the commandos left, all buildings inside the battery perimeter were set on fire. The buildings had also been rifled for documents that might provide useful intelligence.

As Mills-Roberts approached the gully, he was intercepted by the old Frenchman, whose nightdress had been exchanged for a black coat and striped trousers. He offered a glass of red wine, but Mills-Roberts refused for lack of time. Apologizing for his men having trampled the garden, Mills-Roberts carried on.[39]

Corporal Frank Koons also encountered French civilians during the withdrawal. Having volunteered for the rearguard, he had been falling back from one hedge to another while watching for pursuing Germans, when several civilians approached. On learning he was an American, several "grabbed hold of me and shook me by the hand." A man said there were ten Germans covering the road to the gully. Koons and the commandos with him went back carefully but found these Germans had already been killed. Koons looked on his first German corpse, "lying on the road. He looked a strong healthy lad about 22 years old and had been killed by the bursting of one of his own grenades."

Koons was in awe of the commandos. "The English," he wrote, "are very calm and quiet." When he reached the beach, the landing craft waited. Tide out, they stood off to avoid grounding on rocks. Koons and some other commandos located a small French rowboat and put a few of the wounded aboard. The men then wrestled it over rocks and floated the wounded to MGB312. Koons climbed aboard. As the boat headed for Newhaven, he "had the wonderful experience of watching dog-fighting between Spitfires and Messerschmitts fought at a height of not more than 700 or 800 feet."[40]

No. 4 Commando's losses totalled forty-five, of which two officers and ten other ranks were killed. Three officers and seventeen other ranks were wounded and successfully evacuated. Another thirteen men were missing, having been left behind. Included in this tally were the commandos struck on Orange 11 by the German mortar fire and left behind because they were too badly wounded to endure the hard march to reach the battery on schedule. Despite being unwounded, medical orderly Private Jim Pasquale had stayed with these men. All five U.S. Rangers and two French commandos came through unscathed.

Aboard MGB312, Lovat had Lieutenant Commander Mulleneux intercept the main fleet so he could personally report to Major General Ham Roberts aboard *Calpe*. When Roberts did not come out on deck for a personal briefing, someone told Lovat via loudhailer that his commandos "might as well go home."[41] Some of the more seriously wounded were transferred from MGB312 to HMS *Fernie*.[42] At 0850 hours, Lovat sent a signal to Mountbatten at Uxbridge. Claiming to have been met by resistance from about 250 Germans, Lovat ended the message, "Every one of gun crews finished with bayonet. OK by you?"

The German defenders actually numbered no more than 112 men and perhaps as few as 93 (German records differ). Losses were about 30 killed and another 30 wounded, a proportion that, as the Canadian Army historian noted, "reflects the use of the bayonet."[43] The point of the operation, of course, had been to destroy the coastal guns rather than inflicting German casualties. "In this very brilliant affair," as one army commentator wrote, No. 4 Commando carried out an attack that was "a model of bold action and successful synchronization."[44]

For their parts, Lovat received a DSO and Mills-Roberts a Military Cross. When the commandos reached Newhaven, hundreds of civilians were waiting on the docks. All the soldiers had been soaked to the armpits gaining the landing craft, and uniforms were still wet. Faces were streaked with war paint, sweat, and powder burns. Lovat had lost his woollen cap. He stood on the dock, sporting rifle casually slung over a shoulder, chatting with the men. Mobile canteens doled out hot tea and cigarettes, while the sergeants took the roll and a final accounting of losses for the adjutant. A lot of press hung about seeking a telling quote. Special Service Brigade commander Brigadier Bob Laycock, mouth slightly covered by one hand, quietly warned Lovat, "Go easy with the press. The Canadians have taken losses."[45]

15

The Real Thing

A T NO. 11 Fighter Group Headquarters in Uxbridge, Air Vice-Marshal Trafford Leigh-Mallory had set the raid's complex air support program in motion at 0303 hours.[1] With eight hundred aircraft, Leigh-Mallory had to maintain a continuous blanket of protective cover over the navy and army forces for the raid's duration. Simultaneously, attacks were required against the coastal gun batteries. These five batteries were code-named Hess (behind Orange 1), Goebbels (at Berneval), Rommel (inland of Blue Beach), Hitler (on the high ground next to the River Arques behind Dieppe), and Goering (southwest of Dieppe). Also prime targets were the two fortified headlands on either side of Dieppe—Bismarck to the east and Hindenburg to the west. These headlands were to be regularly bombed or wreathed in smoke to blind the defenders. Tactical reconnaissance planes, meanwhile, would fly deep inland to keep "close watch on the movements of the enemy in order to discover any attempt to reinforce the garrison of Dieppe by land." During the night, as the fleet had closed on the French coast, RAF Coastal Command patrolled the channel for signs of German surface vessels—but had failed to detect the convoy that ran into Group 5 to such disastrous effect.[2]

Most of Leigh-Mallory's aircraft were fighters drawn from fifty-six squadrons. Fifty provided the covering force. Forty-six of these flew Spitfires, four American P-51 Mustangs, and the other six Hurricanes.

There were also four bomber squadrons. Two were equipped with Bostons—light two-engine bombers with a two-thousand-pound bomb load capacity—and the others with Hurricane fighters converted to a bombing role. Three squadrons of smoke-laying Blenheim bombers were available, either carrying smoke bombs or fitted with sci (Smoke Curtain Installation) aerial spray tanks that spewed out smoke in the manner of a crop-duster. Typhoon fighter-bombers from four Army Co-Operation Force squadrons also supported the raid.[3]

A detailed mission schedule had been set in place, but it was not inflexible. Leigh-Mallory realized the normal chaos of battle would require rapid responses to unforeseen emergencies. Aboard *Calpe* and *Fernie*, RAF personnel maintained continuous wireless links to Uxbridge. Under Commodore Adrian Cole's direction, RAF controllers could communicate with both Uxbridge and the planes directly overhead. The flight leader of the lowest-altitude fighter squadron in the covering force was in wireless contact with RAF controller Acting Squadron Leader James Humphreys Sprott on *Fernie*, who could vector fighters against any threatening German aircraft. Flight Lieutenant Gerald Le Blount Kidd on *Calpe* would link up with the close-support fighters and fighter-bombers as they appeared over the coast. If a target other than their assigned one presented itself, he would redirect them to it. *Calpe* was also linked to Uxbridge, and either Major General Roberts or Captain Hughes-Hallett could at any time request additional fighter or bomber support.

The system would prove its worth. Although pilots of close-support missions were well briefed on their target types and locations, the controller on *Calpe* was often required to help direct them. And in the fury of the dogfights that began raging over the fleet immediately after dawn, it was "the running commentary given by the controller" in *Fernie* that helped covering fighters engage enemy aircraft. "There was no doubt that this local control was largely responsible for the high percentage of interceptions made on enemy aircraft," Leigh-Mallory wrote, "thus greatly minimizing the effectiveness of enemy air strikes on ships and troops."

Just before midnight on August 18–19, Uxbridge Headquarters came alive with RAF personnel. Dozens of signallers manned the elaborate communications system. Plotters hovered over an immense map dominating the centre of the room, quietly shifting pins and markers that designated aircraft, ship, and army unit locations to accord with the latest information streaming in. German dispositions were also plotted. A couple of hours before dawn, Mountbatten and Lieutenant General Harry Crerar joined Leigh-Mallory. Little more than spectators, Crerar and Mountbatten exuded cheerful confidence. Leigh-Mallory remained "grim, barely speaking and rarely smiling." Safeguarding the army and naval forces from air attack weighed heavily.[4]

Across southern England, pilots and crews mustered in the dark at twenty-three bases. Men pulled on clothes intended to keep them warm and comfortable in tight cockpits—roll-neck or pullover sweaters and silk scarves or collarless shirts to prevent neck chafing due to the constant swivelling of heads. Breakfast was special, at least one egg served alongside the normal toast and preserves. In the flying huts, they donned boots, Mae Wests, goggles, gloves, and soft leather helmets.

It was a cold morning, with the coastal bases wrapped in a lingering ground fog. But inland it was clear. Some squadrons reported stars overhead.[5] Although all squadrons were mustered, some would not sortie for hours. Leigh-Mallory's plan called for a slow rollout that corresponded with the increasing visibility and the raid's escalation.

The first planes to arrive over Dieppe were Spitfires from Squadrons 65 and 111. Taking off in darkness at 0420 and 0415 respectively, they arrived over Dieppe at 0445. Scheduled to arrive at the same time were six Bostons, two each from three squadrons. They were to attack the Hitler and Goering batteries. Although one Boston was forced to abort because of landing gear failing to retract, the others appeared at 0459 hours. Each released two 500-pound and sixteen 40-pound bombs on either battery. Light was too poor to truly measure the effect, but several large explosions were noted that might have resulted from exploding munitions.[6]

SPITFIRES SUDDENLY APPEARING over the coast, followed by the bomber attacks on the batteries, erased any doubts the Germans might have had that they were under attack. But the nature of the attack remained unclear. At 0430 hours, the Dieppe signal station reported to the port commander hearing "motor sounds" just off the coast. Still expecting the convoy from Boulogne, the port commander thought this was the likely source. Five minutes later, the harbour-protection boat west of Dieppe's harbour mouth reported "unknown vessels approaching Pourville" and flashed a challenge. When the ships failed to respond, alert rockets were fired to warn coastal defence units.

Two other harbour-protection boats stood off Dieppe along with a tugboat waiting to meet the convoy. All four boats reported sighting destroyers and other vessels about one and a half nautical miles from the coast. The German vessels prudently ran for Dieppe's inner harbour. As the tug steamed in, the pilot signalled that many landing craft were steering towards beaches on either side of the moles sheltering the harbour mouth. At 0450 hours, he signalled that two landing craft "burst into flame on the beach of Pourville." Seconds later, smoke smothered the coast, and the pilot's view was obscured. At 0500, the signal station signalled that "enemy forces were probably attempting to land at Pourville." The port commandant had already ordered all naval personnel to move to assigned battle stations, and they were soon ready for action.[7]

AS THE SOUTH Saskatchewan Regiment's twelve landing craft closed on Pourville at 0450, Captain G.B. "Buck" Buchanan saw "lights shining in some windows and smoke curling from a few chimneys. We thought how peaceful it was and how soon we would disturb this quiet seaside town by rifle and gunfire." If not for the "grim and determined look on these prairie lads' faces," they might have been on just another exercise. "But this was the real thing and we all knew it."[8]

Aboard an LCA, Private Victor Story saw an anti-aircraft gun on the eastern headland firing at low-flying fighters. The plane engines were loud, masking the quieter boat motors.[9]

Having lost 17 wounded by the earlier grenade explosion, the battalion was 506 strong, and 'C' Company had 93 men compared to the 110 in the other companies. Another 30 men formed a special force under Lieutenant Les England, and the first-aid contingent numbered about 20. On the right flank, Major Claude Orme's 'C'

Company would seize the western headland. Pourville was to be secured by Major Elmer "Lefty" White's 'B' Company. Once the village was taken, White would advance men two thousand yards inland to eliminate a strongpoint west of the River Scie. The radar station and eastern headland—including two batteries, a searchlight tower, and a battery of light anti-aircraft guns—were the objectives of Captain Murray Osten's 'A' Company. Flight Sergeant Jack Nissenthall, field security Sergeant Roy Hawkins, and ten 'A' Company minders would then carry out the special intelligence mission. 'D' Company, under Major Mac MacTavish, would advance alongside the eastern headland to capture Quatre Vents Farm and silence a nearby field artillery battery. England's special force was to take out a German strongpoint carved seventy-five feet up the eastern headland's face, which covered the intersection of two roads at its base. One of these roads ran east over the headland to Dieppe, the other up the Scie valley to the airfield and the divisional headquarters mistakenly believed to be located at Arques-la-Bataille. Eliminating this strongpoint and capturing Quatre Vents Farm would open the way for the Queen's Own Cameron Highlanders to advance to the airfield and headquarters.

According to plan, 'A' and 'D' Companies, along with the special force, were to land east of the river mouth and the other two companies to its west. Lieutenant Colonel Cecil Merritt's battalion headquarters would also land to the west and set up inside the village.[10]

The LCA carrying the special force was just yards from the beach when a light machine gun opened up to the left. More machine guns fired over the wire entanglement topping the seawall as the boat grounded. Sergeant W.A. Richardson's No. 3 Section waited impatiently at the back of the LCA for the first two sections and Lieutenant English to clear off. Then Richardson led a dash up the beach to where the entire force pressed hard against the seawall for cover.[11]

Second-in-command of No. 1 Section, Sergeant R.K. Kerr, saw that the machine guns were concentrating on the landing craft. In the gloomy pre-dawn darkness, the Germans seemed not to have seen the men unload. Kerr noted his men "were lightly nervous."[12]

Not everyone got ashore. The LCM carrying twenty-five headquarters men and a Bren carrier loaded with wireless equipment was five minutes later than the rest reaching the beach. When its ramp dropped, Captain N.A. Adams and ten men raced to the seawall. The Bren carrier and a cluster of bicycles prevented the other men from getting off. When the carrier driver edged forward, the vehicle stalled two feet short of the ramp. Sergeant R.A. Pollard tried to lead the men over the bicycles and carrier, but heavy machine-gun fire tore into the LCM, and several fell badly wounded. The LCM lurched clear of the beach and turned away. After attempting to land twice more, only to be met by withering fire, it withdrew and transferred the remaining Sasks aboard to the destroyer *Albrighton*.[13]

On Green Beach, Private T.J. Rands with 'D' Company's headquarters section was at first astonished by the quiet landing. But "as soon as we reached the wall hell seemed to open up. I was a bit scared."[14]

Most fire was still high, and the German gunners shot along predetermined fixed lines, with none of the guns able to sight along the seawall. They fired instead down the length of the promenade and adjacent road. This made the seawall a safe place, while going beyond would be deadly. There was also the need to get through the wire topping the wall, which Private Ernest Clarke noted with unease had barbs "about an inch long and ... curved like a fish hook."[15]

'A' Company's Sergeant Basil Smith got over the seawall by slithering through an unmanned pillbox firing slit, whose back door exited onto the promenade. Private L.R. Thrussell was close behind. Both men realized they would have died on the beach if the Germans had manned that pillbox.[16]

Lieutenant John Edmondson, 'D' Company's second-in-command, worried less about surmounting the seawall than the fact that the landing had been screwed up. All of 'A' and 'D' Companies had been landed west of the river. They now must cross it to reach objectives. Edmondson's men were getting enmeshed with 'B' Company, and cohesion was dissolving. No option but get over the damned wall, organize people, and find a river crossing. The wall varied in height from eight to ten feet. Edmondson's complaints during Isle of Wight training had eventually been heard, so there were scaling ladders. He yelled for one to be brought up. It duly appeared. "Wire cutters," he shouted. "Someone get up there and cut the wires." A wire cutter slapped into his hand. "Officers lead," Edmondson thought and climbed the ladder. Machine-gun slugs pinged the wire as he cut. Three rolls of concertina wire had to be cut away.[17]

Edmondson noted that the machine-gun fire traced an unwavering line, a constant eighteen inches high. "Just slide over the wall," he told the men below, "and then dash for the cover of the buildings." Edmondson slithered through the wire and ran to the buildings. In the semi-darkness, the situation in the village proved confused. Canadians, civilians, and Germans ran every which way. Frenchmen screamed at soldiers not to shoot, while the Canadians and Germans sought to engage each other. Coming face-to-face with a German, Edmondson squeezed his Sten's trigger and heard the dull thud of a misfire. Stunned, the German failed to raise his gun. Edmondson dodged behind a corner and tried again to fire. The Sten thudded uselessly. He chucked it away, picked up a dropped Lee-Enfield. After firing it to make sure the gun worked, Edmondson turned the corner to face the German. He was gone. The main street, which ran east to west through the village and included a bridge that crossed the river, was raked by machine-gun fire.[18]

EVERYWHERE, SOLDIERS WERE crossing the seawall and getting on with assigned missions. Passage was easier to the west. Lieutenant Leonard Kempton's No. 14 Platoon of 'C' Company crossed without incident and headed for a suspected motor transport works eight hundred yards inland, on the slope ascending the western headland. Kempton's men jogged through the village and into the countryside. Dawn light now illuminated the beach, but here a gloom was cast by the headland and the woods lining the road. Kempton feared that the darkness concealed Germans lying in ambush. Signalling his men to stay with Sergeant M. Lehman, Kempton ghosted forward alone to check the trees bordering the road ahead. Seeing the large building near and no Germans about, he returned and gathered the men for an advance. As they closed in, Kempton led one section in a charge that quickly secured the empty building. He then took several men to search a scatter of farm buildings on either side of the road. Sergeant Lehman was so impressed by Kempton's "wonderful leadership," he believed every man in the platoon would "follow him wherever he went."[19]

Although the Saskatchewan Regiment's officers prided themselves on leading from the front, Major Claude Orme was the most insistent on this point. Such leadership, he believed, steadied the men and ensured they did as Lehman thought No. 14 Platoon would. The rest of 'C' Company had been close behind Kempton's platoon with Orme's headquarters section, heading for a large hotel that faced the promenade at the village's western end. Sergeant H.E. Long led No. 13 Platoon around the hotel's left side and broke in the back door. A machine-gun crew firing on the beach from inside the building was quickly killed.

The hotel proved to be quarters for a large group of foreigners, many of them Belgians forced to work as slave labourers on the coastal defences. After calming these civilians down, 'C' Company advanced up the slope of the western headland, with Long's platoon leading. As Long crested the summit, a shot rang out and he fell wounded. The platoon sergeant froze uncertainly, and Corporal Guy Berthelot realized, "If we don't do something very soon we will all be dead." The platoon was "in a pretty compact bunch"; a single mortar round could kill them. Berthelot shouted to Private William Haggard: "We should advance. One section on the right and two sections on the left." Haggard nodded agreement. The two men quickly explained the idea to the platoon sergeant, who agreed to it, evidently relieved at their having assumed the responsibility for making decisions.

Haggard led the two leftward platoons while Corporal Scotty Mathieson guided the right-hand section in a loose hook towards the summit. Berthelot set up his Bren gun at the corner of a house to provide covering fire. On the other side of the crest, the road was bordered by low banks, with Germans manning gun pits on one side. Shots were traded without noticeable effect. When Berthelot came running up, he was stunned to see the formerly hesitant platoon sergeant standing in the centre of the road, "hollering at the boys to advance and charge the Germans in the pits. No one wanted to start out, so I took my Bren and shooting from the hip... advanced into the pit area, firing almost directly straight down in the pits as I went along. Soon after I started advancing... up comes Corporal Mathieson from the opposite side, firing his Tommy gun from the hip. A few of the boys then dashed in from both sides and threw hand grenades into the pits. In about 15 minutes, from the time I walked out with my Bren, we had about twenty dead Germans and 30 prisoners on our hands. Two men escorted the prisoners to [the main-street garage set up as battalion headquarters]."[20]

Lieutenant Ross MacIlveen's No. 15 Platoon, meanwhile, advanced to the transport building taken by No. 14 Platoon. MacIlveen's objective was a strongpoint on the cliff edge overlooking the beach. Rather than going straight at it, he had decided to hook through No. 14 Platoon and close from above and behind. Sweeping into the position, his men found it abandoned and in "a disused condition." 'C' Company held all its objectives and controlled the western headland. MacIlveen sent a signal back to Orme—now headquartered alongside No. 14 Platoon—reporting this. Down the slope facing Pourville stood a large white mansion that he then decided to clear. No. 15 Platoon met several Germans there, killing all but two, who surrendered. Had the Germans been organized, they could have offered a stiff fight. The building contained two medium machine guns and a 2-inch mortar with ten bombs. After firing off the ammunition and destroying the machine guns, MacIlveen saw that No. 13 Platoon was under fire from four snipers in nearby woods. He had a man "engage the enemy with the captured mortar. Their fire ceased and we destroyed the mortar." The two platoons then formed an all-round defensive position on top of the headland.[21]

ABOUT THIRTY MINUTES after the Sasks landed, Orme reported 'C' Company's success to battalion headquarters. Pourville had also fallen to 'B' Company. Wallace Reyburn, a *Montreal Standard* correspondent, left the headquarters to follow men clearing houses. At each house, Bren gunners and men with Stens covered it "for their companions to go in. They went forward and battered the door down with their rifle butts, kicked through windows at the side, and climbed in. It was the same stuff I'd seen them do times without number at deserted houses near their training camps in England. Now here they were doing it with a precision and thoroughness that looked as though they'd been clearing enemy houses ever since the war began."

On one such detail, Private Ernest Clarke tried advancing up a street heading inland, only to discover a machine gun firing up its length. His section worked forward via a series of narrower lanes. When one man set a slow-burning fire inside a house with an incendiary grenade, "several Frenchmen came out... dressed in blue denim shirts and trousers, and some carried what appeared to be lunches... They were rather panicky and ran gibbering and waving their hands above their heads... To our left was a house and on the veranda of the second storey appeared French women. These women were crying and they were quieted by the words of a French Canadian." Clarke's platoon assaulted "houses with heavy rifle and MG fire, supported by hand grenades. We went past [a] house, throwing a few more hand grenades, then down the road throwing grenades, [and] into the main street. As we went up the road a brick wall lined each side and a side road which was heavily defended with barbed wire joined this road... An enemy mortar was at the end of the road, but we fired on it and destroyed it. The Jerries seemed surprised and rather snivelling although several of the larger sullen looking creatures still had that arrogant look which made me want to pull the trigger."[22]

Reyburn returned to the garage and, from the cover of a vehicle bay, sized up Pourville: a typical small French resort. Holiday hotels and *pensions* lined the broad promenade. Behind that, Pourville stretched inland for three or four blocks—"a pleasant little spot, with red brick, grey stone, and wooden buildings, with white picket fences in front of the gardens." The headlands loomed on either side. Inland, the ground right of the river was hilly and terraced. Thick woods were interspersed by small hotels, a few mansions, and small cottages. The headland left of the river rose steeply.[23]

Resistance inside Pourville soon slackened to occasional sniping. But on the village's eastern flank, the situation remained deadly. Many buildings burned, and German mortars on the headland and at strongpoints guarding the road leading to Quatre Vents Farm hit the village with intense, accurate fire. Despite RAF smoke-laying planes and smoke shells fired by HMS *Albrighton* and other support ships, German observers on the headland were obviously still able to direct the mortars. Captain Buck Buchanan at battalion headquarters saw that much of the damage resulted from hidden 81-millimetre mortars and a light artillery field gun. Their fire made "the town echo with . . . continuous explosions."[24]

The battalion's second-in-command, Major Jim McRae, was forced to move the headquarters when the garage was heavily shelled. He set up again in one corner of the village's grassy main square, in the lee of several buildings. The signallers had just finished tuning in their wireless sets when a mortar round smacked into the middle of the square. Reyburn "caught a glimpse of a young officer who was standing up with his back to the explosion. Spurts of blood shot out from the front part of his neck and shoulder as the shell-splinters went right through him. He toppled forward into the arms of a companion." Spattered by pebbles, Reyburn thought nothing of it until an hour later, when he realized his trousers and shirt were damp. "It was a hot, sunny day, and at first I concluded it was merely perspiration. But it was blood, and those 'pebbles' had been shell fragments."[25]

Several men had been hit, including Regimental Sergeant Major Roger Strumm. Renowned for a thundering parade ground drill voice, the Great War veteran had suffered a severe leg wound from shrapnel. Lieutenant Colonel Merritt, who had been checking on the rifle companies, arrived several minutes after the explosion to find Strumm on a stretcher. He knelt and said, "I'm very sorry to see you hit, Mr. Strumm." Smiling broadly, the RSM replied, "They told me I was too old to go into action but I fooled them."[26]

McRae again relocated the headquarters, this time next to a swampy area that had been inundated when the Germans blew small dykes and dams controlling the flow of the River Scie.[27] He would move the headquarters six times in all. Captain Buchanan thought McRae "was gifted with a sixth sense. Every time we moved, the previous spot was bombed out."[28]

As casualties mounted and German fire pursued the headquarters doggedly from one place to another, battalion medical officer Captain Frank Hayter had to adapt his methods. Normally, the wounded would be kept at the Regimental Aid Post, but as this had to remain close to the headquarters, Hayter kept men there just as long as was required to treat their wounds. They were then either carried on stretchers or sent as walking wounded "to the beach... by the seawall which helped to protect them from enemy fire."[29]

THE LANDING OF 'A' and 'D' Companies on the wrong side of the river threw that Saskatchewan attack awry. Only Lieutenant Les England's special force had been set down correctly east of the river. Here Sergeant R.K. Kerr's No. 1 section used a scaling ladder to get up the seawall and then created a bridge across the thick wire tangle by throwing another ladder on top.[30] England led Nos. 1 and 2 sections towards a roadblock and abandoned pillbox about a hundred yards beyond the wall. As they closed in, a machine gun fired. Falling wounded, England shouted at Sergeant R.R. Neil to take over.[31]

Meanwhile, Sergeant W.A. Richardson had brought No. 3 section up on the left flank "under heavy fire from MG posts on the hill." Richardson heard England hand the force to Neil. Somebody had thrown out a smoke grenade, and under its covering veil Richardson jumped on top of the abandoned pillbox to try spotting the machine-gun positions. As the smoke cleared, he saw one about twenty-five yards distant and dug into a hole in the side of the bank. Instead of a Sten gun, Richardson carried a Thompson submachine gun. Standing on the pillbox, he loosed a long burst of .45-calibre that killed the gunners. Richardson then charged his section towards the face of the cliff to get under the fire of a second machine gun that "seemed to be high on the hill and to the right." At least one more machine gun was firing, and the lines of fire crossing in "the area of the pillbox and roadblock was very accurate. In this advance my section became split and presumably suffered casualties as I had now only two men with me, and on looking back could see two bodies [by the] pillbox."

As they reached the cliff face, one of his privates shouted a warning. "A grenade had been thrown from above... landing not more than 25 feet from us. We dropped flat." Richardson stared at the grenade. It was about eighteen inches long and two inches in diameter, and it had a wooden handle about eight inches long on one end. He had never seen a German stick grenade or been briefed on their existence. It seemed forever before it exploded; when it did, though, nobody was harmed. "As soon as it went off, another landed in the same spot. While waiting [for] its explosion I pulled a [No.] 36 [grenade] from my belt. As soon as [the stick grenade] exploded, I stood up and threw my 36 as high up the cliff as I could in the general area of the enemy grenadier. The 36 went off and as we were no longer interfered with, we crossed the road in hopes of finding the rest of the section." Finding only Sergeant Neil and another man, the little party moved inland until it came upon the other two special force sections pinned down by more machine-gun and sniper fire. The men spread out and returned fire. Although the range seemed to be about 550 yards, the German fire "was extremely accurate." Riddled by bullets, twenty-four-year-old Private Donald Daniel John Tyman of Regina fell dead, and another man was badly wounded. The special force had lost too many men to reach and eliminate the strongpoint. Richardson realized they would be lucky not to be wiped out but then observed that although the Germans were "good fighters at long range," they "showed no inclination to counterattack, although he seemed to be in a good position to cut [us] off... if he showed initiative and guts." This allowed the special force to tie in with some 'A' Company men when they arrived.[32]

ON THE WRONG side of the river, 'A' and 'D' Companies had surmounted the seawall and immediately confronted a single narrow bridge, about eighty feet long, that crossed the river just off the beach. Its eastern exit faced the headland. Both 'A' Company's Captain Murray Osten and 'D' Company's Major Mac MacTavish knew they must cross this bridge to gain assigned objectives. The main street, which was also the coastal highway, was under continuous machine-gun fire from a pillbox set alongside the road at the base of the eastern headland. Several other machine guns on the sloping headland also had the bridge zeroed in, as did heavy mortars.

Men from both companies dashed for the bridge. Private J. Krohn's section of 'D' Company's No. 16 Platoon came off the seawall, turned hard left, and belted onto the bridge. They were halfway across when machine guns caught them. The leading three men "made a mad dash for the other side," but Krohn hesitated when three men beside him fell wounded. "It was too late for us to be able to make the dash. One more boy fell right beside me, so I flattened out, rolled myself over the side, into the canal, at the same time dragging one of the boys with me. The bridge was under heavy fire by this time." More of 'D' Company slithered down the bank to the river; a 3-inch mortar dropping smoke rounds to the east provided some cover.[33]

Major Osten, meanwhile, had led some of 'A' Company across in another mad dash that left more dead and wounded scattered along the bridge's length. Sergeant Basil Smith and another section "came under very heavy [machine-gun] fire." More men fell, and the rest of his platoon slid down the riverbank and swam across.[34] Corporal H. McKenzie "had a tough time swimming the river, as my equipment dragged me down."[35]

The second-in-command, Lieutenant John Edmondson, had meanwhile set up 'D' Company's headquarters in a gas station 150 yards short of the bridge. Just as the wireless signallers settled, Edmondson noticed a Bren gunner firing at the pillbox across the river from behind an empty gas pump—a typical one, with a glass cylinder on top and a hand pump fixed to the side. Edmondson dashed out and took cover behind an adjacent pump. Acting as spotter, he gave the Bren man an estimated range. After each short burst, Edmondson called adjustments until the Bren gun fire was "peppering around the [pillbox's] machine-gun slot.

"That German machine gunner caught sight of us though, because bullets flew down both sides of us. We could see the sparks as the bullets hit the pavement." Suddenly the gun went silent, and Edmondson thought the Bren gunner's fire had perhaps struck home.[36]

The pillbox had actually fallen to thirty-two-year-old Private Charlie Sawden. Having crossed the bridge, he and a group of men under

'A' Company's Lieutenant C. Stiles were pinned down by the pillbox gun. A laconic farmer from Consul, Saskatchewan, Sawden turned to Corporal Charles Devlin and drawled, "If somebody will hold my rifle, I'll knock out those guys."[37] Stiles took the gun. Sawden stepped into the gunfire and "nonchalantly strolled up to the pillbox and tossed in two 36 grenades, wiping it out and killing four Jerries," Private Victor Story wrote later.[38] A bullet soon afterwards shattered Sawden's leg. He was carried to the beach after having the injury crudely splinted with bayonets. Sawden would die in the evacuation.

About half of 'D' Company and all that remained of 'A' Company had yet to cross the river. The bridge was strewn with wounded and dead. Edmondson decided the best way over was to string a line under the bridge by looping toggle ropes together. With the bridge concealing them, men could then pull themselves across in single file. He was busy working on this when Lieutenant Colonel Merritt showed up. "That's too slow," Merritt shouted. "Go across the top."

Edmondson hollered at Major Lefty White, headquartered in a large hotel on the north side of the road just beside the bridge, to cover his group with smoke rounds from 'B' Company's 2-inch mortar. White complied, and Edmondson led three men in a dash onto the bridge. Suddenly, Edmondson was lifted off his feet, hurled through a hedge, and thrown down an embankment to land on his side amid rocks next to the river. His legs were paralyzed, and blood streamed from a forehead gash. Two stretcher-bearers quickly dressed the minor scalp wound. Every time Edmondson tried to stand up, though, his legs failed. Merritt told the stretcher-bearers to evacuate him, but Edmondson called back that he would be okay.

Edmondson watched Merritt walk back towards the bridge. Helmet held in one hand, Merritt called out to the men hunkered on the wrong side. "Come on, fellows. There's no trouble here. They can't hit anything. Get across."[39] A clutch of men responded, dashing through the fire. Others stayed put. Captain H.B. Carswell, a 6th Field Regiment forward observation officer (FOO) who was to direct the guns of HMS *Albrighton* against German targets, saw Merritt lead "several parties across the bridge... which was swept by machine-gun, mortar and [field] gun fire continuously. He was constantly exposing himself. On many occasions he crossed over the bridge, urging his men forward and calling, 'See, there is no danger here.' The men followed him splendidly but were shot down time after time."[40]

Four times Merritt guided a party of men over. Once he was seen to "take off his hat and twirling it, for all the world like a boy with his school books, sauntered across the bridge calling back, 'Come on, boys, they can't hit a thing, come on, let's go and get 'em.'"[41]

By the time Merritt finished, Edmondson had regained mobility. He set up 'D' Company's new headquarters in a two-storey pub on the bridge's east side. Looking at the bridge, he saw the dead piled two deep.[42]

It was now 0550 hours, and Edmondson heard a strange sound from seaward. Curious, he ducked across to the seawall. Out on the water, a line of landing craft approached. Edmondson realized the noise was the skirl of bagpipes played by the Queen's Own Cameron Highlanders' pipers. The Sasks were about to be reinforced, Edmondson realized. He also knew that 'A' and 'D' Companies had failed to clear the headland and capture Quatre Vents Farm. The Camerons would land under the fire of German guns.[43]

16

Hell of a Fix

THE QUEEN'S OWN Cameron Highlanders had crossed the channel in R-Boats without incident. They were to land at 0520 hours. Lieutenant Colonel Al Gostling's gut told him the South Saskatchewan Regiment would be unable to seize both headlands in just thirty minutes. So he asked naval officer Commander H.V.P. McClintock to delay the landing ten minutes. After agreeing, McClintock made several critical errors. "Had we trusted to our dead reckoning and continued at a steady course and speed from our turn on to the last leg of the track laid down we would have made the correct beach about 10 minutes late, which was the time we were aiming for," he later admitted. "Unfortunately when we sighted the coast we thought we seemed rather close and made a reduction in speed... Later when we could see a bit more we thought that we were rather too far to the eastward and made an unnecessary alteration of course which we later had to correct."[1]

It was broad daylight as the R-Boats closed on the beach. Aboard one carrying a 'B' Company platoon that included Private G.L. Bird, "everybody was in the best of spirits, singing and joking." A thousand yards offshore, the Germans began firing from the eastern headland with machine guns, mortars, and light artillery.[2] Shells threw up spouts of water.[3] Gostling "was very cool and collected," explaining the different types of fire. "Listen to that, that's mobile artillery," he shouted.[4] Amid the explosions and firing guns, the Camerons heard also the skirl of pipes. 'B' Company's piper, Corporal Alec Graham, stood defiantly at one boat's bow. Company Sergeant Major George Gouk recognized "A Hundred Pipers," 'B' Company's march-past music. Then the boats grounded "on a gravel beach with shells bursting pretty close." Captain Norman Young leading, the men jumped off the bow.[5]

Touchdown was 0550 hours, twenty minutes later than Gostling had desired. The entire battalion was to have been put down east of the river but instead ended up scattered all along Green Beach. This left the Camerons divided by the river. The largest group, consisting of Major Norman Ross's 'A' Company, two 'B' Company platoons, most of the men in three 'C' Company platoons, and battalion second-in-command Major Andy Law's headquarters section, landed west of the river.[6]

Gostling's landing craft correctly landed east of the river but right next to the headland. As Gostling led the men off the boat, a burst of fire from a pillbox killed him instantly. Captain John Runcie, leading 'D' Company, saw Gostling fall—likely the first Cameron to die.[7] More men died in the dash for the seawall. They had been led to believe the beach was mostly sand and light gravel. Instead, Law encountered shingle "about the size of eggs and terrible to cross." The seawall, also reportedly only two to three feet high, presented an eight-foot-tall obstacle.[8]

The Camerons with Runcie "crowded in front of it, taking shelter from machine-gun and mortar fire coming from the left... The plan had been for 'A,' 'B,' and 'C' Companies... to cross the wall and assemble in a designated area beyond it; but 'B' and 'C' Companies had been pinned down by enemy fire and up to this time had not been able to cross the wall." Runcie conferred with 'B' Company's Captain Norman Young and 'C' Company commander Captain R.M. Campbell. The fire was coming from the eastern headland or positions close by. Nothing emanated from Pourville. Runcie said he would reconnoitre that way to see if they might advance from the village. Accompanied by his orderly, Runcie crawled along the seawall to the river. Spreading widely as it discharged into the sea, the river was little more than "a trickle."

On the western side of the river, Runcie found that Camerons here had already cleared the wall and entered the village. He sent his runner to tell Young and Campbell to bring everyone from the eastern side of the river to Pourville.[9]

Although 'A' Company had landed in good order west of the river, it had been held up by the wire entanglements on the seawall. Corporal J.S. Thomas's section required fifteen minutes to cut a path through the wire while under "considerable mortar fire" that intensified with each passing minute. The promenade was swept by machine-gun fire. Thomas saw that the pillbox at the base of the eastern headland enjoyed a clear field of fire along the promenade's entire length.[10]

Once through the wire, Major Ross led his men across the main road to the buildings bordering it. Seeing the bridge, he advanced 'A' Company towards it by working through backyards. Ross kept outrunning his troops. Puzzled, he turned to see them carefully climbing fences, ensuring gates were closed after passing, trying not to damage vegetable gardens. What the hell? They were acting like men on a training scheme in England, where a claims officer would follow close behind to compensate civilians for damaged property. Ross yelled, "This is war, fellows. No claims officer here. Get going." Men started ripping down fences and smashing anything that slowed their advance. As 'A' Company approached the bridge, Ross saw the corpses piled upon it and held up a halting hand. "We can't get across there," he told the company sergeant major. "If we're going to get to that airfield, we've got to go up this side of the river."[11]

EAST OF THE river, the Sasks were embroiled in fierce firefights and making little progress. Lieutenant Colonel Cecil Merritt seemed everywhere at once. After the fourth bridge crossing, he went forward and caught up to the special force stuck in front of the pillbox dug in on the slope of the headland above the roadblock. With him were Sergeant Basil Smith and Private Ernest Clarke of 'A' Company. "We have got to get the bastards out of here," Merritt shouted. Private L.R. Thrussell and some others "took all the smoke bombs we had and threw them between us and [the] pillbox and rushed immediately to dead ground between the pillbox and roadblock. We then crawled up nearer to the pillbox." With Thrussell providing covering fire, Merritt, Smith, and Clarke ran forward and "threw four grenades in the box."[12]

This opened the way for 'A' Company to advance up the headland towards the radar station. Down the slope from the radar station, the Sasks controlled a grey house. Two large villas stood between this house and the station. Lieutenant C. Stiles and a small group that included Private Victor Story attempted to fight through to the radar station "but found it impossible" because of fire from the villas. Stiles decided to clear the Germans out of them. "As we approached the houses," Story wrote, "Jerry opened fire on us with 81-millimetre mortar and we were very fortunate in getting away, having to withdraw and wait for reinforcements. Every now and then a few men would come up and finally we went back to the hedgerow near the grey house, and that's as far as we were able to advance."[13]

Sergeant Jack Nissenthall recognized that his intelligence-gathering mission was no longer feasible. Although Captain Murray Osten had arrived with twenty-five more 'A' Company men, they were still unable to make any progress. Nissenthall decided to creep around the back of the radar station. Although getting inside to discover its secrets was clearly impossible, perhaps he could force the operators to unwittingly reveal them. Armed with two grenades, his special tool kit, and a pistol, Nissenthall somehow managed to elude detection. Approaching the station from the rear, he cut a hole through the perimeter wire and then crossed fifty yards of open ground to reach a telephone pole. Until recently, cryptographers in England had regularly intercepted coded wireless signals sent from the radar stations. But these had recently ceased, and Nissenthall saw that the stations were now using land lines. Cut these and for at least a short interval, this station would have to revert to wireless communication. Some secrets might be revealed. The pole was fifteen feet high, and when Nissenthall climbed to the crossbar supporting eight different wires, he was exposed to German and Canadian fire from all directions.

Working fast, Nissenthall severed all eight lines, free-fell to the ground, and rolled downslope towards the Canadian position. Bullets spattered all around as he sprang to his feet and dashed to

'A' Company's lines. Nissenthall's efforts bore fruit. Moments after the lines were clipped, radar expert Ken Dearson, aboard HMS *Prince Albert*, picked up a radio message from the station. So did two operators in an intelligence listening station in Sussex. For several days the Germans failed to repair the lines, and a significant amount of intelligence on radar technology and procedures was gathered.[14]

While 'A' Company made its abortive attempt to take the radar station, Merritt had recrossed the bridge to check his battalion headquarters. Out front and personally leading his men, Merritt consistently left his signaller—dogging along under the thirty-two-pound No. 18 set—far behind. This meant that Merritt was "often out of touch with [battalion headquarters]," leaving Major Jim McRae to direct the battalion's overall operations.[15] McRae "controlled the movements of reinforcements as the battle shifted and as much as reception of the [No.] 18 sets would allow... throughout the whole morning. He was outstanding in his indifference to the heavy bombardments," one after-action report stated.[16]

Merritt had just crossed the bridge when he saw Captain Runcie of the Camerons come off the beach with about thirty men from 'D' Company and Captain R.M. Campbell's remnant of 'C' Company that had landed on the eastern side. Runcie was disgruntled. Rather than his runner returning with all the Camerons east of the river, he had rounded up only these men. Runcie's second-in-command, Lieutenant P. Jackson, reported that Captain Norman Young had advanced 'B' Company across the seawall and most of 'D' Company's platoon commanders had followed.[17]

Unable to raise anybody at battalion headquarters by wireless, Young had decided "we would carry on and do as much damage as possible," Company Sergeant Major George Gouk later explained. About a mile inland, they encountered a cluster of houses on the eastern slope overlooking the road. Every house was alive with snipers and machine guns. "So we got busy... and were doing a fairly good job cleaning them out with rifles and grenades when all of a sudden they opened up on us with their mortars... it sure was hell. Our casualties... started mounting then, every corner you turned you seemed to run into mortar fire and they sure could place their shots. Well there was no stopping the boys then, they were seeing their pals for the first time being killed and wounded at their side and the only thought that seemed to be in everyone's mind was to have revenge. It sure was great to see the boys with blood all over their faces and running from wounds in their arms and legs, not worrying about getting first aid but carrying on in a systematic manner, clearing out the 'Nazis' from the houses just the same way as they learned to do on the Isle of Wight," Gouk said.[18]

Young dashed about boldly, rallying his men and pointing out the enemy. Private Clarence Flemington confessed to being "kind of worried about all those bullets" flying around. The forty-one-year-old Young overheard and said the Germans "weren't very good shots during the last war and that he didn't think they had much practice since." Flemington decided to take "his word for it and keep going." Young was abruptly hit in the stomach by a machine-gun burst, and then mortar round shrapnel killed him. The advance sputtered out. The Camerons were down to little more than a dozen men.[19]

RUNCIE, MEANWHILE, HAD intercepted Merritt and asked whether he should cross the bridge to rejoin his company and push inland as planned. Merritt instead said the element of Camerons with Runcie and Campbell should come under his command and reinforce the Sasks across the river. Managing to raise Major Andy Law by wireless, Runcie advised him that Gostling was dead. This meant Law now commanded the regiment and needed to decide if Runcie should conform to Merritt's intention. Law immediately agreed he should. Campbell had suffered a severe facial wound on the beach that Runcie thought provided "ample justification for retiring to the RAP." Despite suffering "further painful wounds," Campbell doggedly refused. He remained "indefatigably active, setting a fine example to his men."[20]

Reinforced by these Camerons, Merritt returned to the fight across the river. Sergeant Pat McBride was among a group of Sasks pinned down by fire from a pillbox alongside the road that elements of 'D' Company had bypassed on their way to Quatre Vents Farm. Merritt arrived shouting, "We must get ahead lads. We need more men up front as quick as possible—who's coming with me?"

"We are all going with you," McBride growled.

"Good lads," Merritt said. "Let's go." The men ran up the road about forty yards and then went to ground again, until Merritt asked, "Are you ready again?"

They all answered, "Okay, sir," went right through to the pillbox, and silenced it.[21] Merritt then led the group towards Quatre Vents Farm and soon picked up the remnant of Captain Young's men. The strengthened force managed to eliminate a 120-millimetre mortar position. But Merritt realized that by now his force was too small to gain the farm and clear out the strong German positions there. The situation was rapidly deteriorating along the entire eastern flank. 'A' Company had stalled well short of the headland summit. It was over this summit that the battalions landed at Pourville were to advance through to Dieppe for withdrawal off the main beaches there. This route was unlikely to be forced open, and there was no sign of the Royal Hamilton Light Infantry coming in from Dieppe to link up with them.

Merritt decided that a last effort to break through via the headland must be made. He therefore ordered the men with him to withdraw and join 'A' Company. He also sent a runner to 'D' Company's headquarters at the pub alongside the bridge with instructions for Lieutenant John Edmondson to contact Major Mac MacTavish and order their attack on the farm broken off. Everyone was to concentrate on 'A' Company's position.

'D' Company was by now stuck on a slope leading up to the farm. "The interlocking line of German defences with wire, machine gun nests, snipers, mortar and artillery was too strong," Lieutenant John Edmondson learned. MacTavish was somewhere at the head of the company, and Edmondson had no wireless contact with him. Edmondson sent runners to pass him the word, but none of them ever returned. So Edmondson had no idea if MacTavish received the break-off order or not. Pourville, meanwhile, was now being hammered by increasingly heavy and accurate shellfire.

Edmondson, desperately wanting to hit back with fire of his own, asked artillery FOO Captain H.B. Carswell to have *Albrighton* fire its 4-inch guns on likely German gun positions. Carswell "refused because I could not pinpoint exactly where the forward line was. We had quite a heated argument. I said it could not matter less where the forward troops are because I know they are not within the danger area of the objective I want you to have shelled. But to no avail, the forward troops were to have no fire support."[22]

Although Edmondson was unaware of it, Carswell had been attempting to support the forward troops but was unable to accurately spot any artillery or heavy mortar positions against which to direct *Albrighton*'s guns. Carswell thought most of the fire plaguing 'A' and 'D' Companies came from a point on the headland close to the coast and midway between Dieppe and Pourville. Three times Carswell arranged for *Albrighton* to hit this area with indirect fire but was unable to see any effect. "He also indicated targets on the cliff between Dieppe and Green Beach for direct bombardment," the destroyer's captain later reported, "and I think [the] ship silenced the fire of one light gun position. The ship could not remain stationary long as the enemy gunners soon started getting close."

Carswell was also plagued by German retaliatory fire. Whenever his wireless went live to direct fire, the FOO was targeted by extremely accurate mortar fire that forced him to shut down and run for a new position. It was during one such relocation that Carswell and Edmondson argued. The simple fact was that the raiding plan contained a basic flaw that Carswell could not rectify. No provision for land-based artillery or any other kind of heavy support had been made for the battalions landing on the flanks at either Green or Blue Beach. "The only artillery available to support the troops ashore was that of the destroyers," the Canadian Army historian later wrote, "and in these circumstances it could not be effective."[23] Carswell also had no ability to call in air support, nor was anybody else ashore able to directly request that the RAF carry out bombing or strafing runs against specific targets. All calls for such support had to be routed through *Calpe* or *Fernie* for transmission to Uxbridge for action—resulting in delays that, even when the support was given, often came too late to be of assistance.

THE "VERY HEAVY fire, chiefly from mortars," striking Pourville shocked the Camerons. "This fire," Major Law noted, "was extremely accurate and it was necessary to move wireless sets after sending one or two messages, as they always became targets." Yet "while the blast effect of the German mortar-bombs was considerable, the splinter effect [spray of shrapnel] was much less, and bombs burst close to some of our men without injuring them."[24]

When Major Ross arrived at the headquarters, he quickly briefed Law on the impossibility of advancing inland through Quatre Vents Farm and proposed advancing 'A' Company up the right side of the river to Petit Appeville and forcing a crossing over the bridges there to attack the airfield. Law said he would follow with the battalion headquarters and every other Cameron he could round up. Once across the river, they could push on to the Bois des Vertus.[25] This was a small wood next to the airfield, where they were supposed to link up at about 0630 hours with a Calgary regiment squadron of tanks coming from Dieppe. The combined force would then overrun the airfield and push on to the suspected German headquarters at Arques-la-Bataille.[26]

Law had no idea whether the tanks had reached the woods on schedule or would wait for the badly delayed Camerons. The battalion set off at 0700 hours, with 'A' Company on point.[27] Ross moved while Law was still rushing to get more Camerons following. Having passed Captain Runcie's group to Merritt's command, he scrounged up only Nos. 10 and 11 Platoons from 'B' Company, under command of Captain E.R. "Tommy" Thompson; most of three 'C' Company platoons; and his battalion headquarters group. As the Camerons' 3-inch mortars had all been destroyed by shellfire, there were no heavy weapons.[28]

Ross started up a road bordering the river, only to immediately come under machine-gun fire from Quatre Vents Farm, and the mortars pummelling Pourville quickly shifted to the Camerons. Having anticipated this would happen, Ross kept to the road only as long as it took to reach the woods behind the village. Slipping into the cover of the trees, he advanced along a rough road leading to Brenouvelle Farm. Lieutenant W.S.M. Lang's No. 7 Platoon was on 'A' Company's point, and in short order the Camerons had covered about four thousand yards to close on the farm. Lang's platoon had already passed by when two Germans burst out from one of the buildings, and the trailing No. 8 Platoon fired so rapidly that Ross figured "every man could claim a hit." Hooking left onto a track that led a thousand yards to the Petit Appeville crossing, 'A' Company kept moving quickly. There were two bridges here, one for the road and the other the railway.[29]

Coming out of the wood, Ross saw the two bridges and deployed his men on a height of ground to the right. With 'A' Company covering, the elements of 'B' and 'C' Companies descended through a draw towards the hamlet and bridges. Law set the battalion headquarters on ground closely overlooking the bridges. A few hundred yards east of the river lay Bois des Vertus, and Law saw no sign of tanks there. All he could see were Germans, particularly a bicycle platoon heading towards the coast. It was 0900 hours. Law decided he could forget about getting tank support. His Camerons were too few to fight through to the airfield, but they might be able to cross the river and strike Quatre Vents Farm from the rear. Eliminate this strongpoint, and the Camerons could link up with the men fighting alongside Merritt. All together they might be able to fight through to Dieppe for the withdrawal.[30]

Law's battalion headquarters group and its support platoon opened fire on the bicyclists. Two snipers, Private A. Huppe and Private E. Herbert, quickly shot about fifteen men off their bicycles before the others scattered for cover.[31]

'A' Company had, meanwhile, started descending the slope towards the bridges when suddenly a horse-drawn 81-millimetre mortar detachment appeared on the road immediately below them. The leading platoon shot down the mortar crew and then rushed forward and "wrecked the mortar." One prisoner was taken and put to work carrying the heavy and so far useless Boys anti-tank rifle the battalion was packing.[32] One of the two horses was dead, but Private H.P.L. Hutton saw that the other was lying wounded in its traces. He cut it free, but another man declared the horse doomed and shot it.[33]

While 'A' Company had been eliminating the mortar detachment, more Germans were flooding into the area. A detachment of three horse-drawn light artillery guns came up the road immediately west of the river and crossed one bridge to set up a blocking position on the eastern side. The rate of machine-gun and sniper fire from the eastern heights overlooking the bridges also ramped up. The Camerons had nothing capable of engaging either the artillery or the heights.[34]

It was now about 0930 hours, and Law recognized that crossing the bridges was no longer possible. He had no wireless contact with 6th Brigade or with Merritt. The Camerons were effectively in the blue—nothing for it but to withdraw back to Pourville. About a mile and a half inland, theirs was the deepest penetration that would be achieved during Jubilee. Law's signaller reported intercepting a 6th Brigade signal to the Sasks. The message read: "Vanquish from Green Beach at 1000 hours, get in touch with the Camerons." Law's signaller managed to reach the Sasks and told them the Camerons were heading back to Green Beach.[35]

Ross considered the withdrawal a bitter pill but one that must be swallowed. A single tank would have saved the situation. He remembered the insistent intelligence briefings claiming that it was impracticable to land tanks at Pourville instead of Dieppe. The bridges over the Scie would surely be rigged with demolition charges and blown before the tanks could cross. But none of the bridges had been wired, and the Germans defending Pourville lacked anti-tank guns. Their mortars and artillery would have had little effect on tanks, which could have overrun them with virtual impunity. But the plans could not be undone, so the Camerons must now extricate themselves from an increasingly dangerous situation.[36]

WHEN ROSS ORDERED 'A' Company's withdrawal, a man rushed over and pleaded with him to first send a platoon to where his friend lay well out front and badly wounded. "Can't sacrifice a company to save one wounded man," Ross replied. That sort of risk was the heroic stuff of old films and dime novels. To get as many men home as you could, an officer had to make hard choices.

Realizing a withdrawal was under way, the Germans were starting to press hard. "Tremendous disorder set in as we tried to fold the battalion back to a position from which it was not to have been evacuated. There had been no provision for a retreat in the planning," Ross remembered.

To Regimental Sergeant Major J.W. Dumma, the "withdrawal was the toughest job we had, but even the best the enemy had to throw at us did not for a minute unnerve the boys."[37] Private Hutton ended up on one side of a gully swept by machine-gun fire and "had to run the gauntlet." Reaching the other side, he and his sergeant turned to provide covering fire that enabled the others to get across. Then the group "proceeded along the edge of the gully... through to a large copse of trees at the edge of a field of grain. We had to stop now and again to give covering fire to the rest of our boys and they in turn... for us."[38]

'A' Company's Corporal A. Eastman felt he was fleeing through "overwhelming opposition. It seemed... that the positions of the enemy were all prearranged and though they were in isolated areas [they had] an inexhaustible supply of ammo and men. The machine-guns were constantly firing on fixed lines and were ranged on all gaps and places where we were forced to cross. Their tactics seemed to be to pin us down with heavy machine-gun and rifle fire and then to range on us with their mortars, which [were] the most dangerous weapon we encountered. Also, I noticed as the enemy moved in on our right flank and tried to cut our retirement off, that they moved very quickly and had some trucks and motorcycles with them." The Germans were "either very young men or very old. There seemed to be a complete lack of men of middle age. The positions of enemy machine-guns were difficult to pinpoint and well camouflaged. The enemy, once we closed with them, were very easily overcome, but were dangerous at long range and their weapons were very accurate."[39]

Germans dogging their heels, the Camerons "re-entered Pourville with about 80 percent of their strength intact, at 0956 hours." Law had expected to hit the beach running with the evacuation beginning in mere minutes, but there was no sign seaward of landing craft. He rushed to the Saskatchewan headquarters and learned from Merritt that the evacuation had been pushed back to 1100 hours. In turn, Law warned Merritt that the Germans were closing in strength from the south, and he would send two Cameron companies to hold the west side of the bridgehead to prevent their breaking into the village.[40]

At about the same time, the Sasks on the western headland also reported enemy closing from the south. The 302nd Infantry Division's Generalleutnant Konrad Haase had earlier decided Pourville represented the "greatest danger in the divisional sector." Consequently, just twenty minutes after the Camerons had begun landing, 571st Regiment's 1st Battalion was ordered to advance on Pourville from the southwest. It was this battalion, along with the regiment's anti-tank company and infantry gun platoon, the Camerons had encountered.[41]

Closest to the approaching enemy were 'C' Company's No. 14 Platoon under Lieutenant Leonard Kempton. About 0945 hours, Sergeant M. Lehman saw "the enemy moving out of the trees and a section started down the road in our direction, followed shortly afterwards by larger bodies of troops. We allowed them to get into range and opened fire with all we had, taking our toll of them before they had a chance to get cover on the sides of the road. They moved back to the cover of the trees again and proceeded to pull a pincer on us."

Kempton informed Major Claude Orme that he was in trouble and then prepared to meet the attack. "We are in a hell of a fix," he told Lehman, "as our flanks are unprotected except for what fire we can produce ourselves. I hate to keep the boys [here], but we have to stick it out until they get in on top of us and then make the best of getting out." Everyone in Pourville was "relying on us."

No. 14 Platoon was caught in the vice as a nasty firefight erupted. But the men had good cover and kept the Germans back. Knowing the situation could not hold, Kempton started slowly leapfrogging men back, while a single Bren gun team covered each move. As the gun team followed after one backward hop, one man was hit crossing the road. Lehman grabbed Kempton's arm as he started to go to the man's aid. "You're needed worse than I am," Lehman said. "Give me covering fire and I'll get him." Kempton nodded and ordered smoke grenades thrown. Through fire, Lehman dashed to the fallen man. Discovering he suffered only a light leg wound, Lehman helped him reach the platoon's new position. Going along the road, Lehman saw Kempton lying dead by the roadside.[42] He had been shot between the eyes.[43]

When Major Orme had received Kempton's signal, he ordered Lieutenant Ross MacIlveen to go to assist No. 14 Platoon with No. 15 Platoon. MacIlveen had barely started moving when Kempton's men fell back upon his. Orme ordered MacIlveen to cover the battered platoon's withdrawal into the village and then to also fall back. No way could 'C' Company stand on the headland against the Germans coming at it. MacIlveen remained in position, "inflicting heavy casualties on the enemy," until about 1000 hours, when the Germans started firing machine guns from the headland's crest into his right flank. Under this heavy fire, MacIlveen pulled back towards Pourville.[44]

Major Jim McRae had been apprised of 'C' Company's situation at the outset and approved the withdrawal to the edge of the village. He also dispatched a small party of Camerons to support the company. At 1000 hours, he reported to HMS *Calpe* that an enemy battalion was "looming up to counterattack."[45]

Forced to surrender the western headland, the Canadians were powerless to prevent the Germans setting up machine guns and mortars on it. Beach and village were soon raked by fire from both headlands, meaning the evacuation would be more costly. Still, the Sasks and Camerons remained organized and held the lower slopes of the eastern headland. Wounded were gathered by the seawall or buildings across the promenade.

Merritt and Captain Runcie prepared to defend the village perimeter. The village's westernmost sector was covered mostly by Camerons—sections of 'C' and 'D' Companies and the battalion headquarters.[46] On the eastern flank, Lieutenant John Edmondson led a covering force consisting primarily of Saskatchewan Regiment troops. He had two ten-man sections. One group under Corporal E. Hart held the north side of the road near the intersection at the base of the headland. Corporal R. Jackson's group was with Edmondson in the second storey of the pub by the bridge. When the troops still fighting on the eastern headland withdrew past these positions to the beach, Edmondson's men would provide a rearguard and then try to escape at the last moment.

Major Norman Ross took charge of organizing the Camerons who were to evacuate first. Realizing all the companies were intermingled and also mixed up with Sasks hoping to get away, Ross designated areas along the promenade where various houses offered some cover. Ross grabbed officers and sergeants as they appeared. "That's your area over there. Get your men into it," he said. "There wasn't any great panic. It was a case of what do we do now?"[47]

Also preparing for the evacuation was the naval beach master, Lieutenant Commander Redvers Prior. He had realized at about 0900 hours that evacuating from Dieppe was unlikely to happen for the troops who had landed at Pourville. Already a large number of wounded were by the seawall, and he sought to get them taken off. Unable to establish wireless contact with the ships offshore, Prior had jumped onto a pillbox and, under fire, waved semaphore flags to get their attention. *Invicta*'s LCA521 approached at 0930 hours, only to be driven off by enemy fire. At 1000 hours, LCA315 made an attempt, its captain seeing only Prior's beach party "taking cover under the wall, being held there by fire from light machine-gun posts on the West Cliff and by heavy calibre fire from the East Cliff which covered their line of retreat. One man was seen to attempt to reach the boat but was instantly killed. The boat was then forced to retire."[48]

Although several times wounded, Prior calmly imposed order on chaos. He thrust wire cutters at Private William Haggard "and told him to cut passages through the wire to facilitate passage to the beach." Inspired by the "fine job" Prior was doing, Haggard zealously attacked the task and completed it just as the beach was smothered by mortar fire that drove him to cover.[49]

It was about 1030 hours. Men huddled against the seawall or in the buildings. Correspondent Wallace Reyburn stood in a doorway of the hotel the Sasks were using for headquarters and RAP. He watched stretcher-bearers carry wounded across the promenade under fire. Merritt and several officers discussed the fate of their many prisoners. "It looked as though we were going to have a tough enough job getting our dead and wounded and ourselves off the beach without the trouble of taking Germans along. So it was decided that when we left we'd just leave them there."

Reyburn "looked out to sea, and there was still no sign of the boats. The German troops behind us were getting closer now. We knew that, because their bullets were now splattering on the upper storey of the house."[50]

17

Such a Carnage

WHITEWASHED VILLAS CLUSTERED on a narrow gully's slopes directly overlooked the Royal Regiment of Canada's Blue Beach. The holiday villas of Puys were modestly opulent, but the village's overall situation was unappealing. The beach was barely 250 yards long and fifty feet wide at high tide. Headlands jutting up sharply on either flank created a sense of confinement. A seawall stretching from one headland to the other added to the oppressive air. Depending on how deeply the sharp, fist-sized rocks washed up against the seawall, its height varied from eight to twelve feet.

Headlands, villas, seawall, and tightly confined beach all served as natural defences, and the Germans had capitalized on these to prepare for staving off any amphibious landing. Triple coils of concertina wire now topped the seawall.[1] Landward, four to five feet of open ground lay between the wall and more "bundled" wire.[2] On the gully's east side, the front garden of a brick house contained a concrete pillbox disguised as a summer cottage. Its firing slits commanded the seawall and beach from very short range. Another pillbox was sited at the western end of the seawall and was flanked by two stone stairways that ascended the cliff. These were blocked by more wire. Three more pillboxes stared down from the gully and enjoyed excellent fields of fire.[3] "All in all," the Royal Regiment's historian wrote, "it would have been difficult to discover, anywhere on the coast of Europe, a less favourable area for an assault landing."[4]

Yet it was here the Royals must land—their mission of securing the eastern headland that stood between Puys and Dieppe was considered essential to overall success. Bismarck, the four-gun coastal battery on this headland, dominated Dieppe's waterfront. Therefore, the Royals must destroy Bismarck and several nearby heavy and light anti-aircraft batteries. Once this task was complete, they would drive through to Dieppe for evacuation.

Poised to land with the Royals were artillery detachments from the 3rd Light Anti-Aircraft Regiment and 4th Field Regiment. The anti-aircraft personnel would assist in capturing headland guns and "use them against ground and air targets." They were also to purloin two new German gunsights for analysis. After aiding in Bismarck's capture, the artillery detachment would turn its guns on Goering— the inland coastal battery south of Dieppe—and other targets of opportunity. 'C' Company of the Black Watch, less its company headquarters, was also assigned to the Royals. Designated "Edwards Force," the Black Watch was aboard the LSI *Duke of Wellington* and under command of the Royals' Captain Raymond Hicks. The artillerymen were on *Queen Emma* with one component of the Royals, and *Princess Astrid* carried the majority of the battalion.[5] There were 554 Royals in all, 26 officers and 528 other ranks. Four officers and 107 other ranks had been added from the Black Watch. Two officers and 24 other ranks comprised the 4th Field Detachment, whereas the anti-aircraft group consisted of 2 officers and 24 other ranks drawn from the regiment's 16th Field Battery. Also in the group were artillery forward observation officer Captain George Browne, his signaller, Canadian Press journalist Ross Munro, and a small naval beach party. In all, about 750 men were to land on Blue Beach.[6]

The landing flotilla lowered from the LSIS on schedule at 0300 hours. So that the assaulting wave was hidden by darkness, the landing was scheduled for 0450. For the Royals to overwhelm the Blue Beach's heavy defences, surprise was considered essential. Royal Navy's Lieutenant Commander Harold Goulding, aboard MGB316, was to guide the flotilla in.

The approach plan ran into trouble as soon as the flotilla cast free of the LSIS at 0310 hours. Five LCAS mistook the passing MGB315 for Goulding's boat and followed it. Goulding spent a frantic fifteen minutes shepherding them back on course. Anxious to get back on schedule, Goulding increased speed to 6.5 knots. This was too fast for the two LCMS, which each carried a hundred vital men. The LCMS, with four LCAS astern, fell back in a straggling line that Goulding lost all sight of at 0350. They kept on course only by trailing MGB315's wake.

Goulding lost faith in his ability to find Blue Beach by dead reckoning and arbitrarily decided to home first on the easily recognizable Dieppe harbour. Once he had it in sight, Goulding would have to lead the flotilla in a dogleg along the coast to Puys.[7]

Seated aboard one of the struggling LCMS, Ross Munro could see over the gunwale the eastward Dieppe mole "in the light of flak and the bomb bursts and searchlights" erupting as the main attack got under way. Darkness was fast fading. "The Royals were very late. They should have been on the beach before dawn but it was grey light of morning by now," he wrote.[8]

The battalion was to land in three successive waves. The first consisted of 'A,' 'B,' and 'C' Companies, with 'C' landing on the right, 'A' in the centre, and 'B' to the left. Second-in-command Major George Schofield's advance headquarters and the navy beach party would land with this wave. Lieutenant Colonel Doug Catto's headquarters would come ashore ten minutes later with the second-wave 'D' Company. Edwards Force, comprising the third wave, would follow in another ten minutes.[9]

With formation lost, this phased landing plan was shot. Instead, landing craft headed shoreward in a loose gaggle that shook out into two separate intermixed waves. Edwards Force had not yet even launched from *Duke of Wellington*.

The first LCAS were about a hundred yards offshore, still somewhat hidden in semi-darkness, when Private H.E. Wright of the headquarters company's No. 3 Platoon heard directly overhead the roar of waves of RAF fighters headed inland. Streams of anti-aircraft fire from the headlands streaked skyward.[10] "A huge white flare [suddenly] lit up the whole sky."[11] Private J. Brooks knew "right then that the Jerry was expecting us."[12]

German light machine guns on the sloping gully opened fire. It was 0507 hours and seventeen critical minutes too late. Dawn was breaking as more flares burst and stole the last protective cloak of darkness. The fire from the gully was at such an angle that it punched into the interior of some LCAS. Major George Schofield suffered a slight wound just before his LCA touched down. Schofield, the senior commander in this wave, piled out at the head of his men.[13]

As the ramps dropped, the Royals were met by a deluge of fire. "Jerry fired straight into the boats," Private J.E. Creer recalled.[14] It was the same for Private R.G. Jones of the battalion's support platoon. "Bullets flew into and surrounded" everyone on his LCA. Jones wrestled a 3-inch mortar mounted on a dolly, together weighing about four hundred pounds, off the ramp and plunged into water over his head. Unable to "budge the dolly under water," he abandoned it. Up on the beach, other men were dragging another mortar dolly towards the seawall. "All the men around the mortar in front of me were getting hit. Most of the men ran for the base of the cliff for protection... which wasn't very good."[15]

Corporal W. Duggan, however, refused to abandon this 3-inch mortar. "I found myself alone trying to pull it onto the beach and set the mortar up. Sergeant [Johnny] Carroll came to my assistance and he was standing beside me when he was shot. He disappeared and I knew then that I could never hope to get the mortar to the beach, so I opened fire on a machine-gun post with my rifle and after firing around 30 to 40 rounds my rifle jammed with sand and a rusty cartridge."[16]

One man saw Sergeant Carroll down on the beach, his hands holding his entrails. He ran to Carroll and dragged him into an LCA full of other wounded men. The LCA pulled away and ran for safety.[17]

The first fifteen men exiting the LCA ahead of Private M. Hamilton were cut down, and the survivors could "only... take cover against the wall and fire back the best we could. The enemy had us in between crossfire from houses on our left and right flank on the cliff top. It was hard to find targets to fire back at."[18]

Peering over an LCA's ramp, Corporal Leslie Ellis had watched uneasily as things "formerly only vaguely distinguishable [became] clearly visible" in the growing light. The boat hit the beach, and its ramp jammed when partly open. Ellis jumped onto it but could not jog it loose, so he leapt ashore. Getting only his feet wet, Ellis ran to the seawall "and crouched against it waiting for the other men to join him. Looking back, he saw these men being cut down, chiefly by machine-gun fire... sweeping the beach." Those not hit crowded up against the seawall, but fire from the pillbox disguised as a summer cottage "was able to enfilade the wall effectively and caused very heavy casualties."[19]

Corporal H. Hoxie had to swim thirty feet before being able to touch bottom. "Most of our company was wiped out on the beach before they could reach the wall... It seemed the fire was on fixed lines. You couldn't see Jerry at all. There were quite a few snipers evidently to pick off our officers and NCOS... The NCOS had been issued with Sten guns but for the position we had to take they were useless as far as I could see." Having lost his rifle swimming in, Hoxie saw that "quite a few [other] fellows lost their rifles and were defenceless."[20]

Most of what was left of 'A' Company sought shelter beside the western cliff face where the stone steps led upward. But the pillbox firing from the eastern end of the wall still hit them. Although wire tangles blocked the stairs, Ellis clawed a way through. To one side of the stairs stood a silent pillbox that proved unmanned. Crossing over the wall, Ellis ascended the other stairs until he came to a "wire obstacle so thick that he could not shoot through it."

Moments later, Captain George Sinclair and his batman, who was armed with a Sten, arrived. Sinclair and Ellis crammed a bangalore torpedo into the wire, which created a decent hole when it exploded. As Sinclair began shouting for the men down on the beach by the cliff to join them, Ellis pushed past and headed up the stairs. Over his shoulder, he saw the second wave arriving.[21]

THIS WAVE CONSISTED of the two LCMS and four LCAS left in the wake by Lieutenant Commander Goulding's increased flotilla speed.

It grounded at 0535.[22] "When we hit the beach," Sergeant John Legate wrote, "the battle was really in shape... dead and wounded were lying all over the place. We just had to stay close to the wall... The crossfire coming at us made it impossible to move two feet from the wall... There was nobody around to look after the wounded and... it was impossible to get near them. The Germans... were getting the range with their mortars and the shells were dropping around us and... it was impossible to give orders... It turned out to be every man for himself."

Lieutenant John Woodhouse, the only officer left standing near Legate, kept shouting orders despite being "badly shot up."[23] Unable to rouse the men, Woodhouse charged the eastern pillbox while firing a Bren gun from the hip. Badly wounded by a machine-gun burst, he collapsed alongside the seawall.

Twenty-seven-year-old Lieutenant William Wedd's platoon had been shredded to about ten men by fire from a pillbox on top of the seawall—from there, the Germans were able to fire point-blank into Wedd's platoon. Unable to flank the pillbox, Wedd used a bangalore to blow a hole in the wire and led the platoon in a charge straight into the teeth of the German fire. Although riddled by bullets, Wedd threw a grenade through the firing slit, killing the Germans before he collapsed dead in front of the pillbox.[24]

The second wave's arrival corresponded with the Germans suddenly bringing 81-millimetre mortars into play. "Every time a... mortar bomb landed on that stoney beach it accounted for a number of casualties." As a smoke-laying boat spewed a thin screening cloak along the beach, thirty-four-year-old Sergeant Ewart Peaks and three men dashed to the water and dragged a 3-inch mortar onto the shingle. "They didn't get many more than three bombs away when Heinie found them with his machinegun and they were cut to pieces," Private M. Hamilton recalled.[25]

Virtually every man in the LCA with Private J.E. Creer was struck down seconds after gaining the beach. Creer reached the seawall just as Lieutenant William Patterson tried unsuccessfully to shove a bangalore into the wire.[26] Although bangalores were designed to be joined together so they could be pushed deeper into wire obstacles, when Patterson tried linking up two, the fitting mechanism proved to be fouled with grit. As he extracted the detonating fuse from one bangalore to clean the mechanism, Patterson was shot. The fuse ignited, setting his equipment and clothes on fire. He was immolated.[27]

Creer turned from this grisly spectacle to see Private John Stevenson firing his Bren while lying in the open on the beach. Suddenly the man shouted, "Fight. Keep fighting." Then "he was hit ... and ... died right on the beach. There was very heavy opposition there and there was a big house just back from the wall and there seemed to be a machinegun firing from every window."[28]

Corporal Fred Ruggles was aboard an LCM with one platoon from 'C' Company, a mortar detachment, the twenty-six-man 3rd Light Anti-Aircraft Regiment, stretcher-bearers of 11th Field Ambulance, the navy's beach master and his party, and correspondent Ross Munro. It was standing room only; Ruggles was port side in the stern, with Bren gunner Private James Murphy beside him. As the LCM approached the beach, Ruggles and Murphy started shooting at the houses.[29]

Looking at the house on the eastern flank of the seawall, Murphy "saw fire from this one and fired into each of the windows of the first floor. I think each floor had six windows. By the time I would get to the sixth window the first one would open up again. After I had fired six magazines, I ran down the craft to get to the beach."[30]

Ruggles tried to follow, climbing "over many wounded men. Before I reached the unloading platform the boat was on its way out and I was unable to get off... As we were backing out I had one brief glimpse of men crouched against the cliff or wall and many others lying on the beach and some in the water." Murphy was also caught still on board when the LCM withdrew. Only later would the two frustrated young men realize the lucky hand chance had dealt by placing them at the LCM's back.[31]

Munro had fully witnessed the LCMs' landing effort. As the craft approached the beach, the faces of the men around him were tense and grim. Hands tightly gripped weapons. When the ramp fell, the leading troops "plunged into about two feet of water and machinegun bullets laced into them. Bodies piled up on the ramp. Some staggered to the beach and fell. Bullets were splattering into the boat...wounding and killing.

"I was near the stern and to one side. Looking out the open bow over the bodies... I saw the slope leading a short way up to a stone wall littered with Royal casualties. There must have been sixty or seventy of them, lying sprawled... A dozen Canadians were running along the edge of the cliff towards the stone wall. They carried their weapons and some were firing as they ran. But some had no helmets, some were already wounded, their uniforms torn and bloody. One by one they were cut down and rolled down the slope to the sea... On no other front have I witnessed such a carnage. It was brutal and terrible and shocked you almost to insensibility to see the piles of dead and feel the hopelessness of the attack at this point."

One young soldier kept trying to get off the LCM, only to be driven back by fire. Despite a wounded arm, he again "lunged forward and a streak of red-white tracer slashed through his stomach. I'll never forget his anguished cry as he collapsed on the blood-soaked deck: 'Christ, we gotta beat them; we gotta beat them!' He was dead in a few minutes." Captain Jack Anderson was right next to Munro when he was hit in the head and fell across the correspondent's leg, bleeding heavily. A naval rating lay dying with "a sickening gash in his throat."[32]

When the LCM door had dropped, Private S.T. Bertram was stunned, as "the most terrific machine-gun fire poured into our craft from five large pillboxes... At the same time heavy fire came in at us from the left flank from a large house and the same from the right of us. Men started falling before they ever took a step and the rest that did reach shore were laying still on the beach. It seemed to me that only four or five men from our craft reached the wall, a distance of 40 yards. I opened fire on the house on the left to try and stop the crossfire." The LCM drifted out, and a stretcher-bearer shouted for the men in the boat to help wounded get aboard. Bertram dropped his rifle and managed to pull Private H. Seaton, shot in the ankle, into the boat. He then shifted several wounded back to the stern to make room for more to board.[33]

A 'D' Company platoon approached the beach in one of the second-wave LCAS. Seeing the machine-gun fire raking the beach, Private N.E.H. Blair and his compatriots planned their moves. All three platoon sections would dash for the seawall and then move along it to attack and silence the pillbox on the western flank. Blair was to cover the others with his Bren gun as they unloaded. A sensible plan, it unravelled the moment the ramp dropped. Blair burned off magazines until the last man left, then turned to follow and stopped dead just off the ramp, "as my platoon was getting cut down before me from fire from the pillboxes. Everyone before me was dead or wounded. A few of the fellows made the wall but were cut down by machine-gun fire from the house on the left of the pillboxes. I continued to fire at the pillboxes and then they started mortar at us. A naval officer shouted to get back in the [LCA]. But I continued firing. So then he said it was an order for me to get aboard. I realized he was right; it was impossible to make the wall." As he turned towards the LCA, Blair heard a call for help. He and a naval rating dashed to where two badly wounded men were half-drowning in the water. They dragged the two men aboard and the LCA withdrew.[34]

A RARE EXCEPTION, Corporal Leslie Ellis crossed the seawall. After pushing past Captain George Sinclair by the steps ascending the western cliff, Ellis crawled a short distance before again being blocked by wire. Using cutters, he opened a hole and worked his way up to the house overlooking the beach. Slipping around back, Ellis opened a door and threw a grenade down the length of the room within. On the heels of the explosion, Ellis ran to the next room. It was empty, but warm cartridges were scattered near the windows facing the beach. Pulling a grenade's pin, Ellis started up the stairs. He was halfway to the second floor when a naval vessel's 20-millimetre Oerlikon ripped into the building. Pitching the grenade aside, Ellis fled downstairs and jumped out a back window.

After following a trail to woods on the headland, Ellis realized he could do nothing useful alone and should return to the beach. En route he encountered Sinclair's batman and sent him back to bring up the captain and more troops. Returning to the headland, Ellis discovered another abandoned pillbox and then three empty weapon pits.

Across the gully leading to Puys, Ellis saw the pillbox camouflaged as a summer cottage. Bullets were chipping away at the concrete, but no fire seemed to be coming from the pillbox. Instead, Ellis saw tracers streaming from a bush next to the pillbox's beach side. A closer look revealed a gleam of white that Ellis assumed was the machine gunner's face. Trained as a sniper, Ellis set his rifle sights for 650 yards and fired—seeing "the stream of tracer bullets change direction from the beach up into the air, as though the gunner had been struck and had fallen back with his finger still on the trigger. No more fire came from the bush."

When Ellis sniped other German positions in the buildings of Puys, he drew return fire. A bullet creased his helmet, convincing him to again return to the beach. Crawling past the house he had earlier explored, Ellis came upon a Royals officer he didn't know. Ellis warned him that the house was drawing naval fire. Ignoring Ellis, the man went inside just as a salvo of 4-inch shells from HMS *Garth* tore through it. Ellis decided against investigating the man's fate.

Instead, seeing that an LCA was taking on troops, he scrambled down the slope towards the beach. Happening upon a soldier paralyzed by a bullet, Ellis half dragged and half carried him to the wire obstacle. Climbing through the hole, he saw a wire that looked like telephone cable. Ellis had earlier cut such cables and gave it a hard pull, only to trigger an explosive booby trap. The paralyzed man was killed, and Ellis's face, right hand, and left foot were all gashed open by shrapnel. His eardrum was also punctured. Crawling to the wire topping the seawall, Ellis discovered he had lost the cutters. So he "jumped right over it and landed on the beach" atop another wire tangle.[35]

All along the beach, a growing sense of panic was building. Suddenly, Private J.E. Creer heard an officer shout that "it was hopeless. If you can get back in the boats do so." Creer "took the chance and just as I got to water's edge the boat pulled out." Plunging into the sea, Creer started swimming. He was eventually rescued by a destroyer.[36]

Sergeant John Legate joined a rush towards the second wave's last LCA to depart the beach. This was LCA209, commanded by Royal Navy lieutenant N.E.B. Ramsay.[37] About fifty men gained the boat.

Legate managed to join the clutch aboard. Others clung to its sides. The combined weight proved too much for the boat's engine and it grounded.[38] Private Ed Simpson also joined "the terrible scramble." The men were completely exposed to fire, and "the slaughter was awful."[39] Corporal Ellis ran up as Ramsay shouted for the men to get out and shove the LCA free. Ellis organized some of the men into making a concerted effort. Then, as the boat slipped free, he helped several badly wounded men get aboard. Captain Jack Catto, the battalion commander's brother, was one. He "appeared to be in bad shape," with one eye shot out.[40]

Shortly before the mad rush, Private H.E. Wright had been knocked unconscious when a shrapnel sliver from a mortar round pierced his helmet. He awoke unhurt save for a splitting headache and blood gushing down his face from a flesh wound. Wright realized "we were practically wiped out and [there was] no hope of gaining the cliff to clear the opposition." So he headed for the boat and came upon his chum Private Norman Orpen, who "was lying with a bullet through the leg and one hand practically blown off. I managed to drag him to the [LCA] and heaved him aboard."

With men pushing and Wright and Sergeant Morris Greenberg pulling on it from seaward, the LCA finally floated free.[41] Ellis remained on shore, watching as the naval ratings forced men to let go of the badly overloaded boat by hitting their hands with boat hooks.[42] So many dead and wounded lay on the ramp that Ramsay was unable to close it, and water gushed in. Fifty yards out the LCA capsized, and many men—including Ramsay—drowned. "She turned over, about ten of us got away and had to swim for it," Legate wrote.[43] Wright saw Greenberg, now badly injured, assist several wounded men to swim to the boat and climb up on the hull. "The last I saw of him," Wright said, "he was sinking through exhaustion." Greenberg's body later washed ashore.

The Germans started shooting the men off the exposed hull. Wright and several others "swam out to sea but mortar bombs and snipers picked us off till there were only five or six of us. After getting fairly well out of range I stripped off my uniform and boots and hat." Encountering Legate, Wright swam with him for a couple of hours, the sergeant finally towing the exhausted Wright by having him cling to a strip of tape on Legate's Mae West. It was "a respite that enabled me to keep going," Wright said.[44] Legate tried repeatedly to attract the attention of passing boats, but none responded to his waving and shouting. Eventually he came upon an abandoned rowboat that contained two Stens and a Bren gun. He guessed some other Royals had escaped the beach in it and been rescued. After helping Wright aboard, Legate discovered a paddle and then saw three men swimming nearby. When he paddled over to them, Legate recognized Sergeant Ernest Thirgood. All three men were wounded. He had just got them on board when a naval vessel came to the rescue. While a medical officer began treating the other wounded men, a sailor stripped Legate's uniform off and put him to bed with "six blankets, two hot water bottles and a big shot of rum."[45]

WHILE THOSE ON Blue Beach were trying to escape it, the commanders of Edwards Force were considering whether to reinforce it. Canadian naval reservist Lieutenant Jack Koyl commanded *Duke of Wellington*'s landing craft flotilla. Most of his crews were also Canadian. The flotilla had cast off from *Wellington* at 0334 hours and closed slowly on Blue Beach in order to land behind the other waves. It was now 0525, and the five landing craft, loaded with Black Watch infantrymen and 4th Field Regiment artillerymen, drifted about a mile offshore. Koyl and Edwards Force's commander, Captain Raymond Hicks, waited in vain for a wireless signal that the beach was secure. Nor could they raise anyone on the beach. Checking in with *Calpe*, they learned there had been no wireless contact with the Royals since an initial signal reporting the second wave touching down.

Nobody offshore knew the chaos that had descended on Blue Beach. The beach master and his party had never landed. The Royals had carried ashore only a single No. 18 wireless that was disabled when it became soaked in seawater. Only FOO Captain George Browne's No. 66 wireless set remained, but it was netted to *Garth* so he could direct the fire of the destroyer's guns. Although Browne was regularly sending *Garth* messages for forwarding to *Calpe*, these were being passed on well after receipt, and often the contents were badly garbled.[46]

In the absence of news, Hicks and Koyl agreed to close upon the beach and decide at the last moment whether or not to land. Drawing closer, they saw bodies strewn everywhere and most of those Royals still alive huddled at the western end of the seawall where some rocks provided a little cover. Koyl ordered his LCA's Lewis gunner to open fire on Germans moving around on the western headland above the Royals. Although agreeing the situation looked dire, Koyl and Hicks decided to land Edwards Force under the headland on a narrow strip of beach west of the seawall. The men would then reinforce the Royals. At 0545 hours, Edwards Force duly landed a hundred yards west of the seawall.[47]

Barely getting boots wet, the men dashed through fire across a fifty-yard-wide rocky shelf to the cliff face. Lieutenant Mark Mather "was right beside [Lieutenant] Jack Colson when he got his—a burst of machine gun (fire) right through the eyes and head... Except for poor Jack, the [Black Watch] didn't lose a man!"

They did suffer wounded. Ahead of Private Reg Hall, three men were cut down immediately. Hall could see German machine guns on top of the horseshoe-shaped headland. "There were German snipers on the top throwing potato mashers and sniping at us. That's where the majority of the casualties came from, the grenades. The fire was so heavy we couldn't do anything except take shelter."[48] Mortars quickly transformed the beach shingle into deadly shrapnel. Edwards Force was trapped in a vise from which escape was impossible. The angle of the cliff prevented their even seeing the Royals on Blue Beach, and moving along the fire-swept shelf to reach them would be suicide. "There was no point in creating further havoc for our wounded comrades, so we stopped firing. There was nothing we could do, we didn't have a chance."[49]

While exiting an LCA, Private Albert O'Toole had lost his footing and wrenched an ankle. Pulled back aboard the hurriedly departing LCA, O'Toole would be the only Black Watch soldier landed who returned from the raid. All the rest were taken prisoner.[50]

AS THE DISASTER of Blue Beach began drawing inevitably to its close, some Royals still refused to give up. Lieutenant Colonel Doug

Catto and a party of men primarily from 'D' Company ended up in "a sort of re-entrant on the western side of [the] seawall's end spur." Around the corner was a remnant of 'C' Company. Gathering these men together at 0600 hours, Catto discovered that nobody had any bangalore torpedoes to blow holes through the wire on the seawall. So Sergeant Edward Coles and two other men started cutting while Lieutenant Bob Stewart stood up to cover them with a Bren gun. The officer was promptly shot and fell badly wounded. Ten minutes later, however, the hole was opened. Captain Browne signalled *Garth:* "Doug still on beach. Casualties heavy. MG and mortar fire. 0610." But Catto was passing through the hole, shouting for the men to follow him.

Browne, meanwhile, gave his signaller a second message to send and told him to follow the party once it was gone.[51] Although Browne was sure it was futile, the message eventually relayed from *Garth* to *Calpe* read: "From Blue Beach. Is there possible chance of getting us off?"[52] Browne and Catto both thought it impossible for LCAs to successfully pass through the German fire to save men from the beach. Their only chance was to fight overland to Dieppe, which was what they would now try.

As Catto and his small party of twenty-one men ascended the cliff, those Royals left behind were pasted by mortars and stick grenades thrown down from its top. German artillery burst "precisely at the water-line at impeccably correct intervals and timing." Browne's prediction was confirmed when two LCAs trying to land were "sunk by hits or splinters from this fire. From a gunner's point of view, it was admirable shooting." Browne "sprinted up the cliff after the colonel." He was the last man through the wire. German machine guns zeroed the hole, preventing its further use. The time was 0700 hours.[53]

On the beach, it was a time of decision—escape by swimming, surrender, or fight to the death? Corporal Leslie Ellis "looked about... and saw no movement on the beach, on which many dead men were lying." He calmly stripped off boots and equipment before walking into the sea. When he started crawl stroking, a sniper smacked a bullet in front of his nose. Ellis floated, played dead for a few minutes, and was not fired on after that. Dragged down by clothes and his seemingly damaged Mae West, Ellis wriggled free of them. He swam for two hours and was nearing exhaustion when a corpse bumped him. Ellis liberated it of a lifebelt and then took the lifebelt and jacket from a second body. Each of the men had been killed by a single bullet to the head—testimony to the accuracy of the German snipers. When Ellis tried just floating, he started losing consciousness. If he didn't keep swimming, he realized, he would die. Finally, he happened upon a rowboat, possibly the one abandoned by Legate's group. Climbing aboard, Ellis passed out and later awoke to find he was on an LCF, whose anti-aircraft guns were firing relentlessly. Ellis discovered that his watch had stopped the moment it was exposed to seawater—the time locked at 0630 hours. With a kind of dazed wonder, Ellis realized that during all the slaughter on Blue Beach, he had seen only a single German—the flashing white of the machine gunner's face.[54]

Despite the constant fire directed at it, a few men still clung to the keel of the overturned LCA. Private Ed Simpson was one. He saw no signs of life on the beach. "Slowly we were being picked off by snipers on the cliff. How long I hung on, I do not know." He was losing all hope when two LCAS from the *Duke of Wellington* braved the fire to reach the overturned vessel. Canadians under command of Sub-Lieutenant John Boak crewed one LCA; the other had a Royal Navy captain, Sub-Lieutenant Ben Franklin, but a mostly Canadian crew. Both boats "came under a perfect hurricane of fire from artillery, mortars and machineguns," but Boak's LCA reached the overturned craft. His crew "shouted to the soldiers to jump" and grab a rope strung over the side.[55]

Simpson and fellow privates Thomas Miller Armstrong, L.W. Roberts, and J.N. Wallace grasped the line. "As soon as we grabbed the rope the boat swung out to sea at top speed. A mile or so from where we were picked up, Armstrong let go." Presumed drowned, he was never found. When the LCA stopped, Simpson "clambered aboard unassisted and helped the seaman to bring Roberts and Wallace on deck."[56]

The other boat lifted the rest of the men from the overturned craft, but two of its naval crew died in this "act of gallantry."[57] One was Ordinary Seaman Joseph Alphonsus McKenna, a nineteen-year-old from

Prince Edward Island. Perched on the gunwale, McKenna had fired at the cliffs with a Lewis gun until he was shot in the chest. "I am afraid I am hit, Sir," he cried, "spun round and fell dead."[58] Franklin was also wounded. Although several other landing craft attempted to reach Blue Beach, they were driven back by drenching fire. It was no longer possible for men to swim away without being shot and killed.

Inland, Catto's party comprised four Royal officers and eleven other ranks, an officer and three 3rd Light Anti-Aircraft Regiment men, and foo Browne. As they moved up the slope towards the headland, Browne realized he no longer heard any fire from the east side of the beach, and from the centre and western flanks there were only "intermittent bursts of German automatic fire and the steady detonation of their mortar bombs." When a light machine gun on a hill to their left opened up, they realized any return to the beach was impossible. Gaining the top of the headland, Catto advanced a small patrol under Lieutenant Sterling Ryerson, whose grandfather had founded the Canadian Red Cross Society. Within minutes, Ryerson returned with word that a strong German patrol was approaching from the fortified house at the east side of the beach.

The party hurried westward towards Dieppe via a walled road overarched by tree branches, but soon left it for the security of a small wood. Emerging from the wood, they found a road bordered by walls that on the map connected Puys to Dieppe. An anti-aircraft battery was visible across about a hundred yards of open ground to the south. Two to three hundred yards northward, several light machine guns on the edge of the cliff fired at RAF fighters. Ryerson, on trail, reported that the patrol of about two full platoons was closing fast. It was about 1000 hours. A scout sent forward to explore a path leading into a second wood bumped into a machine-gun position and was killed. Catto and the others took refuge in the wood. Unable to proceed farther and eventually hearing all signs of fighting fade away, they surrendered to a Luftwaffe officer at 1620 hours.[59]

On Blue Beach, the surrender had come much earlier—shortly before 0830—and little more than three hours after the first landing. At 0835, a report from 571st German Infantry Regiment to 302nd Division stated tersely: "Puys firmly in our hands; enemy lost about 500 men prisoners or dead." Very few Royals had escaped—just two officers, Captains Jack Anderson and Jack Catto, and sixty-five men. Most of these had been on the second-wave LCM that had pulled out with mostly wounded men aboard. Both officers had been wounded, as had thirty-one other ranks. Two of these died later. Including 18 men who died in captivity, 227 of the 554 men embarked perished. Of the 26 3rd Light Anti-Aircraft Regiment men, 9 were killed. Only 7 returned to England, most of them having never landed. The Black Watch had only Lieutenant Jack Colson killed. "The episode at Puys," the army's official historian wrote, "was the grimmest of the whole grim operation, and the Royal Regiment had more men killed than any other unit engaged. Along the fatal seawall the lads from Toronto lay in heaps."[60]

The disaster had stark ramifications for the raid as a whole. With the headland between Puys and Dieppe not taken, its guns ranged on the frontal landings at Dieppe. For as the Royals had lunged onto Blue Beach, the leading assault waves of the main force had almost simultaneously touched down on Red and White Beaches.

18

Murderous Crossfire

"IT IS VITAL to the success of the operation as a whole that White and Red Beaches be in our hands with minimal delay," Operation Jubilee's military plan had asserted. The beach facing Dieppe was about a mile long. White Beach stretched a half mile from the western headland, with Red Beach then extending east to the harbour mouth. The Royal Hamilton Light Infantry was to capture White Beach, the Essex Scottish Red Beach. A first flight of nine Calgary Regiment tanks would land alongside the infantry assault wave. Detachments of signallers, engineer assault teams, and ordnance and provost personnel tasked with assisting the engineers were also included. The engineers were carrying ashore large amounts of equipment and explosives to "clear the necessary beach roadways and remove obstacles to enable the tanks to enter the town."[1] Touchdown was slated for 0520 hours, immediately following an "intense direct bombardment by four destroyers and *Locust*." Between 0515 and 0525, five cannon-firing Hurricane squadrons would repeatedly strafe the beachfront.[2]

As the landing craft headed shoreward, Lieutenant Colonel Bob Labatt realized his earlier misgivings about the operation had "completely disappeared. We were launched upon a daring expedition—undoubtedly the most hazardous operation ever undertaken by Canadian troops," the Riley commander wrote. "I was elated to think that we had been amongst those chosen to carry it out. I was pleased to realize that I was not scared." The men around him in the LCA sat with "gas capes slipped on back to front as a protection against the spray. There was no false bravado. They talked in low voices, checking over their various tasks in the coming operation."

As the sky lightened, Labatt discerned "vegetation and buildings showing black on top of white cliffs. Soon we were able to pick out landmarks made familiar by previous study of the model. We were headed dead for our beach, the piece of black horizon between the West Cliff and the Eastern Heights. We kept steadily on. The light became better and soon the buildings of the town showed up." Labatt's LCA made directly for the casino, with the other landing craft formed alongside in line. "The sea presented an inspiring picture. Hundreds of small craft heading for the land with fast support boats zigzagging well ahead—and astern the large tank carriers pushing up milk white cushions under their square bows. Everything was deathly quiet on the beach... Suddenly there was a roar overhead and a flight of hurricanes swept low over the water and attacked the buildings immediately ahead with M.G. and cannon fire. Flashes of flame ran up and down the esplanade as the bursts exploded... It was all over quickly, too quickly. The men who had been standing up to watch... were disappointed. 'Is that all?' they asked." The landing craft were about five hundred yards from shore and had not yet been fired on.[3]

As the beach became visible, Captain Denis Whitaker realized things were "terribly wrong. Everything was intact! We expected a town shattered by the RAF's saturation bombing the previous night. We thought we would see a lot of damage to the seafront buildings from the shelling. There was no sign of bombing. The window panes were glittering, unbroken, in the reflections of the sun's first rays."[4]

Fellow Riley Lieutenant Lou Counsell and his No. 16 Platoon of 'D' Company "were all a little disappointed by the smallness of the air support... the fighter attack seemed to be over in a moment." Bafflingly, only senior regimental officers knew there would be no saturation bombing of Dieppe and had not passed this information down to junior officers. On seeing "no evidence of bomb damage as they landed," Counsell said later, "you felt let down."[5]

Signaller Private Alf Collingdon was in Counsell's LCA. Pointing out the castle on the headland, he asked, "Sir, are you going to be king of the castle when we take it?"

"You can bet on it," Counsell replied. "But we're going to have to get there first!"[6]

Observing from *Calpe*, Captain John Hughes-Hallett thought the air support and fire from destroyers "appeared to be as effective as could be expected."[7] *Albrighton*, *Bleasdale*, *Berkeley*, and *Garth* had begun shooting at 0515 hours. American brigadier Lucien Truscott, on *Fernie* as an observer, was surprised by "the relative ineffectiveness of the 4-inch destroyer guns." A naval officer nearby said they had known "such support was inadequate, but that it was the only solution possible since cruisers could not be risked in such restricted waters."[8]

Fifty-eight Hurricanes mounting four 20-millimetre cannons each carried out the strafing attack. The first thirty-four-strong wave targeted light-gun positions, and the pilots reported shells striking "gun-posts, buildings and wireless masts." Both headlands were wreathed in thick smoke clouds as the destroyers fired smoke shells and smoke-laying aircraft swept in. More smoke roiled along the beach. While the smoke provided protective cover for the Hurricanes, it also prevented the pilots from targeting specific machine-gun or artillery positions. So they just wildly strafed the beach and buildings behind. Anti-aircraft fire was immediate and intense, hitting seven Hurricanes. Flight Sergeant Stirling David Banks, a nineteen-year-old RCAF pilot from Prince Edward Island serving in RAF's No. 3 Squadron, was struck by heavy flak. Last seen "trying desperately to ditch on the sea," he died in the crash. After two strafing runs, the leading squadrons broke for home. The two following squadrons attacked anti-aircraft batteries on the western headland, but due to smoke and poor light were unable to gauge the damage caused. Five Hurricanes failed to return from the attack.[9]

None of the supporting fire hindered the waiting Germans. From an observation post alongside the western headland's castle, Dieppe's naval port commandant saw the artillery and machine-gun positions cease firing blindly the moment the fighters departed. They now switched to observed fire "on the transports," which had now "become visible."[10]

"SUDDENLY ALL HELL broke loose." No. 2 Provost Company's Corporal Bob Prouse aboard LCT5 saw "mortar shells... exploding all around us... As we drew closer the Navy gunner... handling the Bofors gun suddenly disappeared in a puff of smoke."[11] Essex Scottish private Stanley Carley's hell started "two hundred yards from the beach [with] a terrific amount of machine-gun fire and artillery... being sent at us."[12]

"They greeted us not only with M.G. fire, but also mortars and anti-tank and infantry guns from concrete emplacements along the seawall. The surface of the water was hidden by spray," Lieutenant Colonel Labatt wrote. "The towers of the casino loomed above us. We could see them firing from the upper windows and gun emplacements on the ground floor level. I shouted to [Captain Denis Whitaker] to get busy with the Bren and everyone else to prepare to move. Gas capes were thrown under foot and the Mae Wests deflated. Whitaker had time to get off two mags from the Bren before we touched down."[13]

"Where was that weak demoralized enemy with puny weapons that we had been told was defending the town?" Whitaker wondered. "Dieppe was a fortress, and the Germans were obviously ready and waiting."[14]

Lieutenant Fred Woodcock, commanding No. 17 Platoon of 'D' Company, was in the LCA landing closest to the western headland and under intense fire from positions around the castle and casino. He thought it "unbelievable that anyone survived." Woodcock yelled at Private W.A. Korenblum, "Take the Bren." Korenblum "fired a clip at the flashes on the cliff... Then we were hit. The Bangalore torpedoes exploded among the toggle ropes and grappling irons. I only remember the sound, because I was blinded. The boat filled with water and I was soon up to my neck. I couldn't hear at all after that for a long while, but later there were faraway noises as if I were listening to something over a very poor connection on a long distance phone call. It seemed that my limbs wouldn't move. I wanted to brush the blood from my eyes, and I couldn't. Then, a long time later, I would feel something touching my face and I realized that it was my hand." Only Woodcock, blinded for life, and Korenblum survived. The rest of No. 17 Platoon died before landing.[15]

The first landing craft reached White Beach at 0520 hours and Red Beach three minutes later. Lieutenant Commander Colin McMullen, responsible for navigation, reported none of the LCAS or LCMS sunk on the approach.[16]

"The keel grated, the ramp swung down," and the Rileys "surged out" behind Labatt. "Drinks—Newhaven—tonight," the LCA captain shouted, as Labatt passed. "There was a momentary lull in the firing as we touched down, then it opened up again with terrific intensity."[17]

Thirty-five Rileys and eight 7th Field Company engineers piled out of one LCM. Despite the rain of fire, engineer Sergeant George Hickson calmly assessed the casino's defences. The Germans had recently begun demolishing the three-storey white building to create a large strongpoint amid its ruins. But so far, only the southwest corner had been torn down. The strongpoint's defences were, however, well advanced.[18]

A 40-millimetre rapid-fire gun was concealed by a heavy pillbox directly in front of the casino, and a heavy gun in a solidly constructed emplacement anchored the northwest corner. Two machine guns fired from either flank of the casino. The northeast corner was guarded by a large sandbagged emplacement. East of the casino, just back of the promenade, was a very large, low building. Aerial photographs had failed to reveal its purpose, but Hickson saw now that it housed at least one anti-tank gun and numerous machine guns. All around Hickson, men were falling or already lay dead on the rocks. Fire seemed to be coming from every which way. Hickson ran for two dense wire obstacles fronting the casino, which was where his "Hicks Party" of engineers and thirty-five Rileys were to rendezvous. They would then push into the town to destroy the post office's telephone exchange, blast its safe and loot any documents found, and then rig a torpedo dump under the eastern headland for demolition. Hickson already knew this tidy scheme was doomed.[19]

"THE INSTANT WE jumped from our boats... we were... swept with a murderous crossfire, which took a heavy toll of our ranks," 'C' Company's Private J. Johnston reported. "We raced to the first wire entanglements and threw ourselves flat. We crawled under the wire and made a dash for a low brick wall which was three bricks high. We then returned the fire which was still intense."[20]

Private Herb Prince realized "the German sniper is a real specialist. They are wonderful shots and go for the officers and NCOs. We found that they are mostly all planted on roofs or in very high buildings... The Germans seemed able to lay down mortar bombs where they damn well pleased." Having only just gained the wall, his 'C' Company platoon had its officer wounded and all NCOs killed. Company commander Major C.G. Pirie crawled over to Prince "and told us to stay put."[21]

'D' Company was shredded. The company was to have consolidated next to some houses at the western headland's base, and it was towards those that Lieutenant Lou Counsell had led No. 18 Platoon. Counsell saw two wide gaps in the wire obstacle ahead. Unaware that none of the beach was mined, he warned his men to keep clear of the gaps and instead began opening a path with wire cutters. Corporal Percy Haines joined Counsell.[22] While they were cutting, Haines heard Counsell yell to him. "I went over... and found he was wounded. I put a dressing on the wound. While I was doing that he got another in the hip, so I told him we would have to move. I helped him back to the water's edge. On the way back he got hit a third time. I then got dressings on all wounds and told him to lie quiet, while I went for a stretcher... On the way I received a shrapnel wound in the shoulder and before I could get back to Lieutenant Counsell I was all battered up myself."[23]

Captain Jimmy Brown, meanwhile, had been knocked down by a bullet in the side when he tried to reach the gap Counsell had started. Private Alf Collingdon tumbled behind a low shingle ridge nearby and looked around to see his two fellow signallers from 'D' Company—Private Stanley Chadwick and Corporal Clarence Foster—lying dead. Also dead was 'D' Company commander Captain Bud Bowery. Company Sergeant Major H.E. Bell, face slashed by shrapnel, crouched close to Collingdon. Private Tod Sullivan simply sat down, dazed, blood streaming from a head wound. 'D' Company was effectively finished.

To the left of 'D' Company, 'B' Company had charged straight for the casino. Slipping and sliding in the loose rock, Captain

George Matchett got halfway there before a machine-gun burst killed him.[24]

Lieutenant Jack Halladay and Major Frederick Wilkinson, the battalion's second-in-command, reached a shale ridge facing the casino and began shooting at a nearby pillbox. Wilkinson was shot in the shoulder and fell wounded. Halladay crawled ahead to the seawall and hunkered with some 'B' Company men. Germans in the casino chucked grenades at them. Private Harvey Dicus was killed, and several men, including Halladay and Lieutenant Johnny Webster, were wounded. After having his arm and leg wounds bandaged, Halladay crawled along the seawall to find 'B' Company's commander. Halladay saw Major Norry Waldron—he of the Groucho Marx moustache, who had been the bane of all Rileys during training—walking calmly along, about twenty yards away. Suddenly, a sniper's bullet struck and killed Waldron. Spotting the sniper in a casino window, Halladay fired a Sten burst that sent the man sprawling out of sight.

Spotting some 'B' Company Rileys trying to knock out a machine gun firing from the top corner of the tobacco factory, Halladay went down to the tide line, where a 3-inch mortar crew was set up. He pointed out the target, but each time the mortar fired, its base slipped in the loose rock and the round was thrown astray. After several failed shots, the crew abandoned the mortar and crawled towards the seawall. On the way, the mortar team leader, Sergeant William Joseph Bennett, and two men were killed by fire from a hidden machine gun to their left. Lieutenant John Counsell of 'C' Company's No. 14 Platoon was wounded. Shrapnel wounded Halladay again in the arm and leg, rendering him incapable of crawling up the sloping beach. He instead found cover behind a low hump of tide-piled rocks.[25]

Lieutenant Colonel Labatt, meanwhile, saw a "terrific fight" developing in front of the casino and "scrambled towards it. To stand up on that beach meant instant death. Halfway through the wire I stuck, the strands above me thrumming like banjo strings as they were hit. This wire was on the crest of a roll on the beach and while very exposed, it commanded an excellent view. From a hollow just ahead a section was firing like mad at the pillbox [fifteen yards] ahead [and on the casino's northeast corner]. Then I noticed one lone man worming his way through the jungle of wire surrounding the emplacement. He reached it, then having pulled the pin from a grenade, he stood up and shoved it through a loophole. Without waiting he rushed around to the back and seconds later I saw his helmet being jerked up and down on the end of his bayonet as a sign of victory." Private Hugh McCourt was quickly joined by his platoon section and led them into the casino. Within a few minutes, however, the twenty-one-year-old from Eganville, Ontario, was killed.[26]

Lieutenant Johnny Webster and Corporal C.W. Cox managed to blow a gap in the wire that enabled a handful of men through. One of these, Corporal P. Sandy of No. 12 Platoon, saw a pillbox full of Germans about ten feet away. The platoon sergeant and Corporal T. Wilkinson "were closest to the pillbox and they each dropped 36 grenades which temporarily stopped the fire from this point. Just beyond the pillboxes, against the Casino, near the corner, was a round barricade... of sandbags. There was no roof over it. By this time at least seven of the boys were either dead or dying. I made a dive into the sandbag position where Lieutenant Webster, Privates Wheeler and Addis and about six men were. Lieutenant Webster's legs were pretty badly shot up from shrapnel. Private Wheeler had got the fingers of his left hand shot off while aiming a Bren. Private Addis had a wound near the left eye. Private [Harry] Minnett had a wound on the left side of his mouth." The men regrouped and snuck along the seaward wall until they ducked into the casino. They found it jammed with remnants of the entire battalion.[27]

'B' Company had been blocked by a pillbox containing a machine gun that "practically wiped out No. 11 Platoon," Corporal T. Wilkinson recalled. "It was quite impossible to get near the casino as long as this pillbox was in operation as it was [able] to sweep the beach with fire. We therefore put smoke over a low wall behind which we were taking cover. Private [Harry] Wichtacz went over the wall, around the back of the pillbox and placed in it a bangalore torpedo, destroying the pillbox and its crew of 14 Germans. This brave and hazardous operation opened up the way for the advance on the... casino." Wichtacz "was hit by a burst of machine-gun fire which later necessitated the amputation of his leg." He would be awarded a Distinguished Conduct Medal for bravery.[28]

Captain Tony Hill and Company Sergeant Major Jack Stewart had been pinned down with about fourteen 'B' Company men in a hollow of shingle. "We had better get out of here," Hill shouted, and led a dash to the casino. Going straight through the front door, they were surprised to meet no resistance.[29]

Captain Dennis Whitaker's platoon had reached the casino just ahead of Hill's group. They faced two or three dozen Germans. Most of these men threw up their hands in surrender. A short firefight ensued between the Rileys and a few Germans who chose to fight. Although most of these were quickly killed, a few managed to escape out a back door and fled into the town. Whitaker led his men through a main salon—absent any furniture and partially torn down—to the building's east side. Looking out a window, Whitaker saw below it a long slit trench held by German infantry. Quickly positioning a Bren gunner and a Boys anti-tank rifle manned by Private Tommy Graham at windows, "we took them by surprise and cleared up this position," Whitaker wrote.[30] Spotting a machine-gun post in the hotel next door, Graham "let more shots go... and there was a flash from it and it was never heard from again." Running downstairs, Graham charged into the slit trench without considering that the cumbersome anti-tank rifle was his only weapon. The trench was filled with dead Germans. Creeping forward, Graham peered around a bend and saw two who were unscathed. Quickly loosing a .55-calibre round from the anti-tank rifle, Graham killed one of the men and wounded the other.[31]

For more than an hour, the Rileys battled for control of the casino.[32] Corporal George McDermott glanced into a room and "saw three enemy, one of them had his rifle pointed my way. I left and worked my way close enough to throw a grenade. They didn't seem afraid, and threw one back, hitting me on the right foot. I ran about 25 feet before it went off, knocking the rifle from my hand. I came back and threw another grenade. When I moved ahead this time, they had gone, leaving a pool of blood, a rifle, three grenades and two bayonets."

Captain John Currie, sent by Labatt with reinforcements, joined McDermott in searching rooms towards the building's western end. They were soon driven back by artillery and mortar fire hammering down on the casino from positions on the western headland. Entire sections of the building were shattered, their ceilings and walls collapsing, as Rileys dashed through the warren of rooms.[33]

Labatt, meanwhile, had established his headquarters against the headland's cliff face so that he was sheltered from the positions above. Deafened by a shell blast, Labatt shouted into the wireless handset, "Get Johnny Forward, get Johnny forward." "Johnny" was the call sign of Calgary Tank Regiment's Lieutenant Colonel Johnny Andrews. (Regiments and brigades were identified by the first names of their commanders.) Labatt knew that the Rileys had to get tank support now, or the assault would run out of steam—if it had not already done so.[34]

THE ESSEX SCOTTISH had been caught in an even more desperate situation. Captain Dennis Guest's 'A' Company set down immediately left of the most easterly Rileys and became entangled in a wire obstacle at the tide line. Raked by machine guns, only thirty-five men followed Guest in jumping the wire. The other seventy-five lay dead or wounded on the wire or in the surf. At the seawall, the survivors faced another wire obstacle that was three feet high and fifteen feet wide. As all the company's mortars and bangalore torpedoes had been lost, they could not get past the wall or return the heavy fire coming from the headlands.[35]

"The first blast of heavy fire" striking No. 9 Platoon "stunned us for a moment," Private Eugene Cousineau wrote. "But we soon recovered and when we reached the protection of the wall most of our section was present. We could not see the fire of the Germans who were hidden in the buildings along the water front, but the machine-gun and mortar fire was very intense, the [81-millimetre] mortar being very effective and apparently laid along a very definite pattern. The beach being all shale made the fire of the mortars and artillery extremely damaging."

Guest led the men along the seawall to a position facing the tobacco factory. Here a concrete support projected from the wall, and nearby was a breakwater. 'A' Company tucked in between these two structures and gained a little flank cover. "At this time the morale of the men was very high," Cousineau noted, "despite the heavy fire and continual casualties. The men were all smoking and laughing."

The seawall "was covered by a large amount of heavy wire, and beyond that lay about 100 yards of open ground, and then the first row of buildings, which were full of machine-gun posts and snipers. We set up two or three Brens on the wall and fired [at] the windows from one end to the other and I believe inflicted considerable damage as we silenced the fire of several machineguns and snipers." Private Robert Kearns "tried to cut through the wire, but was killed almost instantly."[36]

Private Stanley Carley's platoon was tasked with protecting Lieutenant Colonel Fred Jasperson's battalion headquarters. They found cover behind a small embankment of stones pushed against the first wire barrier by the tide. "There were a lot of men killed going from the boats to the barbed wire. Then everyone took cover for a minute as the machine-gun fire was terrific." Carley watched as one company crossed the wire and "a lot of men dropped." Carley's commander, Lieutenant Jack Kent, led the platoon seventy-five yards to the left. After chucking smoke grenades over the wire, the men crossed and used the covering smoke to gain the seawall and take cover in a large hole fronting it. The hole was already crowded with men from 'C' and 'D' Companies. An officer yelled that Jasperson's orders were for everyone to stay put.[37]

Coming off an LCA, 'C' Company's Lieutenant Peter Ambery had been struck in the right side by shrapnel. Waving his men onto the seawall, he slapped on a shell dressing to stem the blood flow and then ran to join them. Carefully raising one eye over the edge of the seawall, Ambery saw two pillboxes on the esplanade.[38] A French tank protected by a concrete surround was near the base of the west mole, and a pillbox on the mole itself held an anti-tank gun that fired along the seawall's length.[39]

Ambery's men thrust bangalore torpedoes deep into the wire but failed to blast open a path. Bodies dangling from the wire testified to the fate awaiting anyone foolish enough to try crawling over it. Ambery realized they were trapped.[40]

By 0545 hours, Captain Donald MacRae, an attached Stormont, Dundas and Glengarry Highlander officer, estimated the Essex Scottish had suffered 40 per cent either killed or wounded. Yet men continued to fight. "The 3-inch mortars were set up but almost instantly were destroyed by bomb or shell fire. Smoke cover was put over by the 2-inch mortars and the crossing of the seawall was attempted [but] met with intensive gun and mortar fire as well as LMG fire and almost all... the assaulting troops were killed or badly wounded." A second attempt under smoke cover from the 2-inch mortars "suffered [a] similar fate to the first. By this time the wireless sets were largely destroyed; there being only the [No.] 18 set in 'C' Company still functioning. A third attempt on a reduced scale... to cross the wall... was met by a hail of fire causing most of the personnel to become casualties."[41]

Joined by Captain Walter McGregor, Ambery, meanwhile, had crept along the seawall to Jasperson's headquarters. They found the situation there a shambles. Everyone hugged the wall, and Jasperson reported having no wireless contact with either his companies or *Calpe*. Only tanks could break the impasse.[42]

19

A Death Trap

ALL ALONG THE fire-wracked beach, men looked seaward through billowing smoke clouds for the three LCTs bearing nine tanks that were to have landed with the infantry.

Tragically, the LCTs had been led too far westward when the guide ship commander provided incorrect navigational fixes—an error not realized until 0502 hours. Although hurried course corrections were made, the LCTs were still two miles from Dieppe at 0515 and did not enter the offshore smokescreen until 0530. Five minutes later, they began landing.[1] "In any opposed landing," the Canadian Army historian observed, "the first minute or two after the craft touch down are of critical importance; and it may be said that during that minute or two the Dieppe battle, on the main beaches, was lost. The impetus of the attack ebbed quickly away, and by the time the tanks arrived the psychological moment was past."[2]

In addition to the tanks, the LCTs carried parties of Essex Scottish and Rileys; most of the engineers, support personnel, and medical teams; and a collection of scout cars, Bren carriers, and beach buggies. When the large front doors dropped, the men aboard looked upon a scene from hell. Through the thick, drifting smoke clouds, bodies, parts of bodies, and wounded men could be seen strewn across the beach. Most of the still living hunkered along the seawall. Exploding shells and mortar bombs sprayed shards of rock in every direction. Tracer rounds flickered back and forth.

LCT1 grounded on the eastern end of Red Beach, close to the mole. Aboard was 'C' Squadron's headquarters troop, consisting of three tanks: *Chief, Company,* and *Calgary.* The tanks exited fast, with *Chief* leading. *Calgary,* towing a scout car, brought up the rear.[3] Also aboard was Captain D.A. Deziel's Essex Scottish platoon. As the leading men stepped on the ramp, an 81-millimetre mortar round struck it, and shrapnel wounded Deziel in the stomach and chest. "He dropped immediately, and wiggled back into the ship where a stretcher bearer took charge of him," Private R.A.M. Baker recalled. "Let's go, boys," Lieutenant Bill Scott shouted, and the men piled out behind him.[4] As LCT1 backed away, several artillery shells holed and sunk her.

Chief's commander, Major Allen Glenn, deployed the chespaling roll to enable the tank to claw a path up a steep, stony ridge. Gaining the crest, Glenn looked into a seven-foot cavern created by tidal action and German stone-mining operations. Backing downslope to a hull-down position that exposed only the main gun in the turret, Glenn decided this "was a logical place to set up a command post to observe all action and give support."

Captain G.T. Valentine's *Company* had been following *Chief* when a shell broke a track pin on the left front drive wheel and immobilized the tank. *Company* was soon targeted by mortars. Although the explosions filled the tank with smoke, they caused the men inside no injury. Yet the tankers could do little but endure the fiery rain.[5]

Lieutenant Scott's Essex party initially found cover behind *Company* before sprinting for the seawall. A bangalore torpedo shoved into the wire exploded and "[Private] Morris St. Louis had both his legs crushed when a great bunch of the wall toppled over on him." Attempts to use the gap created by this collapse to gain the promenade were driven back by machine-gun fire.[6]

Having seen the other two tanks head for the steep slope, Lieutenant Brice G. Douglas in *Calgary* had moved out to the right flank. When he released the scout car fifteen feet from the LCT, tracers slashed into the fifty-pound bags of explosives strapped to the hood. The scout car exploded, reduced to a flaming wreck. *Calgary* was paralleling the seawall, seeking a way to gain the promenade, when a shell shattered its left track about midway across White Beach. Douglas began shelling the tobacco factory and casino with its 6-pounder gun. Trooper Dennis G. Scott wrote later that when they "observed horses pulling mortars or guns along the top of the [west] cliff, [Trooper Ken] Smethurst hesitated because he really did not want to shoot the horses. Meanwhile, we were attracting a lot of gunfire. We took some direct hits on the turret, hard enough that the paint was melting and running down on the inside. The heat inside, along with the smell of the smoke and cordite, was almost unbearable, so much so that Sergeant 'Al' Wagstaff, who was down in the co-driver's seat was put out of action." *Calgary* kept firing until it ran out of ammunition but likely to little effect. Although the 6-pounder was the most powerful Churchill gun, its only ammunition was armour-piercing, at a time when high-explosive shell would have had more effect.[7]

LCT2 had also landed near the west mole, immediately drawing heavy artillery, mortar, and machine-gun fire. Captain A.L. MacLaurin commanded a Black Watch mortar platoon consisting of four mortar teams totalling twenty-two men. A Royal Navy beach party, thirty No. 11 Canadian Field Company engineers, and thirty Les Fusiliers Mont-Royal assigned to help unload the heavy explosives and equipment were also aboard. The engineers were commanded by Major Bert Sucharov. As soon as the ramp dropped, machine-gun and rifle fire showered in, and men began falling in droves.

MacLaurin thought the tanks of No. 13 Troop were taking forever to get off, possibly because each paused upon gaining the beach to set off the explosive charges that would blast the waterproofing clear of the hull. The explosions stalled the tank engine, which then had to be restarted. The mortar team was to be last off. As the men waited impatiently, they unloaded mortar rounds from ammunition boxes and readied them for carrying ashore. There were 640 rounds, and MacLaurin estimated that each man would have to make four trips between the LCT and a firing position by the seawall, which was three hundred yards away.

LCT2 was absorbing a lot of damage from artillery and mortar strikes. The gunners manning its 2-pounder guns were killed or wounded. Both magazine lockers were hit, but the ammunition inside failed to detonate. A shell punching through the stern penetrated the engine room and opened a hole in the hull through which water poured in. Another shell knocked out one engine. As the last tank with its scout car in trail exited, the LCT captain backed four hundred yards offshore.[8]

Major Sucharov approved, certain his engineers would have been slaughtered trying to unload at that part of the beach. He was just asking the captain to shift 450 yards west for another landing attempt when a shell cut the cable and chains that raised and lowered the ramp, which now hung open.[9]

MacLaurin was frantically trying to get instructions from 4th Brigade headquarters by wireless. His mortars were to have gone into action at 0520 hours by hammering the eastern headland with smoke and high explosive until 0558. It was well past that time, and LCT2 drifted helplessly seaward as the crew tried to stem the water flowing through the hole in the hull before attempting a second landing.[10]

It soon became evident that the LCT was too severely damaged, and its captain ordered her to withdraw. Sucharov, developer of many techniques for assisting tanks in surmounting the seawall, stared helplessly towards a beach he would never reach.[11] So too did MacLaurin.

ASHORE, NO. 13 Troop had successfully reached the seawall, with *Cougar* unfurling its chespaling and lumbering up it to gain the promenade. *Cat* followed suit, but *Cheetah*'s driver, Trooper Fred Hilsabeck, felt his tank beginning to bog down in the rocks. To avoid clogging the bogey wheels with stones, he turned head on to the seawall and climbed straight up it. This exposed the lightly armoured underside, which was immediately struck by a shell. The floor turned "red hot at my feet, so it came mighty close to coming through," Hilsabeck recalled. "It blew all the fuses in the tank, so we rolled back down in behind the wall. I got all the fuses changed and then we went up over the wall... Once we were on the promenade we were like a bunch of rats in a treadmill. We didn't know where to go or just what to do."[12]

Despite having its turret jammed by a 75-millimetre shell strike, *Cougar* fired several shells into the tobacco factory before a buildup of rocks between the tread and bogey wheel broke the left track. Lieutenant T.R. Cornett kept *Cougar* fighting until a shell smashed the other track, rendering the tank helpless. Cornett ordered his crew out. Trooper G.M. Ross was last out, setting off an incendiary sticky bomb that gutted the tank's interior.[13]

The rocks that broke *Cougar*'s track exposed another grave intelligence error. No analysis had been performed of Dieppe's beach stones. It was simply assumed they mirrored the cobble of Sussex beaches. Calgary Tank trooper Stan Kanik [a geological engineer after the war] later determined and reported that Dieppe's stones were chert—"an exceedingly *hard rock*... allied to flint." Beach erosion shaped it "into rounded and oblong stones... that resist cracking or breaking... The entire beach [was] composed of chert stones, boulders and rubble... many metres in depth... When a tracked or wheeled vehicle tries to climb up this slope, it immediately digs itself down; when the tracks are turned to either side the stones roll in between the drive sprocket and track and the object that first gives way is the pins holding the track links—end of locomotion!"[14]

Six months earlier, the German port commander had staged a mock tank attack on the beach. "Within a short time the tank was stuck so firmly that it could no longer be moved. The tracks had to be removed and cleaned." In his report, the port commander concluded, "Now we know that the British cannot land here with tanks."[15]

Only the driving skill of the Canadians allowed so many tanks to cross the beach and gain the promenade. Roaming freely along its length, they were able to engage German positions. *Cat* silenced the 75-millimetre gun at the base of the eastern headland and then joined *Cheetah* in firing up German positions inside the buildings and slit trenches behind the Boulevard de Verdun.[16] *Cat* also engaged the French tank entrenched by the western mole, scoring a direct hit that caused its turret "to explode into the air."[17]

Overhead, German and Allied fighters were tangled in a massive dogfight through which Junkers 87 (Stuka) dive-bombers swooped down to try attacking the tanks. A bomb punched into *Cat*'s engine compartment, the explosion's flash temporarily blinding loader/ operator Trooper G.L. Blair and burning the gunner, Trooper Lloyd McLellan. *Cheetah* hovered protectively as the crew bailed out. No sooner had they dropped behind the cover of the seawall than the same Stuka dropped a bomb on *Cheetah*'s engine deck. "The motor went wild, there was no clutch or steering and the radio was out," Hilsabeck remembered. Everyone bailed out and took cover beside the tank.[18]

LCT3, THE LAST of the first flight to reach the beach, carried three tanks each mounting an experimental flame-throwing device. Also aboard were the primary naval and Calgary Regiment beach parties. Captain Dick Eldred, Captain A. Turney, and four other ranks comprised the tank beach party. Their job was to guide the tanks of the later flights to predetermined positions, direct medical and ammunition parties, and coordinate the tank regiment's actions with those of the more experienced naval beach parties to ensure that the beach did not become overly congested. There was also an engineering party with a bulldozer and other road-building equipment.

In *Bull*, the lead tank, Captain Douglas Gordon Purdy grumbled to Trooper Percy W. Aide, the loader/operator, "We are running behind time." Suddenly, the LCT's ramp dropped. Assuming they were on the beach, Purdy ordered *Bull* to charge. In fact, the LCT was still a hundred yards from landing, and the weight of the tank on the floating ramp severed the left chain, causing a sideways sag. *Bull* "nosed right down" into the water, which started pouring in "from a thousand different sources." The tank struck bottom in ten feet of water, and the crew swam clear. Despite Aide's attempts to help him, Purdy—a non-swimmer—drowned. Trooper William Steward also drowned, trying to swim to the LCT, which had pulled away the moment the tank fell clear of the ramp. The three survivors swam to shore. Aide would be one of only two tankers landed at Dieppe to return to England.[19]

During LCT3's second run in, a shell killed its captain, Sub-Lieutenant W.H. Cooke, and wounded everyone else on the bridge. Lieutenant Peter Ross of the naval beach party managed to stop the engines just as the LCT grounded with such momentum that the ramp folded back on itself, high-ending the front of the craft ten feet into the air.[20] The LCT lay at an angle to the beach, about thirty yards west of the tobacco factory.

The commander of *Boar* ordered it off, even though this meant hurtling off the ramp. The tank crashed so heavily onto the rocks that its flame-thrower fuel tank flew free. Trundling over to the casino, *Boar* gained the promenade and supported the Rileys. *Beetle*, meanwhile, was unable to get moving at all. Realizing a chock holding the tank in place had not been removed, Lieutenant Gordon Drysdale ordered his driver to reverse free of it. Two wounded men lying behind the tank were crushed. After plunging off the LCT, *Beetle* lost a track to the chert. Although immobilized, the tank acted as a vital pillbox and sheltering point set precisely at the juncture of White and Red Beaches.[21]

In the few minutes required for *Beetle* to unload, most of the soldiers and naval personnel aboard LCT3 were killed or wounded. Eldred estimated that of sixty men, 80 per cent were casualties. Only four engineers managed to land, dashing for the seawall through intense machine-gun fire. The Calgary beach party stayed aboard, assisting the wounded. Half-beached, LCT3 was "littered with dead and wounded" and continuously battered by machine-gun and mortar fire.[22]

THE FIRST LCT flight's late landing meant it had gained the beach only minutes before the second flight. LCT4 landed just east of the tobacco factory with 'B' Squadron's headquarters troop. Squadron commander Major Charles Page led off in *Burns*. With *Bolster* and *Backer* following, the tanks cleared in less than three minutes. As the LCT began backing away, it was sunk by artillery fire.

Tearing through a wire obstacle, *Burns* ground to the top of the ridge behind which the deep cavern formed a natural tank trap that the Germans had been deepening with a mechanical digger, abandoned nearby.[23] "I gave the orders to turn to the right and that's when I was hit," Page said. "The right track was blown off. The left one went on for a few seconds and kind of pulled me into the trench." This left *Burns* with guns pointing downward. Armed with Brens and Stens, the crew ran to the seawall. Corporal G.M. Mowat was soon wounded, and a little later Trooper Thomas Gorman was killed.

A shell jammed *Backer*'s turret, and seeing that *Burns* was disabled, Lieutenant Dick Wallace headed towards it to surrender his tank to Page. About ten yards short of the other tank, the left track broke, and the tank slewed to a halt with its 2-pounder pointing uselessly along the length of the beach. Trooper Jack Chapman crawled out and attached a heavy cable to the gun turret. Then the driver, Trooper E.M. Snider, reversed the still functioning track. The tank slewed so its gun pointed towards the promenade. Soon, after its ammunition was expended, Wallace had the tank interior burned by a sticky bomb after the crew evacuated. Everyone belly-crawled to a nearby hole, which proved too shallow for Trooper Charles Lyman Provis, whose nickname was "Heavy." Unable to get his head below the rim, Provis was shot between the eyes by a sniper. *Bolster*, meanwhile, had lost both tracks to the chert.[24]

'B' Squadron's No. 9 Troop landed from LCT5 east of the casino. Lashed by machine-gun and mortar fire, the LCT began backing off the moment the tanks cleared, without waiting for the soldiers aboard to exit. At first, Provost Corps's Corporal Bob Prouse tried "to hug the side of the craft" for cover but quickly "tired of being a sitting duck." Stepping over bodies, he ran forward and jumped off the ramp. "I was up to my thighs in water and still don't know how I got ashore without being hit. I threw my body on the coarse gravel beach and squirmed … towards the concrete seawall. I had to get through a mess of barbed wire already strewn with bodies and finally pushed myself up to the wall where a soldier lay dead, draped over the barbed wire that ran along the top. I made my way to a burning scout car which afforded some protection. I flopped down behind it and found three or four men from our company. There was a blinding explosion as a mortar shell hit the scout car. All I could feel was a numbing sensation in my legs as shrapnel entered my flesh."[25]

Engine room and bridge destroyed, LCT5 had meanwhile grounded on the beach directly in front of the casino. The few surviving crew and soldiers aboard abandoned her. Detonating ammunition and explosives set the craft ablaze.[26]

No. 9 Troop's Sergeant J.D. Morrison managed to get the lead tank, *Buttercup*, over the seawall by deploying the chespaling. The tank alternated its fire between targets on the western headland and the buildings east of the casino. In *Blossom*, Lieutenant Marcel Lambert had tried to follow Morrison. "We were doing a turn to get lined up with the wall...when our right track broke...we had never run into that kind of stuff before...once we had broken our track we were pretty much sheltered by the casino." Lambert's gunner fired at a 37-millimetre gun in a pillbox beside the casino, but the 6-pounder's armour-piercing shells were ineffective. It was "just like chipping away with a handpick...or spitting at it; we were terribly under-gunned," Lambert said. *Blossom* lay at such an angle to the pillbox that the German gun could not retaliate.

Towing a scout car, *Bluebell* became bogged down in the loose chert. Able to move no more than a couple of feet in either direction, the tank fired at gun flashes coming from buildings across the promenade. Spotting a sniper on the casino roof, the gunner killed him with a 6-pounder shell. Trooper G. Volk, meanwhile, had slithered out of the tank, only to be wounded while scooping rocks away from the track. Volk would be the second and last tanker evacuated from the beach to England.

During each of three attempts to land, the sailor manning LCT6's helm was killed. The fourth attempt succeeded only because the captain grounded her behind the cover of the sinking LCT1. No. 6 Troop's *Bob*, *Bert*, and *Bill* quickly unloaded. As *Bert*'s waterproofing was blown off, it failed to clear and jammed the turret traverse. Climbing out, Trooper T.A. Dunsmore hacked the waterproofing away with a machete. All three tanks surmounted the seawall just west of the casino. Proceeding around back of the large building, they fired at strongpoints near the castle. When Lieutenant Lambert warned them by wireless of the 37-millimetre gun position, Lieutenant Jack Dunlap moved *Bob* "into position and we fired into an opening at the rear of the bunker. We also fired the turret Besa [machine gun] but it... jammed." Leaving *Bert* to finish the job, Dunlap moved "to fire the 6-pounder at a sandbagged gun emplacement at the side of a building facing the promenade. We destroyed it."

Dunlap kept seeking an exit into the town, but large concrete roadblocks plugged every street. The three tanks joined the others motoring along the promenade and Boulevard de Verdun, firing at the headlands and into the seaside buildings.[27]

AS THE FIRST tanks had gained the promenade, an intrepid group of unlikely Essex Scottish succeeded in surmounting the seawall. Company Sergeant Major Cornelius Stapleton's platoon of cooks and drivers were to safeguard battalion headquarters and carry out special assignments. Stapleton had reached the seawall with only ten of his men still following. The rest had been killed or wounded crossing the beach. Unable to locate Lieutenant Colonel Jasperson's headquarters, Stapleton assumed it would be in the buildings fronting Boulevard de Verdun. Seeing several gaps in the wire created by German mortar fire, Stapleton led his men through one and out onto the promenade. Pausing next to a tank for cover, Stapleton waited until the mortar fire eased for a moment and then led his men in "one mad dash" across the wide, grassy strip separating the promenade from Boulevard de Verdun. Private Charlie Hoskin fell wounded, but the rest got through unscathed.[28]

Not so a second party. Seeing Stapleton's men making their move, Private J.T. Fleming, Corporal C.H. Grondin, and seven other men tried following. Having missed Stapleton's men, the Germans were ready. Everyone but Fleming and Grondin was killed. The two survivors found refuge by plunging through a hotel's open front door.[29]

Stapleton "had been expecting to find the buildings facing the promenade destroyed by the pre-landing fire support and was disappointed" that they were largely undamaged. Finding the door to the hotel in front of him locked, Stapleton chucked a grenade through a window. The blast blew out the glass.[30] As the men climbed through the opening, the tobacco factory next door erupted in flames, because of either tank fire or Essex Scottish firing incendiary grenades.[31]

Inside the hotel, Stapleton surprised and killed two German snipers. All the gunfire coming from the surrounding buildings seemed to be German, and Stapleton realized he had been mistaken. The Essex Scottish headquarters must be back on the beach.

Deciding that since he was here, he might as well cause some mischief, Stapleton cautiously led the men through the hotel and into the street beyond.[32]

Meanwhile, Fleming and Grondin had become separated. Chancing upon two men from Stapleton's group, Corporal C.E. Stevenson and Private T.E. Hood, Fleming joined them in clearing snipers from the front row of buildings. They killed four or five with Bren and Thompson submachine-gun fire but lost sight of Stevenson. Encountering Stapleton, the two men joined his group. Grondin also turned up. Passing through several buildings, the men entered "a sort of courtyard" and then moved south in short rushes along a narrow street towards the inner harbour. Along the way, they engaged and killed several more snipers. Private R.I. Richards was hit in the eye by a ricocheting bullet, and Stapleton ordered him back to the beach. The others soon came to a row of houses on Quai du Hable directly facing the narrow passage between the port mouth and outer harbour. Suddenly, a sniper, firing from the eastern headland, shot Fleming in the right arm. Stapleton sent Fleming back.

On his return, Fleming entered a hotel that served as a German billet and discovered a company-sized store of grenades and ammunition, which he blew up with a grenade. As he ran towards the seawall, Fleming was shot again—this time in the left arm. Diving into a small anti-aircraft position on the promenade, Fleming found Richards hiding there.[33]

Stapleton, meanwhile, watched from the third storey of an old house as a small tug approached a nearby dock. When the tug came into range, his men opened fire and drove the crew to cover. Realizing they lacked the firepower to sink the sturdy vessel, Stapleton withdrew into the maze of streets comprising Dieppe's old quarter. A French civilian pointed out a window. Peeking around a corner, Stapleton saw German infantry exiting a building and boarding a truck. Once the truck was loaded and driving off, Stapleton shouted for his men to form a line and open fire. Two Brens, one Thompson, and three or four rifles spoke as one. The truck stalled, its lights came on, and one of his men shouted, "Bingo!" Before the Germans could react, the Canadians withdrew.

Two young French women soon appeared and tried to lead off two of Stapleton's men. Suspecting a trap, Stapleton sternly shooed the women away and then led the men down a narrow alley that dead-ended. Suddenly, a sniper opened up, his men scattered, and Stapleton was alone in a building and pinned down. To draw the sniper's fire, Stapleton stuck his head out a window. When the sniper fired, Stapleton charged. As he closed in, one of his men appeared and killed the sniper with a grenade.

Deciding their luck was turning sour, Stapleton led the men back to the hotels. As they sprinted to the seawall, a couple of Calgary tanks mistook them for Germans and opened fire. But all the men made the crossing safely. Finally locating Jasperson, Stapleton reported his adventure.[34] Having been informed that a party of Essex Scottish had gone into Dieppe, Jasperson had just moments before used the battalion's single remaining wireless set to contact Lieutenant Bob Labatt. "Twelve of our men in the buildings. Have not heard from them in some time," he said. Stapleton's party had been inside Dieppe for about thirty minutes. Although several other Essex Scottish parties were reported to have gone beyond the seawall, the army's official historian disproved these accounts. Stapleton was awarded a Distinguished Conduct Medal.[35]

IN FACT, THE Essex Scottish were, as early as 0630 hours, "unable to continue organized fighting" because "they had suffered at least 75% casualties," Captain Donald MacRae realized. "A large number of officers [had been] either killed or very severely wounded." Yet MacRae noted that "the troops were marvellously cool and there was not the slightest evidence of fear. The men [were] fighting all the time and words are inadequate to pay proper tribute to the excellence of all these officers and men. Unless they were so badly wounded that they could not carry on, all ranks fought stubbornly in spite of their wounds.[36]

Jasperson remained unhurt. "Mortar and shell splinters were whistling all around me, some as close as 8 feet but none got me. The most I suffered was periodic showers of stone... on my tin hat and body which did me no harm."[37]

Except for some Rileys and engineers inside the casino and a couple of nearby buildings, the Canadians were pinned behind the seawall. Several tanks prowled the promenade. Others strewn along the beach with damaged tracks still fired at the seaside buildings. Several Churchills burned; others had been abandoned.

Inside the casino, Captain Tony Hill collected about fourteen men and led them out a back exit into the street beyond. Company Sergeant Major Jack Stewart provided covering fire with a Bren gun as the rest sprinted across the street—one man falling wounded—and gained the buildings. After Stewart joined them, the men tried to pass a concrete roadblock plugging the street east of Rue de Sygogne. Thick wire tangles alongside the roadblock made it impossible to get through. Instead they broke a window and crawled into a building that proved to be a cinema.

Hill—"a bold and aggressive leader," in Stewart's estimation—was "determined to push on into the town." Exiting the cinema, they advanced east through a square centred on St. Rémy Church. Meeting a German patrol, the Rileys fell back as Stewart kept the enemy at bay with his Bren gun. Near the church square, they spotted a group of Germans milling around an apparent headquarters. Stewart loosed a burst and two Germans fell dead. The Germans lashed back. Corporal Samuel Howard Harris, carrying a broken wireless set, was killed by a sniper. Other Germans rushed forward with heavy machine guns. Hill led the men fleeing across the square and into the cinema. Firing out windows, they drove the Germans into cover. Bolstered by the arrival of Major Harold Lazier and a small group of men, the Rileys engaged the Germans in a desultory gun battle.[38]

By this time, Lieutenant Colonel Labatt fully appreciated that the Rileys were in a "pretty desperate state... On the right the enemy held the west cliff, the castle and the buildings on the town level. From these positions every inch of the beach was covered by observation and fire. In the centre, he held emplacements in the esplanade and all the buildings covering it. On the left he had the east hill from which he covered the esplanade and the eastern end of the beach and from behind the mole his automatic weapons were raking the beach from one end to the other."

Labatt's most rightward company had "been practically annihi-
lated before reaching the wire and its survivors were pinned to the
little hollows in the beaches. In the centre we had got through the
wire, captured the casino and small parties were in the town. This
operation had been costly and had used up the centre and most of
the reserve companies. The left company had got through to the
esplanade, there to be practically wiped out. Its survivors had moved
to the right, joining up with the units around the casino... The
beach was a death trap."

Suddenly, a signaller handed Labatt a message from Brigadier
Sherwood Lett. "What is the situation? Where are you?" Still deaf,
Labatt could not talk directly into the wireless. "Brigadier Lett is
going to land," the signaller told him. Labatt hurriedly dictated a
message that the situation was hopeless and "on no account" should
Lett land.[39]

LABATT'S WARNING WENT unheeded. At 0605 hours, right on
schedule, the next flight of four LCTS approached. Brigadier Lett was
aboard LCT8, Brigadier Bill Southam LCT7. As Southam climbed a
ladder to the bridge, "there was a flash which seemed to be almost in
my face... I was tumbled off the ladder, and landed on a man below
me... I saw that the centre tank was afire, and a soldier with fire
blackened face was attempting to put it out."[40]

The soldier was Lieutenant Ed Bennett, commanding 'B' Squadron's No. 10 Troop. He had been standing on the turret of *Bellicose*,
attempting to figure out in which direction the squadron should go.
The smokescreens obscured his view. All he could see were buildings
rising up out of the smoke, but Bennett "knew there was lots of action
on the beach" because he "could hear all the firing." Suddenly, a shell
from the gun emplacement on the mole punched through the LCT's
left side, hit the barrage balloon storage area, and exploded the hydro-
gen cylinders. Bennett was caught "in the middle of the blast. My face
was burnt—all my hair was gone." A sliver of metal lodged in his
right eye.[41] "But we were coming into action and I picked myself up
and we went into shore." Bennett's loader/operator, Trooper Archie
Anderson, clambered out with a fire extinguisher and doused the

flames—one of a series of brave actions eventually recognized with a Military Medal.[42] As the two men climbed back inside, Bennett, whose left eye was unhurt, saw that some of the brigade's wireless equipment had been destroyed by the blast. The explosion had also jammed *Bellicose*'s turret.

As *Bellicose* exited on the heels of *Beefy*, Bennett saw tanks stranded on the beach. Realizing the tanks had broken their tracks on the rocks, Bennett ordered his driver to hug the tide line. The last tank out was *Bloody*, towing a scout car with the Calgary Regiment's signals officer, Major Gordon Rolfe, and two No. 19 wireless sets aboard. Rolfe was to use the signals equipment in three scout cars to establish the regiment's communications link to both brigade head-quarters and 2nd Division's headquarters on *Calpe*. Sergeant Ron B. Lee, commanding *Bloody*, first headed for the seawall before turning to follow Bennett. As he reversed, Lee's tank crushed Rolfe's scout car. Releasing the scout car, *Bloody* trundled off along the beach. Partly squashed, pressed deep into the chert, the scout car appeared destroyed. But Rolfe was unhurt and had one operational No. 19 set inside. Shortly, Corporal A.G. Wills arrived to report the other two scout cars and their wireless sets destroyed by shellfire.[43]

The "scene on the beach was one of utter confusion," Southam realized. "Men both living and dead were lying about." He checked his gear. Everything was in order, including the army attaché case that contained a copy of the Jubilee military plan. Spotting his signal-lers dragging the brigade's No. 19 set on a dolly, he ran over to help as a Churchill bore down upon them. "We waved at it, and attempted vainly to move the 19 set from its path; some fast jumping saved us from being bumped but the 19 set was not so fortunate." The brigade major had another No. 19 set, but a sergeant reported all other officers in the headquarters had been wounded and remained aboard LCT7. So too had the wireless set. Realizing his brigade headquarters now consisted of one officer—himself—and a few other ranks, Southam ran to Rolfe's scout car and the last remaining wireless.[44] Rolfe assured Southam he could "handle all frequencies needed, including tanks." He and Wills were "able to keep the Brigadier in communica-tion forward to his battalions and back to [*Calpe*], and by switching frequency Rolfe was able to keep in touch with the tank C.O. and Squadron Commanders and give situation reports to Force Headquarters. This task . . . was not an easy one . . . requiring rapid and accurate changes of frequency on the operator's part."[45] Southam tried unsuccessfully to raise his South Saskatchewan Rifles and Queen's Own Cameron Highlanders at Pourville and soon realized—wireless links aside—that he was effectively marooned.[46]

Bennett's No. 10 Troop, meanwhile, had ground down the length of the beach to gain the promenade near the casino. "The Germans who were pinning down the infantry on the beach were entrenched in front of the buildings . . . We made a dash for them and to our surprise they poured out from everywhere running like hell for the buildings. Both gunners opened up and we got plenty of them. Even had the pleasure of running down one who tried to dodge us. We passed their trench defences and came back for more. By this time we were starting to receive something in return. We moved east again and tried to get into the town back of the casino. All the side streets were very narrow and . . . blocked with solid concrete about five feet high. We were finally hit properly and our steering was buggered. I think it was the idler wheel. We backed up to where the trench was and when I tried to fire through the pistol port at a stray German running for cover I realized that I was unable to see clearly any longer. The burns had closed up the left eye."[47]

LCT8 HAD NOT only Brigadier Sherwood Lett's 4th Brigade headquarters aboard but also the Calgary Regiment's three-tank-strong headquarters. The regiment's adjutant, Captain Austin Stanton, commanded the lead tank, *Ringer*. Lieutenant Colonel Johnny Andrews was in the second tank, *Regiment*. Major John Begg, the regiment's second-in-command, was in *Rounder*. *Ringer* immediately mired in the chert in front of the ramp.[48] A dozen engineers from 7th Field Company under command of Captain John Eric Bright dashed off the LCT with chespaling rolls but were unable to free the tank. Most of Bright's men were killed or wounded, and he suffered two wounds before the LCT captain ordered the engineers back aboard.[49] As LCT8 backed out to sea under intense fire, Andrews signalled Major Allan Glenn of 'C' Squadron to temporarily take command ashore.[50]

Once the LCT left, *Ringer* backed up and freed itself. The tank started following the beach in the lowest gear, "because of all those damnable round stones that no one mentioned before," Trooper Tom H. Pinder recalled. After only a short distance a track broke, and the tank was stranded.[51]

Every tanker cursed the chert. 'B' Squadron's No. 7 Troop landed easily from LCT9. *Brenda, Betty,* and *Blondie* picked their way warily to the promenade across a "beach with stones the size of baseballs."[52] Like the other tanks there, they found no passage into the town, so they cruised the promenade and Boulevard de Verdun.

Because the engineers ashore had not managed to off-load many explosives, they were unable to demolish the roadblocks. A mixed party, commanded by 7th Field Company's Lieutenant William Alexander Ewener, tackled the roadblock barring Rue de Sygogne—which intersected the western end of Boulevard de Verdun. Gathering up explosives found on the beach, the men made for the casino. Burdened by the weight of their loads, few survived the heavy fire. Ewener, severely wounded in the chest, staggered into the casino carrying fifty pounds of explosives. He collapsed, unable to go farther. The 11th Field Company's Corporal Milton Douglas Sinasac took over, leading six men towards the roadblock. Four men died gaining the roadblock, and the charges set failed to breach the obstruction. Sinasac ran back to the casino through murderous machine-gun fire. Finding two more heavy charges, Sinasac and another engineer returned to the roadblock. Although wounded, Sinasac was able to place and detonate the explosives, only to barely scratch the roadblock's surface. During the withdrawal, Sinasac was again wounded. Explosives exhausted, the engineers were forced to give up. For their efforts Ewener received a Military Cross and Sinasac a Distinguished Conduct Medal.[53]

LCT10, carrying 'C' Squadron's No. 15 Troop, touched down at 0610 hours. Lieutenant Pat Patterson was leading in *Caustic*. As the ramp dropped, a flurry of artillery fire struck. Water, shrapnel, and whirling rocks showered down. Patterson directed *Caustic* towards a ramp leading up onto the promenade. *Canny* and *Confident* followed. Trooper Lee Patterson, driving *Confident,* remembered getting across the beach by "turning a bit, backing up, then going ahead again, then turning a bit and so on." All three tanks gained the promenade, but *Confident* was immediately struck by concentrated shellfire, and Patterson plunged it back onto the beach. Unable to escape the German fire, *Confident* played at jack-in-the-box by darting quickly up the ramp, firing several shots, and then backing fast down to the beach. *Caustic* and *Canny,* meanwhile, joined the other tanks promenading back and forth along the esplanade.[54]

Behind the tanks on LCT10 were sixty-two engineers under senior engineer Lieutenant Colonel Frank Barnes. As *Confident* had left, it had severely damaged the ramp, disabling the LCT. The engineers were trapped aboard as LCT9 took the boat under tow and dragged it seaward. It was 0630 hours and, aboard *Calpe,* time for dire decisions.

20

Situation Very Grim

TWO MILES AT sea off Dieppe, Captain John Hughes-Hallett was certain "things were going badly, partly through the sight of so many damaged landing craft limping back through the smoke and making for the 'boat pool' which had been established four miles out to sea, and partly because the reports being received by Major General Roberts in his improvised Operations Room below the bridge were chaotic and uninformative."[1]

The communication problems were not due to *Calpe* lacking resources. Roberts had "major command links to his brigadiers, there were 'listening sets' tuned on other nets (such as brigade command nets) and each operator was expected to write down everything, no matter how trivial, that came over his particular network," the Canadian Corps of Signals official historian wrote. "Complete as were these facilities, they were useful only in exact proportion to the number of forward sets that were able to remain on the air. The Senior Signals NCO aboard reported later that the entire communications pattern was satisfactory until the battalions made actual contact [with the enemy], 'at which time you could almost hear their sets going off the air.'"[2]

Aboard *Calpe* and *Fernie*, other problems also plagued communications. Lieutenant Colonel J.D. Macbeth, 2nd Division's chief signals officer, noted that one intercept receiver on *Fernie* was manned by clerks who "turned in very few records of traffic on this wave and merely listened." A second monitoring wireless tuned to a different wavelength was "operated by a Signals Officer, who fed Brigadier [Church] Mann extracts from all conversations." Macbeth decided all receivers should henceforth "be manned jointly by Signals (who can note breakdowns on the intercepted wireless group) and clerks who can write down ALL intercept traffic which can be sorted out by [Mann] as pertinent or otherwise."[3]

Brigadier Lucien Truscott thought the handling of communications on *Fernie* unprofessional. "Radio was the only means of communications... between military elements afloat and ashore. Practically all communication from the division downward was by voice radio and the greater part that I observed was in the clear. Considerable confusion resulted from 'bogus messages' of which a number were received... It would seem dangerous in the extreme to use voice radio as freely... without greater use of code and identification than was observed.

"Throughout the operation... Brigadier Mann and his principal assistant actually received and transmitted most of the messages that passed through the headquarters." Truscott thought "that trained signal operators might be more efficient from a technical point of view, as well as from a security point of view. Also, the use of trained operators would free staff officers for consideration of other matters."[4]

Of course, no amount of reorganizing of communications aboard *Calpe* or *Fernie* could compensate for the fact that as soon as a unit landed, it started losing wireless sets and signallers at an alarming pace. Under almost constant fire, signallers and officers resorted to sending truncated and—due to the literal fog of war—often confused or inaccurate signals. Consequently, Roberts and Hughes-Hallett had no real idea what was happening on the beaches. At 0450, for example, the only concrete information Roberts received was a South Saskatchewan Regiment signal: "Cecil landed." There was no news from Yellow, Orange, or Blue Beaches.[5]

Adding to the confusion was the fact that few of the wireless sets that survived ashore were directly netted to either command ship. Instead, wireless sets like that of artillery officer Captain George Browne on Blue Beach were netted to destroyers for fire-support direction. Although from 0541 to 0747 hours Browne remained in steady communication with *Garth*, whose captain duly ordered the signals forwarded to *Calpe*, none of them were received—leaving Roberts completely in the dark about events on Blue Beach.[6]

As the morning wore on, the wireless equipment on the two command destroyers also became increasingly unreliable as the anti-aircraft gunners fended off Luftwaffe air attacks and the ships undertook increasingly violent evasive action to throw off the aim of coastal batteries. The wireless-set tubes became prone to problems that made receiving or sending messages impossible until the ship steadied.[7] Such was the potential for concussion damaging the radios that neither destroyer was permitted to fire its main 4-inch guns.[8]

The most reliable news proved to be that delivered in person. This was how Hughes-Hallett and Roberts finally learned the cause and consequences of the naval battle to the east. Forced to play hopscotch from one vessel to another—each time being unable to establish wireless connection to *Calpe*—Group 5 Commander Derek Wyburd and Lieutenant Colonel John Durnford-Slater finally arrived to report in person.[9] Both "bleeding profusely from head wounds," they told Hughes-Hallett of No. 3 Commando's fate.[10] Even then the information was erroneous, for they believed none of the commando had landed.

Not surprisingly, below decks Durnford-Slater found Roberts "in a mood of the deepest depression."[11] His knowledge of events ashore was vague. *Calpe's* wireless log reported both the Essex Scottish and Rileys landed by 0550 hours. He had received no word from Blue Beach. The signal "Doug in faint comm[unication] with Sherwood" at 0555 clarified nothing, as Brigadier Sherwood Lett added no details about what Lieutenant Colonel Doug Catto reported, if anything. Precisely at 0600, a signal from Cecil reported the Camerons landing on Green Beach. At 0610, Lett's 4th Brigade further muddied the waters by reporting having "no word" from the Royals, and ten minutes later an unattributed signal reported the battalion had "not landed."[12] This was followed at 0615 hours by a signal from a naval beach officer aboard a landing craft off Blue Beach that reached *Calpe* as "impossible to land Blue Beach." The original signal had actually read, "impossible to land any more troops on Blue Beach."

Convinced that the Royals were still all at sea, Roberts sent a signal to Catto directing him to land at Red Beach and assist the Essex Scottish in an advance up the eastern headland overlooking Dieppe.[13]

At 0610, meanwhile, Lieutenant Colonel Fred Jasperson's signal to Lieutenant Colonel Bob Labatt that a dozen Essex Scottish were inside Dieppe reached *Fernie* in such distorted form that Brigadier Church Mann was happily telling Roberts that the entire battalion was "across the beaches" and in the town.[14] This was followed at 0615 by Labatt's reporting the Rileys had taken the casino.[15]

For Roberts, 0615 was a time for decisions. He understood that No. 4 Commando had destroyed the battery at Varengeville. On Green Beach, the Sasks and Camerons appeared to be doing well. The Essex Scottish and Rileys were making progress in front of Dieppe, and at least two flights of tanks had landed in support. Most of his problems, he thought, lay to the east, where the Royals apparently were still at sea and No. 3 Commando had been scattered without having landed. Although the Berneval battery appeared not to be firing, the reason for this was a mystery. Ominously, the German guns on the eastern headland were heavily shelling Dieppe's beach and the landing craft offshore. If the raid were to succeed, those guns must be silenced.

That the raid's success was no longer possible eluded Roberts. Isolated in his headquarters below deck, he could not see the obvious. Had he gone to the bridge, the evidence would have been plain. *Calpe* had a crew of about one hundred men. Already its decks, wardrooms, infirmary, and most other available space were crowded with wounded Canadians transferred from landing craft for treatment by the doctors aboard. Limping towards the boat pool were LCTS, LCMS, and LCAS jammed with casualties—most of their naval crews included—and decks streaming blood. Intermittently, the smoke thinned sufficiently for the flash of the guns on the headlands and out on the mole to be seen spitting fire at Red and White Beaches.

Roberts would also have seen the gallant sacrifice of LCF2 as it steamed with guns blazing to within point-blank range of White Beach. Despite being straddled by artillery fire, raked by machine guns, and pummelled by mortars, she hammered the buildings around the casino and positions on the headlands with her 20-

millimetre Oerlikons and 2-pounder guns until Captain E.L. Graham and all other naval officers were killed. Then surgeon Lieutenant M.P. Martin took command, keeping her fighting until all the guns aboard "were put out of action one by one." As LCF2 sank, Martin "swam away, was picked up and transferred... to *Calpe* [and there] helped the Surgeon on board with the wounded."[16]

Roberts witnessed none of this. And Hughes-Hallett, curiously, decided not to communicate his own forebodings. Having never previously shied away from interfering in military planning, he now decided that as "a professional sailor," it was not for him "to adjudicate."[17]

Consequently, Roberts decided that the "information received indicated that RED beach was sufficiently cleared to permit the landing of the floating reserve." Turning to Lieutenant Colonel Joe Ménard, who had been standing by since 0610, Roberts ordered Les Fusiliers Mont-Royal "to land, and, moving to the west, establish themselves on WHITE beach and on the edge of the town of Dieppe."[18]

As Ménard departed, Lieutenant Commander Colin McMullen reported to Hughes-Hallett the news that he had overseen landing the Royals on Blue Beach and that they had met with disaster. "There was," he concluded, "no prospect of the east cliffs being captured" from the direction of Puys.

According to plan, the Royal Marines No. 40 Commando was to enter Dieppe harbour at 0700 hours aboard the gunboat HMS *Locust* and seven French *chasseurs*. Hughes-Hallett immediately summoned *Locust*'s captain, Commander Red Ryder, and said he doubted the mission "was feasible." Ryder replied "that he felt certain... any attempt to enter the harbour would be attended by the loss of all the ships concerned, since they would have to run the gauntlet at pointblank range of batteries of medium calibre guns concealed in caves dug into the side of the cliff." After consulting with Roberts, the harbour mission was abandoned.[19] *Locust* and the *chasseurs* stood offshore.

BEFORE LEADING HIS 584-strong force of Fusiliers towards Dieppe, Ménard cruised along the broad line of twenty-six fragile R-Boats at about 0700, shouting orders through a loudhailer.[20] The entire battalion was going to charge directly at Red Beach, he said. Ménard had come to know his men well. "They were nearly all French Canadians like myself. I'd seen snapshots of their wives, kids, mothers and girls. I wondered how many of them would be coming back and I started praying—not for myself particularly, but in a general sort of way: 'O God, please let as many of us as possible come back.'

"Every man in the battalion knew a lot of us were going to get killed or hurt. But I didn't think that I was going to get killed and I don't believe a single man thought he was... That's why I say the first element of what they call bravery is a sort of optimism or egoism. It brings you up to the action itself—sort of pays your bus fare to the battlefield."

Ménard knew "we were going to get hell. There were a lot of guns going, and at first you could pick out the sounds. The heavy, dull thunder of the artillery... The ripping clatter of the machineguns. The boom of the mortars. The whine of the sniper's rifle. Then, as we moved in closer, all these sounds began to merge into one continuous roar that pressed hard on your eardrums... Those last 200 yards were bad. The German fire was getting the range of our boats. I had a dry, hot feeling in my throat. I wanted to do something—not just sit there in that damned boat."[21]

The boats were deployed with 'D' Company on the far right, then 'A' Company, 'C' Company, Ménard's headquarters, and finally 'B' Company. Because Ménard's R-Boat guided directly towards the burning tobacco factory, this meant most of the Fusiliers were actually angling towards White Beach. 'C' Company's Lieutenant Antoine Masson's boat passed through one thin smokescreen and emerged into a wide expanse of clear water. Ahead lay another thin screen of smoke, but for now they were nakedly exposed. The Germans struck with "heavy and accurate fire... either from mortars or howitzers... mainly from the *east* cliff." The boat to his left exploded and sank. Several other craft were hit. Water erupted around his boat, but it suffered no damage. Masson shouted at his Bren gunners, who set up on each side of the boat and began firing bursts at the headlands.

The entire formation was shrinking westward to gain distance from the heavier eastern headland fire. As a consequence, a large number of boats were soon headed for the stretch of the beach that was but a narrow strip under the cliffs to the west of the casino.[22]

From the shore, Brigadier Bill Southam saw the R-Boats approaching the casino area. "I took it to be the FMR and wondered why they were coming in there. I could see quite plainly that they were subjected to murderous fire as they came in."[23]

Lieutenant Peter Ross, the Royal Navy officer beach party commander, had earlier signalled for boats to evacuate the rapidly growing number of wounded, and he assumed these R-Boats were his. "The craft landed along the whole length of White Beach, but at least two which had landed between the casino and cliffs were put out of action owing to coming within point blank range of the honeycomb of machine-gun positions in the face of the cliffs—the bullets penetrating their thin wooden hulls or setting the petrol tanks on fire.

"Owing to the falling tide the remainder of the craft did not touch down on the beach but dropped the troops off knee deep in water and made off as quickly as possible out to sea. As the craft never came within hailing distance of the beach... it was not possible to detain them."[24]

Sergeant Major Lucien Dumais and twenty men from No. 3 (Mortar) Platoon landed fifty yards east of the casino. Dumais and five men leapt ashore. Looking back, Dumais saw that the boat had backed out to sea so quickly that the other fifteen men and mortars were still on board. His cries for it to return were ignored. Dumais and his remaining men stood between two beached LCTs, one burning furiously. A couple of these men were hit as fire came in from both flanks. Leading the survivors westward, Dumais came upon his commander, Lieutenant Pierre Loranger, and the rest of the mortar platoon.[25] Wounded in the leg, Loranger handed Dumais his Sten gun and told him to "take command of the platoon." One man stayed to help Loranger board an R-Boat.[26]

Many Fusiliers were killed or wounded before reaching the beach. Private Joseph Noel's platoon commander, Lieutenant André Vennat, fell mortally wounded beside him. The survivors piled out and ran to the seawall in front of the tobacco factory.[27]

Corporal Robert Berube's platoon came ashore close to the cliffs. "After we landed all that could be done and all that was done was to take cover." The Germans above them were "covering a wide area of the beach" from "well protected emplacements." Machine-gun and mortar fire made it impossible for the men caught on the narrow beach to either move or return fire.[28]

On the opposite flank, Major Guy Vandelac's 'B' Company landed facing the tobacco factory. As Vandelac ran ashore, an officer hiding in a hole with some men shouted at the Fusiliers "not to open fire because we will all be killed." Vandelac retorted that "he was not going to lose his company just standing there, and if he didn't like it, he should... move somewhere else." Vandelac yelled for the company to make for the seawall, "but his men refused to move." Company headquarters in tow, Vandelac continued to the wall. "After a while the men on the beach, suffering casualties from enfilade machine-gun fire and snipers, and without a leader," joined him.

Vandelac ordered Captain Roland Gravel's platoon to investigate the possibility of breaking into the town by advancing from the west jetty along the Quai du Hable. Reaching the jetty, Gravel sent a section forward, but it was immediately eliminated. After several futile attempts, Gravel returned to Vandelac with just two men left. Vandelac next tried calling down smoke shells in front of his position but could get no response on the wireless. Sending one section up on the promenade without any smoke cover only got the men killed. Mortar, machine-gun, and sniper fire shredded 'B' Company as it cowered against the seawall. It was 0730 hours, Vandelac was out of ideas, and his men were helpless.[29]

As Lieutenant Masson's R-Boat landed close to the west cliff, his sergeant was hit. So, too, were the boat captain and a naval rating. No sooner had the Fusiliers vacated the boat than it was smashed by a mortar round. The tide was out, exposing a lot of ridges and holes that provided some cover. Without that, Masson figured everyone near the cliff would have been killed. Instead, "although the fire was very heavy indeed, there were comparatively few casualties."

Germans dropped grenades down the cliff, but most exploded harmlessly overhead. When Masson's men returned fire with their two Bren guns, one jammed and the tracers from the other drew immediate and accurate counter-fire. Masson thought "his men seemed extremely bewildered by the turn events had taken." Deciding to try getting away from the cliff and into the casino, Masson threw a smoke canister to provide cover. It failed to ignite. Struck in the right knee by shrapnel, Masson led his men crawling and rolling to the seawall before the casino. The wire topping the seawall was uncut. When one man attempted to open a path with wire cutters, a bullet struck his helmet and he dived for cover. Masson and his group were stuck.[30]

East of the casino, Ménard had been hit by shrapnel after taking only three steps up the beach. "You say a bullet or a piece of shrapnel hits you but the word isn't right. They slam you the way a sledgehammer slams you. There's no sharp pain at first. It jars you so much you're not sure exactly where you've been hit or what with.

"I felt confused and shaken up, the same feeling you get on the football field after getting tackled from behind. Stunned, surprised, frustrated." Staggering to his feet, Ménard stood dazed for a moment in the open, bullets and shrapnel flying past him. A touch to the right shoulder resulted in blood covering his left hand. As he fumbled out his first-aid kit, Ménard thought, "How the hell can I bandage my shoulder with my left hand?" The question jogged him out of his stupor. Move or die! Straight ahead, a machine gun was spitting bullets at him from a pillbox slit. He yelled at the Fusiliers to flank it in a pincer action. Shrapnel ripped away part of his cheek.

One of Ménard's closest friends fell, clutching his stomach. "A bad place to be hit because nothing outside of a hospital operating room could help him. His face was grey and he was sucking hard for breath." Ménard put a morphine tablet on his tongue. "There was nothing else I could do. He knew it and I knew it."

Before, Ménard had just been surviving. Now rage propelled him. It made him "think harder and faster." As he bounded onto the promenade, a bullet tore through his right arm above the wrist and snapped two bones. Knocked backwards off the wall, he slammed onto a steel picket and seriously injured his spine. Somehow mustering strength, Ménard regained the promenade to discover that the Fusiliers had silenced the pillbox. He established the battalion headquarters next to it. Another chunk of shrapnel gouged into his right leg just above the knee. Ménard remained standing, determined to exert command over a battalion being cut to pieces.[31]

From his headquarters near the casino, Labatt had watched in dismay as the Fusiliers landed. He had tried to head off this catastrophe, but his signals to *Calpe* were never acknowledged. "It was a suicide job, gallantly done, but they never had a chance... Landing near the casino under terrific fire they found the beach littered with dead and wounded and suffered so heavily themselves in crossing it that they could accomplish nothing."[32]

AT 0706 HOURS, Lieutenant Colonel Johnny Andrews signalled *Calpe* and recommended "holding up" landing the last two flights of Calgary tanks.[33] Aboard LCT8, he and Brigadier Sherwood Lett discussed the merits of attempting a second landing themselves. Andrews wanted to personally assess the situation ashore before committing more tanks. Lett was also anxious to land. The wireless traffic from the beach was confused and contradictory. The two men understood "that the tanks could get through at one spot. Some had [perhaps even] gone through [into the town], but it was not possible to find out how many."[34]

Lett said they should have "another go at it." Major Paul Garneau, a brigade headquarters staffer, heard Andrews reply that he "was more than willing to go back. The men on the beach were calling for support and it was more than evident that... penetration by tanks of the beach defences would completely change the picture." As LCT8 headed for White Beach, Lett signalled Lieutenant Colonel Bob Labatt "that we were landing and to give us full support.

"Only M.G. fire was whistling overhead, our naval gunners answering back with 20 mm. Then hell broke loose... arty from that high ground on the left, from the centre of town was firing at us. We kept on moving. A direct hit just below the gun turret on the port side killed Captain [Theodor Marie] Insinger" and seriously injured many others. "By this time it seemed that every half minute we were hit by shellfire... One gun was out of action. We kept on going and were just arriving at the beach when a shell broke the remaining chain that supported the ramp which dropped in, caught the sand, and brought our craft to a standstill."

Andrews ordered his tank *Regiment* forward. "The craft had unfortunately beached too far at sea and Colonel Andrews's tank went right in the water, four inches only of the turret above water... Slowly our craft started drifting sideways along the beach."[35]

The Churchill's waterproofing might have kept the tank water-tight had not a ventilation louvre broken off when it scraped the LCT's side during the exit. Water gushing in, Andrews and his crew evacuated and were taken aboard a motor launch. Struck immediately by shellfire, the launch burst into flames. Andrews was killed by machine-gun fire while swimming shoreward.[36]

LCT8 drifted out of control. Its ramp could not be raised, and gunfire ripped the length of the exposed deck. Both guns had been silenced. Lett was trying to contact *Calpe* by wireless. Hearing that the engine room had been abandoned, Garneau ran below. Managing to restart the engine, he backed the craft away from the beach. Back topside, Garneau found Lett on a stretcher, "seriously wounded," with the medical officer tending him. Lett asked "what was happening, why we were leaving." Garneau explained that the LCT could not be properly beached. There was no hope of successfully landing the heavy wireless sets. Lett signalled Labatt that he was in charge of the brigade.[37]

Labatt had tried to warn Lett against landing, but "apparently he proceeded to do so," Labatt wrote. "Things were certainly hotting up." Managing to get through to Lieutenant Colonel Fred Jasperson, Labatt learned that the Essex Scottish "were pinned down on the beach and could not get on to the esplanade. From the casino, I could see the devilish position they were in." Labatt decided to siphon as many Rileys and Fusiliers through the casino as possible. Once in the streets beyond, the troops could start clearing buildings in an eastward drive to free the Essex Scottish.[38]

ABOARD CALPE, news was increasingly distorted. An 0810 signal reported: "Elements of Johnny have made progress, most in front of Tobacco factory." This was followed by another signal at 0817: "Have control of White Beach."[39] Based on these signals and his belief that "it appeared essential to take the East cliff," Roberts played his last card by sending the 17 officers and 352 other ranks of No. 40 Royal Marine Commando to seize the eastern headland.[40]

Roberts, Hughes-Hallett, and Commander Ryder briefly conferred. Ryder then returned to *Locust* and advised Lieutenant Colonel Joseph Picton-Phillips "that Red and White beaches were clear of opposition and the General wished the marines to go in and support the Essex Scottish through White Beach [actually Red Beach]," Captain Peter Hellings of 'A' Company recorded. "The Colonel gave his orders from *Locust*, the idea being to pass through the beach to the town and there reform and report to the Colonel of the Essex Scottish, the object of the force being to pass around the west and south of the town, and attack the batteries on the eastern cliff from the south."[41]

Amazingly, as one French commentator later said, none of the officers questioned how the marines were supposed to carry out "a mere walk of two to two and a half miles along the rue de Sygogne, where no one had yet advanced more than 20 yards, the Rue Chanzy, the Arques road, the inner harbour and the heights of Neuville!"[42]

Picton-Phillips, his headquarters, and 'A' Company transferred to two LCMS and the commandos in the *chasseurs* to five LCAS. Forming off Green Beach, the landing craft started the run to White Beach— a move that "meant steaming parallel to the shore for a considerable distance. The *chasseurs* formed up on either flank... in an attempt to screen them from the fire of the shore batteries." Lieutenant Malcolm Buist, commanding the *chasseurs*, quickly "realized that this landing was to be a sea parallel of the Charge of the Light Brigade. There was a barrage coming from the cliffs on the east side of the harbour and from the houses on the promenade which showed only too well that White Beach was under a very heavy fire. Added to which there was a blazing LCT high and dry on the beach, and another abandoned alongside it. Shells started to burst... round the group of landing craft, which we endeavoured to screen by smoke; and I shouted to Colonel Phillips to ask what he thought about going on; but I doubt whether he heard me. Anyway he merely waved his arms and grinned to show that he meant to land at all costs."[43]

Struck by shellfire, Buist's damaged *chasseur* fell out of line about three thousand yards off the beach. The LCA carrying Captain J.C. Manners and No. 12 Platoon of 'X' Company also fell behind when both engines failed. Managing to get one stuttering weakly along, the crew reached a spare LCA, and Manners transferred his men to it.[44]

Five hundred yards from the beach, the *chasseurs* broke away before the water became too shallow for their draft. Hellings's LCM had lost power and stalled inside the smokescreen for the two minutes it took to get the engine restarted. As the craft limped out of the smoke, Hellings saw the LCM with Picton-Phillips aboard and an LCA carrying 'B' Company's Captain R.K. Devereaux and No. 8 Platoon approaching a beach "under heavy fire."

Suddenly, Picton-Phillips climbed on the gunwale to direct the landing craft. "Thus, leading the boats and open to most intense M.G., he led his commando into the beach. As the range shortened and the smoke cleared there was no doubt in any man's mind that an attempt to reach the town over that beach would mean certain death to the majority. In spite of all these facts my commanding officer refused to turn back until he had proved the uselessness of the adventure by his personal action. The [LCM] reached the beach and, realizing now the futility of further action, he stood in the stern in full view of all, placing his white... gloves on his hands and waving to the boats astern to return to the cover of the smoke."

As the trailing boats began turning about, Picton-Phillips was shot. A lieutenant "gave him rum, but he died about 5 minutes later." His actions in preventing most of the boats from landing saved about two hundred marines.[45] But his LCM and one LCA carrying Lieutenant Ken Smale's platoon had grounded. Smale looked on a "scene of horror and carnage where people had, quite literally, been blown to pieces. We charged up the beach and took shelter behind a Churchill tank; I never realized I would be so keen to press my nose against a lump of steel."[46]

Captain Devereaux's LCA was twelve feet short of the beach when he saw an LCM lying broadside on the rocks with a dozen dead marines next to it. Turning hard astern, his LCA collided with Hellings's LCM. Holed, the LCA was sinking when a *chasseur* arrived and rescued everyone aboard.[47] Hellings's LCM had the steering gear shot away, and then the engine failed. A *chasseur* took it under tow.[48]

Arriving in the spare LCA, Manners saw that the smokescreen had thinned dramatically and the last thousand yards to the beach would be crossed fully exposed. "We were hit through the stern and the whole engine caught fire. By this time we were the only available target . . . and we were engaged heavily . . . I gave the order to abandon the [LCA] and swim around to avoid the fire. It could be seen by that time that the landing on White Beach had not been successful." After a half hour of swimming, the men were picked up by the destroyer *Brocklesby*.[49]

The marines had reached the beach at 0830 hours. Those ashore were stranded. Corporal W.J. Harvey, who landed with Smale, had come "under strong enemy M.G. fire [and] took cover behind a tank which was still firing but unable to move."[50]

"Of the men who reached the shore," a Royal Marine report concluded, "those who lived to disembark were unable to get further up the beach than about 60 yards."[51]

FIGHTING STILL RAGED in and around the casino, the maze-like building now a nightmarish place. Narrow hallways passed large and small rooms used for gaming, counting winnings, offices, storage, and God knew what else. Rileys, Fusiliers, and engineers fought side by side. The engineer Sergeant George Hickson went on a rampage. Creeping up on a sniper, he set a demolition charge that not only killed the German but knocked down several walls. Liking this technique, Hickson eliminated another sniper by blasting a wall down on him. He then tackled a heavy gun emplacement beside the casino by blowing its door off with three pounds of plastic explosive. The explosion's force killed the five gunners manning the artillery piece. Hickson then wrapped the gun barrel with a one-pound charge that shattered it.

Gathering about eighteen men, Hickson led them into the town. He still hoped to seize the post office and destroy its telephone exchange. Despite heavy sniper resistance, the party got close to St. Rémy Church. Hickson was surprised to see civilians "moving freely about the streets and making no attempt to take cover." Realizing these "civilians" were actually locating individual Canadians for the snipers, he fired a Bren gun burst that "cleared the streets." The Canadians then broke into a house and wiped out the Germans inside in a melee of hand-to-hand fighting. With ammunition all but exhausted, Hickson led the way back to the casino.[52]

Other small parties also made sporadic forays into Dieppe. Sergeant Pierre Dubuc led eleven Fusiliers through the backyards of buildings paralleling Rue de Dumas, which extended east from the cliff to intersect Rue de Sygogne by the casino. Dubuc and his men wriggled through a narrow gap next to the Sygogne's roadblock. As they approached a small park, three Germans in a machine-gun pit there opened fire. A grenade knocked out the machine gun. Finding the Germans playing dead, the Fusiliers killed them with gunfire.

As snipers opened fire from the windows of a school by the park, Dubuc led the men sprinting along Rue Claude Groulard and then Quai Bérigny, which was bordered to the south by a large public garden. A sniper round struck one man in the heel, but he refused to go back alone to the beach. Returning the sniper fire from the school stopped the shooting there. The Fusiliers ran on to the Bassin Duquesne, a small, mostly enclosed part of the harbour, and skirted its southern flank at a dead run while under fire from a machine gun on the other side. They reached Bassin du Canada, another small artificial enclosure in which two vessels similar to R-Boats were tied alongside a couple of miniature submarines. Several Germans guarding the boats were brought under fire and killed. Dubuc led the Fusiliers south alongside the railroad bordering the west side of the Bassin du Canada. As they reached its southwest corner, fifteen heavily armed Germans appeared. Dubuc's Bren gun clicked empty, and several men announced they too were out of ammunition. The Fusiliers surrendered.

The Germans led them into a backyard. An order was shouted in German. Nobody moved. In English they were told to undress. Nobody moved. When the order was repeated in French, the men reluctantly removed uniforms and equipment, piling everything in a heap and retaining just their underwear. After forcing the twelve men to face a wall with arms pressed against it, the Germans gathered the equipment and clothes. Leaving a single guard, they departed.

Dubuc asked the guard if he spoke English. A little English, a little French, the man replied. Dubuc requested water. As the man turned, Dubuc jumped him, and several others joined in. As the men wrestled, one Fusilier grabbed a long piece of pipe and "swinging it over his head cut the German's head in half."

The men sprinted wildly for the beach. There was no plan. Dubuc had no idea what streets to follow. The group became separated. Dubuc burst on alone to the promenade. He never saw any of the other men again and assumed they had been recaptured. A strange stillness had settled over the beach, the fire not as heavy as before. Dubuc ran along the promenade until he was just northeast of the casino. Three knocked-out tanks stood on the shingle below. Dubuc ran to their cover and found Lieutenant Colonel Ménard on a stretcher beside one. Captain Vandelac stood nearby. Many Fusiliers hunkered along the seawall and in the cover of the tanks. Dubuc asked what was happening. Vandelac said they were holding until boats came to withdraw them. It was all they could do.[53]

21

Pretty Shaky All Around

A T 0900 HOURS, Captain John Hughes-Hallett decided "the troops ashore were in difficulties and... unlikely to gain possession of the East and West Cliffs which dominated the main beaches. It was learned also that even some of the buildings on the beach front were still in enemy hands. It was obvious... the military situation was serious, and that it was becoming steadily more difficult for the ships and craft to close [on] the beaches."[1]

Sitting on the floor of Major General Ham Roberts's headquarters, correspondent Quentin Reynolds watched how the general smoked "one cigarette after another and kept a large cup of hot tea beside him."[2] Roberts had "taken off his coat and he was sweating a little but he was calm, alert... Captain Hughes-Hallett came into the room. No one would have thought that he'd been through anything more strenuous than a maneuver. He and Roberts talked. They were like co-captains of a team, each respecting the other's opinion... They discussed the advisability of withdrawing the men to keep pace with the timetable. They decided to withdraw them."

Hughes-Hallett said, "I'd really do it as quickly as possible" and suggested 1030 as the earliest practicable time.[3] This would give Air Vice-Marshal Trafford Leigh-Mallory time to advance the planned air support for the withdrawal. Hughes-Hallett also needed to organize landing craft. The withdrawal should, he said, "be confined to personnel." Tanks, mortars, and other heavy equipment must be abandoned.[4]

Roberts hesitated, "loath to abandon hope and reconcile himself to the failure of the operation."[5] Then he said quietly, "Bring them home."[6] Returning to the bridge, Hughes-Hallett prepared a coded message announcing Vanquish—the order for beginning the withdrawal. Just before he sent it, Roberts asked for a delay to 1100.[7] He needed time to ensure that all units were informed, especially the Queen's Own Cameron Highlanders, believed to be well inland. Air Commodore Adrian Cole supported the delay to buy Leigh-Mallory more time.[8]

Holding offshore were the LCTs carrying two remaining flights of Calgary tanks and about seven hundred men—mostly engineers and additional beach parties.[9] The destroyer *Garth* had fired about six hundred shells—mostly in futile efforts to silence artillery on the headland east of Dieppe. The ship's ammunition almost exhausted, Hughes-Hallett ordered *Garth* to escort the two LCT flights back to England.[10]

Ashore on White Beach, Lieutenant Colonel Bob Labatt faced ever-deteriorating communications. He supposedly commanded all 4th Brigade, but had no link to any battalions except his own Rileys. Not only was wireless reception poor but now German operators were jamming the nets with bogus messages, which meant every signal had to be double-checked. A garbled signal from *Calpe* just after 0900 apparently set the evacuation forward to 0930. This puzzled Labatt, as he "knew that the tide would not be right at that time. Shortly afterwards the evacuation time was changed to 1100 hours.

"The evacuation order changed my plan but little. It was essential to keep pressing and at the same time to plaster West Cliff and the buildings across the esplanade with everything available. I continued to ask for smoke and aerial bombardment for these two targets." Of his headquarters section, operating in an exposed position near the casino, Labatt was the only man unwounded. "It was a grim feeling to be in command of the finest brigade in the Canadian Army only to find it in a position to which there was no tactical solution."

Labatt anticipated hand-to-hand fighting during the withdrawal. He wanted aerial smoke to conceal the men and bombardments to smash the buildings and emplacements sheltering Germans. "The greatest bravery in the world (and much was cheerfully showed all day) could achieve nothing unsupported." But the bombers and smoke-laying planes never came—even though "there was constant activity in the air" that he found "thrilling. Planes chased each other all over the sky."[11]

LEIGH-MALLORY'S DESIRED great air battle was in full play by 0900. The Luftwaffe had reacted hesitantly at first, its response "confined entirely to fighters patrolling the area in small numbers. The German control merely instructed his aircraft to go to Dieppe area where large numbers of British bombers and fighters were operating." Leigh-Mallory realized the Luftwaffe "had not been at a high state of readiness."[12] This was true, as Luftwaffe No. 3 Air Fleet had released a third of its pilots to the night-long party with the Women's Auxiliary.

Most Spitfires covering the raiding ships during the early morning encountered no Germans. Those that did appear either kept warily distant or were easily chased away. Of his thirty-minute sortie by forty-eight Spitfires that ended at 0550 hours, Wing Commander Myles Duke-Woolley reported it "was, in practical terms, a waste of time but a necessary show of force."[13]

The Germans, Leigh-Mallory thought, "did not appear to appreciate the scale of our effort." By 0700, they still seldom had more than twenty to thirty fighters in the skies.[14] Not until 0830 did the first German bomber attack the ships. By then, however, German fighter strength averaged fifty fighters overhead, with dogfights in full swing.[15] Although German fighters within range were greatly outnumbered, their bases were much closer. This meant each plane could remain on station longer and return more quickly than Allied aircraft could.

In Uxbridge, Leigh-Mallory conducted a complex juggling act not only to maintain the vital fighter cover but also to deploy bombers, fighter-bombers, smoke-laying aircraft, and reconnaissance flights.

The complex air plan unfolded on schedule through to 0900. Then, at 0916, *Calpe* called urgently for a squadron to bomb the Hindenburg Battery on the western headland overlooking Dieppe. Up to now, each squadron had had an hour's notice before its presence over the French coast was required. Now Leigh-Mallory demanded that squadrons scramble the instant he called. In this case, a Boston bomber squadron was scrambled at 0926.[16]

As more calls came in for smoke and bombing missions against the headlands, Leigh-Mallory asked Air Commodore Cole for a situation report. "Situation too obscure to give useful report," Cole replied at 0956. "Air co-operation faultless. Enemy air opposition now increasing. Have you any questions?"

A thirty-minute smokescreen along Red and White Beaches was requested for between 1100 and 1130 hours to screen the evacuation. Leigh-Mallory ordered as many aircraft as possible fitted with SCI smoke sprayers to fulfill this purpose. Roberts signalled that Green Beach also required smoke screening.[17]

Of aircraft committed, the smoke-laying planes were fewest in number. As the day wore on, though, they were most in demand. Just two Blenheim IV squadrons and one Boston were available. These had been considered sufficient during planning to fulfill the scheduled smoke-laying missions. No allowance had been made for the "possibility of impromptu sorties." Twenty-three additional requested sorties—including Labatt's—over the course of about three hours left the squadrons hard pressed.

When a sortie requiring smoke bombs to blind a coastal battery was ordered, all available aircraft were already fitted with SCI for covering the withdrawal. "Consequently SCIs had to be removed and small bomb containers fitted, which is a lengthy proceeding on Blenheim aircraft," an RAF analyst reported. Previous sorties also added delay because the planes returned "mostly shot up and careful inspection was necessary before undertaking [another] sortie."[18]

Despite the increasing calls for attacks on the coastal batteries, it was apparent that bomb runs were having little effect. A later report examining ten bombing attacks on 6-inch coastal batteries noted that none were silenced. "The twelve Bostons... sent against Hitler

Battery bombed from 6,000 to 8,000 feet and... the bombs fell some 2,000 yards wide of the target. To neutralize a battery by bombing it is necessary to hit the actual gun pit. These batteries were in prepared positions dug in with sandbags around them so that near misses were ineffective." Attacks by four Hurricane squadrons against gun positions hidden in caves or in concrete positions alongside the buildings facing Red and White Beaches also failed. "This is not surprising," the report concluded, "considering that the target was not susceptible to the cannon fighters and Hurri-bombers. It is... a waste of time attempting to attack such targets with fighters which can only carry light bombs."[19]

When a Hurricane-bomber squadron was dispatched against the headland between White and Green Beaches, two Spitfire squadrons provided covering support. The Spitfires of No. 412 (RCAF) Squadron supported this attack. Flight Lieutenant Jack Godfrey tailed Flying Officer John Brookhouse. "Of all the jobs that could have been assigned to us," Godfrey wrote, "this undoubtedly was the worst." Taking off at 1000 hours, they "met the Hurri-bombers over the southern coast of England, and away we went... We flew about five feet above the waves, cruising quite slowly. About five miles off the French coast we gradually opened up so that we hit the coast going flat out to the right of the town.

"Up over the headland we went and flew inland about three miles, weaving amongst trees. Then we swung to the left. I was following... Brookhouse, slightly to the right and about 75 yards behind. After making our turn we were in a bit of a gully with trees on either side and no trees ahead. The ground started to rise and there at the top was a big flak position. We were on it before we realised it. All hell was breaking loose. There were heavy ack-ack guns and I don't know how many machine-guns blazing away at us from point-blank range. We had come up a funnel completely exposed. The next thing I saw was the tail of Johnny's kite just blow, and the fuselage broke in two right behind the cockpit. His kite seemed to go slowly over on its nose. I didn't see it hit the ground as I was past but one of the other lads saw it and it really spread itself all over the ground. I don't suppose poor Johnny even knew he was hit."[20]

Committing the Hurricanes had been Leigh-Mallory's only option with the support planes available. But he recognized that their effectiveness was likely to be scant. It had quickly become apparent that "attacks by Cannon Fighters are effective only whilst they are engaging their targets, but they have no lasting material effect on well-protected defensive positions. They are extravagant in as much as each aircraft is in action for a few seconds only."[21]

At 1000 hours, the first major flight of German bombers arrived; Leigh-Mallory doubled the continuous fighter coverage to six squadrons in response. No. 416 (RCAF), commanded by Squadron Leader Lloyd Chadburn, scrambled immediately. The Aurora, Ontario, bank clerk had been the first Commonwealth Air Training Plan graduate to command a squadron. In May 1942, he had become the first airman to sink a German E-boat. On August 19, he was two days shy of turning twenty-three.[22]

The squadron flew four sorties over Dieppe, and Chadburn led each one, while his pilots drew two each. Pilot Officer John Maffre of Montreal was "green as grass," flying his first combat mission. The squadron operated off a grass field at Hawkinge in Kent—the RAF base closest to France. "Being dry in August there was a great possibility that if you took off individually you would blind the rest with dust. They'd have to wait until the dust settled. So we would take off, twelve, line abreast—almost like a cavalry charge. It was great!"

Arriving over Dieppe, Maffre saw "a tapestry of aircraft, wheeling all over the place—just nothing but aircraft—mostly fighters. We would see low-level bombers—Bostons and so on—attacking down below. But in the moments we had, when we could look around we'd see pinpricks of light down below, from the navy escort pounding the shoreline. We couldn't see much of the shoreline, because it was wreathed in smoke and flames. And we just chased around. I just followed my leader. And there were aircraft—mostly Me-109s, but a lot of Focke-Wulf 190s, and a lot of Spitfires and Mustangs."

The squadron knew the soldiers below were mostly Canadian, which "gave us a proprietary sense." During one dogfight, Maffre lost contact with his leader. Suddenly, tracers passed his wingtip and "you realize some SOB is trying to kill you. But fortunately he didn't hit me." Maffre fired his guns once, hitting nothing.[23]

Lord Lovat (hatless, with his trademark hunting rifle slung over his shoulder) talks with one of his men of No. 4 Commando while others look on. The unit had just returned to the dock at Newhaven. Photographer unknown. LAC PA–183766.

top left · An unidentified Hunt class destroyer fires at the Dieppe beaches. Photographer unknown. LAC PA–183772.

bottom left · Support ships operate off Red and White Beaches at Dieppe. Photo in the author's possession.

above · Casualties from Red and White Beaches are brought aboard HMS *Calpe*. Photo in the author's possession.

left · For his part in tending the wounded on White Beach and for refusing to be evacuated when the opportunity presented itself, Royal Hamilton Light Infantry padre Captain John Foote was awarded a Victoria Cross. Gordon Jolley photo. LAC PA–501320.

top · Dieppe was a scene of disaster. A beached LCT burns, and strewn around several disabled Churchills lie mostly Canadian dead. The corpse in the foreground is identifiable as an American ranger from his puttees, which were part of the unit's standard uniform. Photographer unknown. LAC C–014160.

bottom · As the soldiers returned from the raid, staff personnel were quick to record their names and units. Photo in the author's possession.

top left · A group of exhausted Canadians return from the Dieppe raid. Some nurse wounds. Photographer unknown. LAC PA–183775.

bottom left · In the aftermath, victorious German officers stand on the beach at Dieppe and take stock of the slaughter. Photographer unknown. LAC C–017293.

top · Canadian prisoners are marched through the streets of Dieppe. Photographer unknown. LAC PA–200058.

bottom · Canadian troops and members of No. 4 Commando crowd the docks at Newhaven following the raid. Photo in the author's possession.

top · The Germans viewed the defeat of the Dieppe raid as an important propaganda victory, which they greatly exploited. This photo is generally believed to have been taken after the dead were removed, with Canadian prisoners made to pose as dead. Note the man in the foreground who has his head pillowed and appears to be sleeping. Photo in the author's possession.

bottom · Canadian war correspondents interview Lieutenant Colonel Cecil Merritt (centre) in 1945 about his Victoria Cross award at a repatriation depot for prisoners of war. Arthur L. Cole photo. LAC PA–161938.

Not so Flight Lieutenant Blair Dalzell "Dal" Russel. He jumped an FW-190 when it's pilot "wasn't looking... I think he was a fairly green pilot." Russel found the wheeling air battle "pretty shaky all around" and considered his downing the plane more due to luck than skill.[24]

THE FIRST GERMAN bombers were single-engine Stuka dive-bombers, but dual-engine Dorniers and Heinkels flying from bases in Holland and Belgium soon arrived. Some were painted black for nighttime operations. A few were training planes flown by trainee crews. The intensity of anti-aircraft fire from the ships and immediate response by covering fighters made it difficult to attack properly. To target a ship, the bombardier needed the plane to hold a steady course until he released the bombs. Instead, the bomber pilots were jinking to escape the Spitfires or avoid anti-aircraft fire. The ships were also constantly zigzagging. Scoring a hit became a matter of chance. Except for some Stuka attacks on the beaches, the bombers concentrated on the ships. By about 1030 hours, all Luftwaffe "resources on the Western Front were in action." Leigh-Mallory increased the covering squadrons to nine.[25]

The fighter cover was terrifically effective. From the deck of *Calpe*, Quentin Reynolds watched three Dorniers fly straight over Dieppe towards the destroyer. Spitfires jumped them immediately, and one Dornier broke left with three giving chase. The leader "dove under the tail... and then climbed up under it, firing... into the fat belly... and a thin, white trail of smoke appeared, as though the belly were leaking and the white smoke changed to black and the Dornier began a slow dive. Then a burst of bright orange flame completely obliterated the smoke, as though the belly of the Dornier had exploded... now the whole nose of the Dornier was a ball of fire as its dive became deeper." The bomber released a dozen bombs, which struck three hundred yards from *Calpe*. "The ship rocked... and the bombs threw up jets of water." A quarter mile distant, the bomber crashed into the sea. Two crewmen had bailed out, the other three consigned to a watery grave.

Calpe's anti-aircraft guns were hammering fire towards the dangerously closing third Dornier. "The gun crew worked in beautiful harmony. Range finders bent over their instruments, men passed shells, men slapped them into guns, breeches slammed shut... Black bursts seemed to surround the Dornier, and then suddenly there was no Dornier... One moment it was streaking at 280 miles an hour, alive, pulsating, vital, and then it was a mass of scattering debris. One wing sluiced crazily down, and thousands of parts too small to see flew in a thousand directions. It was very impersonal, and the thought that men of flesh and blood were parts of that flying debris never presented itself. Aerial warfare is impersonal."[26]

The ships' gun crews seldom bothered distinguishing friend from foe. Any plane in range drew their fire. Aboard LCT16, Captain G.C. Wallace of 3rd Canadian Light Anti-Aircraft Regiment "was standing beneath the bridge when two Bostons escorted by Spitfires flew very low over us. The naval gunner... opened up, followed by several machine guns mounted on the deck, followed by fire from our Oerlikon guns. I dashed up to the bridge and asked the first officer why the goddamn gunner was firing upon our aircraft. His answer was noncommittal so I then dashed over to the gunner and asked him what he was firing at and he replied, 'At a Focke Wulfe Torpedo Bomber.' The planes were now out of range and the firing was stopped. We were recompensed for our mistake by having the escort of Spitfires spray us liberally with machine-gun fire."[27] At least six RAF planes were lost to friendly fire.[28]

The Jubilee plan had foreseen such events and sought their prevention by establishing a minimum altitude, below which friendly aircraft were to operate only when pursuing enemy planes. In the heat of the moment, however, some pilots forgot this instruction. The gunners also fired at planes well above the designated ceiling. Leigh-Mallory felt the naval gunners ill trained in aircraft recognition.[29]

Hughes-Hallett was also displeased but considered the fire largely unavoidable. "It is very difficult for a ship to recognize aircraft flying straight at it and if the aircraft is close ships must engage them otherwise the enemy would get a clear run." He recommended having "noses of single engine aircraft... painted a distinctive colour" for recognition purposes and also that gun crews not fire at low-flying aircraft unless they were coming directly at the ship.[30]

AT 1030 HOURS, Leigh-Mallory released twenty-four American B-17 bombers to carry out a pre-arranged attack on the Abbeville airfield, thirty miles northeast of Dieppe. The intention was to render the base inoperable during the withdrawal. This was the second mission flown by the U.S. Army Air Force in Europe. Four fighter squadrons—including RCAF 401 and 402 Squadrons—covered the bombers. Despite heavy flak, the bombers reached the airfield unscathed. Mechanical failure prevented one dropping its bombs, but the others each released about 1.5 tons of either high-explosive or incendiary bombs. "Many bursts were seen in the northwest dispersal areas and on the runways whilst fires were started in the woods adjoining the dispersal areas. Bursts were also observed on storage sites and clouds of black smoke were seen rising from the whole target area. This very accurate bombing of dispersal areas and runways—bombs fell near to at least 16 aircraft in these areas—caused considerable confusion to the enemy, and he was denied the use of his aerodrome for probably two hours, his aircraft being instructed to land at alternatives."[31]

As the bombers returned to England, three of the Spitfire squadrons were released to engage the German fighters. Squadron Leader Ken Hodson led No. 402's Spitfires in a gradual descent from 25,000 to 10,000 feet. Spotting a flight of Dorniers, Hodson dove towards them. He fired a long burst that smacked rounds into one Dornier's tail and fuselage. Hodson's second, Flight Sergeant B.M. Zobell, hit another Dornier with two bursts. The bomber's gunner replied, punching bullets through his rudder, both wings, shattering the Perspex canopy, and smashing the gunsight. A splinter of glass pierced his left eye. Breaking away, Zobell flew homeward.[32]

Meanwhile, Flight Sergeant Donald Robert Morrison had dived on an FW-190 about 1,500 feet below him. "I did a slipping barrel roll, losing height and levelled out about 150 yards behind and slightly to the starboard and above the enemy aircraft. I opened fire with a 2-second burst closing to 25 yards. I saw strikes all along the starboard side of the fuselage and several pieces which seemed about a foot square flew off from around the cowling. Just as both the enemy aircraft and myself ran into cloud, he exploded with a terrific flash of flame and black smoke. Immediately after this my wind-shield and hood were covered with oil and there was a terrific clatter as pieces of debris struck my aircraft."

Morrison started for home at about a thousand feet of altitude. Suddenly his engine began to sputter. Realizing he must bail out, Morrison nursed the faltering plane to two thousand feet before the engine died. "I took off my helmet and undid my straps and opened the hood. I crouched on the seat and then shoved the stick forward. My parachute became caught somehow and I figured I was about 200–250 feet above the water when I got clear. The aircraft plunged into the water below me as my parachute opened. Almost immediately I pressed the quick release, just as I hit the water. I inflated my dinghy without any trouble and then climbed in." While a couple of Spitfires circled protectively, Morrison raised a flag." This aided the rescue boat to come straight to me ... I had only been in the water for about 15 minutes." Morrison was seventeen miles from Dieppe when a high-speed launch from RAF's Air Sea Rescue Service picked him up.[33] Lightly armed and relying on speed and covering fighter protection, these launches rescued twenty pilots. But of five launches deployed from a base in Dover, the Luftwaffe sunk three, and twenty crew died. "Whilst under the fighter screen," Leigh-Mallory wrote, "they were adequately protected but at times they gallantly went beyond this cover and suffered casualties."[34]

Air operations intensified at 1100 hours. Boston, Hurri-bomber, and Hurricane cannon squadrons repeatedly attacked the headlands, while smoke-laying aircraft swathed them in smoke. Blenheims raced the length of Red, White, and Green Beaches, creating an obscuring screen. Overhead, Leigh-Mallory thickened the covering force by sending a squadron of Spitfire ixs, capable of reaching higher altitudes than other Spitfire models, to intercept German bombers attacking the beaches from 23,000 feet.[35]

SINCE DECIDING TO launch Vanquish, Hughes-Hallett had scrambled to ensure that the navy would be ready on time. As the original plan had foreseen everyone being picked up in front of Dieppe, a new plan had to be improvised on the fly. Commander H.V.P.

McClintock, in charge of the boat pool, was summoned to *Calpe*. Only LCAS and LCMS would lift troops from the beaches, Hughes-Hallett declared. They would then bring the men to LCTS waiting a mile offshore, transfer them, and then rotate back to the beach in a constant shuttle. Hughes-Hallett "considered it out of the question" to send R-Boats or LCTS "inshore in view of the volume of enemy fire."

Still unaware of the Royal Regiment's surrender on Blue Beach, Hughes-Hallett instructed that the LCA and LCM flotillas should return to the same beaches where they had landed troops.

Earlier, Hughes-Hallett had dispatched Lieutenant Commander Harold Goulding, Blue Beach's boat officer, to take three LCAS from *Princess Astrid*'s flotilla with ML291 in support and try landing there. Goulding began the approach at about 1030 hours. The flotilla came "under increasingly heavy fire and he could see no sign of our forces. One LCA... was sunk and the remainder withdrew."[36]

Meanwhile, the main rescue effort was clumsily evolving. No landing craft were equipped with wireless sets, so McClintock gave instructions by loudhailer from the deck of ML187. To speed the process, he ordered his boat pool assistant commander, Lieutenant J.H. Dathan, to inform the flotillas that would approach Green and White Beaches to be ready by 1100. McClintock would take care of those facing Red and Blue Beaches.[37] Dathan diligently warned the respective LCA flotillas. Then, finding twenty LCAS in the boat pool lacking apparent assignment, he tasked ML214 to guide them in to White and Red Beaches.[38]

As these two officers sailed through the flotillas bellowing instructions, *Calpe* was notifying the larger ships of the new plan. Standing off Dieppe, Lieutenant F.M. Foggitt, commanding LCFI, received a signal at 1030 hours "that the withdrawal was ordered for 1100 hours. Subsequently it appeared that the captain read this signal as referring to LCFI. A further signal detailing the action of certain ships during the withdrawal was received at 1045 hours. LCFI was not included and, subsequently, at 1100 hours she turned to seaward and proceeded back to Newhaven in company with a group of LCTS." These were the LCTS under *Garth*'s escort. Aboard LCFI, Royal Marine major G.H. Stockley thought "that the action of the captain was wrong. But, if the signals were read as described, then it was reasonable to suppose that LCFI should withdraw at 1100 hours and provide [anti-aircraft] protection to the group of LCTs."[39]

Fortunately, LCFI's unscheduled departure had no serious consequences, though some later commentators reported otherwise because they believed the LCTs could have been used in the evacuation.[40] All that was lost was an additional gun platform for fending off the Luftwaffe.

Far more serious was McClintock's mishandled organization of the eastern LCAS. Drawing abreast of Dieppe's harbour entrance, ML187 was fired on by German fighters and possibly the gun on the western mole. "I retired very hurriedly to seaward followed by quite a few landing craft. The end of this attack found us rather disorganized as we had 3 or 4 serious casualties." McClintock's intention was to transfer the wounded to a destroyer. However, learning of the failed attempt to reach Blue Beach, he concluded "that it was not possible to evacuate from Blue, White or Red beaches... I then went in search of HMS *Calpe* to report what I knew to the Force Commander and to exchange information, but could not find her so made a signal in plain language to Commander Luce by name. He replied saying, 'If no further evacuation possible, withdraw to 4 miles from shore.' The signal was received by me as 'No further evacuation possible, withdraw.' Foolishly I made no reply to this signal so left the Force Commander in the dark as to what I was doing." Unable to see shoreward through the smoke, McClintock became increasingly unsure of what to do next. The captain of a passing LCT shouted that White Beach had fallen. McClintock realized he did not know where all the landing craft were. "I... was pretty sure... Dathan had a certain number with him, and I knew that a certain number had already started for home by my orders." He rounded up a number of R-Boats but could hardly communicate with them because his loudhailer no longer worked. "After a certain amount of hesitation I decided the best thing to do was withdraw with this group." McClintock lingered, however, seeking other LCAS to shepherd away from the beaches and get them headed back to England.[41]

Happening upon Canadian navy reservist Sub-Lieutenant Johnny O'Rourke's LCA as it headed towards Dieppe's beaches, McClintock shouted, "Follow me," and guided him away.[42] He next encountered Lieutenant Jack Koyl. "I was ordered by the Boat Pool Officer to follow him. We turned about and proceeded seaward at full speed under cover of smoke screen. We were led in the direction of the Main Convoy, waited in company with four LCAS from HMS *Princess Astrid* until 1230 when we were ordered to sail for England."[43] It was never determined how many landing craft McClintock's miscalculations denied the withdrawal, consigning many troops to being left behind.

Very Heartbreaking

AT 1100 HOURS, the Essex Scottish and scattered elements of the Fusiliers on Red Beach remained pinned against the seawall or behind stranded tanks on the beach. The intensely accurate fire made it almost impossible to organize resistance. Any movement drew immediate fire. After losing a foot to a mortar round, Essex Scottish lieutenant Douglas Green had "continued to hobble on, leading his platoon until... a second bomb finished him." 'D' Company's Major John Willis carried on despite such severe chest, arm, and head wounds that Lieutenant Colonel Fred Jasperson thought it "seemed humanly impossible to do so." Seeing a man wounded in the open, Willis suffered a last, fatal wound trying to drag him to cover.[1]

On White Beach, the situation was slightly better because the Rileys controlled the casino and a couple of trenches alongside. They were supported by Fusiliers concentrated around the casino. Under the western cliff, a growing number of Fusiliers were trapped, their numbers increasing as men moved there in a futile search for a better refuge.

Captain Tony Hill's band of Rileys and engineers had abandoned the cinema inside the town after a two-hour standoff. While in the cinema, Company Sergeant Major Jack Stewart had been perplexed that civilians seemed oblivious to the shooting around them. One woman had nonchalantly left home, strolled to a bakery, purchased a baguette, and then walked home again. Despite German bullets whickering through the theatre, an old male caretaker calmly swept the floors. Just before 1000 hours, Private Archie Liss had reported German infantry closing from several directions. With Stewart and Liss providing covering fire, the group withdrew to the casino, suffering one man wounded en route.

Stewart was surprised by how strong a position the casino had become. Probably 150 men, including some wounded, were there. He counted thirty-five Bren guns and saw lots of ammunition for them. Captain Denis Whitaker seemed in charge. He had cut off his rank badges to avoid the special attention snipers gave officers. Captain Hill helped gather the wounded in the building's northeast corner. A sheltered area, it provided a good launching point for a run to the promised boats.[2]

Stewart, Hill, and Major Harold Lazier organized a Bren gun covering party for the withdrawal. Each gunner would have a loader ready to ram home fresh magazines. While they shot up German positions, the rest of the troops would help the wounded to the boats and embark. The gunners would fall back, maintaining a steady rate of fire, and be last off.[3]

Most of the Calgary tanks on the promenade had abandoned their search for exits into the town and were standing close to the casino. Lieutenant Ed Bennett in *Bellicose* discovered that despite his burns, he could see "by lifting up my [left] eyelid." Upon learning the withdrawal was coming, Major Allan Glenn ordered all tanks able to move onto the beach to provide covering fire for the infantry's evacuation. Bennett drove close to LCT3, stranded broadside on the beach, and came to a stop facing the western headland. Moments later, a shell shattered the right track, immobilizing his tank. One after the other, the tanks all suffered similar fates, mostly due to the chert breaking tracks. *Bellicose* happened to be "in a good position to turn our six-pounder turret gun on the high buildings on the cliff. We had pretty well expended our small arms ammunition on the esplanade but we still had some large gun ammunition. I'm very proud of Bill Stannard with his marksmanship with the six-pounder gun because one of the buildings on the cliff had a tower on it and there was machine-gun fire coming from the Germans in that tower. I recall seeing the whole side of the tower where the fire was coming from just crumble. It was a perfect hit. That was the highlight of our shooting on the beach but we continued to fire the gun until... the ammunition was expended."[4]

Because of the severity of Lieutenant Colonel Joe Ménard's wounds, Major Paul Savoy had taken charge of the Fusiliers at the casino. He was trying to contact brigade headquarters by wireless "to get a smoke screen and 3-inch mortar protection on the beach" when a bullet pierced his chest. "I heard him scream," Regimental Sergeant Major R. Levesque recorded, "and I turned... to see what had happened to him when he was hit a second time in the face by what seemed to be a piece of shrapnel. Part of his face was blown off. He fell on his back and did not move again. I spoke to him but I received no answer."[5]

The signallers were unable to contact brigade or *Calpe*. There had, in fact, been virtually no wireless link between the Fusiliers and higher command since the battalion landed. Only two signals were logged by *Calpe* as possibly from the Fusiliers. The first, at 0845, reported "Joe in severe difficulties, must be taken off or will be wiped out." Another message at 0908 declared, "Joe is surrounded." Both were dismissed as bogus. Repeated signals from *Calpe* for any word of the Fusiliers resulted in no news. "The fact is that each group on the beach could report only upon events in its immediate vicinity and could throw very little light on the situation at large."[6]

For the Fusiliers pinned under the western cliff, conditions had by about 1030 become desperate. There were about two hundred of them, many wounded. Lieutenant Antoine Masson had just readied a small party to try getting over the seawall when Captain Sarto Marchand and several Fusiliers "appeared from the west with their hands up, followed by a German officer and some German soldiers with a machinegun. Evidently the Germans had come down to the beach by some track to the west... of where the [Fusiliers] had landed." Marchand told Masson that "further resistance was impossible," and the lieutenant surrendered his men. The prisoners were marched west along the beach and up a steep track onto the headland.[7]

Captain Charles Hector Alleyne, the Fusiliers' medical officer, and the chief stretcher-bearer, Company Sergeant Major W. Gagne, were driven by machine-gun fire on hands and knees towards some rocks promising scant cover. Alleyne "asked me how many [stretcher-bearers] he still had with him. As I was telling him there was only the two of us, he was hit by a bullet on the right side of the chest. He lay still on his stomach... I took his pulse. He was dead. I left him there and crawled forward on the beach."[8]

The medical plan for casualty care had unravelled. All personnel from No. 11 Field Ambulance had been aboard the last two flights of LCTs carrying tanks of the Calgary Tank Regiment and so had never landed. This was the case also for the tank regiment's medical team. The Essex Scottish and Riley medical officers did get ashore with their small teams. Unable to establish a normal regimental aid post, they clustered casualties along the seawall and provided rudimentary first aid. Gathering the wounded, the stretcher-bearers suffered heavy losses.[9] "I found that stretchers in a raid such as this were useless and a dangerous risk to the life of those attempting to use them," Riley stretcher-bearer Sergeant F.B. Volterman reported.[10]

Royal Navy lieutenant Peter Ross managed to improve the situation for some wounded on White Beach. Gathering a small group of Canadian engineers, he led them across the fire-swept beach to collect wounded. These were taken to LCT3, "whose steel sides offered more protection than the open." Two stretcher-bearers there dressed wounds. Ross organized water-carrying parties to draw fresh water in pails from the LCT's water tank for distribution. He also located the boat's first-aid stores, which contained a supply of morphine and bandages. By 1100 hours, about fifty wounded sheltered in the LCT. Believing withdrawal was imminent, Ross "made all preparations necessary, but no craft appeared."[11]

Rileys' Private Alf Collingdon was inside LCT3. "I thought at first that land crabs or some other creatures were moving the stones. Then I realized that it was shell fragments or bullets from the high cliffs." The Germans hammered the LCT and nearby beach mercilessly until Collingdon fashioned a Red Cross flag by ripping the Royal Navy ensign's Cross of St. George off and tying it to the blank white side of a landing craft marker. "There was no more heavy stuff near us after that, only the odd sniper, and every minute or two he'd fire into the ramp just to let us know that we were to stay in the craft with the wounded."[12]

The Rileys had first established their RAP in a slight depression, where work had to be done lying prone. Padre John Foote, a powerful, burly man, who was also a clarinetist in the regimental band, "time and again left this shelter to inject morphine, give first-aid and carry wounded personnel from the open beach to the [RAP]. On these occasions, with utter disregard for his personal safety... Foote exposed himself to an inferno of fire and saved many lives by his gallant action. During the action, as the tide went out, the [RAP] was moved to the shelter of a stranded landing craft [LCT5]... Foote continued tirelessly and courageously to carry wounded men from the exposed beach to the cover of the landing craft. He also removed wounded from inside the landing craft when ammunition had been set on fire by enemy shells," his Victoria Cross citation stated.[13] "The padre and medical officer [Captain Wesley Clare] did very heroic work under heavy enemy fire," stretcher-bearer Private H. Partington reported.[14] Similarly tenacious in his duty was Corporal Al Comfort. Despite being shot in both legs shortly after the landing and since suffering two chest wounds, Comfort "still managed to take care of the wounded. He refused to be looked after himself, but insisted on having as many wounded as possible brought somewhere near so he could attend them," Private Al Oldfield recalled.[15]

LCT5 was a forlorn refuge. She had "a gaping hole amidships from a direct hit. Her bow was a sieve, her anti-aircraft guns... loosely pointed skyward. Black smoke curled from within her and drifted, low and lazily, westward along the beach," the battalion's official history reported. "Exploding ammunition sputtered and ricocheted from the bulwarks."[16]

On the defensive, with the number of wounded rapidly increasing, ever-more officers and men turned from fighting to providing care. 'A' Company's second-in-command, Captain George Donald

Skerritt, arrived as LCT5 caught fire when the shells aboard began exploding. He organized the movement of wounded from inside the craft to the shelter of its lee side. "Large dressings were in great demand," Private J. McQuade remembered. "Most of the men had given their own issue to the cause." Skerritt stripped off shirt, trousers, and boots and tore the clothing into strips for tourniquets. Then Skerritt and Clare "administered morphine to the bad cases."[17]

AT POURVILLE, the South Saskatchewan Regiment and Queen's Own Cameron Highlanders saw the noose tightening around them. They had to get away soon or lose the chance. Lieutenant John Edmondson had about twenty Sasks and Camerons split into two groups holding the village's eastern flank. One group guarded the road intersection at the base of the headland, while Edmondson and ten men held the second storey of the pub next to the bridge. Edmondson's group was amply equipped, with a 3-inch mortar, a couple of Boys anti-tank rifles, several Bren guns, and a few rifles.[18]

Everyone had ditched the Stens. Lieutenant Leonard Dickin spoke for many when he declared, "Sten guns are no damn good. I did not see one, and I have not heard of one, that fired more than a mag and then jammed. One spot of sand and they stop." The battalion's intelligence officer, Dickin, thought Lieutenant Colonel Cecil Merritt's withdrawal plan was good. They held Pourville and the beach "by using a small scattered force in front, heavy with Brens, and the main force about 100 yards back ready to counterattack. At 1100 hours we start back to the beaches by fire and movement." The covering force was intended to be composed of Sasks, with the Camerons being first to evacuate Green Beach.[19] Although the plan was sound, communication problems wrecked it.

The two battalions were badly intermixed. Camerons' Captain John Runcie figured a large proportion of his battalion's 'C' and 'D' Companies, along with part of battalion headquarters, comprised at least half of the covering party.[20] Often men tossed together by chance realized the Germans had to be kept at bay and fought them from the cover of buildings or orchards. Although the Germans were pressing, they did so warily, seemingly content to just close as the Canadians gave ground. There was no determined attempt to overrun Green Beach.

Merritt allowed Major Jim McRae to see to details while he carried the fight to the Germans. The Saskatchewan headquarters had moved so many times that by 1100 hours, some officers no longer knew its location. Edmondson was one of them; he felt that he and his men fought alone. With ammunition for the Boys guns and 3-inch mortar exhausted and Bren ammunition running low, they kept shooting at machine-gun and mortar positions on the headland and also at German infantry riding bicycles in from Quatre Vents Farm. "We managed to knock a few off their bicycles, forcing the others to ground and slowing their advance."

The Germans retaliated with machine-gun and mortar fire "that fell directly on top of the pub" sheltering Edmondson's group. "But we had run downstairs after firing. When there was a lull in their fire... we ran upstairs and fired bursts at them again which brought down more German bombardment, but we had sprinted downstairs again. The upper floor of the inn was steadily disintegrating." Edmondson realized he had seen no sign of anyone withdrawing over the seawall for about twenty minutes. Were he and his men left behind? He sent a runner to find battalion headquarters for news. When the man failed to return, Edmondson sent a second, who also never reappeared. Nobody volunteered to go after that, because it meant crossing the fire-swept bridge.[21]

Lieutenant J. Stiles, meanwhile, had been standing next to Merritt near the western headland when sniper fire suddenly increased. Merritt told Stiles to get the wounded gathered behind the seawall closer to the cover of the cliff. While Stiles turned to this task, Merritt grabbed a Bren gun and headed up the slope alone. "He must have got the sniper," Stiles wrote, "because the firing stopped. He was the life and soul of the attack and showed the utmost courage and personal disregard of danger. He sure had guts."[22]

No sooner did Merritt return than the Germans set up two machine-gun positions on the hill behind the large white hotel on Pourville's eastern flank.[23] Merritt gathered Major Claude Orme,

Lieutenant Ross MacIlveen, and three Bren gunners. The six men charged up the slope and eliminated the positions.[24]

Major Norman Ross oversaw the Camerons preparing to evacuate. Rather than taking cover behind the seawall, he concentrated the men in and around the buildings facing the esplanade. He considered this time "the worst part of the raid, waiting for the boats to come in... being shot at with rifle, M.G. and mortars."[25]

The covering parties were gradually withdrawing—steadily narrowing the perimeter. There was no panic. The tide was out, exposing a long stretch of sand. Scattered across it were LCAS and R-Boats wrecked during the landing. A couple wallowed in shallow water. Ross realized that when the boats came, a long run across about two hundred yards of exposed ground would be necessary.[26]

ABOARD *CALPE*, Captain John Hughes-Hallett sent a coded signal at 1022 hours to all the destroyers, LCFS, SGBS, MGBS, and MLS that had acted as guides for the LCAS earlier, "ordering them to form a line of bearing parallel to the... coast between [Puys] and Pourville." They would follow the landing craft in while the smaller support vessels went ahead to lay a smokescreen. Despite Commander H.V.P. McClintock's premature withdrawal of some landing craft, those organized by boat pool assistant commander Lieutenant J.H. Dathan were well positioned to evacuate troops off Green Beach. As these LCAS headed in, the supporting ships fired over their heads. "The wind carried the smoke screen ahead of the Landing Craft flotillas," Hughes-Hallett recorded, "which consequently came under little fire until they were close inshore." *Calpe* had taken position on the extreme western flank of Green Beach to serve as a boundary marker. "Although this beach was hidden by smoke the high ground to the west of it was visible above the smoke screen and the ship came under heavy... fire before she stopped."[27] The destroyers and other supporting ships found it impossible to identify specific targets through the smoke. But without the smoke, the LCAS would never reach the beaches.[28]

Six LCAS of *Prince Leopold*'s flotilla bound for Red Beach steered too far westward and landed at Green Beach. As planned, four LCAS from *Invicta* also approached this beach.[29] At 1104 hours, they emerged out of the covering smoke.

Major Ross sent men towards the boats. "As soon as the troops began to cross the beach, a very heavy crossfire from machineguns and musketry came down upon it," Major Andy Law reported. "There was also mortar fire and shellfire."[30]

PRIVATE J.L. BRIDGE and other Camerons passed through a gap blown in the seawall. He saw two LCAS approaching. "The beach was being swept by machine-gun fire and shells were falling all round. We split into two groups... I went to the right. As we arrived at the [LCA] we saw it had been abandoned... It was a shambles. I turned toward the other boat and saw two shells hit near the other group. We ran for that [LCA] and climbed aboard over the side. It wouldn't move so some of us climbed out and began to pull it off the beach. Shells were dropping and we could hear bullets striking the [LCA]. After considerable time we managed to get it off the beach. Some of the men assisting were killed... The boat was riddled and was not going to float very long. The sailors started it out to sea and I hung on the side... After going a short way the boat stopped and began to settle. I realized I was going to have to swim for it... Took off my equipment, boots and gaiters. As she started going down I pushed off and watched. I saw a few men get out, not as many as there were in it. The others must have been dead because there was lots of time to leave... before it went down." Rescued by another LCA, Bridge was transferred to a destroyer.[31]

Private Clarence Flemington thought the run across the beach "the worst thing I ever hope to see. To see good men die like flies."[32] Company Sergeant Major George Gouk had known "it was going to be hell going to the boats as we could see the bullets knocking up the sand and shells bursting right along the beach... the 'Nazi' gunners sure took a heavy toll, it was pretty hard to see the boys being knocked out after all they had done. Those left crawled and dragged a pal along with him."[33]

Journalist Wallace Reyburn ran for the boats, cursing as he stumbled in his clumsy army boots. "The sound of explosions and the whistle of bullets rang in my ears, but I didn't think about the prospect of being hit or blown to bits. I thought about only one thing—getting to that boat." It was the one grounded by the weight of men aboard. Reyburn joined in dragging it seaward. When the boat floated, he and the others grabbed hold of long, looping lifelines hanging from the sides. "As we went I noticed the young lad next to me lose his grip. He grabbed frantically at the rope again, but the boat slipped away from him. He was too exhausted to swim after us, and I saw him standing waist-deep in the water, watching us go. I shall never forget the look on that boy's face. It was a look of utter hopelessness. He'd come so far, almost got into the boat, and now we were going without him."

The men hung shoulder-to-shoulder from the lines. Soon Reyburn's hands grew icy cold and numb. The steel side of the LCA was wet and slippery. A bullet whistled past, "went right through the brain of the man next to me... his tin hat clanked against mine as he went down. One moment he'd been alive... and the next split second dead... He floated away face downward on the water."

When the LCA began sinking, Reyburn was surprised to see it was only about two hundred yards offshore. He'd imagined they had made greater gains. He also noticed "dozens of tin hats floating on the surface." Reyburn was finally dragged aboard another LCA. Soon its captain shouted that there were too many aboard and their weight was sinking the boat. All guns, webbing, uniforms, boots, and the dead went over the side. But more men crowded aboard, lowering the craft "almost flush with the water." About the time the boat started sinking, a tug-sized support vessel came to the rescue.[34]

"It was on the beach that we lost quite a number of men who were like brothers to us," Private E.G. Bird wrote. "Under terrific M.G. fire and mortar fire we raced to the beach, missing death by only fractions of an inch. The beach was the most gruesome place I ever saw. Our boys lay there, not a breath of life left. Some were pretty blown to pieces. Although the tide was out we made a mad dash for the boats which we finally succeeded in getting [on] amid heavy fire."[35]

When Private P.J. Gobin reached one LCA after a mad dash across about four hundred yards of bullet-swept beach, he found it already full. Gobin swam until picked up by another LCA.[36]

Major Norman Ross stayed until he was certain most Camerons and some Sasks had either been picked up or killed escaping. Quite a number of men still hugged the seawall, hesitating to risk the beach. Several large, boxy LCMs stood off the beach, just inside the thinning smokescreen, waiting for men to swim to them. Between the low tide and German fire, there was too much risk of losing the LCMs if they tried landing. "Okay fellows, we're going to make it," Ross shouted. "The alternative to sitting here and being captured is to run across that beach and into the water right out to the boats out there. Now who's with me? Line up against that wall and spread out and let's go." Ross led the charge, not looking back, not knowing how many followed and how many stayed behind. Most of the men were prairie boys and did not know how to swim. Ross waded out, shedding his web kit with the revolver and compass. As he started swimming, Ross glanced back. There were more men with him than expected. But some were floating, struck dead by bullets or shrapnel. Bullets spattered the water around him. Ross reached an LCM.[37]

BEHIND THE ESCAPING Camerons, the covering party continued shrinking its lines until it held just the buildings bordering the esplanade. As ordered by Merritt, most of the Sasks had waited until the Camerons were gone before attempting their own escape. Private Victor Story joined a group at the battalion's RAP behind the seawall. There was no organization here, so when a couple of LCAS arrived, "everyone seemed to run to the one boat, this caused [it] to upset." Story got away aboard a different LCA.[38]

Saskatchewan medical officer Captain Frank Hayter tried to coincide the moving of wounded from the seawall to the water's edge with the arrival of LCAS. "This was done under very heavy machine-gun and mortar fire. The majority of those wounded during the crossing... had to be left to look after themselves as it was suicide to try and stop and care for them. Many were wounded after embarking on [LCAS] and were attended by their companions... The majority of casualties among the stretcher bearers were received while carrying wounded across the beach... Some... making repeated trips."[39]

Lieutenant Ross MacIlveen took charge of about 120 Sasks and Camerons close to the western headland. Seeing that the LCAS were all landing at the centre of Green Beach, he had smoke canisters thrown to blind the Germans on the headland. Then the men double-timed it to the LCAS. Merritt was there by the seawall and "wished me luck...We had to swim about 400 to 600 yards through water riddled with MG and sniper bullets, and mortar bombs. The major part of my platoon succeeded in reaching [LCAS] and finally a destroyer."[40]

Merritt, meanwhile, had spotted a wounded man drowning and had run to him. As he carried the man to the safety of the wall, a sniper bullet struck him in the left shoulder. Merritt also suffered a facial wound. "Throughout the day," Captain John Runcie observed, Merritt's "actions were almost incredibly gallant. It wasn't human, what he did."[41] Merritt's heroism, reported by so many, would be recognized with the third Victoria Cross granted in the Dieppe raid.

Wounded, Merritt could have been one of the last evacuated. He never considered the idea. "I did know what to do, which was to continue... and not to evacuate myself. I was to help evacuate the others."[42]

Lieutenant John Edmondson still clung to the pub by the bridge, his group shrinking rapidly due to casualties. Unsure of the overall situation, he ran to the eastern end of the beach and saw no signs of life through the smoke. A loaded LCA was pulling out. Its captain shouted, "Goodbye, fellows. We've been told not to come in again." Disheartened, Edmondson returned to the pub. The men continued holding the Germans back until they became "desperately short of ammunition." When they were sure to be overrun, Edmondson ordered a withdrawal. His men joined some others against the seawall and close by the river, forming a group of about twenty. Between them they had a single 2-inch mortar round and two Bren gun magazines. Some were wounded. Because of the beach's curve, Edmondson was unable to see the main body of Sasks at its centre. He thought his were the only men left. "Couldn't move ten feet from the seawall without getting shot." An LCA appeared well out to sea but headed generally towards them. "Well fellows, this is your chance to get home," Edmondson said. "You want to go, you have to start for that craft. And once you leave the protection of this beach wall, anybody who gets shot, nobody stops for them. If you stop, you're dead." Edmondson dropped his rifle, pulled his pistol and shouted, "Let's go."[43]

He figured about fifteen men followed, the others standing by the wall in doubt. They ran to the water and started wading. "It seemed a hell of a long way to go, almost endless, when I was being shot at... Not more than five or six of us got aboard. The landing craft turned and headed straight out, bullets ricocheting off the metal sides."[44]

Private J. Krohn had watched the first LCA lifts from the safety of the seawall. There seemed then a long interval with no landing craft visible. By noon, "things looked very heartbreaking. Enemy machine-gun firing upon us on the beach, every half minute, boys passed away, blood everywhere. Everybody took it wonderfully and always thought of someone else and never himself." When a couple of LCAS landed, Krohn, Private Bud Evenden, and Corporal Leonard Roy Chilton ran for one. "Chilton was badly wounded so we had to carry him." The LCA had grounded turning about. "Those that could, pushed and heaved to push her off. It took all of twenty minutes to get her free. Fire was heavily laid down by Ack Ack and artillery on our small craft. We got it free eventually and then I climbed on deck. Chilton and Bud were laying there on deck, so I started to drag Chilton under cover. He received an Ack Ack shell in the stomach and a moment later another in the hip. Evenden received a wound in the head, but I managed to get them under cover. Chilton died a few moments later. While this happened our boat was riddled by bullets and started to leak badly. The sailor flagged for a [destroyer] to come to our rescue. We were only halfway out when we were told to swim for the [destroyer]. So I stripped and swam for it. The rest of the boys were transferred to the [destroyer]. I was given a good drink of rum and this was God sent, it gave me more strength. I spent three hours dressing the wounded... How I came out unwounded is a mystery."[45]

"We had a long stretch of beach and a long stretch of water to cover to get to our craft which stayed out in five feet of water," Captain Buck Buchanan wrote. "No words can describe the sheer display of courage and bravery that dominated that half hour of hell. Our stretcher bearers repeatedly carried wounded out to those boats and came back for more. Many of the lads... owe their lives... to the stretcher bearers' coolness and guts.

"And the Navy chaps cannot be forgotten, again and again they came in for us, through that curtain of lead and steel, to take us out to the larger boats. But at last, the ordeal was over and as the last craft left the shore, we saw the fellows who had to stay behind waving us on and still keeping the Jerries away from the seawall."[46]

By the time the LCA carrying Buchanan left, the covering party had withdrawn to the seawall. A long stretch had been under repair and had scaffolding erected alongside. The scaffolding enabled the soldiers to stand and fire over the wall at the Germans taking up position in the buildings facing the beach. Merritt commanded, with Runcie acting as the senior Cameron. They kept fighting "in the hope that boats would come in to take them off. The boats, however, did not return." Runcie thought this best. It "would have indeed been suicidal for the LCAS to have attempted to come in again after the enemy had fully established himself on the headlands on either side of the village." Twice after the last LCAS withdrew, a half dozen Spitfires "swept in and heavily machine-gunned the beach, doubtless under the impression that it was in enemy possession." The attacks caused some casualties.

Scouts reported "the enemy... pressing forward in steadily increasing numbers." Merritt and Runcie discussed options. Runcie suggested that "all the officers should be asked their views, and a 'confab' took place accordingly. There was now comparatively little ammunition left, particularly for the automatic weapons. The officers discussed whether to fight to the last man and the last round, or to surrender in order to prevent further loss of life; and as it seemed clear that no further damage could be done to the enemy it was unanimously decided to surrender. The men on the scaffolding, who were still firing, were called down, and we chucked our weapons down and called it a day." It was about 1500 hours.[47] The Germans arrived within minutes. "We were not very far apart," Merritt said. "They were just soldiers. And I think they were good soldiers. They treated us properly."[48]

At least a dozen LCAS, one LCM, and a French *chasseur* participated in Green Beach's evacuation. Four LCAS were sunk.[49] The decision to end the rescue effort was due to misinformation. By 1215, there were reports that no more soldiers were visible on Green Beach.

Sub-Lieutenant Kenneth Tew of LCA187 had successfully lifted forty men from the beach, including Flight Sergeant Jack Nissenthall, and transferred them to a destroyer. An officer there told Tew "it was impracticable to beach again and this tallied with my own theory, but I took craft beyond the smokescreen where I had a good view of the beach. There was no one there, except a few soldiers in the water who were swimming towards the other boats." A little later, Sub-Lieutenant H.E. Snead returned with LCM21 "to the beach, but saw no live men, either in the water or on the beach."[50]

The Sasks and Camerons suffered heavy casualties—65 per cent of their total strength. But this was far less than on the other Canadian beaches. Total Cameron casualties numbered 24 officers and 322 other ranks. Of these, 5 officers and 55 other ranks were killed. One officer and 7 other ranks died later of wounds, and 8 other ranks died in captivity, for a total fatality count of 76. A further 167 officers and men were taken prisoner. Of the Camerons who returned to England, 9 officers and 94 other ranks were wounded. Saskatchewan casualties totalled 339. Three officers and 75 other ranks were killed, 3 other ranks died of wounds, and 3 died while prisoners, for a total of 84 fatalities. Eighty-nine officers and other ranks captured survived imprisonment. The number of wounded Sasks reaching England was high—7 officers and 159 other ranks.[51]

Sorry, Lads

LIEUTENANT COLONEL Bob Labatt knew the withdrawal from White and Red Beaches in front of Dieppe would be bloody. By 1100 hours, runners had spread the word that boats were expected. A runner even notified Lieutenant Colonel Fred Jasperson, who alerted his Essex Scottish. Fire from the headlands steadily increased as additional mobile artillery and 81-millimetre mortars arrived. Labatt saw machine guns, mortars, and artillery firing on the beach from just 250 yards away. "The day was sunny and the only cover for troops crossing the beach was light smoke from burning tanks, landing craft, bursting projectiles, and the abandoned vehicles themselves. I was just wondering how many would survive the gauntlet when from the east appeared two [Bostons] flying at 200 feet along the water's edge. They laid the most perfect smoke screen I have ever seen, from one end of the beach to the other... Under cover of the smoke which drifted slowly inland, small groups began to climb through the wire and move towards the water. The first and largest was a crowd of German prisoners, carrying our wounded from the casino, some using doors and other makeshift stretchers."[1]

Although the Rileys were able to organize themselves somewhat, the Essex Scottish and most of the Fusiliers were too exposed to make any real preparations. Most of the tank crews were also pinned in place by a reluctance to abandon the comparative safety of their Churchills for open beach. Lieutenant Ed Bennett and his crew were exceptions. After expending their ammunition, they left *Bellicose* for the wrecked LCT5. Bennett sat with his back against the LCT's steel side, occasionally lifting his left eyelid to peek at the surrounding "chaos." With him were Troopers Rinehard "Bob" Cornelsen, Bill Stannard, Len Storvold, and Archie Anderson. "They're bringing in some Assault Craft to take us off," Anderson finally told Bennett. The lieutenant considered, imagining the initial panic. "Well, Archie, we'll take the *second* flight," he decided.[2]

Due to Commander H.V.P. McClintock's premature withdrawal of landing craft, fewer were coming to Red Beach than originally scheduled. This error was exacerbated by the six *Prince Leopold* LCAS bound for Red Beach that lost course and ended up at Green Beach. The first flight of boats was also late, and as it closed on the shore at 1120, the smokescreen was thinning.

Five LCAS landed in front of the casino. From the wrecked scout car where he and Major Gordon Rolfe were maintaining the vital wireless link to *Calpe*, Brigadier Bill Southam watched as the Rileys' plan—to load the wounded first—fell apart. "Their approach was a signal for a headlong rush of several hundred men, who waded into the water—shoulder deep—in an attempt to board them. Some boats were hit, some were swamped—it was my thought that certainly none would get away."[3]

Naval lieutenant Peter Ross, sheltering wounded at LCT3, saw two LCAS knocked out by German fire before gaining the beach. He tried to stop the others from being overwhelmed by the mad rush of soldiers. Plunging into the sea, Ross waded to the nearest loaded LCA and ordered its captain to "go full speed astern in order to get clear, but the few extra men who had managed to scramble aboard, together with timely enemy fire, upset the trim of the craft and she sank. One of the remaining craft received a direct hit and sank but the third managed to get away to sea ... At this stage of the action the beach was strewn with dead and the sea dotted with those who had been killed or drowned in the water."[4]

Sergeant Major Lucien Dumais tried to clamber aboard an LCA by climbing the lifelines. But the weight of his waterlogged field pack and other equipment caused him to lose hold. He plunged into eight feet of water. Dumais crawled along the bottom, swallowing seawater and nearly drowning, until he gained the shallows and lifted his head above the surface. Dumais staggered to LCT5 and helped tend wounded.[5]

Sergeant George Hickson watched "a great rush of infantry down from the centre of the beach towards the boats. Instead of scattering... they seemed to concentrate on a few craft, and the crowd of men around these craft drew heavy fire." Hickson swam to an LCA well offshore, finding it so crammed "that the door could not be closed and it was in danger of sinking." Hickson ordered the men to bail with their helmets, urging them to sing to establish a rhythm. Finding he was "singing alone," Hickson decided "this sounded rather foolish [and] desisted." The LCA soon transferred its passengers to a support boat and headed back towards the beach. For the first time, Hickson checked himself over—two bullet holes in the left sleeve of his tunic, another through a trouser leg. But nothing more than a barbed-wire scratch.[6]

Southam tried to impose order, walking to LCT5 and instructing everyone to give the wounded priority during the next evacuation attempt. Any "disobedience would be settled if necessary by pistols in the hands of officers," he threatened. Southam was struck by how many unwounded men huddled alongside the wounded behind the LCT and nearby tanks. They seemed totally inactive, yet "there was no sign of fear or panic—they seemed to be stunned—and almost incapable of action (and in some cases conversation). I urged those about this area to get busy—look for, and deal with the Germans who were firing at us."[7]

Bennett, meanwhile, had seen things play out as he had expected. "There were some survivors, but there were a great many killed in the water and some wounded trying to get back in." Bob Cornelsen, a thirty-year-old from Stettler, Alberta, squatted beside him. "Mr. Bennett, we're going out to bring some of them in." He and Trooper Anderson "went out and a few minutes later Archie came back and said, 'Well, they got Bobby.'"[8]

The orderly second flight Bennett had anticipated never developed. Each LCA was swarmed by men trying to escape. At times the wounded did get priority. But for the most part it was, in the words of Fusiliers' Corporal Robert Berube, "everyone for himself."[9]

Rather than taking this tack, Berube joined Sergeant Pierre Dubuc in seeing to Lieutenant Colonel Joe Ménard's safety. The Fusiliers commander had been partly sheltered by three tanks close together. Earlier, Ménard had collapsed from blood loss and then drifted in and out of consciousness. During conscious moments, the pain was almost unbearable. He endured by "praying, harder and harder."[10]

Ménard was conscious when several LCAS approached. Dubuc, still clad only in underwear, suggested he should be evacuated. "The colonel replied that he would not do so until all his men had been taken off." Ménard passed out. Dubuc and Berube carried his stretcher to an LCA. Berube remained with Ménard while Dubuc helped another wounded man board before also getting on. The LCA got away safely, transferring its load of largely wounded Fusiliers to an LCF.[11]

Regaining consciousness, Ménard accepted his rescue. German fighters and bombers were attacking the vessel, whose anti-aircraft guns fired back fiercely. Ménard was lying on cases of high-explosive shells. "One bullet would blow the whole works sky high but, by then, I didn't give a damn. I thought, 'What the hell, if they haven't got me by this time they're never going to get me.'" A naval rating gave him a slug of rum, then came back looking alarmed. "Pardon me, Sir, but have you got a stomach wound?" Ménard shook his head. "That's good, Sir, because if you had I shouldn't have given you that rum."

Ménard thought this "the funniest thing I'd ever heard. I began laughing and the only thing that stopped me was the pain burning my side. You see, I knew I'd been through it and I felt pretty damned good."[12]

SOUTHAM, MEANWHILE, was back at the scout car trying to hurry the withdrawal. At 1132 he signalled: "Want lots of support. Enemy engaging craft and they cannot get in. Much smoke and air support wanted." Three minutes later, Southam pleaded, "Can we rush things? Things are getting heavy." Then, at 1140, "Small boats have been sinking. I do not consider it possible to evacuate unless you get everything available in here." This was followed at 1154 by, "Boats hit because no support. High ground to east and west of beaches must be bombed or shelled."[13]

Eight LCAS approaching Red Beach in line abreast came under murderous shell and mortar fire when the smoke thinned, denying them cover. Six were sunk or blown apart. Reaching the remaining two required the Essex Scottish to cross a fully exposed beach. Private J.H. Mizon chucked two smoke canisters over the seawall to blind snipers in the buildings. The beach "was covered with a cross fire and mortar fire. I noticed the tanks were still firing as I crawled behind one before hitting the water. I reached the [LCA] where I had to drop my rifle to climb up. After getting on ... I noticed two of our boys hanging over the side so I pulled them up, one being hit in both legs. The [LCA] was taking in water by now and as a Navy power boat pulled up alongside I hopped onto that."

Corporal R. Carle thought it had been "hell on the beach, but it was worse on leaving. Men were dropping like flies." Jumping on an LCA, Carle realized he was going to get home. "THANK GOD," he wrote later.

Captain B.S. Wilson calmly reminded the men around him to help the wounded to boats. Corporal J. Donaldson started out with Private James Maier, "who was wounded in the stomach and I think a bullet in his neck. It was a very slow walk to the [LCAS] which were beaching about 500 yards to our left. There were still plenty of bullets around and the mortars were still at it. I was lucky and didn't even get scratched. I managed to get Maier on ... but was pushed down just after I got him on. They couldn't close the door so we soon had about a foot and a half of water in the bottom of the boat." Pinned on his stomach by the press of men, Donaldson fought to keep his head above the water until—drawing on all his strength—he managed to struggle to his feet. When another boat came alongside, the press of the mob around him pushed Donaldson into the other LCA.[14]

Having passed out from loss of blood, Maier was thrown overboard along with the dead. Roused by the shock of hitting the water, he swam to another LCA.[15]

Sergeant W.E. Hussey had moved to LCT3 at about 1130 hours. More than 250 men were gathered there. "We were under intense fire from the flanks. We set Bren guns up on either flank and returned their fire. [When] the first [LCAS] began to come in . . . we started to wade out in the water to meet them. It was at this time that the enemy took advantage of our inability to protect ourselves and there were extremely heavy casualties. Many men . . . drowned."

Hussey boarded an LCA. "We couldn't get the landing door . . . closed because of the men hanging on to it. We finally did get it closed and we were ordered by one of the naval men to throw all the dead overboard and also all the blankets and equipment. We did all this and spent the rest of the time bailing water with our steel helmets. Quite a few of the personnel on board were wounded by machine-gun fire."[16]

Captain Donald MacRae, the Stormont, Dundas and Glengarry Highlander observer, saw the German fire destroy "so many [LCAS] that very few of the troops got off. I got away myself with a small party of wounded in a small wooden row boat and we were eventually picked up by a smoke-laying ship."[17] Just three Essex Scottish officers and forty-nine other ranks returned to England.[18] Most of these, however, were aboard LCTs that had never landed. While no formal tally was ever compiled, MacRae is known to have been the only officer on Red Beach who got away. Of seventeen Essex Scottish men who provided accounts of the raid, only seven had landed.

LCAS CONTINUED COMING into White Beach. While the loading was still chaotic, there was some order. At LCT5, serving as the battalion's RAP, Captain George Donald Skerritt had pointed to an LCA. "Every man, carry a man," he shouted, and the unwounded complied. Private J. McQuade was uninjured. He noted they were so few in number that many of the wounded "were left on the beach."[19] Although badly overloaded, the LCA managed to withdraw. Skerritt, who had swum out several times to help more wounded aboard, did not try to escape. He returned to the wounded by the LCT.

Private W. McNab also hesitated to leave the wounded. He asked medical officer Captain Wesley Clare "what I could do and was told that the men were all too badly wounded to move and that he was staying with them. I then proceeded to the boats."[20] Carrying a wounded man to an LCA, Padre John Foote was urged to board. "No, there are lots of chaplains back in England," he replied. "I didn't intend to go home because the action wasn't over, my work wasn't done."[21] He joined Clare and Skerritt.

Having seen that the riflemen and wounded had either gotten away, were stranded, or had been killed, the Bren gun covering party at the casino started towards the water. Private J.H. Stuart backed down the beach, firing his Bren, while another man passed magazines to reload.[22] Company Sergeant Major Jack Stewart was also there. He took cover behind a tank until an LCA came in. No sooner did he board the crowded craft than it sank twenty yards offshore. Standing on the edge of the beach, Stewart stripped off most of his clothes and then swam for it. Two and a half hours later, an LCA cruising for survivors scooped him up.[23]

Deciding the time had come for his own departure, Labatt ordered all the wireless sets destroyed, save the one netted to brigade—he hoped to float that set out to an LCA. He, Major Dick McLaren, and Captain Herb Poag walked towards the water. They joined the Bren gunners wading out to sea and were squeezed aboard "a frightfully crowded" LCA. Labatt saw Major Harold Lazier already on board, along with wounded Rileys, Fusiliers, and Royal Marines. Suddenly, the smokescreen completely disappeared. Labatt saw about a dozen similarly loaded LCAS all nakedly exposed. "Every German weapon turned on them and hell let loose. What we had experienced before was nothing to the furious hurricane of fire. In no time the sea was littered with the wreckage of shattered [LCAS] and dotted with heads and waving arms. A shell burst inside the crowded boat next to us with ghastly results.

"I could feel our craft being hit, but was not conscious of anything being amiss until I saw the naval crew jump overboard and found that I was standing in water up to my knees. I told the men to inflate their Mae Wests and either to swim out to meet incoming boats or to go ashore and wait for them there. They could do as they chose." Labatt asked Poag if he was coming. "I still don't like water and I am going ashore, if it's okay by you," Poag replied. As Poag swam shoreward Labatt stripped to underpants and shirt. The LCA had drifted in

and beached in about six feet of water. "Well goodbye, Bob," someone called. Labatt turned to find McLaren leaning against a bulkhead
with left hand extended. "He... had just been hit in the right arm
and figured his number was up. I examined the wound and found it
was nasty but not serious. I assured him that the boat would not sink
and that his best chance was to sit tight right where he was. Several
others also remained in the boat."

Labatt swam towards an LCT a half mile distant. When he was only
two hundred yards away, the LCT suffered two direct artillery hits and
sank. Labatt was very cold and tired. The only ships he saw seemed
miles away. His only choice was to swim back to shore. Landing close
to LCT5, he ran to it. "The fire had increased if anything and I was
horrified by the number of dead washing upon the beach." Between
150 and 200 men from every possible unit were sheltered there now.
Most were wounded and "in shocking condition." Southam, limping
from a slight leg wound, was trying to organize Bren gun parties to
provide covering fire. Labatt thought it futile. Many men had previously tried to reach the LCAS and lost their weapons. So there was
"practically nothing with which to fight."[24]

Southam and Labatt were talking when Poag approached. A
machine-gun burst ripped into his stomach and he fell mortally
wounded.[25] Southam headed back to the scout car. Finding the chert
"hell on bare feet," Labatt donned the overalls and boots of a dead
tanker. Shaking with cold, he layered on a naval rating's duffle coat.
The tide was coming in, threatening to drown the wounded by the
water's edge and beside the LCT. He got two Riley officers, Major C.G.
Pirie and Captain Tony Hill, to organize parties to move wounded
away from the approaching tide. "The behaviour of the wounded...
was wonderful. The injuries were appalling and many could neither
be shifted nor properly tended, but I never heard any complaining—
and if one cried out or groaned, he tried to apologize for it." Labatt
walked along the beach with a stretcher-bearer, pulling wounded
above the high-water mark. Someone called from a wrecked LCA that
had washed in. Labatt saw it was McLaren and helped him to the LCT.
Poag lay there, looking "very pale," and said he was "going out on a
long journey." Other than putting him on a stretcher, there was
nothing Labatt could do for him.

In fact, there was little Labatt could do, period. Water lapped the LCT. No LCAS were to be seen. German infantry along the promenade were only about a hundred yards away, their fire increasingly accurate. There were few able men to offer resistance and "even fewer weapons." If Labatt continued to resist, "we might kill a few more Germans, but while doing so hundreds of our wounded would be drowned."

Labatt looked at Captain Ed Bennett, who was blinded, his face burned practically away. "He must have been in agony yet his spirit was magnificent. I heard him say, 'Remember boys, if it comes, give only your name, rank, and number.'

"I quickly made the most unpleasant decision of my life. I warned the nearby tanks to cease fire and sent [a captured German airman] out with a white towel... Firing died down, mortar shells ceased to fall, thirty to forty Germans leaped up on the seawall and covered us."[26]

AT 1130 HOURS, Captain John Hughes-Hallett ordered *Brocklesby* "to close and give what support she was able" to the troops on White and Red Beaches. Steering through the smokescreen, the destroyer emerged just five hundred yards from shore, opening fire on the headlands and buildings along the promenade while enduring a barrage in return. "Feeling that his fire was ineffective," Lieutenant Commander Nigel Pumphrey "decided to retire behind the smoke." As the ship turned, "both... engines were put out of action by shore fire and the ship grounded by the stern. Repairs were effected in three minutes and still firing at shore targets... *Brocklesby* retired behind the smoke."[27]

The few wireless signals from the beach reported a rapidly deteriorating situation. One at 1211 reported, "Very few personnel have been evacuated."[28]

A Calgary Tank wireless operator monitoring the regimental net intermittently intercepted traffic between Major Rolfe; Major Allen Glenn, who was still manning his tank; and Major Brian McCool, the principal military beach officer. At 1210, McCool advised that it was "getting pretty hot here." This was followed moments later by one of the three—the operator was unable to determine who—

saying, "We better get these fellows back. Just a minute, are these guys dead or not? They don't move, so they must be dead." At 1220, Rolfe asked if Glenn could see him. The operator heard the two, "as if they were playing a game of hide and seek, and nothing more serious, chat back and forth trying to decide whether they can see each other." Glenn announced, "I can see you now. Can you see me?" Rolfe replied, "Yes, I can see you too." It was 1225, and Glenn's last message was, "Unload crews from tanks." The wireless link ceased.[29]

Although Hughes-Hallett "could not see what was happening on the beaches, it was possible to form an opinion of the progress of the withdrawal by watching the diminishing stream of LCA proceeding past *Calpe* on their way seaward. A number of them came alongside and gave us news, and at the same time transferred the more seriously wounded men to the ship."[30]

Unaware that the boat pool officer, Commander H.V.P. McClintock, had long left for England with many LCAs, Hughes-Hallett still believed significant numbers of landing craft operated somewhere in the smoke. In reality, by 1230 hours, *Calpe* and two LCAs alongside were "the only craft left close inshore."[31]

At 1243, Rolfe signalled, "White Beach not good, Red Beach not so bad because of fewer people there."[32] Seven minutes later, Hughes-Hallett ordered *Calpe* "to close the beach... for a final personal inspection." With an LCA on either side, *Calpe* made for the eastern end of Red Beach.[33] "Since the radio equipment seemed by now to be of secondary importance," Hughes-Hallett freed the 4-inch guns to fire. If they saw men ashore, the LCAs would be sent in. "As soon as we were through the smoke several things happened at once. *Calpe* came under very heavy fire from guns whose projectiles threw up vicious little water spouts all round the ship... The sound of *Calpe*'s 4-inch guns firing back cheered up all on board... The ship... stopped slightly under a mile from the beaches, but no Canadian troops could be made out." Then a fighter, mistakenly identified as a Spitfire, swept in and its "wing appeared to turn blue and become incandescent. A stream of cannon shell followed and we all dived for cover... Most of the officers and men on... *Calpe*'s overcrowded bridge received superficial wounds, and as we stood up again we presented a gory sight."[34]

"The concussion rang in my ears and the machine guns and cannon roared," Quentin Reynolds wrote, "and then the sharp clang of bullets hitting and ricocheting from one steel object to another added to the sound... I was dazed, lying there. Then I bit on something and spit out a gold inlay. I picked it up and put it in my pocket...I got up shakily... Two men who had been standing on either side of me lay there on the deck. They were dead. A sailor helped Air Commodore Cole... His face was covered with blood."[35] Cole's wounds proved severe.[36]

Calpe "altered course to gain the cover of smoke, and it appeared certain that any further attempt to take off troops would be unlikely to succeed." Still, Hughes-Hallett and Major General Roberts were loath to give up. *Calpe* closed on *Locust,* Hughes-Hallett thinking Commander Ryder might have been closer to the beach and have more information.[37]

It was 1300 hours, and as Hughes-Hallett and Ryder exchanged semaphore signals, a series of messages from Rolfe were forwarded from *Fernie* to Roberts. The first, at 1301, pleaded, "Bombard buildings and pillboxes along promenade. Enemy closing in." At 1305: "Give us quick support, enemy closing in on beach. Hurry it up please." Then, at 1307, "We are evacuating." A minute later, Rolfe's last message reported: "There seems to be a mass surrender of our troops to the Germans on the beach. Our people here have surrendered."[38]

Hughes-Hallett was still digesting this news when a mighty explosion rocked the nearby destroyer *Berkeley,* its back broken by a direct bomb hit. Once the crew abandoned ship, *Albrighton* sunk her with a torpedo.[39]

"Slowly we turned seaward," Hughes-Hallett wrote, "and shaped course for Newhaven at the best speed of the crippled landing craft, which was under four knots. The mass of small landing craft were formed into an amorphous bunch surrounded by the larger craft armed with Oerlikons or better, while outside them there was a circle of destroyers... enemy aircraft seemed reluctant to press home attacks in the face of what added up to a formidable volume of anti-aircraft fire. Up to this point... *Calpe* had not been seriously damaged, although casualties to personnel had been heavy [25 per cent] and her upper deck was choked with seriously wounded soldiers." A young naval officer asked Hughes-Hallett if he "believed the history books when they spoke of the 'scuppers' running with blood. 'If not, lean over the bridge and take a look along the ship's side.' I did so and as the ship rolled very gently in a long, lazy swell you could see little red rivulets running down out of each scupper."[40]

NEXT TO THE scout car, Brigadier Southam saw a white flag appear on LCT3. "Very soon... numerous white towels or shirts were seen in the direction of the casino. Rolfe and I were by now destroying and burning our papers. Some which were not yet burned were put into the car to be burned. The next report was that German soldiers were closing in across the esplanade. The operator was ordered out of the scout car and—to the best of my knowledge—an incendiary was started inside the car." Southam looked at the Germans on the wall and called out, "Sorry, lads, we might as well pack up too." Then "we raised our hands and that was that."[41]

Southam had made an error of serious consequence for the Canadian prisoners. Instead of first burning the detailed military plan brought ashore, he stuck it inside the scout car. Either the incendiary failed to ignite or was not set off. The plan, including instructions that German prisoners' hands were to be tied, was captured. In retaliation, throughout the fall of 1942, Canadian and British prisoners were sporadically handcuffed or tied. The British and Canadian governments decided upon a tit for tat that saw German prisoners in both countries selectively handcuffed. Shackling German prisoners was abandoned on December 12, 1942. But the Germans only discontinued the practice on November 22, 1943, after intervention by the International Red Cross.[42]

As the Germans approached LCT5, Captain Ed Bennett "was standing... with water up to my knees and I slipped my belt and my pistol into the water so that there were no souvenirs for them. They then led us up the beach and I was taken through the town to the Hôtel Dieu. That was the hospital and Archie [Anderson] left me there. He worked all day on that beach bringing bodies and wounded up and putting them in ambulances. He told me he never was so tired in his life because he worked right until dusk that evening before he was taken away himself. Because my hands and wrists were burned I was never chained... That night we were loaded in railway boxcars—all the wounded were packed in like cattle until we reached Rouen. When we arrived at Rouen we weren't taken off until [eight] in the morning and during that night wounded men were dying and others crying for water. A great many of them died, I'm sure, in the boxcar that night. We were then taken to the hospital in Rouen and I received quite good treatment there... My one eye was good and I could see if I pried it open, but my right eye had gone and I didn't ever recover the sight in that one."[43]

At the time of surrender, Labatt's watch showed it was 1500 hours.[44] But most hostilities had ended an hour earlier, the German artillery ceasing fire at 1358.

The casualty toll in front of Dieppe was dreadful. Although the Essex Scottish suffered the most, the Rileys and Fusiliers had also been savaged. Just 125 Fusiliers returned to England and 217 Rileys. Fifty of these Fusiliers were wounded as were 108 Rileys. The latter battalion had 7 officers, and 172 other ranks were killed. Another officer and 6 other ranks succumbed to wounds, and 2 more officers and 9 other ranks died in captivity. The Fusiliers lost 7 officers, and 98 other ranks were killed. Four wounded other ranks died along with 1 officer and 9 other ranks taken prisoner. The Calgary Tank Regiment had only 2 officers and 10 other ranks killed, with 1 more man dying in captivity. But only 2 tankers who landed reached England.[45]

Aboard *Calpe,* Roberts released a carrier pigeon that flew to 1 Canadian Corps headquarters. "Very heavy casualties in men and ships," the report it carried read. "Did everything possible to get men off but in order to get any home had to come to sad decision to abandon remainder. This was joint decision by Force Commanders. Obviously operation completely lacked surprise."[46]

The convoy steamed homeward under protective air cover. As the voyage wore on, the weather deteriorated. Single German bombers used the increasing cloud cover to slip through and attack the ships but were driven off.

Air Vice-Marshal Trafford Leigh-Mallory's air battle had not developed as hoped. About 106 Allied aircraft were lost, 98 being fighters or tactical reconnaissance planes. Sixty-seven airmen died.

The RCAF lost 13 planes and 10 pilots. Combined Operations Head-quarters claimed 91 German aircraft destroyed and twice this number probably destroyed or damaged. German documents, how-ever, reported only 48 planes lost and 24 damaged.[47]

German Army losses amounted to "five officers and 116 other ranks killed, six officers and 195 other ranks wounded and 11 other ranks missing." Although many Germans surrendered on White and Green Beaches, most were left behind. Just thirty-seven were taken to England.[48] Possessing the complete military plan allowed the Germans to thoroughly critique the raid. They considered it a folly. The 302nd Division's Generalleutnant Konrad Haase acknowl-edged that the Canadians had attacked "with great energy. That the enemy gained no ground at all in Puys, and in Dieppe could take only parts of the beach not including the west mole and the western edge of the beach, and this only for a short time, was not the result of lack of courage, but of the concentrated defensive fire of our divi-sional artillery and infantry heavy weapons. Moreover, his tank crews did not lack spirit. They could not penetrate the anti-tank walls which barred the way into the town... and some of them were unable to get forward over the rolling beach shingle and cross the seawall. In Puys the efforts made by the enemy, in spite of the heavy German machine-gun fire, to surmount the wire obstacles studded with booby traps on the first beach terrace are signs of a good offen-sive spirit... The large number of prisoners at Puys was the result of the hopelessness of the situation for the men who had been landed caught under German machine-gun, rifle and mortar fire between the cliffs and the sea on a beach which offered no cover.

"At Pourville the enemy, immediately after landing, pushed for-ward into the interior without worrying about flank protection... The operations against the coastal batteries were conducted by the Commandos with great dash and skill."

But bravery alone could not suffice. Haase concluded: "It is incomprehensible that it should be believed that a single Canadian division should be able to overrun a German Infantry Regiment reinforced with artillery."[49] Generalfeldmarschall Gerd von Rundst-edt cautioned that it "would be an error to believe that the enemy will mount his next operation in the same manner. He will draw his lessons from his mistakes in planning and from his failure and next time he will do things differently."[50]

"IT WAS TOUGHER than you figured, wasn't it?" Quentin Reynolds asked Major General Roberts. Leaning over a rail, Roberts watched the sea passing. "He looked tired now... He drew a deep breath. 'Yes,' he said slowly. 'It was tougher than we figured. They had more stuff than we knew. Our casualties were heavier.'"[51]

The convoy divided—destroyers sailing for Portsmouth, the smaller craft for Newhaven. Portsmouth's dockyard "was floodlit and a veritable sea of ambulances awaited us," Hughes-Hallett wrote.[52] At Newhaven, the scene was similar. Pre-warned that large numbers of wounded were expected, a hospital train was in place by 1730 hours, and 118 ambulances waited dockside. As the wounded were carried off vessels, they were either transferred to the train or taken by ambulance to a series of hospitals. About six hundred wounded soldiers soon crowded Canadian Army hospitals.[53]

The unwounded were well received. The Queen's Own Camerons were taken to a large hall outside Newhaven "where hot tea and sandwiches waited," Major Norman Ross said. A room had been set aside where men could write brief messages to next of kin in Canada. "I just put down, 'Returned safely.' My wife got this and wondered where the hell I had returned from."[54]

Saskatchewan lieutenant John Edmondson was first subjected to questioning. "What happened? Who came back with you? Who did you see killed or wounded?" Edmondson reported seeing a lot of men killed and wounded but was unable to "remember explicitly anything. Remember, the nine hours ashore seemed like only ten minutes. And in the heat of the moment... you only register someone is hit and do not stop to register, 'Oh, that is John Smith.' As well, it was more than thirty hours since our last meal at lunch the day before. Heavens, even I was reported killed by someone who had probably seen me knocked off the road at the end of the bridge, so you can't be sure of anything. They handed me a mug of rum, but the thought nauseated me so I asked for tea and something to eat. That steaming tea and bully beef on white bread sandwich tasted better than anything I'd ever eaten."[55]

"So ended the brave and bitter day," the Canadian Army official historian wrote. "Under the shaded dockside lights in the English ports, tired and grimy men drank strong tea and told their tales, and the ambulance trains filled and drew slowly out. Back on the Dieppe beaches the Germans were still collecting Canadian wounded, and the Canadian dead in their hundreds lay yet where they had fallen. On both sides of the Channel staff officers were already beginning to scan the record and assess the lessons of the raid; and beyond the Atlantic, in innumerable communities across Canada, people waited in painful anxiety for news of friends in the overseas army—that army which, after three years of war, had just fought its first battle."[56]

DIEPPE IN MEMORY

I STAND ON A German bunker, gazing down Blue Beach's length. From seawall to tide line, this bunker overlooks all. I have visited countless battlefields across Europe where Canadians fought and died, but I find Puys the grimmest and saddest of all. The high headlands close in oppressively upon either side. Remains of bunkers dominate every flank. It is impossible to look across that bleak, rocky beach and not be haunted by images and sounds of young men dying. A stark monument, much like a bunker itself, stands close by the eastern headland. Prime Minister Mackenzie King attended its dedication on August 18, 1946. The bilingual plaque reads: "On this beach officers and men of the Royal Regiment of Canada died at dawn 19 August 1942 striving to reach the heights beyond. You who are alive, on this beach, remember that these died far from home, that others, here and everywhere, might freely enjoy life in God's Mercy." The monument adds to the pervading melancholy.

Touring Dieppe's beaches is a sobering affair, one that confirms the inevitability of Jubilee's failure. As finally planned and executed, the raid was never going to succeed. Yet it was launched and played through to its tragic conclusion. We still ponder the reasons.

From the outset, the planning was fatally flawed. Combined Operations, particularly Mountbatten and Hughes-Hallett, wanted to stage something spectacular—not just to meet strategic goals, such as assuaging Soviet demands for western Allied action, but to cement and extend the influence of Combined Operations Headquarters. As Hughes-Hallett admitted, where the raid happened mattered little. The point was to raid on a larger scale than ever before and to be seen as *doing* something.

Against this backdrop, the operational plan was allowed to develop through a series of compromises that cumulatively ensured failure. The insufficient naval and aerial fire support, Montgomery's insistence on a frontal attack including all the tanks, the execution of this frontal assault in broad daylight against an assuredly alert enemy, and other bad decisions made success impossible. Deciding to remount the raid after Rutter's cancellation, and without significantly correcting the plan's increasingly apparent weaknesses, was yet more poor judgement—not just by Mountbatten and Hughes-Hallett but by all the senior Canadian commanders involved, the British Chiefs of Staff, and Churchill.

As if flawed planning was not enough, there was also spectacularly bad luck. The intelligence failure that reported 302nd Infantry Division being replaced by the much weaker 110th Infantry Division led to gross underestimation of enemy strength. Then came the run-in with the German coastal convoy. While this did not alert the Germans to the actual raid, it critically disrupted No. 3 Commando's part in it and woke up the Germans guarding the beach at Puys. Bad luck and poor judgement then combined to send the Royal Regiment to its doom. Naval lieutenant commander Harold Goulding then landed the Royals late, in daylight, and under the guns of a fully aware enemy. The battle at Blue Beach was lost before the troops stepped onto the baseball-sized chert. On the other beaches, the situation differed only by degrees. Even on Green Beach, the slight advances inland achieved nothing of import.

Throughout, the raid was further undermined by a string of wireless malfunctions and inept handling of communications. Hardly a signal was wholly received or correctly interpreted by the officers on *Calpe* and *Fernie*. A handful of Essex Scottish gaining the town was reported as a breakthrough by the battalion; minor success around the casino became a sign of near victory. Like dominoes falling, these mistakes led to more fatal ones, the most glaring being Major General Ham Roberts's decision to send Les Fusiliers Mont-Royal and the Royal Marines in to reinforce the troops at Dieppe when evidence was pouring in of a catastrophe ashore. Finally, mangled communication prompted Commander H.V.P. McClintock to direct a major share of the landing craft away from the beaches just when they were desperately required for the evacuation. How many troops ashore died or were taken prisoner as a result of one man's mistake will never be known.

No battle in Canadian history has undergone such intense scrutiny, much of it focused on whom to blame. Major General Ham Roberts became the traditional scapegoat. Removed from 2nd Division's command in the spring of 1943, he ran a recruiting depot until the war ended. Still a major general, he retired to Jersey in the Channel Islands. Each year, until his death in 1962, the August 19 mail brought a small box containing a piece of cake—an anonymous, bitter reminder of his alleged prediction of an easy victory. Roberts never attempted to exonerate himself for his part in the raid's failure, except to say that history would do so.

Whether Roberts even made the "piece of cake" statement is disputed. It was a fairly common remark. Uncountable the number of times a Canadian regiment's war diary or report on an Orders Group recorded a commander calling a forthcoming action a piece of cake— when it proved anything but. The phrase came to be often used sardonically.

Roberts's agreement to proceed without major pre-raid bombing and his decision to reinforce the Dieppe beaches were mistakes. Regarding the first point, however, I think Roberts was correct in his belief that had he refused to commit Canadian troops without large-scale bombing, Lieutenant General Harry Crerar would have appointed someone else to command, and the raid would have continued. Reinforcing failure, which was what Roberts did when he sent more troops to Dieppe, is harder to excuse. Yet Roberts had no notion of what was transpiring on any of the beaches. What intelligence he possessed was largely faulty. Hughes-Hallett, who from the deck of *Calpe* saw the boatfuls of wounded washing up and might have suspected a likely disaster, did not protest this reinforcement. If there is blame here, it must be shared by both force commanders.

But ultimately it was not Roberts who decided to remount the raid, the original fatal error. Who made this decision also remains debatable. Some analysts consider Prime Minister Winston Churchill the final culprit—insisting on the raid to satisfy Stalin's Second Front demands. It is true Churchill desired the raid, but he wanted it only if there was a good prospect of success. The last thing Churchill needed was another bloody defeat, which was what he was given.

A great many Dieppe veterans blamed Mountbatten, and a theory developed that relaunching Operation Rutter as Operation Jubilee was in fact never authorized by Churchill or his Chiefs of Staff. Mountbatten is said to have gone behind their backs, independently steamrolling the renewal and execution of the raid without their knowledge. This claim rests less on evidence for guilt than on lack of evidence against it. No Chiefs of Staff minutes mention Operation Jubilee. Assertions made by Mountbatten and Hughes-Hallett and contained in Combined Operations records provide the only indications that restaging the raid had Chiefs of Staff approval. So the reasoning goes that the raid was remounted on the sly by a vainglorious Mountbatten, with the cunning complicity of his Combined Operations staff. I think this theory, which has gained significant momentum and acceptance, improbable and bordering on the fantastic.

The Dieppe raid was too large, too complex, and involved too many chains of command for proper channels not to have been followed. Churchill and Chief of the Imperial General Staff, General Sir Alan Brooke were extremely hands-on superiors. That either they or their sprawling staffs would not have got wind of an unauthorized action mounted literally under their noses is simply not possible.

But if Mountbatten did not mastermind a grand conspiracy, certainly the raid would never have been remounted as Jubilee without him. Mountbatten sold the idea, just as he had previously secured authorization to stage Operation Rutter. He did so despite his grave reservations about the plan as rejigged, principally by Montgomery, and about the decision not to provide major supporting firepower. Montgomery ultimately denied any definite role in the debacle. Despite conclusive evidence to the contrary, he refused responsibility for the fatal decision to attack Dieppe frontally and concentrate the tanks there. Even his official biographer doubted him. In the aftermath, virtually everyone involved in mounting the raid either denied responsibility or reframed the tragedy as a partial success that provided valuable lessons in warfare—an argument widely embraced by veterans and some veteran organizations. Nobody argued this more ardently than Mountbatten. "From the lessons we learnt at Dieppe all subsequent landings in the Mediterranean and elsewhere benefitted directly," he declared, along with the immortal line, "The successful landing in Normandy was won on the beaches of Dieppe."[1]

Primary among these supposed lessons: capturing a port intact and without exceptional casualties was unlikely; specialized armour was needed to support any landing; troops required close and extensive fire support during the landing phase. The Canadian Army's official historian exhaustively examined the so-called lessons. Most were already known or suspected. He concluded that for the few new lessons, "it had not been necessary to attack Dieppe in order to learn them."[2]

Even the claim that Dieppe led to development of the artificial harbours used in Normandy is untrue. Hughes-Hallett is often credited with proposing these "mulberries" after the raid, but he himself said they were Churchill's idea, posed months before Dieppe. Already, initial planning for a major amphibious invasion of occupied Europe had concluded that the invasion must not occur at a port but fall on open beaches, with the buildup of supplies and reinforcements passed over them. As Mountbatten had argued, Dieppe could not be a test for supplying and building up an invasion force—the raiders would not be ashore long enough.

Those contending that the Normandy invasion succeeded because of lessons learned at Dieppe generally ignore that between these two attacks, the western Allies carried out several amphibious operations that were much more instructive than Dieppe for the landings on June 6, 1944. The true dress rehearsal for D-Day happened on July 10, 1943, when Canadian, British, and American troops stormed onto the beaches of Sicily as the opening move of Operation Husky. This was the largest amphibious invasion of the war, putting eight divisions ashore across a broad front.

Another claim to justify the raid was that it gathered vital intelligence. There are two theories. First, that Flight Sergeant Jack Nissenthall's severing of the radar station's communications lines gave the Allies highly classified intelligence when the operators were forced to fall back on sending data via wireless. But that result, though useful, hardly justifies the raid. A second, more current theory is that the sole reason for the raid was to enable No. 30 Assault Unit to capture Ultra-sensitive intelligence, such as codebooks and a four-rotor Enigma machine, from a Dieppe hotel. This more sensational theory has many factual and logical holes and is also not credible. For one thing, the idea that thousands of soldiers and resources would be committed for the sole purpose of looting a hotel—and that total secrecy could be maintained to hide that purpose—is ludicrous. For another, No. 30 Assault Unit did not carry out any mission, so the raid was in vain. Nissenthall and the No. 30 specialists were along because the raid presented an opportunity for intelligence gathering. These claims are two of the many in which unforeseen outcomes are used as after-the-fact justification.

Among the unforeseen outcomes, one that much pleased Churchill was that although a tactical defeat, Dieppe represented a strategic victory because it panicked the German high command. Germany's premier super-unit, the Leibstandarte ss Panzer Division, was transferred from Russia to France in direct response. In the face of increasingly powerful Russian offensives, this loss constituted a serious blow.[3]

A further justification for Dieppe was that it fostered fears of an imminent Allied invasion. For a while, it did. But by November, the German high command belatedly recognized that the raid had preluded nothing. Attention returned dramatically to the eastern theatre. In any case, as South Saskatchewan Lieutenant John Edmondson later wrote, "a strategic success remains a cold comfort when measured against the suffering of the men at Dieppe, and the suffering of their families." I agree, and I believe the strategic-success argument is hollow. Inevitably, further justifications or explanations for the raid will emerge as more classified documents are released or facts unearthed. Even the most convincing raison d'être, however, does not excuse the colossal futility of the plan and its execution.

Immediately after the raid and in the years following, discussion arose over whether its failure could at least partly be attributed to the inexperience of the Canadian troops. Proponents inevitably pointed to the successful assault by Lord Lovat's No. 4 Commando on the Varengeville Battery. If Mountbatten's original desire to use the Royal Marine Division and select commando forces had been followed, the argument went, the raid would have had better odds. This argument ignores the fact that No. 4 Commando's success stemmed as much from luck as skill. Lord Lovat acknowledged that at a decisive moment, had the mortar on Orange II Beach not switched its aim towards the withdrawing LCAS, the commandos there would likely have been slaughtered. The Canadians enjoyed no such luck—the Germans defending their beaches made no mistakes. Wherever the Germans were ready and responded correctly, nobody stood a chance, whether they were Canadians, commandos, or Royal Marines. At Green Beach, where Canadian troops had the benefit of some surprise, they succeeded in crossing the beach, seized Pourville, and largely secured the western headland. Although the Sasks could not defeat the eastern headland defences or fight through to Quatre Vents Farm, this was due to lack of fire support rather than fighting skill. A single tank might have made the difference. The same holds true for the Camerons' advance towards the airfield. They were stymied by superior weaponry. Finally, there is the impartial assessment of Generalleutnant Konrad Haase, who immediately after the raid acknowledged the gallantry and skill of all the troops engaged in the raid while pointing out the hopelessness of their assignment.

HONOURING THE SACRIFICE of those who fought at Dieppe requires no justification for the raid. While Dieppe was the worst military disaster for Canadians in World War II, there were other defeats. Hong Kong, of course, stands out. Other examples are the 2nd Canadian Infantry Brigade's virtual destruction before the Hitler Line during the Liri Valley campaign of May 1944 and the shattering of the South Saskatchewan Regiment, Essex Scottish Regiment, and Black Watch at Verrières Ridge in July 1944. We do not bestow less honour on those killed at Dieppe just because their generals failed by sending them into a battle doomed from the outset by a poor plan.

Thankfully, those who fought at Dieppe are remembered and honoured, particularly in France. Commemorative monuments dedicated to the units that fought there are to be found on or near every beach. Because of the compact battleground, all can be visited in a single day's drive. Some date back to shortly after the war's end; others have been recently erected. All are worth seeing, as are the beaches themselves. It is easy enough to stand on the beach at Dieppe or on Green Beach at Pourville and imagine the soldiers' experience. Scramble across the chert to gain the distant seawall at Dieppe. You will be amazed that as many men gained the wall as did. Or that, despite the chert, at least half the tanks managed to reach the promenade.

At Pourville, the bridge over the Scie is today named Lieutenant Colonel Merritt's Bridge. As you look up to the looming eastern headland, it seems a miracle he managed to go back and forth across it unscathed at least four times, taking many men with him. In the end, it is what the soldiers achieved despite the near-insurmountable obstacles that impresses.

Most of those who died lie in Dieppe Canadian War Cemetery. You find it by driving out of Dieppe onto the Avenue des Canadiens and then turning right onto Rue des Canadiens. A total of 948 Commonwealth servicemen are buried or commemorated here, 187 of them unidentified. Those from the raid tally 783, the rest falling during other operations. Some Dieppe casualties are buried at Rouen, having died of wounds in hospital there. Surrounded by farmland, the cemetery's long rows of well-spaced marble headstones stretch from one bordering hedge to another. When I visited on a sunny day in May, I saw that somebody had recently placed small Canadian flags at the base of many headstones. They are likely remnants of one of the increasingly common tours of Canadians visiting Normandy's battlefields and participating in acts of remembrance.

One of the most recent and unusual memorials I have encountered stands on the promenade facing Red Beach. It is dedicated to the Essex Scottish. The almost eight-foot-high, thin black-granite monument was designed by Rory O'Connor. In 2006, the year the monument was erected in Dieppe, she was an eighteen-year-old art student at the University of Windsor. At the centre of the monument is a stylized cutaway maple leaf. The monument is designed so that every August 19 at precisely 1:00 PM local time, in commemoration of the raid's end, the sun aligns with the cut-out and illuminates a metal maple leaf inlaid in the monument's rock base.

O'Connor had the idea while driving on a sunny day. "I saw some sunshine on the dashboard," she said later, "and I thought, 'wouldn't it be great to use the sundial idea to tell about the time and retreat of these soldiers.'" On August 20, 2010, an identical monument was unveiled in Windsor's Dieppe Park, with about a thousand people in attendance—including Rory and her grandfather, Jack Baker, a World War II veteran.

The Essex Scottish wanted the replica monument to give residents unable to travel to Dieppe the opportunity "to experience this beautiful, solemn tribute to our fallen." City officials embraced the idea, hoping it would "reignite the spirit of remembrance." It is a sound hope, for the spirit of remembrance appears to be growing across Canada. Looking at photographs of the unveiling in Windsor, I am particularly struck by the number of children present. It is a point I have made before but which deserves restating. Our nation's children are remembrance's hope. But they need parents and teachers to instill the reasons for it. If they do not learn why a generation of young people with hopes and dreams of their own set those aside to fight a noble war in faraway lands, then an essential national memory will fade and die away. And Canada will be poorer for it. So it behooves us all to keep that memory alive. In Windsor and in Dieppe, twin monuments designed by a young art student play their vital part in sustaining that remembrance.

APPENDIX A:
PRINCIPAL POLITICIANS, COMMANDERS, AND UNITS INVOLVED IN THE DIEPPE RAID

AMERICAN

President, Franklin Delano Roosevelt

Chair American Chiefs of Staff, Gen. George C. Marshall

War Department General Staff Chief of the Operations Division, then American European Theatre of Operations Commander, Gen. Dwight D. Eisenhower

U.S. Rangers commander and Dieppe raid observer, Brig. Lucien Truscott

BRITISH

Prime Minister, Winston Churchill

Chief of Imperial General Staff, Gen. Sir Alan Brooke

Chief of Combined Operations, Vice-Adm. Lord Louis Mountbatten

Commander-in-Chief, Home Forces, Gen. Bernard Paget

South-Eastern Command, Maj. Gen. Bernard Law Montgomery

Operation Rutter and Jubilee Air Force Commander, Vice-Air Marshal Trafford Leigh-Mallory

Operation Rutter Naval Force Commander, Rear-Adm. Tom Baillie-Grohman

Operation Jubilee Naval Force Commander, Capt. John Hughes-Hallett

No. 3 Commando, Lt. Col. John Durnford-Slater

No. 4 Commando, Lt. Col. Lord Lovat

No. 40 Royal Marines, Lt. Col. Joseph Picton-Phillips

CANADIAN

Prime Minister, Mackenzie King

First Army, Lt. Gen. Andrew McNaughton

1 Canadian Corps, Lt. Gen. Harry Crerar

2nd Infantry Division and Military Force Commander, Operations
    Rutter and Jubilee, Maj. Gen. John Hamilton "Ham" Roberts

2nd Infantry Division Chief Operations, Brig. C.C. "Church" Mann

4th Brigade, Brig. Sherwood Lett

6th Brigade, Brig. William Southam

Calgary Tank Regiment, Lt. Col. John Gilby "Johnny" Andrews

Essex Scottish Regiment, Lt. Col. Fred Jasperson

Les Fusiliers Mont-Royal, Lt. Col. Dollard "Joe" Ménard

Queen's Own Cameron Highlanders, Lt. Col. Alfred "Al" Gostling

Royal Hamilton Light Infantry, Lt. Col. Ridley "Bob" Labatt

Royal Regiment of Canada, Lt. Col. Doug Catto

South Saskatchewan Regiment, Lt. Col. Cecil Merritt

GERMAN

Commander-in-Chief, West, Generalfeldmarschall Gerd von
    Rundstedt

Fifteenth Army, Generaloberst Kurt Haase

302nd Infantry Division, Generalleutnant Konrad Haase

APPENDIX B:
ALLIED ORDER OF BATTLE,
OPERATION JUBILEE

MILITARY UNITS

CANADIAN

HQ 2nd Canadian Division

Intelligence Section

Field Security Section

4th Canadian Infantry Brigade

Royal Regiment of Canada

Royal Hamilton Light Infantry

Essex Scottish Regiment

5th Canadian Infantry Brigade

Three infantry platoons, Black Watch
    (Royal Highland Regiment)
    of Canada

Mortar Platoon, Calgary Highlanders

6th Canadian Infantry Brigade

Les Fusiliers Mont-Royal

Queen's Own Cameron Highlanders of Canada

South Saskatchewan Regiment

Calgary Tank Regiment (14th Canadian Tank Battalion)

Royal Canadian Engineers

2nd Field Company

7th Field Company

11th Field Company

1st Field Park Company

2nd Road Construction Company

Mechanical Equipment Company

Other Supporting 2nd Division Detachments
Toronto Scottish Regiment (MG)
Royal Canadian Ordnance Corps
Provost Company
Signals
3rd Light Infantry Anti-Aircraft Regiment
4th Field Regiment, Royal Canadian Artillery
8th Canadian Reconnaissance Regiment (14th Hussars)
11th Canadian Field Ambulance

BRITISH
No. 3 Commando
No. 4 Commando
No. 30 Commando (Assault Unit)
'A' Section No. 40 Commando, Royal Marines
Royal Engineers (beach gradient parties)

OTHER NATIONALS
Detachment 1st U.S. Ranger Battalion
Detachment No. 10 (Inter-Allied) Commando

NAVAL FORCE
Destroyers
HMS *Calpe* (HQ ship)
HMS *Fernie* (2nd HQ ship)
HMS *Albrighton*
HMS *Berkeley*
HMS *Bleasdale*
HMS *Brocklesby*
HMS *Garth*
ORP *Slazak*

Sloop
HMS *Alresford*

Motor Gunboat
HMS *Locust*

Minesweeping Flotillas
9th Minesweeping Flotilla (8 ships)
13th Minesweeping Flotilla (8 ships)

Landing Ships
HMS *Glengyle*—LSI(Large)
HMS *Queen Emma*—LSI(Medium)
HMS *Princess Beatrix*—LSI(Medium)
HMS *Duke of Wellington*—LSI(Small)
HMS *Prince Albert*—LSI(Small)
HMS *Princess Astrid*—LSI(Small)
HMS *Invicta*—LSI(Small)
HMS *Prince Charles*—LSI(Small)
HMS *Prince Leopold*—LSI(Small)

Landing Craft on LSIS Numbered:
60 Landing Craft Assault (LCA)
8 Landing Craft Support (LCS)
7 Landing Craft Mechanized (LCM)

First Flotilla Group 5 (Yellow Beach)
Landing Craft, Personnel—R-Boats Nos. 1, 80, 81, 85,
    86, 87, 95, 118, 128, 145, 157

Second Flotilla Group 6 (Green Beach)
R-Boats Nos. 19, 88, 94, 119, 124, 125, 129, 147, 156

Fourth Flotilla Group 7 (Floating Reserve)
R-Boats Nos. 28, 53, 170, 172, 173, 174, 175, 186, 187,
    188, 192, 196, 199, 212

Fifth Flotilla Group 7 (Floating Reserve)
R-Boats Nos. 31, 45, 155, 163, 165, 166, 167, 208, 209, 210, 614

Sixth Flotilla Group 6 (Green Beach)
R-Boats Nos. 127, 130, 131, 132, 134, 135, 136, 153, 158

Seventh Flotilla Group 6 (Green Beach)
R-Boats Nos. 83, 84, 99, 101, 102, 104, 110, 113, 159, 160

Twenty-fourth Flotilla Group 5 (Yellow Beach)
R-Boats Nos. 3, 4, 13, 15, 23, 24, 34, 40, 41, 42, 43, 44, 79, 115

Second Landing Craft Tank (LCT) Flotilla
LCT Nos. 121 (LCT5), 124 (LCT7), 125 (LCT8), 126 (LCT4),
    127 (LCT2), 145 (LCTI), 163 (LCT6), 165 (LCTIO), 166 (LCT9),
    169 (LCT3)

Fourth Landing Craft Tank (LCT) Flotilla
LCT Nos. 302, 303, 304, 305, 306, 307, 308, 309, 310, 318, 325,
    360, 361, 376

ESCORTING CRAFT
First Landing Craft Flak (LCF) Flotilla
LCF Nos. 1, 2, 3, 4, 5, 6

Motor Gun Boats (MGB)
MGB Nos. 50, 51, 52, 57, 312, 315, 316, 317, 320, 321, 323, 326

Steam Gun Boats (SGB)
SGB Nos. 5, 6, 8, 9

Motor Launches (ML)
ML Nos. 114, 120, 123, 171, 187, 189, 190, 191, 193, 194, 208,
    214, 230, 246, 291, 292, 309, 343, 344, 346

Free French Chasseurs
Nos. 5, 10, 13, 14, 41, 42, 43

AIR FORCE UNITS
RAF FIGHTER COMMAND NO. II GROUP
Spitfire Squadrons
19, 41, 64, 65, 66, 71, 81, 91, 111, 118, 121, 122, 124, 129, 130,
    131, 133, 154, 165, 222, 232, 242, 302, 303, 306, 307, 308,
    309, 310, 312, 317, 331, 332, 340, 350, 400 (RCAF) 401 (RCAF),
    402 (RCAF), 403 (RCAF), 411 (RCAF), 412 (RCAF), 414 (RCAF),
    416 (RCAF), 418 (RCAF) [two aircraft only], 485, 501, 602, 610,
    611, 616

Hurricane Squadrons
3, 32, 43, 87, 174, 175, 245, 253

Typhoon Squadrons
56, 266, 609

Boston Squadrons
88, 107, 226, 418, 605

Blenheim Squadrons
13, 614

Mustang Squadrons
26, 239, 400, 414

Beaufighter Squadron
141

USAAF 97TH BOMBARDMENT GROUP
B-17 *Squadrons*
340, 341, 342, 414

NOTES

Abbreviations: ADM–Admiralty Papers (U.K.). AHQ–Army Headquarters.
CMHQ–Canadian Military Headquarters. CWM–Canadian War Museum.
DND–Department of National Defence. DEFE–Ministry of Defence (U.K.).
DHH–Director of Heritage and History. LAC–Library and Archives Canada.
PRO–Public Records office (U.K.). TNA–The National Archives of the U.K.
UVICSC–University of Victoria Special Collections. WO–War Office (U.K.).

PREFACE

1. C.P. Stacey, *Six Years of War: The Army in Canada, Britain and the Pacific*, vol. I
   (Ottawa: Queen's Printer, 1957), 387–89.

INTRODUCTION: A CRESCENDO OF ACTIVITY

1. John Mosier, *Deathride: Hitler vs. Stalin—The Eastern Front, 1941–1945* (New York:
   Simon & Schuster, 2010), 200–01.
2. Quentin Reynolds, *Dress Rehearsal: The Story of Dieppe* (Garden City, NY: Blue Ribbon
   Books, 1943), III.
3. Arthur Bryant, *The Turn of the Tide, 1939–1943: A study based on the diaries and autobiographical notes of Field Marshal the Viscount Alanbrooke* (London: Collins, 1957), 360.
4. Chester Wilmot, *The Struggle for Europe* (London: Collins, 1952), 101.
5. C.P. Stacey, *Six Years of War: The Army in Canada, Britain and the Pacific*, vol. I
   (Ottawa: Queen's Printer, 1957), 311.
6. Gordon A. Harrison, *Cross-Channel Attack: United States Army in World War II;
   The European Theater of Operations* (Washington: Center of Military History,
   U.S. Army, 1993), 6–8.
7. Ibid., 9–10.
8. Ibid., 9.
9. Stacey, *Six Years of War*, 311.
10. Robin Neillands, *The Dieppe Raid: The Story of the Disastrous 1942 Expedition*
    (London: Aurum Press, 2005), 71.
11. Stacey, *Six Years of War*, 311–12.
12. Wilmot, 103.
13. Harrison, 12–13.

14. Bryant, 354–60.

15. Neillands, 76.

16. Wilmot, 104.

17. Harrison, 18.

18. Stacey, *Six Years of War*, 313.

I A BOLDLY IMAGINATIVE GROUP

1. The Earl Mountbatten of Burma, "Address to the Dieppe Veterans and Prisoner's-of-War Association, 29 September, 1973," pamphlet in the author's possession, 2.

2. *Combined Operations: The Official Story of the Commandos* (New York: Macmillan, 1943), 49.

3. Robin Neillands, *The Dieppe Raid: The Story of the Disastrous 1942 Expedition* (London: Aurum Press, 2005), 80.

4. Quentin Reynolds, *Dress Rehearsal: The Story of Dieppe* (Garden City, NY: Blue Ribbon Books, 1943), 17–18.

5. Ibid., 14–15.

6. Neillands, 34.

7. Reynolds, 18–22.

8. *Combined Operations*, 26.

9. Ibid., 4–5.

10. Ibid., 6–7.

11. Neillands, 89–90.

12. Arthur Bryant, *The Turn of the Tide, 1939–1943: A study based on the diaries and autobiographical notes of Field Marshal the Viscount Alanbrooke* (London: Collins, 1957), 370–71.

13. John Hughes-Hallett, unpublished memoir, MG30 E463, LAC, 110–111.

14. Ibid., 106.

15. Ibid., 112.

16. Ibid., 106.

17. Ibid., 112.

18. "COHQ–War Cabinet–Yalta," *Combined Operations*, accessed Oct. 3, 2011, www.combinedops.com/zCOHQ.htm.

19. Denis Whitaker and Shelagh Whitaker, *Dieppe: Tragedy to Triumph; A Firsthand and Revealing Critical Account of the Most Controversial Battle of World War II* (Whitby, ON: McGraw-Hill Ryerson, 1992), 90.

20. Hughes-Hallett memoir, 113.

21. "Military Intelligence Service, Special Series No. 1, August 9, 1942: Commando Operations–Section 1. Vaagso (Norway) Raid," *Lone Sentry*, accessed Sept. 27, 2011, www.lonesentry.com/manuals/commandos/vaagso-norway-raid.html.

22. *Combined Operations*, 70.

23. Hughes-Hallett memoir, 117.

24. *Combined Operations*, 70–72.

25. Terence Robertson, *Dieppe: The Shame and the Glory* (London: Pan Books, 1965), 45–46.

26. *Combined Operations*, 73.

27. Ibid., 77–78.
28. Ibid., 88–99.
29. Ibid., 99.

2 FOR THE SAKE OF RAIDING

1. John Hughes-Hallett, unpublished memoir, MG30 E463, LAC, 118.
2. "Report No. 159, Operation 'Jubilee,' Additional Information on Planning," Appendix A, CMHQ, DHH, DND, 2.
3. C.P. Stacey, *Six Years of War: The Army in Canada, Britain and the Pacific,* vol. 1 (Ottawa: Queen's Printer, 1957), 324.
4. "Report No. 159," Appendix A, 5.
5. Stacey, *Six Years of War,* 324.
6. The Earl Mountbatten of Burma, "Address to the Dieppe Veterans and Prisoner's-of-War Association, 29 September, 1973," pamphlet in the author's possession, 2.
7. Terence Robertson, *Dieppe: The Shame and the Glory* (London: Pan Books, 1965), 61.
8. Ibid.
9. Brian Loring Villa, *Unauthorized Action: Mountbatten and the Dieppe Raid* (Toronto: Oxford University Press, 1989), 168.
10. Hughes-Hallett memoir, 118.
11. Mountbatten, 2.
12. "Report No. 159," Appendix A, 1.
13. Villa, 170.
14. Hughes-Hallett memoir, 106.
15. Nigel Hamilton, *Monty: The Making of a General, 1887–1942* (London: Coronet, 1984), 517.
16. Robertson, 61.
17. "Report No. 153, Operation 'Jubilee': New Light on Early Planning," Appendix A, " CMHQ, DHH, DND, 1.
18. Hughes-Hallett memoir, 151–52.
19. TNA:PRO DEFE 2/324, "Operation 'Jubilee': Lecture to Staff College, Notes for CCO," 1.
20. Hughes-Hallett memoir, 154.
21. Hamilton, 516.
22. Hughes-Hallett memoir, 152–53.
23. Ronald Atkin, *Dieppe 1942: The Jubilee Disaster* (London: Macmillan London, 1980), 11.
24. Hughes-Hallett memoir, 153.
25. Ibid., 153–54.
26. Hamilton, 521–22.
27. "Report No. 100, The Preliminaries of the Operation," CMHQ, DHH, DND, 13.
28. Mountbatten, 2–3.
29. "Report No. 153," Appendix IV, 1.
30. Ibid., Appendix III, 2–3.
31. Mountbatten, 3.
32. Hughes-Hallett memoir, 154.
33. "Report No. 100," 14.
34. TNA:PRO DEFE 2/323, "Operation 'Jubilee': Lecture," 2.

35. Atkin, 12.
36. TNA:PRO DEFE 2/550, "Inter-Service Topographical Department–18 April, 1952, Appendix 21: Tank Exits at Dieppe," 1–2.
37. Ibid., "Appendix 22: The Rivers Scie, Saane, Arques, Bethune, Varenne, and Eaulne," 1–2.
38. Ibid., "Operation Rutter, Intelligence Reports," 1–4.
39. *Combined Operations: The Official Story of the Commandos* (New York: Macmillan, 1943), 110.
40. "Letter from Mountbatten to Guy Simonds, Feb. 4, 1969, Hughes-Hallett fonds, MG30 E463, LAC, 2.

3 A FANTASTIC CONCEPTION

1. Terence Robertson, *Dieppe: The Shame and the Glory* (London: Pan Books, 1965), 83–84.
2. C.P. Stacey, *Six Years of War: The Army in Canada, Britain and the Pacific*, vol. 1 (Ottawa: Queen's Printer, 1957), 329.
3. Paul Douglas Dickson, *A Thoroughly Canadian General: A Biography of General H.D.G. Crerar* (Toronto: University of Toronto Press, 2007), 203.
4. Ibid., 193.
5. "Report No. 87, Situation of the Canadian Military Forces in the United Kingdom, Autumn, 1942: 11, Recent Changes in Commands and Staffs," CMHQ, DHH, DND, 2.
6. Dickson, 192.
7. Stacey, *Six Years of War*, 308.
8. J.L. Granatstein, *The Generals: The Canadian Army's Senior Commanders in the Second World War* (Toronto: Stoddart, 1993), 55–67.
9. Ibid., 70.
10. C.P. Stacey, *The Canadian Army, 1939–1945: An Official Historical Summary* (Ottawa: King's Printer, 1948), 47.
11. Stacey, *Six Years of War*, 96.
12. Dickson, 182.
13. Granatstein, 86.
14. Ibid., 101.
15. Ibid., 98.
16. Denis Whitaker and Shelagh Whitaker, *Dieppe: Tragedy to Triumph, A Firsthand and Revealing Critical Account of the Most Controversial Battle of World War II* (Whitby, ON: McGraw-Hill Ryerson, 1992), 72.
17. Dominick Graham, *The Price of Command: A Biography of General Guy Simonds* (Toronto: Stoddart, 1993), 66.
18. Dickson, 185–86.
19. Granatstein, 186–87.
20. Dickson, 186–88.
21. Whitaker and Whitaker, 74.
22. Stacey, *Six Years of War*, 308.
23. Ibid., 309–10.
24. Granatstein, 71.

25. "Report No. 100, Operation 'Jubilee': The Preliminaries of the Operation,"
    CMHQ, DHH, DND, 21–23.

26. Robertson, 85.

27. "Report No. 100," 23–24.

28. Ibid., 24–26.

29. Robertson, 88.

30. Stacey, *Six War Years*, 280–82.

31. Whitaker and Whitaker, 95.

32. "Dieppe, 1942: Lecture Notes, Combined Services Raid on Dieppe, 19 Aug 42 by
    Brig. CC Mann, GS, 1 Cdn Corps," 222C1.011(D1), vol. 10772, box 201, RG24, LAC, 3.

33. Whitaker and Whitaker, 96.

34. "Report No. 100," 27.

35. Robertson, 93.

36. "Report No. 100," 27–28.

4 OF CONSIDERABLE DIFFICULTY

 1. "Report No. 100, Operation 'Jubilee': The Preliminaries of the Operation,"
    CMHQ, DHH, DND, 15–16.

 2. Ibid., 10–12.

 3. Brereton Greenhous, *Dieppe, Dieppe* (Montreal: Art Global, 1992), 46.

 4. Terence Robertson, *Dieppe: The Shame and the Glory* (London: Pan Books,
    1965), 94–95.

 5. "Report No. 100," 29–31.

 6. Robertson, 96.

 7. Bernard Law, Viscount Montgomery of Alamein, *The Memoirs of Field-Marshal
    The Viscount Montgomery of Alamein, K.G.* (London: Collins, 1958), 77.

 8. Robin Neillands, *The Dieppe Raid: The Story of the Disastrous 1942 Expedition*
    (London: Aurum Press, 2005), 95.

 9. Arthur Bryant, *The Turn of the Tide, 1939–1943: a study based on the diaries and autobio-
    graphical notes of Field Marshal the Viscount Alanbrooke* (London: Collins, 1957), 372.

10. Robertson, 97.

11. "Trafford Leigh-Mallory," *World War II Database*, accessed Nov. 2, 2011,
    ww2db.com/person_bio.php?person_id=125.

12. Robertson, 97–98.

13. "Report No. 100," 31.

14. C.P. Stacey, *Six Years of War: The Army in Canada, Britain and the Pacific*, vol. 1
    (Ottawa: Queen's Printer, 1957), 244.

15. D.J. Goodspeed, *Battle Royal: A History of the Royal Regiment of Canada, 1862–1962*
    (Toronto: Royal Regt. of Canada Assoc., 1962), 384–85.

16. Stacey, *Six Years of War*, 334.

17. Goodspeed, 385.

18. Sandy Antal and Kevin Shackleton, *Duty Nobly Done: The Official History of the Essex
    and Kent Scottish Regiment* (Windsor, ON: Walkerville, 2006), 389–90.

19. *Cent ans d'histoire d'un régiment canadien-français: Les Fusiliers Mont-Royal, 1869–1969*
    (Montreal: Éditions Du Jour, 1971), 125.

20. "Report No. 100," 31–32.

21. "Report No. 65, Situation of the Canadian Military Forces in the United Kingdom, Spring 1942: Recent Changes in Commands and Staffs," CMHQ,DHH, DND, 2.

22. *Cent ans d'histoire*, 123.

23. Robertson, 28–29.

24. "Lt-Col A.C. Gostling Killed Leading Cameron Highlanders," *Toronto Star*, Aug. 22, 1942, Veteran Affairs Canada, accessed Nov. 4, 2011, www.veterans.gc.ca /eng/collections/virtualmem/photoview/2317090/55185.

25. R.W. Queen-Hughes, *Whatever Men Dare: A History of the Queen's Own Cameron Highlanders of Canada, 1936–1960* (Winnipeg: Bulman Bros., 1960), 52.

26. Norman H. Ross, interview by Chris Main, July 20 and Aug. 16, 1979, UVICSC.

27. "What a Man He Was," *Vancouver Courier*, Nov. 7, 2008, accessed Nov. 6, 2011, www.canada.com/vancouvercourier/news/story.html?id=c2bfeb1b-a86b-4b10 -b584-5ab4bcefe980&p=3.

28. Robertson, 24.

29. "Lt-Col Cecil Merritt, VC," *The Telegraph*, UK, accessed Nov. 6, 2011, www.telegraph.co.uk/news/obituaries/1349057/Lt-Col-Cecil-Merritt-vc.html.

30. John Edmondson, interview by Chris Bell, June 6, August 4 and 12, 1982, UVICSC.

31. "Lieutenant Colonel John Gilby Andrews," in *Onward 1: The Informal History of the Calgary Regiment, 14th Canadian Armoured Regiment*, ed. Dick Maltby and Jessie Maltby (Vancouver: 50/14 Veterans' Assoc., 1989), 1.

5 TRIAL AND ERROR

1. "Report No. 100, Operation 'Jubilee': The Preliminaries of the Operation," CMHQ, DHH, DND, 33.

2. Denis Whitaker and Shelagh Whitaker, *Dieppe: Tragedy to Triumph; A Firsthand and Revealing Critical Account of the Most Controversial Battle of World War II* (Whitby, ON: McGraw-Hill Ryerson, 1992), 125–26.

3. Norman H. Ross, interview by Chris Main, July 20 and Aug. 16, 1979, UVICSC.

4. *Cent ans d'histoire d'un régiment canadien-français: Les Fusiliers Mont-Royal, 1869–1969* (Montreal: Éditions Du Jour, 1971), 129.

5. Whitaker and Whitaker, 126.

6. "Conversations with Dick Maltby, August 1989," UVICSC.

7. A.J. Kerry and W.A. McDill, *History of the Corps of Royal Engineers*, vol. 2 (Ottawa: Military Engineers Assoc., 1966), 98.

8. *Canadian Army Overseas Honours and Awards Citation Details*, DHH, DND, accessed Nov. 8, 2011, www.cmp-cpm.forces.gc.ca/dhh-dhp/gal/cao-aco/details-eng .asp?firstname=Lyman Franklin&lastname=Barnes&rec=id1456.

9. "Canadian and Allied Jews at the Raid on Dieppe," Jewish Virtual Library, accessed Nov. 8, 2011, www.jewishvirtuallibrary.org/jsource/ww2/sugar7.html.

10. Ronald Atkin, *Dieppe 1942: The Jubilee Disaster* (London: Macmillan, 1980), 47.

11. Whitaker and Whitaker, 124–25.

12. Terence Robertson, *Dieppe: The Shame and the Glory* (London: Pan Books, 1965), 107.

13. Kingsley Brown Sr., Kingsley Brown Jr., and Brereton Greenhous, *Semper Paratus: The History of the Royal Hamilton Light Infantry (Wentworth Regiment), 1862–1977* (Hamilton: RHLI Historical Assoc., 1977), 184.

14. Brereton Greenhous, *Dieppe, Dieppe* (Montreal: Art Global, 1992), 50–51.

15. Whitaker and Whitaker, 125–26.

16. W.A.B. Douglas, Roger Sarty, and Michael Whitby, *A Blue Water Navy: The Official Operational History of the Royal Canadian Navy in the Second World War, 1943–1945*, vol. II, part 2 (St. Catharine's, ON: Vanwell Publishing, 2007), 107.

17. "Report No. 100," 33–34.

18. John Edmondson, interview by Chris Bell, June 6, Aug. 4 and 12, 1982, UVICSC.

19. D.J. Goodspeed, *Battle Royal: A History of the Royal Regiment of Canada, 1862–1962* (Toronto: Royal Regt. of Canada Assoc., 1962), 386.

20. "Report No. 100," 34.

21. Edmondson interview.

22. Brown, Brown, and Greenhous, 184.

23. John Marteinson and Michael R. McNorgan, *The Royal Armoured Corps: An Illustrated History* (Toronto: Robin Brass Studio, 2000), 142.

24. "Conversations with Dick Maltby."

25. Kerry and McDill, 98–99.

26. "Engineer Training Report: Exercise 'Rutter' and Operation 'Jubilee,'" Appendix IV, 232C2.033(D4), vol. 10873, box 252, RG24, LAC, I.

27. John Hughes-Hallett, unpublished memoir, MG30 E463, LAC, 155–56.

28. "Engineer Training Report," Appendix 9, 1–2.

29. Kerry and McDill, 99–100.

30. Edmondson interview.

31. Ross interview.

32. Norm Bowen, interview by A.E. "Tony" Delamere, 28 Sept. 2000, Ottawa, Oral History Project Collection, CWM.

33. Ross interview.

34. "Report No. 100," 35.

35. Ross interview.

36. Hughes-Hallett memoir, 156–58.

37. Brian Loring Villa, *Unauthorized Action: Mountbatten and the Dieppe Raid* (Toronto: Oxford University Press, 1989), 182.

38. Hughes-Hallett memoir, 158.

39. Arthur Bryant, *The Turn of the Tide, 1939–1943: A study based on the diaries and autobiographical notes of Field Marshal the Viscount Alanbrooke* (London: Collins, 1957), 396–408.

40. "Report No. 153, Operation 'Jubilee': New Light on Early Planning," Appendix III, CMHQ, DHH, DND, 1–2.

41. "Report No. 100," 19.

42. "Dieppe, 1942: Lecture Notes, Combined Services Raid on Dieppe, 19 Aug 42 by Brig. CC Mann, GS, I Cdn Corps," 222C1.011(DI), vol. 10772, box 201, RG24, LAC, 2.

43. Robertson, 129.

44. "Report No. 153," Appendix III, 3.
45. Bernard Law, Viscount Montgomery of Alamein, *The Memoirs of Field-Marshal The Viscount Montgomery of Alamein, K.G.* (London: Collins, 1958), 76.

6 THESE ARE ANXIOUS DAYS

1. John Hughes-Hallett, unpublished memoir, MG30 E463, LAC, 161–63.
2. Norman H. Ross, interview by Chris Main, July 20 and Aug. 16, 1979, UVICSC.
3. "Report No. 100, Operation 'Jubilee': The Preliminaries of the Operation," CMHQ, DHH, DND, 35–36.
4. "Yukon 1," 232C2(D54), vol. 10873, box 252, RG24, LAC, 5–6.
5. Charles Cecil Ingersoll Merritt interview, Aug. 21, 1997, *Heroes Remember,* accessed Dec. 7, 2011, www.veterans.gc.ca/eng/collections/hrp/alpha_results/123.
6. "Yukon 1," 5–6.
7. Ibid., 7–8.
8. Robin Neillands, *The Dieppe Raid: The Story of the Disastrous 1942 Expedition* (London: Aurum Press, 2005), 105–06.
9. Ross interview.
10. "Yukon 1," 5.
11. Ross interview.
12. "Yukon 1," 6.
13. John "Jack" Abernathy Poolton interview, undated, *Heroes Remember,* Veterans Affairs Canada, accessed Dec. 7, 2011, www.veterans.gc.ca/eng/collections/hrp/alpha _results/40.
14. "Yukon 1," 7.
15. "Report No. 100," 37–38.
16. Neillands, 96.
17. The Earl Mountbatten of Burma, "Address to the Dieppe Veterans and Prisoner's-of-War Association, 29 September, 1973," pamphlet in the author's possession, 5.
18. "Report No. 100," 38.
19. R.W. Queen-Hughes, *Whatever Men Dare: A History of the Queen's Own Cameron Highlanders of Canada, 1936–1960* (Winnipeg: Bulman Bros., 1960), 59.
20. Royal Regiment of Canada War Diary, June 1942, RG24, LAC, June 23 entry.
21. Ross Munro, *Gauntlet to Overlord* (Toronto: Macmillan, 1945), 301.
22. Hughes-Hallett memoir, 164–65.

7 WHAT A BLOW!

1. "Report No. 100, Operation 'Jubilee': The Preliminaries of the Operation," CMHQ, DHH, DND, 38–44.
2. Norman H. Ross, interview by Chris Main, July 20 and Aug. 16, 1979, UVICSC.
3. "Report No. 100," 48–49.
4. Ross Munro, *Gauntlet to Overlord* (Toronto: Macmillan, 1945), 302.
5. Denis Whitaker and Shelagh Whitaker, *Dieppe: Tragedy to Triumph; A Firsthand and Revealing Critical Account of the Most Controversial Battle of World War II* (Whitby, ON: McGraw-Hill Ryerson, 1992), 136–39.
6. "Report No. 100," 49.

7. Whitaker and Whitaker, 138–39.

8. Ross interview.

9. Sandy Antal and Kevin R. Shackleton, *Duty Nobly Done: The Official History of the Essex and Kent Scottish Regiment* (Windsor, ON: Walkerville, 2006), 392.

10. Whitaker and Whitaker, 139.

11. Munro, 303.

12. John Hughes-Hallett, unpublished memoir, MG30 E463, LAC, 165–66.

13. "Report No. 159, Operation 'Jubilee': Additional Information on Planning," Appendix A, CMHQ, DHH, DND, 3.

14. "Report No. 100," 42.

15. Ibid., 44–48.

16. Munro, 303.

17. Antal and Shackleton, 392.

18. Ross interview.

19. R.W. Queen-Hughes, *Whatever Men Dare: A History of the Queen's Own Cameron Highlanders of Canada, 1936–1960* (Winnipeg: Bulman Bros., 1960), 60.

20. Hughes-Hallett memoir, 166.

21. Kingsley Brown Sr., Kingsley Brown Jr., and Brereton Greenhous, *Semper Paratus: The History of the Royal Hamilton Light Infantry (Wentworth Regiment), 1862–1977* (Hamilton: RHLI Historical Assoc., 1977), 185.

22. Whitaker and Whitaker, 139.

23. D.J. Goodspeed, *Battle Royal: A History of the Royal Regiment of Canada, 1862–1962* (Toronto: Royal Regt. of Canada Assoc., 1962), 386.

24. Ross interview.

25. Hughes-Hallett memoir, 166.

26. Goodspeed, 386.

27. "Report No. 100," 50.

28. Whitaker and Whitaker, 169.

29. "Report No. 100," 50.

30. "Report No. 153, Operation 'Jubilee': New Light on Early Planning," Appendix IV, CMHQ, DHH, DND, 3.

31. Whitaker and Whitaker, 169.

32. Queen-Hughes, 61.

33. "Report No. 100," 51.

34. Goodspeed, 387.

35. Ross interview.

36. Munro, 305–06.

8 A BRAINWAVE

1. Terence Robertson, *Dieppe: The Shame and the Glory* (London: Pan Books, 1965), 163.

2. Ibid., 166–67.

3. "Report No. 100, Operation 'Jubilee': The Preliminaries of the Operation," CMHQ, DHH, DND, 52.

4. Bernard Law, Viscount Montgomery of Alamein, *The Memoirs of Field-Marshal The Viscount Montgomery of Alamein, K.G.* (London: Collins, 1958), 75–77.

5. "Report No. 100," 52.

6. Ibid., 54–55.

7. Nigel Hamilton, *Monty: The Making of a General, 1887–1942* (London: Coronet, 1984), 524–25.

8. Montgomery, 76.

9. Hamilton, 526–27.

10. J. Hughes-Hallett, "The Mounting of Raids," *Royal United Service Institution Journal*, vol. 95 (Feb.–Nov., 1950), 585.

11. "Report No. 159, Operation 'Jubilee,' Additional Information on Planning," Appendix A, CMHQ, DHH, DND, 3.

12. C.P. Stacey, *Six Years of War: The Army in Canada, Britain and the Pacific*, vol. 1 (Ottawa: Queen's Printer, 1957), 340.

13. Brian Loring Villa, *Unauthorized Action: Mountbatten and the Dieppe Raid* (Toronto: Oxford University Press, 1989), 186–87.

14. "Report No. 159," Appendix A, 3.

15. Stacey, *Six Years of War*, 342.

16. Hughes-Hallett, "Mounting of Raids," 585.

17. Robertson, 169.

18. The Earl Mountbatten of Burma, "Address to the Dieppe Veterans and Prisoner's-of-War Association, 29 September, 1973," pamphlet in the author's possession, 6.

19. Arthur Bryant, *The Turn of the Tide, 1939–1943: A study based on the diaries and autobiographical notes of Field Marshal the Viscount Alanbrooke* (London: Collins, 1957), 420.

20. Mountbatten address, 6.

21. Winston Churchill, *The Second World War: The Hinge of Fate*, vol. 4 (London: Houghton Mifflin, 1950), 444.

22. Denis Whitaker and Shelagh Whitaker, *Dieppe: Tragedy to Triumph; A Firsthand and Revealing Critical Account of the Most Controversial Battle of World War II* (Whitby, ON: McGraw-Hill Ryerson, 1992), 185.

23. Villa, 194.

24. Robin Neillands, *The Dieppe Raid: The Story of the Disastrous 1942 Expedition* (London: Aurum Press, 2005), 112.

25. Robertson, 172.

26. "Report No. 159," Appendix A, 3.

27. "Dieppe, 1942: Lecture Notes, Combined Services Raid on Dieppe, 19 Aug 42 by Brig. CC Mann, GS, 1 Cdn Corps," 222C1.011(D1), vol. 10772, box 201, RG24, LAC, 6.

28. Villa, 198.

29. Mountbatten address, 7.

30. Whitaker and Whitaker, 186.

31. Mountbatten address, 7.

32. Villa, 198.

33. Montgomery, 76.

34. Hamilton, 515.

35. "Report No. 100," 60–61.

36. Robertson, 172.

37. "Report No. 100," 57.

38. Stacey, *Six Years of War*, 343.

39. Robertson, 173.

40. John Hughes-Hallett, unpublished memoir, MG30 E463, LAC, 167–68.

41. TNA:PRO DEFE 2/551, "Combined Report on the Dieppe Raid, 1942," 8.

42. "Report No. 100," 65.

43. TNA:PRO DEFE 2/551, "Combined Report," 8.

44. "Report No. 100," 64–66.

45. Stacey, *Six Years of War*, 344.

46. "Report No. 100," 58–59.

47. Ibid., 60–61.

48. Stacey, *Six Years of War*, 341.

49. "Report No. 159," Appendix B, 1–3.

50. H. Paul Jeffers, *Command of Honor: General Lucien Truscott's Path to Victory in World War II* (New York: NAL Caliber, 2008), 64–69.

51. Whitaker and Whitaker, 187–88.

52. "Report No. 159," Appendix A, 4.

9 FRAUGHT WITH ALARMING WARNINGS

1. "Brigadier The Lord Lovat," *The Pegasus Archive*, accessed Dec. 12, 2011, www.pegasusarchive.org/normandy/lord_lovat.htm.

2. "John Durnford-Slater," *Fernand(o) Family History Site*, accessed Dec. 12, 2011, www.ferdinando.org.uk/john_durnford-slater.htm.

3. Lord Lovat, *March Past: A Memoir* (New York: Holmes & Meier, 1979), 231–37.

4. Ibid., 238–40.

5. Ronald Atkin, *Dieppe 1942: The Jubilee Disaster* (London: Macmillan, 1980), 42.

6. Lovat, *March Past*, 241–42.

7. Jim DeFelice, *Rangers at Dieppe: The First Combat Action of U.S. Army Rangers in World War II* (New York: Berkley Caliber, 2008), 86–89.

8. Ibid., 111.

9. D.J. Goodspeed, *Battle Royal: A History of the Royal Regiment of Canada, 1862–1962* (Toronto: Royal Regt. of Canada Assoc., 1962), 387–88.

10. Kingsley Brown Sr., Kingsley Brown Jr., and Brereton Greenhous, *Semper Paratus: The History of the Royal Hamilton Light Infantry (Wentworth Regiment), 1862–1977* (Hamilton: RHLI Historical Assoc., 1977), 191.

11. R.W. Queen-Hughes, *Whatever Men Dare: A History of the Queen's Own Cameron Highlanders of Canada, 1936–1960* (Winnipeg: Bulman Bros., 1960), 62.

12. C.P. Stacey, *Six Years of War: The Army in Canada, Britain and the Pacific*, vol. 1 (Ottawa: Queen's Printer, 1957), 342.

13. John Hughes-Hallett, unpublished memoir, MG30 E463, LAC, 169–171.

14. "Dieppe Raid—1942" file, "Op 'Jubilee' 19 Aug 43 Combined Plan, Capt. H. Hallett, Maj-Gen JH Roberts, Air Marshal TL Leigh-Mallory, Operation Jubilee: Instructions for Passage through Enemy Mined Area," 225C1.013(D6), vol. 10796, box 213, RG24, LAC, 1–3.

15. "Report No. 159, Operation 'Jubilee': Additional Information on Planning," Appendix A, CMHQ, DHH, DND, 4.

16. "'Jubilee' Miscellaneous, Special 'Jubilee' Instructions," 232C2(D52), vol. 10873, box 252, RG24, LAC, 2.

17. Terence Robertson, *Dieppe: The Shame and the Glory* (London: Pan Books, 1965), 198–99.

18. Headquarters, 2nd Canadian Infantry Division (G Branch) War Diary, August 1942, RG24, LAC, n.p.

19. 4th Canadian Infantry Brigade War Diary, August 1942, Appendix, "4 CDN. INF. BDE Combined Ops. TEWT: Exercise Foothold," RG24, LAC, 1.

20. Arthur Bryant, *The Turn of the Tide, 1939–1943: A study based on the diaries and auto-biographical notes of Field Marshal the Viscount Alanbrooke* (London: Collins, 1957), 440.

21. Denis Whitaker and Shelagh Whitaker, *Dieppe: Tragedy to Triumph, A Firsthand and Revealing Critical Account of the Most Controversial Battle of World War II* (Whitby, ON: McGraw-Hill Ryerson, 1992), 227.

22. 6th Canadian Infantry Brigade War Diary, August 1944, RG24, LAC, 5.

23. Sandy Antal and Kevin Shackleton, *Duty Nobly Done: The Official History of the Essex and Kent Scottish Regiment* (Windsor, ON: Walkerville, 2006), 394.

24. "Dieppe—The Plans," Royal Regt. of Canada Assoc., accessed Dec. 15, 2011, www.rregtc-assoc.ca/Dieppe%20Plans%20.html.

25. 6th Canadian Infantry Brigade War Diary, 5.

26. "Dieppe Raid—1942" file, "Op 'Jubilee' 19 Aug 43 Combined Plan, Capt. H. Hallett, Maj-Gen JH Roberts, Air Marshal TL Leigh-Mallory, 'Withdrawal Plan Appendix F, sketch maps with code words,'" 225C1.013(D6), vol. 10796, box 213, RG24, LAC, 1–13.

27. "Report No. 101, General Outline and Flank Attacks," CMHQ, DHH, DND, 1–7.

28. "Report No. 159," Appendix A, 4.

29. "Report No. 101," 7–8.

30. "Dieppe Raid—1942" file, "Operation Jubilee: Naval Operation Order No. 1," 225C1.013(D6), vol. 10796, box 213, RG24, LAC, 1–6.

31. Ibid., "Orders for Withdrawal of Troops and Return Passage, (J.N.O.6)" 1.

32. Ibid., Appendix A to "J.N.O.6," 1.

33. TNA:PRO DEFE 2/324, "Operation 'Jubilee': Lecture to Staff College, Notes for CCO," 6–7.

34. Stacey, *Six Years of War,* 348.

35. "Op 'Jubilee' Reports, Air Force," 232C2(D5), vol. 10870, box 250, RG24, LAC, 1.

10 OUR HISTORIC TASK

1. "Dieppe Raid—1942" file, "Op 'Jubilee' 19 Aug 42 Combined Plan, Capt. H. Hallett, Maj-Gen JH Roberts, Air Marshal TL Leigh-Mallory, Operation Jubilee: '110 INF DIV Order of Battle,'" 225C1.013(D6), vol. 10796, box 213, RG24, LAC, 1.

2. "Intelligence Control Station France: Evaluation of Dieppe Operation, 14 Sep 42," 981GInt(DI), vol. 20488, box 218, RG24, LAC, 5.

3. Ibid., 9.

4. TNA:PRO DEFE 2/551, "Combined Report on The Dieppe Raid, 1942," 90.

5. TNA:PRO DEFE 2/330, "Combined Operations Headquarters Intelligence Section Enemy Order of Battle Information–7 August, 1942," 1–2.

6. TNA:PRO DEFE 2/551, "Combined Report," 90.

7. TNA:PRO DEFE 2/330, "Combined Operations," 2.

8. TNA:PRO DEFE 2/551, "Combined Report," 90.

9. "Report No. 36, Information from German War Diaries," AHQ, DHH, DND, 3.

10. "Konrad Haase," accessed Dec. 19, 2011, www.ww2gravestone.com/general /haase-konrad.

11. Jason Pipes, "302.Infanterie-Division," *Feldgrau*, accessed Dec. 19, 2011, www.feldgrau.com/InfDiv.php?ID=206.

12. "Report No. 36," 5–7.

13. Ibid., appended section, "Divisional Order No. 27 for Coast Protection," 1–11.

14. Ibid., 11–13.

15. "Combat Report and Experience Gained During the British Attack on Dieppe 19 August 1942," 981.023(D10), vol. 20438, box 168, RG24, LAC, 1–2.

16. "Report No. 10, Information from German War Diaries," AHQ, DHH, DND, 3.

17. "Report of the Port Commandant Dieppe on the Fighting on 19 Aug 42," 981GN(D13), vol. 20488, box 218, RG24, LAC, 1.

18. "Report No. 36," 28.

19. C.P. Stacey, *Six Years of War: The Army in Canada, Britain and the Pacific*, vol. 1 (Ottawa: Queen's Printer, 1957), 354.

20. TNA:PRO DEFE 2/330, "Interrogation of Prisoners Captured on Dieppe Raid, Martian Report No. 13, Fire Tasks and Coastal Batteries," 3.

21. "Report No. 10," Appendix B, "Report of 302 German INF DIV (Operations Section–1a) on the Dieppe Raid," DHH, DND, 2–5.

22. "Operation Jubilee: Intelligence Report on Dieppe Raid, 19 Aug 42, Part III—Enemy Defences and Weapons," 215C1.98(D357), vol. 10707, box 156, RG24, LAC, 2.

23. TNA:PRO WO 106/4195, "Report on Information Obtained from Ps/W Captured at Dieppe–19/20 August, 1942," 5.

24. Ibid., 7.

25. "Report No. 10," Appendix B, 2–5.

26. Stacey, *Six Years of War*, 356–57.

27. "Report No. 36," 27.

28. "German 12-cm Mortar Battalions," *Tactical and Technical Trends*, no. 40 (Dec. 16, 1943), accessed Dec. 28, 2011, www.lonesentry.com/articles/ttt/german-12-cm-120 -mm-mortar-battalions.html.

29. "Report No. 36," 27.

30. TNA:PRO DEFE 2/330, "Order of the Day, C-in-C 15 Army, 10.8.42," 1.

31. TNA:PRO WO 106/4195, "Report on Information from Ps/W," 10.

32. Ibid., 23.

33. Ibid., 10.

34. Terence Robertson, *Dieppe: The Shame and the Glory* (London: Pan Books, 1965), 252.

35. TNA:PRO DEFE 2/330, "Interrogation of Prisoners," 2.

11 THE DIE WAS CAST

1. Royal Regiment of Canada War Diary, August 1942, RG24, LAC, 6.

2. C.P. Stacey, *Six Years of War: The Army in Canada, Britain and the Pacific*, vol. 1 (Ottawa: Queen's Printer, 1957), 344.

3. Sandy Antal and Kevin Shackleton, *Duty Nobly Done: The Official History of the Essex and Kent Scottish Regiment* (Windsor, ON: Walkerville, 2006), 394.

4. Stacey, *Six Years of War*, 344.

5. Royal Regiment War Diary, August 1942, 7.

6. Les Fusiliers Mont-Royal War Diary, August 1942, RG24, LAC, n.p.

7. Kingsley Brown Sr., Kingsley Brown Jr., and Brereton Greenhous, *Semper Paratus: The History of the Royal Hamilton Light Infantry (Wentworth Regiment), 1962–1977* (Hamilton: RHLI Historical Assoc., 1977), 191–92.

8. Royal Hamilton Light Infantry War Diary, August 1942, RG24, LAC, n.p.

9. Calgary Tank Regiment War Diary, August 1942, RG24, LAC, 5.

10. Hugh Henry, "The Tanks of Dieppe: The History of The Calgary Regiment (Tank), 1939 to August 19, 1942," MA thesis, University of Victoria, 1985, 73.

11. "Churchills Don't Float," *Onward 1: The Informal History of the Calgary Regiment, 14th Canadian Armoured Regiment*, ed. Dick Maltby and Jessie Maltby (Vancouver: 50/14 Veterans' Assoc., 1989), 1.

12. Calgary Tank War Diary, August 1942, 6.

13. "Part of Appx 'C' to Detailed Mil Plan Op 'Jubilee' Dieppe 19 Aug 42 re: Allotment of Personnel, Eqpt & stores," 225C1.013(D5), vol. 10795, box 213, RG24, LAC, 19–28.

14. Calgary Tank War Diary, 6.

15. TNA:PRO ADM 199/107, "Operation 'Jubilee,' Detailed Narrative—Enclosure No. 3 to the Naval Force Commander's No. NPJ.0221/92 of 30th August, 1942," 1.

16. John Hughes-Hallett, unpublished memoir, MG30 E463, LAC, 174–77.

17. Terence Robertson, *Dieppe: The Shame and the Glory* (London: Pan Books, 1965), 231–33.

18. TNA: PRO DEFE 2/551, "Combined Report on the Dieppe Raid," 10.

19. Hughes-Hallett memoir, 77.

20. "The History of the Third Canadian Light Anti-Aircraft Regiment (3LAA)," accessed Dec. 16, 2011, www.ww2f.com/wwii-general/25386-history-third-canadian-light-anti-aircraft-regiment-3laa.html.

21. Ronald Atkin, *Dieppe 1942: The Jubilee Disaster* (London: Macmillan, 1980), 67.

22. A.J. Kerry and W.A. McDill, *History of the Corps of Royal Engineers*, vol. 2 (Ottawa: Military Engineers Assoc., 1966), 101.

23. "Report on Combined Operations by Lt. Col. L.F. Barnes, CRE, 2 CDN DIV," 232C2. (D2), vol. 10870, box 250, RG24, LAC, 1–7.

24. "2nd Canadian Infantry Division Tp Carrying Exercise: Ford 1—Appx 'B' to Director's Notes for Control Movements Involved," 232C2.(D52), vol. 10873, box 252, RG24, LAC, 2.

25. Norman H. Ross, interview by Chris Main, July 20 and Aug. 16, 1979, UVICSC.

26. Atkin, 62.

27. "Part of Appx 'C' to Detailed Mil Plan," 29.

28. Atkin, 62.

29. Queen's Own Cameron Highlanders War Diary, August 1942, Appendix 9, RG24, LAC, I.

30. Atkin, 63.

31. Lord Lovat, *March Past: A Memoir* (New York: Holmes & Meier, 1979), 244–45.

32. South Saskatchewan Regiment War Diary, August 1942, Appendix 7, RG24, LAC, 2.

33. John Edmondson, interview by Chris Bell, June 6, Aug. 4 and 12, 1982, UVICSC.

34. "Part of Appx 'C' to Detailed Mil Plan," 2–3.

35. Edmondson interview.

36. South Saskatchewan War Diary, Appendix 9, 2.

37. Ibid., 2.

38. "Part of Appx 'C' to Detailed Mil Plan," 2.

39. TNA:PRO DEFE 2/551, "Combined Report on the Dieppe Raid, 1942, Appendix L to Annex 2–Intelligence Plan," 2.

40. James Leasor, *Green Beach* (London: William Heinemann, 1975), 47–98.

41. TNA:PRO DEFE 2/551, "Combined Report," 3.

42. Essex Scottish War Diary, August 1942, Appendix VII, RG24, LAC, I.

43. "Part of Appx 'C' to Detailed Mil Plan," 3.

44. Essex Scottish War Diary, RG24, LAC, 4.

45. Ibid., Appendix VI, I.

46. Denis Whitaker and Shelagh Whitaker, *Dieppe: Tragedy to Triumph; A Firsthand and Revealing Critical Account of the Most Controversial Battle of World War II* (Whitby, ON: McGraw-Hill Ryerson, 1992), 228–29.

47. Atkin, 64.

48. Les Fusiliers War Diary, n.p.

49. Atkin, 64.

50. Royal Regiment War Diary, 7.

51. Robertson, 241.

52. Atkin, 67.

53. "In Memory of Private Emile Phillipe Williams," Veterans Affairs Canada, accessed Dec. 31, 2011, www.veterans.gc.ca/eng/collections/virtualmem/Detail/2929447.

54. "Report No. 101, General Outline and Flank Attacks," CMHQ, DHH, DND, 9.

55. Ross Munro, *Gauntlet to Overlord* (Toronto: Macmillan, 1945), 309–10.

56. Hughes-Hallett memoir, 177.

57. Atkins, 69.

12 THE MOST REMARKABLE THING

1. Quentin Reynolds, *Dress Rehearsal: The Story of Dieppe* (Garden City, NY: Blue Ribbon Books, 1943), 91–92.

2. C.P. Stacey, *Six Years of War: The Army in Canada, Britain and the Pacific*, vol. I (Ottawa: Queen's Printer, 1957), 345.

3. Reynolds, 97.

4. TNA:PRO ADM 199/107, "Operation 'Jubilee,' Detailed Narrative—Enclosure No. 3 to the Naval Force Commander's No. NPJ.0221/92 of 30th August, 1942," I.

5. Terence Robertson, *Dieppe: The Shame and the Glory* (London: Pan Books, 1965), 251–52.

6. Reynolds, 105–06.

7. John Hughes-Hallett, unpublished memoir, MG30 E463, LAC, 178.

8. "Dieppe Raid—1942" file, "Op 'Jubilee' 19 Aug 43 Combined Plan, Capt. H. Hallett, Maj-Gen JH Roberts, Air Marshal TL Leigh-Mallory, Appendix 'A' to JNO1—List of Ships, Groups, and Superior Officers," 225CI.013(D6), vol. 10796, box 213, RG24, LAC, 1–4.

9. TNA:PRO DEFE 2/334, "Narrative by Lt. W.K. Rogers, R.M. O.C.R.M. Detachment in L.C.F.(L) 6, 28 Dieppe Raid," 1.

10. "Report No. 101, General Outline and Flank Attacks," CMHQ, DHH, DND, 8.

11. Hughes-Hallett memoir, 178.

12. Ross Munro, Gauntlet to Overlord (Toronto: Macmillan, 1945), 319–20.

13. TNA:PRO ADM 199/107, "Operation 'Jubilee,' Detailed Narrative," 1.

14. Munro, 321.

15. TNA:PRO ADM 199/107, "Operation 'Jubilee,' Detailed Narrative," 1.

16. Ibid., 2.

17. "Report No. 101," 9.

18. Reynolds, 129.

19. TNA:PRO ADM 199/107, "Operation 'Jubilee,' Detailed Narrative," 2–3.

20. Munro, 322.

21. Reynolds, 138–39.

22. John P. Campbell, Dieppe Revisited: Documentary Investigation (Portland, OR: Frank Cass, 1993), 169.

23. "UJ-1411 (Treff III) (+1944)," Wreck Site, accessed Jan. 3, 2012, www.wrecksite.eu /wreck.aspx?133368.

24. Campbell, 169.

25. Stacey, Six Years of War, 358.

26. Brereton Greenhous, "Operation Flodden: The Sea Fight Off Berneval and the Suppression of the Goebbels Battery, 19 August 1942," Canadian Military Journal, vol. 4, no. 4 (Autumn 2003), 49–50.

27. TNA:PRO DEFE 2/334, "Preliminary Report on Activities of Group 5 During Operation Jubilee by Commander D.B. Wyburd," 1.

28. Greenhous, "Operation Flodden," 49.

29. Angus Konstam, British Motor Gun Boat, 1939–45 (Oxford: Osprey Publishing, 2010), 42.

30. Greenhous, "Operation Flodden," 49.

31. TNA:PRO DEFE 2/334, "Preliminary Report by Wyburd," 1.

32. TNA:PRO DEFE 2/335, Appendix v, "Personal Account of Sub-Lieutenant D.J. Lewis, RCNVR" 5–6.

33. Combined Operations: The Official Story of the Commandos (New York: Macmillan, 1943), 118.

34. TNA:PRO DEFE 2/334, "Preliminary Report by Wyburd," 1.

35. TNA:PRO DEFE 2/239, "Jubilee (Operation Flodden) Official Account Lieutenant Colonel J.F. Durnford-Slater," 1.

36. Greenhous, "Operation Flodden," 52.

37. TNA:PRO DEFE 2/334, "Preliminary Report by Wyburd," 1.

38. Ronald Atkin, *Dieppe 1942: The Jubilee Disaster* (London: Macmillan, 1980), 77.

39. Peter Young, *Storm from the Sea* (London: Greenhill Books, 2002), 62–63.

40. TNA:PRO DEFE 2/239, "Official Account Durnford-Slater," 1.

41. TNA:PRO DEFE 2/335, "Personal Account of Lewis," 6.

42. Young, 63.

43. Reynolds, 139.

44. "Dieppe, 1942" file, "Lecture Notes, Combined Services Raid on Dieppe, 19 Aug 42 by Brig. CC Mann, GS, 1 Cdn Corps," 222C1.011(D1), vol. 10772, box 201, RG24, LAC, 7.

45. Greenhous, "Operation Flodden," 53.

46. "Report No. 10, Operation 'Jubilee': Information from German War Diaries," Appendix A, AHQ, DHH, DND, 2.

47. "Report of the Port Commandant Dieppe on the Fighting on 19 Aug 42," 981GN(D13), vol. 20488, box 218, RG24, LAC, 1.

48. "Report No. 10," Appendix B, 6.

49. Reynolds, 139.

50. Greenhous, "Operation Flodden," 51–52.

51. Hughes-Hallett memoir, 186–87.

13 GOOD LUCK TO ALL OF YOU

1. "Personal Accounts Dieppe—Narrative of Experiences at Dieppe, 19 Aug 42 by Lt.-Col. R.R. Labatt, OC, RHLI," 592.011(D3), DHH, DND, 1–3.

2. TNA:PRO DEFE 2/239, "Jubilee (Operation Flodden) Report by Major P. Young," 1.

3. TNA:PRO DEFE 2/335, Appendix V, "Personal Account of Sub-Lieutenant D.J. Lewis, RCNVR," 2.

4. TNA:PRO DEFE 2/239, "Report by Young," 1.

5. Ibid., 2.

6. Ronald Atkin, *Dieppe 1942: The Jubilee Disaster* (London: Macmillan, 1980), 82–84.

7. Ibid., 82–83.

8. TNA:PRO DEFE 2/551, "Combined Report on the Dieppe Raid," 13.

9. Brereton Greenhous, "Operation Flodden: The Sea Fight Off Berneval and the Suppression of the Goebbels Battery," 19 August 1942," *Canadian Military Journal*, vol. 4, no. 4 (Autumn 2003), 54–55.

10. *Combined Operations: The Official Story of the Commandos* (New York: Macmillan, 1943), 118.

11. Greenhous, "Operation Flodden," 54.

12. Terence Robertson, *Dieppe: The Shame and the Glory* (London: Pan Books, 1965), 269.

13. "Report No. 10, Information from German War Diaries," Appendix B, AHQ, DHH, DND, 7.

14. TNA:PRO DEFE 2/239, "Report by Young," 2–3.

15. TNA:PRO DEFE 2/335, "Personal Account of Lewis," 2.

16. TNA:PRO DEFE 2/239, "Report by Young," 2–3.

17. TNA:PRO DEFE 2/335, "Personal Account of Lewis," 2.

18. TNA:PRO DEFE 2/239, "Report by Young," 2–3.

19. TNA:PRO DEFE 2/335, "Personal Account of Lewis," 2.

20. TNA:PRO DEFE 2/239, "Report by Young," 3.

21. "Report No. 10," Appendix B, 8.

22. Jim DeFelice, *Rangers at Dieppe: The First Combat Action of U.S. Army Rangers in World War II* (New York: Berkley Caliber, 2008), 142–44.

23. TNA:PRO DEFE 2/335, "Personal Account of Lewis," 1.

24. Atkin, 89–91.

25. Greenhous, "Operation Flodden," 54.

26. "Soldats Alliés tués combat, disparu, décédes de leurs blessures ou morts en captivité, ayant participé à l'opération sur Berneval le 19 août 1942," memorial plaque, Berneval, France.

27. Greenhous, "Operation Flodden," 55.

14 SMASH AND GRAB

1. Lord Lovat, *March Past: A Memoir* (New York: Holmes & Meier, 1979), 247.

2. Atkin, 95–96.

3. Lovat, *March Past*, 248.

4. TNA:PRO DEFE 2/328, "Story from Corporal Frank Koons—1st Rangers, of the State of Iowa," 1.

5. Lovat, *March Past*, 248.

6. TNA:PRO DEFE 2/328, "Story from Koons," 1.

7. Lovat, *March Past*, 248.

8. Terence Robertson, *Dieppe: The Shame and the Glory* (London: Pan Books, 1965), 275.

9. Lovat, *March Past*, 248.

10. TNA:PRO DEFE 2/337, "Jubilee: Operation Cauldron, Report on Orange Beach 2 Landing by Lt. Col. The Lord Lovat," 1.

11. TNA:PRO DEFE 2/328, "Additions to Lord Lovat's Official Report on Operation 'Jubilee,'" 1.

12. "Finney, William," Fdn. for Information on the Second World War, accessed Jan. 2012, www.ww2awards.com/person/44280.

13. TNA:PRO DEFE 2/328, "Additions to Lovat's Report," 1.

14. TNA:PRO DEFE 2/337, "Jubilee: Operation Cauldron," 1.

15. TNA:PRO DEFE 2/328, "Additions to Lovat's Report," 1.

16. TNA:PRO DEFE 2/337, "Report on Orange Beach One Landing by Major D. Mills-Roberts," 1.

17. TNA:PRO DEFE 2/328, "Story from Koons," 1.

18. TNA:PRO DEFE 2/337, "Report on Orange Beach One," 1.

19. Lovat, *March Past*, 250.

20. TNA:PRO DEFE 2/337, "Report on Orange Beach One," 3.

21. Ibid., 1–2.

22. *Combined Operations: The Official Story of the Commandos* (New York: Macmillan, 1943), 121.

23. TNA:PRO DEFE 2/328, "Story from Koons," 2.

24. TNA:PRO DEFE 2/337, "Report on Orange Beach One," 2.

25. Lovat, *March Past*, 253.

26. TNA:PRO DEFE 2/337, "Jubilee: Operation Cauldron," 2.

27. TNA:PRO DEFE 2/328, "Additions to Lovat's Report," 2.

28. TNA:PRO DEFE 2/337, "Jubilee: Operation Cauldron," 2.

29. "Additions to Lord Lovat's Official Report," 2.

30. TNA:PRO DEFE 2/337, "Jubilee: Operation Cauldron," 2.

31. TNA:PRO DEFE 2/337, "Report on Orange Beach One," 2.

32. TNA:PRO DEFE 2/337, "Jubilee: Operation Cauldron," 2.

33. Lovat, *March Past*, 260.

34. "Colonel Pat Porteous, VC," *The Telegraph*, UK, accessed Jan. 2012, www.telegraph
   .co.uk/news/obituaries/1369771/Colonel-Pat-Porteous-vc.html.

35. TNA:PRO DEFE 2/337, "Jubilee: Operation Cauldron," 2.

36. Lovat, *March Past*, 260.

37. TNA:PRO DEFE 2/337, "Jubilee: Operation Cauldron," 2.

38. *Combined Operations: The Commandos*, 123.

39. Lovat, *March Past*, 255.

40. TNA:PRO DEFE 2/328, "Story from Koons," 2–3.

41. Atkin, 109–10.

42. "Report No. 101, Operation 'Jubilee': General Outline and Flank Attacks," CMHQ, DHH,
   DND, 21.

43. C.P. Stacey, *Six Years of War: The Army in Canada, Britain and the Pacific*, vol. 1 (Ottawa:
   Queen's Printer, 1957), 363.

44. "Report No. 101," 21.

45. Lovat, *March Past*, 263–64.

15 THE REAL THING

1. TNA:PRO DEFE 2/233, "Report by the Air Commander on the Combined Operation
   Against Dieppe—August 19th, 1942, Appendix D," 21.

2. TNA:PRO DEFE 2/551, "Combined Report on the Dieppe Raid, 1942," 29–30.

3. TNA:PRO DEFE 2/233, "Report by the Air Commander, 4.

4. Terence Robertson, *Dieppe: The Shame and the Glory* (London: Pan Books, 1965), 285.

5. Norman L.R. Franks, *Greatest Air Battle: Dieppe, 19th August 1942* (London: William
   Kimber, 1979), 32.

6. Ibid., 38–39.

7. "Report of the Port Commandant Dieppe on the Fighting on 19 Aug 42," 981GN(D13),
   vol. 20488, box 218, RG24, LAC, 1–3.

8. "Personal Accounts Dieppe—South Saskatchewan Reports," 592.011(D3), DHH, DND,
   16.

9. Ibid., 10.

10. "Report No. 101, General Outline and Flank Attacks," CMHQ, DHH, DND, 68–69.

11. "Personal Accounts Dieppe—South Sask. Reports," 2.

12. Ibid., 4.

13. South Saskatchewan Regiment War Diary, Appendix 7, RG24, LAC, 4.

14. South Saskatchewan War Diary, Appendix 9, 4.

15. Ibid., 19.

16. "Personal Accounts Dieppe—South Sask. Reports," 7–9.

17. John Edmondson, interview by Chris Bell, June 6, Aug. 4 and 12, 1982, UVICSC.

18. John S. Edmondson and R. Douglas Edmondson, "Memories and Reflections on the Dieppe Raid of 19 August 1942," *Canadian Military History*, vol. 13, no. 4 (Autumn 2004), 51.

19. South Saskatchewan War Diary, Appendix 9, 2.

20. "Personal Accounts Dieppe—South Sask. Reports," 15.

21. Ibid., 10–11.

22. Ibid., 19–20.

23. Wallace Reyburn, *Glorious Chapter: The Canadians at Dieppe* (Toronto: Oxford University Press, 1943), 63–64.

24. "Personal Accounts Dieppe—South Sask. Reports," 16.

25. Reyburn, 71–72.

26. Ronald Atkin, *Dieppe 1942: The Jubilee Disaster* (London: Macmillan, 1980), 138.

27. "Report No. 101," 85.

28. South Saskatchewan War Diary, Appendix 9, 17.

29. Ibid., 12.

30. Ibid., 4.

31. Ibid., 5.

32. Ibid., 3.

33. Ibid., 14.

34. Ibid., 7.

35. Ibid., 21.

36. Edmondson and Edmondson, 52.

37. "Charles Edward Sawden," Veterans Affairs Canada, accessed Jan. 14, 2012, www.veterans.gc.ca/eng/collections/virtualmem/photoview/2317422/21197.

38. "Personal Accounts Dieppe—South Sask. Reports," 10.

39. Edmondson interview.

40. "Personal Accounts Dieppe—South Sask. Reports," 5.

41. South Saskatchewan War Diary, Appendix 9, 16.

42. "Op 'Jubilee,' Personal account (S Sask R)," 232C2.(D66), vol. 10873, box 252, RG24, LAC, 4–5.

43. Edmondson interview.

16 HELL OF A FIX

1. "Report No. 101, General Outline and Flank Attacks," CMHQ, DHH, DND, 86–87.

2. "Op 'Jubilee,' Personal accounts (Cam Highrs of Cda)," 232C2.(D65), vol. 10873, box 252, RG24, LAC, 150.

3. "Report No. 101," 87.

4. TNA:PRO DEFE 2/335, Appendix V: "Interview with Sub-Lieut. J.E. O'Rourke, RCNVR," 1.

5. "Op 'Jubilee,' Personal accounts (Cam Highrs of Cda)," 125.

6. C.P. Stacey, *Six Years of War: The Army in Canada, Britain and the Pacific*, vol. 1 (Ottawa: Queen's Printer, 1957), 371.

7. "Report No. 89, The Operation at Dieppe, 19 Aug 42: Personal Stories of Participants," CMHQ, DHH, DND, 75.

8. Ibid., 68.

9. Ibid., 76.
10. "Op 'Jubilee,' Personal accounts (Cam Highrs of Cda)," 109.
11. Norman H. Ross, interview by Chris Main, July 20 and August 16, 1979, UVICSC.
12. South Saskatchewan Regiment War Diary, August 1942, RG24, LAC, 9.
13. Ibid., 10.
14. Martin Sugarman, "Jack Nissenthall—The VC Hero Who Never Was," Harry Palmer Gallery, Dieppe Raid Gallery, accessed Apr. 10, 2012, www.aportraitofcanada.ca/?p=2216.
15. "Personal Accounts Dieppe—Memorandum of Interview with Major J.E. McRae," 592.011(D3), DHH, DND, 2.
16. South Saskatchewan War Diary, Appendix 7, 7.
17. "Report No. 89," 76.
18. "Op 'Jubilee,' Personal accounts (Cam Highrs of Cda)," 125.
19. "Report No. 101," 93–94.
20. "Report No. 89," 77.
21. "Op 'Jubilee,' Personal accounts (S Sask R)," 232C2.(D66), vol. 10873, box 252, RG24, LAC, 8.
22. John S. Edmondson and R. Douglas Edmondson, "Memories and Reflections on the Dieppe Raid of 19 August 1942," Canadian Military History, vol. 13, no. 4 (Autumn 2004), 55.
23. "Report No. 101," 81–82.
24. "Report No. 89," 68.
25. Ross interview.
26. Queen's Own Cameron Highlanders War Diary, August 1942, Appendix 9, 2.
27. Ross interview.
28. Stacey, Six Years of War, 373–74.
29. "Op 'Jubilee,' Personal accounts (Cam Highrs of Cda)," 1.
30. "Report No. 101," 99–100.
31. "Report No. 89," 71–72.
32. "Report No. 101," 100.
33. "Op 'Jubilee,' Personal accounts (Cam Highrs of Cda)," 50.
34. "Report No. 101," 100–101.
35. "Report No. 89," 71.
36. Ross interview.
37. "Op 'Jubilee,' Personal accounts (Cam Highrs of Cda)," 33.
38. Ibid., 50–51.
39. Ibid., 107–08.
40. "Report No. 89," 71.
41. "Report No. 10, Information from German War Diaries," AHQ, DHH, DND, 12–13.
42. South Saskatchewan War Diary, Appendix 9, 2.
43. "Op 'Jubilee'—Courts of Inquiry," 232C2.(D83), vol. 1085, box 252, RG24, LAC, 49.
44. South Saskatchewan War Diary, Appendix 7, 2.
45. "Report No. 101," 108.
46. "Report No. 89," 78.
47. Ross interview.

48. "Report No. 101," 110.
49. "Memorandum of Interview with Private W.A. Haggard," 592.011(D3), DHH, DND, 3.
50. Wallace Reyburn, *Glorious Chapter: The Canadians at Dieppe* (Toronto: Oxford University Press, 1943), 107.

17 SUCH A CARNAGE
1. "Report No. 101, General Outline and Flank Attacks," CMHQ, DHH, DND, 30–31.
2. "Op 'Jubilee,' Personal accts (R Regt of C)," 232C2.(D61), vol. 10873, box 252, RG24, 1.
3. "Report No. 101," 31.
4. D.J. Goodspeed, *Battle Royal: A History of the Royal Regiment of Canada, 1862–1962* (Toronto: Royal Regt. of Canada Assoc., 1962), 394.
5. "Report No. 101," 23–24.
6. Ibid., 64–65.
7. TNA:PRO ADM 199/107, "Operation 'Jubilee,' Detailed Narrative—Enclosure No. 3 to the Naval Force Commander's No. NPJ.0221/92 of 30th August, 1942," 7.
8. Ross Munro, *Gauntlet to Overlord* (Toronto: Macmillan, 1945), 324–25.
9. "Report No. 101," 27–28.
10. "Op 'Jubilee,' Personal accts (R Regt of C)," 9.
11. Ibid., 22.
12. Ibid., 17.
13. "Report No. 101," 30.
14. "Op 'Jubilee,' Personal accts (R Regt of C)," 11.
15. Ibid., 10.
16. Ibid., 13.
17. Ibid., 10.
18. Ibid., 20.
19. Ibid., 3.
20. Ibid., 22.
21. Ibid., 3.
22. "Report No. 89, The Operation at Dieppe, 19 Aug 42: Personal Stories of Participants," CMHQ, DHH, DND, 7.
23. "Personal Accounts Dieppe—Action of Royal Regiment of Canada (Blue Beach): Statement of Sgt. Legate," 592.011(D3), DHH, DND, 1.
24. "In Memory of Lieutenant William George Rogers Wedd," Veterans Affairs Canada, accessed Jan. 18, 2012, www.veterans.gc.ca/eng/collections/virtualmem/Detail/2317531.
25. "Op 'Jubilee,' Personal accts (R Regt of C)," 20.
26. Ibid., 11.
27. Royal Regiment of Canada War Diary, August 1942, Appendix 7, RG24, LAC, 1.
28. "Op 'Jubilee,' Personal accts (R Regt of C)," 11.
29. Ibid., 12.
30. Ibid., 15.
31. Ibid., 12.
32. Munro, 325–28.

33. "Op 'Jubilee,' Personal accts (R Regt of C)," 14.
34. Ibid., 16.
35. Ibid., 3–5.
36. Ibid., 11.
37. C.P. Stacey, *Six Years of War: The Army in Canada, Britain and the Pacific,* vol. 1 (Ottawa: Queen's Printer, 1957), 367.
38. "Op 'Jubilee,' Personal accts (R Regt of C)," 6.
39. Ibid., 8.
40. Ibid., 4.
41. Ibid., 9.
42. Ibid., 4.
43. "Personal Accounts Dieppe—Statement of Sgt. Legate," 6.
44. "Op 'Jubilee,' Personal accts (R Regt of C)," 9.
45. "Personal Accounts Dieppe—Statement of Sgt. Legate," 6–7.
46. "Report No. 101," 48–49.
47. TNA:PRO DEFE 2/335, Appendix v, "Report by Lieutenant J.E. Koyl," 8.
48. Denis Whitaker and Shelagh Whitaker, *Dieppe: Tragedy to Triumph; A Firsthand and Revealing Critical Account of the Most Controversial Battle of World War II* (Whitby, ON: McGraw-Hill Ryerson, 1992), 247.
49. Ronald Atkin, *Dieppe 1942: The Jubilee Disaster* (London: Macmillan, 1980), 123.
50. "Report No. 101," 39–40.
51. "Report No. 89," 8–9.
52. Stacey, *Six Years of War,* 367.
53. "Report No. 89," 8–9.
54. "Op 'Jubilee,' Personal accts (R Regt of C)," 5.
55. "Report No. 101," 57–58.
56. "Op 'Jubilee,' Personal accts (R Regt of C)," 8.
57. "Report No. 101," 58.
58. TNA:PRO DEFE 2/335, Appendix v, "Interview with Sub-Lieut. J.E. Boak," 15.
59. "Report No. 86," 7–10.
60. Stacey, *Six Years of War,* 367–69.

18 MURDEROUS CROSSFIRE

1. "Report No. 108, The Attack on the Main Beaches," CMHQ, DHH, DND, 7–9.
2. C.P. Stacey, *Six Years of War: The Army in Canada, Britain and the Pacific,* vol. 1 (Ottawa: Queen's Printer, 1957), 374.
3. "Personal Accounts Dieppe—Narrative of Experiences at Dieppe, 19 Aug 42 by Lt.-Col. R.R. Labatt, OC, RHLI," 592.011(D3), DHH, DND, 4–5.
4. Denis Whitaker and Shelagh Whitaker, *Dieppe: Tragedy to Triumph; A Firsthand and Revealing Critical Account of the Most Controversial Battle of World War II* (Whitby, ON: McGraw-Hill Ryerson, 1992), 242.
5. TNA:PRO DEFE 2/338, "Memorandum of Interview with Lieut. L.C. Counsell," 1.
6. Kingsley Brown Sr., Kingsley Brown Jr., and Brereton Greenhous, *Semper Paratus: The History of the Royal Hamilton Light Infantry (Wentworth Regiment), 1962–1977* (Hamilton: RHLI Historical Assoc., 1977), 198.

7. TNA:PRO ADM 199/107, "Operation 'Jubilee,' Naval Force Commander's Narrative, No. NPJ.0221/92 of 30th August, 1942," 3.

8. TNA:PRO DEFE 2/335, "Observations on 'Jubilee' by Brigadier General L.K. Truscott," 2.

9. Norman L.R. Franks, *Greatest Air Battle: Dieppe, 19th August 1942* (London: William Kimber, 1979), 44–48.

10. "Report of the Port Commandant Dieppe on the Fighting on 19 Aug 42," 981GN(DI3), vol. 20488, box 218, RG24, LAC, 2.

11. Andrew R. Ritchie, *Watchdog: A History of the Canadian Provost Corps* (Toronto: University of Toronto Press, 1995), 53.

12. "Op 'Jubilee,' Personal accts (RCE)," 232C2.(D57), vol. 10873, box 252, RG24, LAC, 25.

13. "Personal Accounts Dieppe—Labatt," 5.

14. Whitaker and Whitaker, 243.

15. Brown Sr., Brown Jr., and Greenhous, 197.

16. "Report No. 108," 11.

17. "Personal Accounts Dieppe—Labatt," 5.

18. Stacey, *Six Years of War,* 375–76.

19. "Report No. 89, The Operation at Dieppe, 19 Aug 42: Personal Stories of Participants," CMHQ, DHH, DND, 55.

20. Royal Hamilton Light Infantry War Diary, August 1942, Appendix 18, RG24, LAC, 24.

21. Ibid., 21.

22. TNA:PRO DEFE 2/338, "Memorandum of Interview with Counsell," 2.

23. Royal Hamilton War Diary, Appendix 18, 47.

24. Brown Sr., Brown Jr., and Greenhous, 198–99.

25. Royal Hamilton War Diary, Appendix 18, 41.

26. "Personal Accounts Dieppe—Labatt," 6.

27. Royal Hamilton War Diary, Appendix 18, 2.

28. Ibid., Appendix A, "Recommendations for Awards and Mentions," 16.

29. "Report No. 89," 81.

30. Whitaker and Whitaker, 253.

31. Royal Hamilton War Diary, Appendix 18, 38.

32. Stacey, *Six Years of War,* 375.

33. Royal Hamilton War Diary, Appendix 18, 29.

34. Kingsley Sr., Kingsley Jr., and Greenhous, 200.

35. Sandy Antal and Kevin Shackleton, *Duty Nobly Done: The Official History of the Essex and Kent Scottish Regiment* (Windsor, ON: Walkerville, 2006), 404.

36. "Op 'Jubilee,' Personal accts (RCE)," 13.

37. Ibid., 25.

38. Antal and Shackleton, 405.

39. Stacey, *Six Years of War,* 376.

40. Antal and Shackleton, 405.

41. Essex Scottish Regiment War Diary, August 1944, Appendix 6, "Attack on Dieppe, 19 Aug 42," RG24, LAC, 2.

42. Antal and Shackleton, 405.

19 A DEATH TRAP

1. "Report No. 108, The Attack on the Main Beaches," CMHQ, DHH, DND, 12–13.

2. C.P. Stacey, *Six Years of War: The Army in Canada, Britain and the Pacific,* vol. 1 (Ottawa: Queen's Printer, 1957), 375.

3. Hugh Henry, "The Tanks of Dieppe: The History of The Calgary Regiment (Tank), 1939 to August 19, 1942," MA thesis, University of Victoria, 1985, 75.

4. "Op 'Jubilee,' Personal accts (RCE)," 232C2.(D57), vol. 10873, box 252, RG24, LAC, 3.

5. Henry, 76–77.

6. "Op 'Jubilee,' Personal accts (RCE)," 3.

7. Henry, 77–78.

8. "Op 'Jubilee,' Personal accts (RCE)," 6.

9. TNA:PRO DEFE 2/328, "Major Sucharov, Royal Canadian Engineers," 1.

10. "Op 'Jubilee,' Personal accts (RCE)," 6.

11. TNA:PRO DEFE 2/328, "Major Sucharov," 1.

12. Henry, 78–79.

13. Ibid., 80.

14. Stan Kanick, "Chert Beach—Alias Dieppe," in *Onward 1: The Informal History of the Calgary Regiment, 14th Canadian Armoured Regiment,* ed. Dick Maltby and Jessie Maltby (Vancouver: 50/14 Veterans' Assoc., 1989), 1.

15. "Report of the Port Commandant Dieppe on the Fighting on 19 Aug 42," 981GN(D13), vol. 20488, box 218, RG24, LAC, 4.

16. Ibid., 80–81.

17. "Personal Accounts Dieppe—Statement of Sgt. J.W. Marsh, Black Watch with Mortar Platoon on LCT2," 592.011(D3), DHH, DND, 132.

18. Henry, 80–81.

19. Ibid., 83–84.

20. Ronald Atkin, *Dieppe 1942: The Jubilee Disaster* (London: Macmillan London, 1980), 163.

21. Henry, 84–85.

22. "Personal Accounts Dieppe—Report on Dieppe by Captain C.R. Eldred," 2.

23. "Report No. 107, The Operation at Dieppe, 19 Aug 42: Further Personal Stories of Participants, CMHQ, DHH, DND, 5.

24. Henry, 87–88.

25. Andrew R. Ritchie, *Watchdog: A History of the Canadian Provost Corps* (Toronto: University of Toronto Press, 1995), 53.

26. Atkin, 165.

27. Henry, 88–93.

28. Sandy Antal and Kevin Shackleton, *Duty Nobly Done: The Official History of the Essex and Kent Scottish Regiment* (Windsor, ON: Walkerville, 2006), 408.

29. "Report No. 107," 10.

30. Antal and Shackleton, 408.

31. John Mellor, *Dieppe—Canada's Forgotten Heroes* (Scarborough, ON: Signet, 1975), 87.

32. Antal and Shackleton, 408.

33. "Report No. 107," 10.

34. Antal and Shackleton, 408–09.

35. "Report No. 108," 4.

36. Essex Scottish Regiment War Diary, August 1944, Appendix 6: "Attack on Dieppe, 19 Aug 42," RG24, LAC, 2–4.

37. "Op 'Jubilee,' Personal accts (RCE)," 232C2.(D57), vol. 10873, box 252, RG24, 1.

38. "Personal Accounts Dieppe—Memorandum of Interview with CSM J. Stewart, RHLI, 26 Oct. 42," 1–2.

39. "Personal Accounts Dieppe—Narrative of Experiences at Dieppe, 19 Aug 42 by Lt.-Col. R.R. Labatt, OC, RHLI," 7.

40. "Personal Accounts Dieppe—Report on Approach, Landing and Subsequent Events Dieppe by Brig. W. Southam," 2.

41. Ed Bennett, "Dieppe 1942," in *Onward 1: The Informal History of the Calgary Regiment, 14th Canadian Armoured Regiment*, ed. Dick Maltby and Jessie Maltby (Vancouver: 50/14 Veterans' Assoc., 1989), 1.

42. Henry, 94.

43. John S. Moir, ed., *History of the Royal Canadian Corps of Signals, 1903–1961* (Ottawa: Corps Comm., Royal Cdn. Corps of Signals, 1962), 120.

44. "Personal Accounts Dieppe—Southam," 2–3.

45. Moir, 121.

46. "Personal Accounts Dieppe—Southam," 3.

47. "Dieppe: Report of Tank Action," 594.011(D1), DHH, DND, 2.

48. Henry, 99–100.

49. A.J. Kerry and W.A. McDill, *History of the Corps of Royal Engineers*, vol. 2 (Ottawa: Military Engineers Assoc., 1966), 106.

50. Henry, 101.

51. Ibid., 100.

52. Ibid.

53. Kerry and McDill, 105.

54. Ibid., 101–06.

20 SITUATION VERY GRIM

1. John Hughes-Hallett, unpublished memoir, MG30 E463, LAC, 182.

2. John S. Moir, ed., *History of the Royal Canadian Corps of Signals, 1903–1961* (Ottawa: Corps Comm., Royal Cdn. Corps of Signals, 1962), 123.

3. "Communications, Operation 'Jubilee,'" 232C2.(D6), vol. 10870, box 250, RG24, LAC, 2.

4. TNA:PRO DEFE 2/335, "Observations on 'Jubilee' by Brigadier General L.K. Truscott," 2.

5. 2nd Canadian Infantry Division (G Branch) War Diary, August 1942, "Operation 'Jubilee' Intelligence Log," RG24, LAC, 1.

6. C.P. Stacey, *Six Years of War: The Army in Canada, Britain and the Pacific*, vol. 1 (Ottawa: Queen's Printer, 1957), 368.

7. Colonel Ed Rayment (Retd.) correspondence with author, Feb. 8, 2012.

8. Hughes-Hallett memoir, 169.

9. TNA:PRO DEFE 2/334, "Preliminary Report on Activities of Group 5 During Operation Jubilee by Commander D.B. Wyburd," 2.

10. Hughes-Hallett memoir, 186.

11. John Durnford-Slater, *Commando* (London: W. Kimber, 1953), 105.

12. 2nd Canadian Infantry Division War Diary, "Intelligence Log," 1–2.

13. Stacey, *Six Years of War*, 368.

14. "Report No. 108, The Attack on the Main Beaches," CMHQ, DHH, DND, 43.

15. Robin Neillands, *The Dieppe Raid: The Story of the Disastrous 1942 Expedition* (London: Aurum Press, 2005), 234.

16. TNA:PRO DEFE 2/328, "Dieppe: Stories of Raid," 5.

17. Hughes-Hallett memoir, 182.

18. 2nd Canadian Infantry Division War Diary, "Report on Operation Jubilee," 2.

19. Hughes-Hallett memoir, 185.

20. *Cent ans d'histoire d'un régiment canadien-français: Les Fusiliers Mont-Royal, 1869–1969* (Montreal: Éditions Du Jour, 1971), 138–39.

21. Dollard Ménard and C.B. Wall, "The Meaning of Bravery," *The Canadians at War, 1939/45*, vol. 1 (Montreal: Reader's Digest Assoc. [Canada], 1969), 196.

22. "Report No. 90, The Operation at Dieppe, 19 Aug 42: Further Personal Stories of Participants," CMHQ, DHH, DND, 30–31.

23. "Personal Accounts Dieppe—Report on Approach, Landing and Subsequent Events Dieppe by Brig. W. Southam," 592.011(D3), DHH, DND, 4.

24. "Personal Accounts Dieppe—Report on the Dieppe Raid on 19th August, 1942 by Lt. P. Ross (RNVR)," 4.

25. "Report No. 89, The Operation at Dieppe, 19 Aug 42: Personal Stories of Participants," CMHQ, DHH, DND, 31.

26. "Personal Accounts Dieppe—Personal Account of Sergeant Major L.A. Dumais," 1.

27. "Op 'Jubilee' Personal Accounts (Fus M.R.)," 232C2.(D55), vol. 10873, box 252, RG24, LAC, 14.

28. Ibid., 39.

29. "Memorandum of interview with Major Guy Vandelac, 6 Nov 46," 594.011(D5), DHH, DND, 1–2.

30. "Report No. 90," 33.

31. Ménard and Wall, 196–97.

32. "Personal Accounts Dieppe—Narrative of Experiences at Dieppe, 19 Aug 42 by Lt.-Col. R.R. Labatt, OC, RHLI," 8–9.

33. 2nd Canadian Infantry Division War Diary, "Intelligence Log," 4.

34. 4th Canadian Infantry Brigade War Diary, August 1942, "Major P. Garneau account," RG24, LAC, 1.

35. Ibid., 2.

36. Hugh Henry, "The Tanks of Dieppe: The History of The Calgary Regiment (Tank), 1939 to August 19, 1942," MA thesis, University of Victoria, 1985, 102.

37. 4th Canadian Infantry Brigade War Diary, "Garneau account," 3.

38. "Personal Accounts Dieppe—Labatt," 7.

39. 2nd Canadian Infantry Division War Diary, "Intelligence Log," 6.

40. TNA:PRO DEFE 2/330, "Analysis of preliminary reports made to CCO by Force Commanders and their Staff on Operation 'Jubilee' 20th August 1942, Room 21, Montagu House," 9.

41. TNA:PRO DEFE 2/337, "Report on Events on 19 Aug 42, of Dieppe of A. Coy, Royal Marine Commando by Capt. P.W.C. Hellings," 1.

42. Jacques Mordal [pseud.], *Dieppe: The Dawn of Decision* (Toronto: Ryerson Press, 1962), 211.

43. "Report No. 108," 50–51.

44. TNA:PRO DEFE 2/337, "Report on Events on 19 Aug 42, of Dieppe of 12 Pl. x. Coy and half Coy H.Q. by Captain J.C. Manners, R.M.," 1.

45. TNA:PRO DEFE 2/239, "Jubilee: RM Commando—19 August 1942," 1–2.

46. Neillands, 242.

47. TNA:PRO DEFE 2/239, "Statement of O.C. 'B' Company, Captain R.K. Devereaux," 1.

48. TNA:PRO DEFE 2/239, "Jubilee: RM Commando," 2.

49. TNA:PRO DEFE 2/337, "Report by Manners," 1.

50. TNA:PRO DEFE 2/239, "Statement by Cpl. Harvey," 1.

51. TNA:PRO DEFE 2/239, "Jubilee: RM Commando," 2.

52. "Personal Accounts Dieppe—Memorandum of Interview with L/Sgt. G.A. Hickson, 7 Fd Coy, RCE, 13 Oct. 42," 4.

53. "Report No. 89," 24–29.

21 PRETTY SHAKY ALL AROUND

1. TNA:PRO ADM 199/107, "Operation 'Jubilee'—Enclosure No. 3 to the Naval Force Commander's No. NPJ.0221/92 of 30th August, 1942," 14.

2. Quentin Reynolds, *Dress Rehearsal: The Story of Dieppe* (Garden City, NY: Blue Ribbon Books, 1943), 167.

3. Ibid., 181–82.

4. TNA:PRO ADM 199/107, "Operation 'Jubilee'—Enclosure," 14.

5. "Report No. 159, Additional Information on Planning," Appendix A, CMHQ, DHH, DND, 4.

6. Ronald Atkin, *Dieppe 1942: The Jubilee Disaster* (London: Macmillan, 1980), 198.

7. TNA:PRO ADM 199/107, "Operation 'Jubilee'—Enclosure," 14.

8. Terence Robertson, *Dieppe: The Shame and the Glory* (London: Pan Books, 1965), 429.

9. TNA:PRO DEFE 2/336, "Report by Military Force Commander—Operation 'Jubilee,'" 2.

10. TNA:PRO ADM 199/107, "Naval Force Commander's Narrative," 5.

11. "Personal Accounts Dieppe—Narrative of Experiences at Dieppe, 19 Aug 42 by Lt.-Col. R.R. Labatt, OC, RHLI," 592.011(D3), DHH, DND, 8–9.

12. TNA:PRO DEFE 2/233, "Report by the Air Force Commander on the Combined Operation Against Dieppe—August 19th, 1942," 10.

13. Norman L.R. Franks, *Greatest Air Battle: Dieppe, 19th August 1942* (London: William Kimber, 1979), 58.

14. TNA:PRO DEFE 2/233, "Report by the Air Force Commander," 10.

15. Michael Schoeman, "Air Umbrella—Dieppe," *Military History Journal*, vol. 1, no. 5 (Dec. 1969), accessed Feb. 11, 2012, samilitaryhistory.org/vol015ms.html.

16. TNA:PRO DEFE 2/233, "Report by the Air Force Commander," 27.

17. Ibid., 11.

18. TNA:PRO DEFE 2/333, "Multiple reports," 129–30.

19. Ibid., 124–26.

20. Atkin, 202–03.

21. TNA:PRO DEFE 2/233, "Report by the Air Force Commander," 15.

22. "Lloyd Vernon 'Chad' Chadburn," accessed Feb. 13, 2012, www.acesofww2.com /Canada/aces/chadburn.htm.

23. Jim and John Maffre, interview by Serge Durflinger, Ottawa, Aug. 13, 1999, Oral History Project Collection, CWM.

24. "Blair Dalzell 'Dal' Russel," *Canadian Aces of World War II*, accessed Feb. 13, 2012, www.acesofww2.com/Canada/aces/russel.htm.

25. TNA:PRO DEFE 2/233, "Report by the Air Force Commander," 12–13.

26. Reynolds, 160–62.

27. "Report No. 108, The Attack on the Main Beaches," CMHQ, DHH, DND, 56.

28. Schoeman.

29. TNA:PRO DEFE 2/233, "Report by the Air Force Commander," 3.

30. TNA:PRO ADM 199/107, "Operation 'Jubilee,' Detailed Narrative," 6.

31. TNA:PRO DEFE 2/233, "Report by the Air Force Commander," 12.

32. Franks, 100.

33. *The R.C.A.F. Overseas* (Toronto: Oxford University Press, 1944), 63–64.

34. TNA:PRO DEFE 2/233, "Report by the Air Force Commander," 2.

35. Ibid., 30.

36. TNA:PRO ADM 199/107, "Operation 'Jubilee,' Detailed Narrative," 14.

37. Atkin, 211.

38. "Report No. 108," 73.

39. TNA:PRO DEFE 2/239, "Major G.H. Stockley, R.M. Report on Operation Jubilee," 2.

40. Atkin, 211.

41. "Report No. 108," 72.

42. TNA:PRO DEFE 2/335, Appendix V, "Interview with Sub-Lieut. J.E. O'Rourke" 13–14.

43. Ibid., "Report by Lieutenant J.E. Koyl," 8–9.

22 VERY HEARTBREAKING

1. "Op 'Jubilee,' Personal accts (RCE)," [mistitled file containing Essex Scottish accounts], 232C2.(D57), vol. 10873, box 252, RG24, 1.

2. "Personal Accounts Dieppe—Memorandum of Interview with CSM J. Stewart," 592.011(D3), DHH, DND, 2.

3. Royal Hamilton Light Infantry War Diary, August 1942, Appendix 18, RG24, LAC, 18.

4. Ed Bennett, "Dieppe 1942," in *Onward 1: The Informal History of the Calgary Regiment, 14th Canadian Armoured Regiment*, ed. Dick Maltby and Jessie Maltby (Vancouver: 50/14 Veterans' Assoc., 1989), 3–4.

5. "Op 'Jubilee'—Courts of Inquiry," 232C2.(D83), vol. 10875, box 252, RG24, LAC, 58.

6. "Report No. 108, The Attack on the Main Beaches," CMHQ, DHH, DND, 57–58.

7. "Report No. 90, The Operation at Dieppe, 19 Aug 42: Further Personal Stories of Participants," CMHQ, DHH, DND, 33.

8. "Op 'Jubilee'—Courts of Inquiry," 58.

9. W.R. Freasby, ed., *Official History of the Canadian Medical Services, 1939–1945*, vol. 1, *Organization and Campaigns* (Ottawa: Queen's Printer, 1956), 116.

10. Royal Hamilton War Diary, Appendix 18, 14.

11. "Personal Accounts Dieppe—Report on the Dieppe Raid on 19th August, 1942 by Lt. P. Ross (RNVR)," 4–5.

12. Kingsley Brown Sr., Kingsley Brown Jr., and Brereton Greenhous, *Semper Paratus: The History of the Royal Hamilton Light Infantry (Wentworth Regiment), 1962–1977* (Hamilton: RHLI Historical Assoc., 1977), 205.

13. "Victoria Cross—Second World War, 1939–1945: John Weir Foote," accessed Feb. 16, 2012, www.cmp-cpm.forces.gc.ca/dhh-dhp/gal/vcg-gcv/bio/foote-jw-eng.asp.

14. Royal Hamilton War Diary, Appendix 18, 14.

15. Ibid., 30.

16. Brown Sr., Brown Jr., and Greenhous, 208.

17. Royal Hamilton War Diary, Appendix 18, 36.

18. John S. Edmondson and R. Douglas Edmondson, "Memories and Reflections on the Dieppe Raid of 19 August 1942," *Canadian Military History*, vol. 13, no. 4 (Autumn 2004), 55.

19. South Saskatchewan Regiment War Diary, August 1942, Appendix 9, RG24, LAC, 6.

20. "Report No. 89, The Operation at Dieppe, 19 Aug 42: Personal Stories of Participants," CMHQ, DHH, DND, 78.

21. Edmondson and Edmondson, 55–56.

22. "Op 'Jubilee,' Personal account (S Sask R)," 232C2.(D66), vol. 10873, box 252, RG24, LAC, 4.

23. Ibid., 9.

24. "Personal Accounts Dieppe—Report on Dieppe Raid by Lieut. L.R. MacIlveen," 2.

25. "Op 'Jubilee,' Personal accounts (Cam Highrs of Cda)," 232C2.(D65), vol. 10873, box 252, RG24, LAC, 1.

26. Norman H. Ross, interview by Chris Main, July 20 and Aug. 16, 1979, UVICSC.

27. John Hughes-Hallett, unpublished memoir, MG30 E463, LAC, 187-88.

28. TNA:PRO ADM 199/107, "Operation 'Jubilee,' Detailed Narrative—Enclosure No. 3 to the Naval Force Commander's No. NPJ.0221/92 of 30th August, 1942," 14.

29. "Report No. 101, General Outline and Flank Attacks," CMHQ, DHH, DND, 115–18.

30. "Personal Accounts Dieppe—Memorandum of Interview with Major A.T. Law," 4.

31. "Op 'Jubilee,' Personal accounts (Cam Highrs of Cda)," 11–13.

32. Ibid., 141.

33. "Personal Accounts Dieppe—Statement of Company Sgt-Major G. Gouk, 'B' Coy, Camerons of C," 1–2.

34. Wallace Reyburn, *Glorious Chapter: The Canadians at Dieppe* (Toronto: Oxford University Press, 1943), 114–25.

35. "Op 'Jubilee,' Personal accounts (Cam Highrs of Cda)," 155–56.

36. Ibid., 163.

37. Ross interview.

38. "Personal Accounts Dieppe—Report on Dieppe by Pte. Story, V.A.," 1.

39. South Saskatchewan War Diary, Appendix 9, 12.

40. "Personal Accounts Dieppe—Report by MacIlveen," 2.

41. "Report No. 89," 79.

42. Charles Cecil Ingersoll Merritt, interview, August 21, 1997, *Heroes Remember,* accessed Dec. 7, 2011, www.veterans.gc.ca/eng/collections/hrp/alpha_results/123.

43. John Edmondson, interview by Chris Bell, June 6, Aug. 4 and 12, 1982, UVICSC.

44. Edmondson and Edmondson, 57.

45. South Saskatchewan War Diary, Appendix 9, 15.

46. Ibid., 17.

47. "Report No. 89," 79.

48. Merritt interview.

49. "Report No. 101," 117–18.

50. Ibid., 122–23.

51. C.P. Stacey, *Six Years of War: The Army in Canada, Britain and the Pacific,* vol. 1 (Ottawa: Queen's Printer, 1957), 389.

23 SORRY, LADS

1. "Personal Accounts Dieppe—Narrative of Experiences at Dieppe, 19 Aug 42 by Lt.-Col. R.R. Labatt, OC, RHLI," 592.011(D3), DHH, DND, 10.

2. Ed Bennett, "Dieppe 1942," in *Onward 1: The Informal History of the Calgary Regiment, 14th Canadian Armoured Regiment,* ed. Dick Maltby and Jessie Maltby (Vancouver: 50/14 Veterans' Assoc., 1989), 4.

3. "Personal Accounts Dieppe—Report on Approach, Landing and Subsequent Events Dieppe by Brig. W. Southam," 4.

4. "Personal Accounts Dieppe—Report on the Dieppe Raid on 19th August, 1942 by Lt. P. Ross (RNVR)," 5.

5. "Report No. 89, Historical Section CMHQ: The Operation at Dieppe, 19 Aug 42: Personal Stories of Participants," DHH, DND, 33–34.

6. Ibid., 60–61.

7. "Personal Accounts Dieppe—Southam, 4–5.

8. Bennett, 5.

9. "Op 'Jubilee' Personal Accounts (Fus M.R.)," 232C2.(D55), vol. 10873, box 252, RG24, LAC, 39.

10. Dollard Ménard and C.B. Wall, "The meaning of bravery," in *The Canadians at War, 1939/45,* vol. 1 (Montreal: Reader's Digest Assoc. [Canada], 1969), 197.

11. "Report No. 89," 29.

12. Ménard and Wall, 197.

13. "Report No. 108, The Attack on the Main Beaches," CMHQ, DHH, DND, 68.

14. "Op 'Jubilee,' Personal accts (RCE)" [mistitled file containing Essex Scottish accounts], 232C2.(D57), vol. 10873, box 252, RG24, 15–20.

15. TNA:PRO DEFE 2/327, "Canadians at Dieppe: Awards for Gallantry Citations," 9.

16. "'Op 'Jubilee,' Personal accts (RCE)," 26.

17. Essex Scottish Regiment War Diary, August 1942, Appendix VI, RG24, LAC, 3.

18. C.P. Stacey, *Six Years of War: The Army in Canada, Britain and the Pacific,* vol. 1 (Ottawa: Queen's Printer, 1957), 389.

19. Royal Hamilton Light Infantry War Diary, August 1942, Appendix 18, RG24, LAC, 36.
20. Ibid., 28.
21. Ronald Atkin, *Dieppe 1942: The Jubilee Disaster* (London: Macmillan, 1980), 233.
22. Royal Hamilton War Diary, Appendix 18, 18.
23. "Report No. 89," 85–86.
24. "Personal Accounts Dieppe—Labatt," 10–12.
25. "Personal Accounts Dieppe—Southam," 4–5.
26. "Personal Accounts Dieppe—Labatt," 12–13.
27. TNA:PRO ADM 199/107, "Operation 'Jubilee,' Detailed Narrative—Enclosure No. 3 to the Naval Force Commander's No. NPJ.0221/92 of 30th August, 1942," 16.
28. "Report No. 108," 70.
29. "Op 'Jubilee,' Personal Accounts (14 Cdn A Tk Bn)," 232C2.(D56), vol. 10873, box 252, RG24, LAC, 8.
30. John Hughes-Hallett, unpublished memoir, MG30 E463, LAC, 188.
31. TNA:PRO ADM 199/107, "Operation 'Jubilee,' Naval Force Commander's Narrative," 6.
32. "Report No. 108," 70.
33. TNA:PRO ADM 199/107, "Operation 'Jubilee'—Enclosure," 16.
34. Hughes-Hallett memoir, 189–90.
35. Quentin Reynolds, *Dress Rehearsal: The Story of Dieppe* (Garden City, NY: Blue Ribbon Books, 1943), 220–21.
36. "Report No. 108," 56.
37. TNA:PRO ADM 199/107, "Operation 'Jubilee'—Enclosure," 16.
38. "Report No. 108," 71–72.
39. Ibid., 55.
40. Hughes-Hallett memoir, 190–91.
41. "Personal Accounts Dieppe—Southam, 5.
42. Stacey, *Six Years of War,* 396–97.
43. Bennett, 5.
44. "Personal Accounts Dieppe—Labatt, 13.
45. Stacey, *Six Years of War,* 387.
46. Ibid., 386.
47. Ibid., 388.
48. Ibid., 390.
49. "Report No. 10, Information from German War Diaries, AHQ, DHH, DND, 21–22.
50. Ibid., 22.
51. Reynolds, 242.
52. Hughes-Hallett memoir, 193.
53. W.R. Freasby, ed., *Official History of the Canadian Medical Services, 1939–1945,* vol. I, *Organization and Campaigns* (Ottawa: Queen's Printer, 1956), 120–21.
54. Norman H. Ross, interview by Chris Main, July 20 and Aug. 16, 1979, UVICSC.
55. John S. Edmondson and R. Douglas Edmondson, "Memories and Reflections on the Dieppe Raid of 19 August 1942," *Canadian Military History,* vol. 13, no. 4 (Autumn 2004), 58.
56. Stacey, *Six Years of War,* 386.

EPILOGUE: DIEPPE IN MEMORY

1. The Earl Mountbatten of Burma, "Address to the Dieppe Veterans and Prisoner's-of-War Association, 29 September, 1973," pamphlet in the author's possession, 9–10.

2. C.P. Stacey, *Six Years of War: The Army in Canada, Britain and the Pacific,* vol. 1 (Ottawa: Queen's Printer, 1957), 401.

3. John Mosier, *Deathride: Hitler vs. Stalin—The Eastern Front, 1941–1945* (New York: Simon & Schuster, 2010), 265.

BIBLIOGRAPHY

Abbreviations: ADM–Admiralty Papers (U.K.). AHQ–Army Headquarters.
  CMHQ–Canadian Military Headquarters. CWM–Canadian War Museum.
  DND–Department of National Defence. DEFE–Ministry of Defence (U.K.).
  DHH–Director of Heritage and History. LAC–Library and Archives Canada.
  PRO–Public Records office (U.K.). TNA–The National Archives of the U.K.
  UVICSC–University of Victoria Special Collections. WO–War Office (U.K.).

BOOKS

Antal, Sandy, and Kevin R. Shackleton. *Duty Nobly Done: The Official History of the Essex and Kent Scottish Regiment.* Windsor, ON: Walkerville, 2006.

Atkin, Ronald. *Dieppe 1942: The Jubilee Disaster.* London: Macmillan, 1980.

Brown, Kingsley Sr., Kingsley Brown Jr., and Brereton Greenhous. *Semper Paratus: The History of the Royal Hamilton Light Infantry (Wentworth Regiment), 1862–1977.* Hamilton: RHLI Historical Assoc., 1977.

Bryant, Arthur. *The Turn of the Tide, 1939–1943: A study based on the diaries and autobiographical notes of Field Marshal the Viscount Alanbrooke.* London: Collins, 1957.

Campbell, John P. *Dieppe Revisited: Documentary Investigation.* Portland, OR: Frank Cass, 1993.

Cent ans d'histoire d'un régiment canadien-français: Les Fusiliers Mont-Royal, 1869–1969. Montreal: Éditions Du Jour, 1971.

Churchill, Winston. *The Second World War: The Hinge of Fate.* Vol. 4. London: Houghton Mifflin, 1950.

Combined Operations: The Official Story of the Commandos. New York: Macmillan, 1943.

DeFelice, Jim. *Rangers at Dieppe: The First Combat Action of U.S. Army Rangers in World War II.* New York: Berkley Caliber, 2008.

Dickson, Paul Douglas. *A Thoroughly Canadian General: A Biography of General H.D.G. Crerar.* Toronto: University of Toronto Press, 2007.

Douglas, W.A.B., Roger Sarty, and Michael Whitby. *A Blue Water Navy: The Official Operational History of the Royal Canadian Navy in the Second World War, 1943–1945.* Vol. II, part 2. St. Catharine's, ON: Vanwell Publishing, 2007.

Durnford-Slater, John. *Commando.* London: W. Kimber, 1953.

Franks, Norman R. *Greatest Air Battle: Dieppe, 19th August 1942*. London: William Kimber, 1979.

Freasby, W.R., ed. *Official History of the Canadian Medical Services, 1939–1945*. Vol. 1: *Organization and Campaigns*. Ottawa: Queen's Printer, 1956.

Goodspeed, D.J. *Battle Royal: A History of the Royal Regiment of Canada, 1862–1962*. Toronto: Royal Regt. Of Canada Assoc., 1962.

Graham, Dominick. *The Price of Command: A Biography of General Guy Simonds*. Toronto: Stoddart, 1992.

Granatstein, J.L. *The Generals: The Canadian Army's Senior Commanders in the Second World War*. Toronto: Stoddart, 1993.

Greenhous, Brereton. *Dieppe, Dieppe*. Montreal: Art Global, 1992.

Hamilton, Nigel. *Monty: The Making of a General, 1887–1942*. London: Coronet, 1984.

Harrison, Gordon A. *Cross-Channel Attack: United States Army in World War II, The European Theater of Operations*. Washington: Center of Military History, United States Army, 1993.

Jeffers, H. Paul. *Command of Honor: General Lucien Truscott's Path to Victory in World War II*. New York: NAL Caliber, 2008.

Kerry, A.J., and W.A. McDill. *History of the Corps of Royal Engineers*. Vol. 2. Ottawa: Military Engineers Assoc., 1966.

Konstam, Angus. *British Motor Gun Boat, 1939–45*. Oxford: Osprey Publishing, 2010.

Leasor, James. *Green Beach*. London: William Heinemann, 1975.

Lovat, Lord. *March Past: A Memoir*. New York: Holmes & Meier, 1979.

Maltby, Dick, and Jessie Maltby, eds. *Onward 1: The Informal History of the Calgary Regiment, 14th Canadian Armoured Regiment*. Vancouver: 50/14 Veterans' Assoc., 1989.

Marteinson, John, and Michael R. McNorgan. *The Royal Armoured Corps: An Illustrated History*. Toronto: Robin Brass Studio, 2000.

Mellor, John. *Dieppe—Canada's Forgotten Heroes*. Scarborough, ON: Signet, 1975.

Ménard, Dollard, and C.B. Wall, "The Meaning of Bravery," *The Canadians at War, 1939/45*. Vol. 1. Montreal: Reader's Digest Assoc. (Canada), 1969.

Moir, John S., ed. *History of the Royal Canadian Corps of Signals, 1903–1961*. Ottawa: Corps Committee, Royal Canadian Corps of Signals, 1962.

Montgomery, Bernard Law. *The Memoirs of Field-Marshal the Viscount Montgomery of Alamein, K.G.* London: Collins, 1958.

Mordal, Jacques [pseud.]. *Dieppe: The Dawn of Decision*. Toronto: Ryerson Press, 1962.

Mosier, John. *Deathride: Hitler vs. Stalin—The Eastern Front 1941–1945*. New York: Simon & Schuster, 2010.

Munro, Ross. *Gauntlet to Overlord*. Toronto: Macmillan, 1945.

Neillands, Robin. *The Dieppe Raid: The Story of the Disastrous 1942 Expedition*. London: Aurum Press, 2005.

Queen-Hughes, R.W. *Whatever Men Dare: A History of the Queen's Own Cameron Highlanders of Canada, 1936–1960*. Winnipeg: Bulman Bros., 1960.

The RCAF Overseas. Toronto: Oxford University Press, 1944.

Reyburn, Wallace. *Glorious Chapter: The Canadians at Dieppe*. Toronto: Oxford University Press, 1943.

Reynolds, Quentin. *Dress Rehearsal: The Story of Dieppe*. Garden City, NY: Blue Ribbon Books, 1943.

Ritchie, Andrew R. *Watchdog: A History of the Canadian Provost Corps*. Toronto: University of Toronto Press, 1995.

Robertson, Terence. *Dieppe: The Shame and the Glory*. London: Pan Books, 1965.

Stacey, C.P. *The Canadian Army, 1939–1945: An Official Historical Summary*. Ottawa: Queen's Printer, 1948.

———. *Six Years of War: The Army in Canada, Britain and the Pacific*. Vol. 1. Ottawa: Queen's Printer, 1957.

Villa, Brian Loring. *Unauthorized Action: Mountbatten and the Dieppe Raid*. Toronto: Oxford University Press, 1989.

Whitaker, Denis, and Shelagh Whitaker. *Dieppe: Tragedy to Triumph; A Firsthand and Revealing Critical Account of the Most Controversial Battle of World War II*. Whitby, ON: McGraw-Hill Ryerson, 1992.

Wilmot, Chester. *The Struggle for Europe*. London: Collins, 1952.

Young, Peter. *Storm from the Sea*. London: Greenhill Books, 2002.

JOURNAL ARTICLES

Edmondson, John S., and R. Douglas Edmondson. "Memories and Reflections on the Dieppe Raid of 19 August 1942," *Canadian Military History*. Vol. 13, no. 4 (Autumn 2004), 47–61.

Greenhous, Brereton. "Operation Flodden: The Sea Fight Off Berneval and the Suppression of the Goebbels Battery, 19 August 1942." *Canadian Military Journal*. Vol. 4, no. 4 (Autumn 2003), 47–57.

Hughes-Hallett, J. "The Mounting of Raids." *Royal United Service Institution Journal*. Vol. 95 (Feb.–Nov. 1950), 580–88.

WEBSITES

"Blair Dalzell 'Dal' Russel." *Canadian Aces of WW2*. Accessed Feb. 13, 2012. www.acesofww2.com/Canada/aces/russel.htm.

"Brigadier The Lord Lovat." *The Pegasus Archive*. Accessed Dec. 12, 2011. www.pegasusarchive.org/normandy/lord_lovat.htm.

"Canadian and Allied Jews at the Raid on Dieppe," Jewish Virtual Library. Accessed Nov. 8, 2011. www.jewishvirtuallibrary.org/jsource/ww2/sugar7.html.

Canadian Army Overseas Honours and Awards Citation Details. DHH, DND. www.cmp-cpm.forces.gc.ca/dhh-dhp/gal/cao-aco/index-eng.asp.

"Charles Edward Sawden." Veterans Affairs Canada. Accessed Jan. 14, 2012. www.veterans.gc.ca/eng/collections/virtualmem/photoview/2317422/21197.

"COHQ–War Cabinet–Yalta." *Combined Operations*. Accessed Oct. 3, 2011. www.combinedops.com/ZCOHQ.htm.

"Colonel Pat Porteous VC." *The Telegraph*, UK. Accessed Jan. 10, 2012. www.telegraph.co.uk/news/obituaries/1369771/Colonel-Pat-Porteous-vc.html.

"Dieppe—The Plans." Royal Regt. of Canada Assoc. Accessed Dec. 15, 2011.
    www.rregtcassoc.ca/Dieppe%20Plans%20.html.

"Finney, William." Fdn. for Information on the Second World War.
    Accessed Jan. 9, 2012. www.ww2awards.com/person/44280.

"German 12-cm Mortar Battalions." *Tactical and Technical Trends.* No. 40
    (Dec. 16, 1943). Accessed Dec. 28, 2011. www.lonesentry.com/articles/ttt
    /german-12-cm-120-mm-mortar-battalions.html.

"The History of the Third Canadian Light Anti-Aircraft Regiment (3LAA)." Accessed
    Dec. 16, 2011. www.ww2f.com/wwii-general/25386-history-third-canadian
    -light-anti-aircraft-regiment-3laa.html.

"In Memory of Lieutenant William George Rogers Wedd." Veterans Affairs Canada.
    Accessed Jan. 18, 2012. www.veterans.gc.ca/eng/collections/virtualmem/
    Detail/2317531.

"In Memory of Private Emile Phillipe Williams." Veterans Affairs Canada. Accessed
    Dec. 31, 2011. www.veterans.gc.ca/eng/collections/virtualmem/Detail/2929447.

"John Durnford-Slater." *Ferdinand(o) Family History Site.* Accessed Dec. 12, 2011.
    www.ferdinando.org.uk/john_durnford-slater.htm.

"Konrad Haase." Accessed Dec. 19, 2011. www.ww2gravestone.com/general
    /haase-konrad.

"Lloyd Vernon 'Chad' Chadburn." Accessed Feb. 13, 2012. www.acesofww2.com
    /Canada/aces/chadburn.htm.

"Lt-Col A.C. Gostling Killed Leading Cameron Highlanders." *Toronto Star,* Aug. 22,
    1942. Veterans Affairs Canada. Accessed Nov. 4, 2011. www.veterans.gc.ca/eng
    /collections/virtualmem/photoview/2317090/55185.

"Lt-Col Cecil Merritt, vc," *The Telegraph.* Accessed Nov. 6, 2011. www.telegraph.co.uk
    /news/obituaries/1349057/Lt-Col-Cecil-Merritt-vc.html.

Merritt, Charles Cecil Ingersoll. Interview, Aug. 21, 1997. *Heroes Remember.* Veterans
    Affairs Canada. Accessed Dec. 7, 2011. www.veterans.gc.ca/eng/collections/hrp
    /alpha_results/123.

"Military Intelligence Service, Special Series No. 1, August 9, 1942: Commando
    Operations—Section 1. Vaagso (Norway) Raid." *Lone Sentry.* Accessed Sept. 27, 2011.
    www.lonesentry.com/manuals/commandos/vaagso-norway-raid.html.

Pipes, Jason. "302.Infanterie-Division." *Feldgrau.* Accessed Dec. 19, 2011.
    www.feldgrau.com/InfDiv.php?ID=206.

Poolton, John "Jack" Abernathy. Interview, undated. *Heroes Remember.* Veterans Affairs
    Canada. Accessed Dec. 7, 2011. www.veterans.gc.ca/eng/collections/hrp
    /alpha_results/40.

Schoeman, Michael. "Air Umbrella—Dieppe." *Military History Journal.* Vol. 1, no. 5
    (Dec. 1969). Accessed Feb. 11, 2012. samilitaryhistory.org/vol015ms.html.

Sugarman, Martin. "Jack Nissenthall—The vc Hero Who Never Was," Harry Palmer
    Gallery, Dieppe Raid Gallery. Accessed Apr. 10, 2012. www.aportraitofcanada
    .ca/?p=2216.

"Trafford Leigh-Mallory." *World War II Database.* Accessed Nov. 2, 2011. ww2db.com
    /person_bio.php?person_id=125.

"UJ-1411 (Treff III) (+1944)." *Wreck Site*. Accessed Jan. 3, 2012.
    www.wrecksite.eu/wreck.aspx?133368.
"Victoria Cross—Second World War, 1939–1945: John Weir Foote."
    Accessed Feb. 16, 2012. www.cmp-cpm.forces.gc.ca/dhh-dhp/gal/vcg-gcv
    /bio/foote-jw-eng.asp.
"What a Man He Was." *Vancouver Courier,* Nov. 7, 2008. Accessed Nov. 6, 2011.
    www.canada.com/vancouvercourier/news/story.html?id=c2bfeb1b-a86b
    -4b10-b584-5ab4bcefe980&p=3.

UNPUBLISHED MATERIALS

Calgary Tank Regiment War Diary, August 1942. RG24, LAC.
"Combat Report and Experience Gained During the British Attack on Dieppe 19 August
    1942." 981.023(D10), vol. 20438, box 168, RG24, LAC.
"Communications, Operation 'Jubilee.'" 232C2.(D6), vol. 10870, box 250, RG24, LAC.
"Conversations with Dick Maltby, Aug. 1989." UVICSC.
"Dieppe, 1942" file. 222C1.011(D1), vol. 10772, box 201, RG24, LAC.
"Dieppe Raid—1942" file. 225C1.013(D6), vol. 10796, box 213, RG24, LAC.
"Dieppe: Report of Tank Action." 594.011(D1), DHH, DND.
The Earl Mountbatten of Burma. "Address to the Dieppe Veterans and Prisoner's-
    of-War Association, 29 September, 1973." Pamphlet in the author's possession.
"Engineer Training Report: Exercise 'Rutter' and Operation 'Jubilee,'" Appendix IV.
    232C2.033(D4), vol. 10873, box 252. RG24, LAC.
Essex Scottish Regiment War Diary, August 1942. RG24, LAC.
4th Canadian Infantry Brigade War Diary. August 1942. RG24, LAC.
Headquarters, 2nd Canadian Infantry Division (G Branch) War Diary, August 1942,
    RG24, LAC.
Henry, Hugh. "The Tanks of Dieppe: The History of The Calgary Regiment (Tank),
    1939 to August 19, 1942." Master's thesis, University of Victoria, 1985.
Hughes-Hallett, John. Unpublished memoir. MG30 E463, LAC.
"Intelligence Control Station France: Evaluation of Dieppe Operation, 14 Sep 42."
    981GINT(D1), vol. 20488, box 218, RG24, LAC.
"'Jubilee' Miscellaneous, Special 'Jubilee' Instructions." 232C2(D52), vol. 10873, box
    252, RG24, LAC.
Les Fusiliers Mont-Royal War Diary, August 1942. RG24, LAC.
"Memorandum of interview with Major Guy Vandelac, 6 Nov 46." 594.011(D5), DHH,
    DND.
"Operation Jubilee: Intelligence Report on Dieppe Raid, 19 Aug 42, Part III—Enemy
    Defences and Weapons." 215C1.98(D357), vol. 10707, box 156, RG24, LAC.
"Op 'Jubilee'—Courts of Inquiry." 232C2.(D83), vol. 10875, box 252, RG24, LAC.
"Op 'Jubilee,' Personal Accounts (14 Cdn A Tk Bn)," 232C2.(D56), vol. 10873, box 252,
    RG24, LAC.
"Op 'Jubilee,' Personal accounts (Cam Highrs of Cda)." 232C2.(D65), vol. 10873,
    box 252, RG24, LAC.
"Op 'Jubilee' Personal Accounts (Fus M.R.)." 232C2.(D55), vol. 10873, box 252, RG24,
    LAC.

"Op 'Jubilee,' Personal accts (RCE)." [Mistitled file containing Essex Scottish accounts.] 232C2.(D57), vol. 10873, box 252, RG24, LAC.

"Op 'Jubilee,' Personal accts (R Regt of C)." 232C2.(D61), vol. 10873, box 252, RG24.

"Op 'Jubilee,' Personal accounts (S Sask R)." 232C2.(D66), vol. 10873, box 252, RG24, LAC.

"Op 'Jubilee' Reports, Air Force." 232C2(D5), vol. 10870, box 250, RG24, LAC.

"Part of Appx 'C' to Detailed Mil Plan Op 'Jubilee' Dieppe 19 Aug 42 re: Allotment of Personnel, Eqpt & stores." 225C1.013(D5), vol. 10795, box 213, RG24, LAC.

"Personal Accounts Dieppe." 592.011(D3), DHH, DND.

Queen's Own Cameron Highlanders War Diary, August 1942. RG24, LAC.

"Report No. 10, Operation 'Jubilee': The Raid on Dieppe, 19 Aug 42, Information from German War Diaries." AHQ, DHH, DND.

"Report No. 36, The Development of the German Defences in the Dieppe Sector (1940–1941), Information from German War Diaries." AHQ, DHH, DND.

"Report No. 65, Situation of the Canadian Military Forces in the United Kingdom, Spring 1942: Recent Changes in Commands and Staffs." CMHQ, DHH, DND.

"Report No. 87, Situation of the Canadian Military Forces in the United Kingdom, Autumn, 1942: II, Recent Changes in Commands and Staffs." CMHQ, DHH, DND.

"Report No. 89, The Operation at Dieppe, 19 Aug 42: Personal Stories of Participants." CMHQ, DHH, DND.

"Report No. 90, The Operation at Dieppe, 19 Aug 42: Further Personal Stories of Participants." CMHQ, DHH, DND.

"Report No. 100, Operation 'Jubilee': The Preliminaries of the Operation." CMHQ, DHH, DND.

"Report No. 101, General Outline and Flank Attacks." CMHQ, DHH, DND.

"Report No. 107, The Operation at Dieppe, 19 Aug 42: Further Personal Stories of Participants." CMHQ, DHH, DND.

"Report No. 108, Operation 'Jubilee': The Attack on the Main Beaches." CMHQ, DHH, DND.

"Report No. 153, Operation 'Jubilee': New Light on Early Planning." CMHQ, DHH, DND.

"Report No. 159, Operation 'Jubilee': Additional Information on Planning." CMHQ, DHH, DND.

"Report of the Port Commandant Dieppe on the Fighting on 19 Aug 42." 981GN(D13), vol. 20488, box 218, RG24, LAC.

"Report on Combined Operations by Lt. Col. L.F. Barnes, CRE, 2 CDN DIV." 232C2.(D2), vol. 10870, box 250, RG24, LAC.

Royal Hamilton Light Infantry War Diary, August 1942. RG24, LAC.

Royal Regiment of Canada War Diary, August 1942. RG24, LAC.

2nd Canadian Infantry Division (G Branch) War Diary, August 1942, RG24, LAC.

"2nd Canadian Infantry Division Tp Carrying Exercise: Ford 1—Appx 'B' to Director's Notes for Control Movements Involved." 232C2.(D52), vol. 10873, box 252, RG24, LAC.

6th Canadian Infantry Brigade War Diary, August 1944. RG24, LAC.

"Soldats Alliés tués combat, disparu, décédes de leurs blessures ou morts en captivité, ayant participé à l'opération sur Berneval le 19 août 1942." Memorial plaque, Berneval, France.

South Saskatchewan Regiment War Diary, August 1942. RG24, LAC.

TNA:PRO ADM 199/107.

TNA:PRO DEFE 2/233.

TNA:PRO DEFE 2/239.

TNA:PRO DEFE 2/324.

TNA:PRO DEFE 2/327.

TNA:PRO DEFE 2/328.

TNA:PRO DEFE 2/330.

TNA:PRO DEFE 2/334.

TNA:PRO DEFE 2/335.

TNA:PRO DEFE 2/336.

TNA:PRO DEFE 2/337.

TNA:PRO DEFE 2/338.

TNA:PRO DEFE 2/550.

TNA:PRO DEFE 2/551.

TNA:PRO WO 106/4195.

"Yukon 1," 232C2(D54), vol. 10873, box 252, RG24, LAC.

INTERVIEWS AND CORRESPONDENCE

Bowen, Norm. Interview by A.E. "Tony" Delamere. Ottawa, Sept. 28, 2000. Oral History Project Collection, CWM.

Rayment, Col. Ed (Retd.). Correspondence with author, Feb. 8, 2012.

Edmondson, John. Interview by Chris Bell. Victoria, June 6, Aug. 4 and 12, 1982. UVICSC.

Mountbatten, Vice-Admiral Lord Louis. Letter to Guy Simonds, Feb. 4, 1969. Hughes-Hallett fonds, MG30 E463, LAC.

Maffre, Jim, and John Maffre. Interview by Serge Durflinger. Ottawa, Aug. 13, 1999. Oral History Project Collection, CWM.

Ross, Norman H. Interview by Chris Main. Victoria, July 20 and Aug. 16, 1979. UVICSC.

INDEX OF FORMATIONS, UNITS, AND CORPS

433

ABOUT THE AUTHOR

THIS IS THE tenth volume in Mark Zuehlke's Canadian Battle Series—the most extensive published account of the battle experiences of Canada's Army in World War II. The series is also the most exhaustive recounting of the battles and campaigns fought by any nation during that war to have been written by a single author. These best-selling books continue to confirm Zuehlke's reputation as the nation's leading popular military historian. In 2006, *Holding Juno: Canada's Heroic Defence of the D-Day Beaches* won the City of Victoria Butler Book Prize.

In 2011, Zuehlke began adapting stories told in the Canadian Battle Series to appeal to reluctant readers and those wanting a quick and easily digestible account. His Rapid Reads titles to date are *Ortona Street Fight* and *Assault on Juno*.

He has written four other historical works, including *For Honour's Sake: The War of 1812 and the Brokering of an Uneasy Peace*, which won the 2007 Canadian Author's Association Lela Common Award for Canadian History. Also a novelist, he is the author of the popular Elias McCann series. The first in the series, *Hands Like Clouds*, won the 2000 Crime Writers of Canada Arthur Ellis Award for Best First Novel.

Zuehlke lives in Victoria, British Columbia, and is currently working on his next Canadian Battle book, which returns to First Canadian Army's advance across Northwest Europe in 1945 by detailing its Rhineland Campaign of February–March 1945. He can be found on the web at www.zuehlke.ca and Mark Zuehlke's Canadian Battle Series Facebook site.